'*Understanding International Politics: The Student Toolkit* is an ideal introductory International Relations text for the 21st century undergraduate. Dee engages students from the outset by putting the variety of their lived experiences front and center. She cultivates critical engagement in the study of international affairs through concrete and timely exercises designed to progressively build skills and confidence, from fundamental study skills and research and writing protocols to conducting literature reviews and presenting independent research findings. The text provides an exacting yet accessible entrance to the mainstream theoretical approaches, but what distinguishes it is the essential and substantial incorporation of critical and postcolonial approaches throughout its comprehensive presentation of the actors and issues of international politics. This is an indispensable resource to empower students and leave them eager – and equipped – to influence the direction of 21st century international relations.'

– **Professor Katie Verlin Laatikainen**, Adelphi University, USA

'*Understanding International Politics: The Student Toolkit* is a brilliant resource for both students and instructors. This book provides an excellent introduction to key concepts combined with up to date empirical examples and exercises to develop and craft essential research skills. I wish this book had been around when I was an undergrad! But I am very happy to be able to assign this book to my current students to give them the tools, skills and knowledge to find their way studying international relations, security studies, and global political economy.'

– **Dr Lucy Hall**, University of Amsterdam, the Netherlands

'This book offers an invaluable set of tools to help students understand and interpret the world of international politics. The Toolkit that Dee develops will help students to grow as scholars, equipping them with the skills to make sense of a rapidly changing world. This book is highly recommended for undergraduates at all levels and will help them tackle the thorny challenges of writing, research, and critical analysis.'

– **Adam Fishwick**, Associate Professor and Reader at De Montfort University, UK, and Research Director at the University of Akureyri, Iceland

'Dee's new *Understanding International Politics* textbook stands out from the rest because it is truly written for today's student. It includes unique features such as a toolkit for each chapter, and practical how to guides on writing, critical thinking, and referencing.'

– **Brian C. Schmidt**, Professor of Political Science, Carleton University, Canada

'Dee offers a new and refreshing approach to the study of international affairs. Ever-present throughout the work, her toolkit provides students with a practical way of approaching the topic that will help them to confront and solve the issues posed by an increasingly complex and chaotic world.'

– **Dr Ben Rich**, Senior Lecturer in International Relations & History, Curtin University, Western Australia

'This textbook stands out in an otherwise crowded market. Written with students in mind, it is academically rigorous yet approachable. Its main strength lies in the combination of theoretical insights, empirical illustrations and academic skills development. Up until today, I did not believe that it is possible to have a book which would be a jack-of-all-trades but Megan Dee accomplished just that.'

– **Professor Michal Onderco**, Erasmus University Rotterdam, the Netherlands

'This is the book I wish I'd had to introduce me to the study of international politics. It is superbly conceived in getting the reader to interrogate their own understanding of key issues – and then using that as a platform to develop a sophisticated comprehension of key concepts, ideas and practices in international politics.'

– **Professor Richard Whitman**, University of Kent, UK

'From metatheory to the study of race relations as a precursor to IR, *Understanding International Politics* provides an approachable text that builds understanding of how our theoretical toolkit influences who, what, and how we study. It is unusual to find such a concise and clearly written explanation of these concepts in an introductory textbook. Issues that today's students most want to unpack are explored via this theoretical toolkit, including energy and the environment, religion, and the security implications of public health.'

– **Dr Kathryn Starnes**, Senior Lecturer in Politics and International Relations, Manchester Metropolitan University, UK

'This textbook provides an intuitive structure for the study of international relations. It also provides the student a toolkit to comprehend the relationships between important concepts and the real world, and gives them the ability to understand "how to" engage in research.'

– **Dr Richard Johnson**, Senior Lecturer in the Department of Politics of International Relations, University of Strathclyde, UK

'*Understanding International Politics* is a timely addition to historically informed and practically oriented pedagogical resources. It centres the student's own experiences and offers students hands-on tools to develop a systematic understanding of major debates on the international system, the actors in it, and its contemporary issues. This book critically and reflectively engages with a range of materials in preparation for different modes of writing and presentation. These tools will contribute to students' success during their studies and transferrable skills after.'

– **Dr Anastasia Shesterinina**, The University of York, UK, and co-editor of *Uncertainty in Global Politics*

UNDERSTANDING INTERNATIONAL POLITICS

THE STUDENT TOOLKIT

MEGAN DEE
UNIVERSITY OF STIRLING, UK

BLOOMSBURY ACADEMIC
LONDON • NEW YORK • OXFORD • NEW DELHI • SYDNEY

BLOOMSBURY ACADEMIC
Bloomsbury Publishing Plc
50 Bedford Square, London, WC1B 3DP, UK
1385 Broadway, New York, NY 10018, USA
29 Earlsfort Terrace, Dublin 2, Ireland

BLOOMSBURY, BLOOMSBURY ACADEMIC and the Diana logo are trademarks
of Bloomsbury Publishing Plc

First published in Great Britain 2024

Cover design: Eleanor Rose
Cover image © Ground Picture/Shutterstock

A catalogue record for this book is available from the British Library.

Names: Dee, Megan, author.
Title: Understanding International Politics: The Student Toolkit / Megan Dee.
Description: [New York]: [Bloomsbury Publishing PLC], [2024] |
Includes bibliographical references and index.
Identifiers: LCCN 2023026767 (print) | LCCN 2023026768 (eBook) |
ISBN 9781350381650 (paperback) | ISBN 9781350381667 (hardback) |
ISBN 9781350381674 (pdf) | ISBN 9781350381681 (epub)
Subjects: LCSH: International relations–Study and teaching. | World Politics–Study and teaching.
Classification: LCC JZ1237 .D43 2024 (print) | LCC JZ1237 (eBook) |
DDC 327.071-dc23/eng/20230927
LC record available at https://lccn.loc.gov/2023026767
LC eBook record available at https://lccn.loc.gov/2023026768

ISBN: HB: 978-1-3503-8166-7
PB: 978-1-3503-8165-0
ePDF: 978-1-3503-8167-4
eBook: 978-1-3503-8168-1

Typeset by Integra Software Service Pvt. Ltd.
Printed and bound in Great Britain by Bell and Bain Ltd, Glasgow.

To find out more about our authors and books visit www.bloomsbury.com
and sign up for our newsletters.

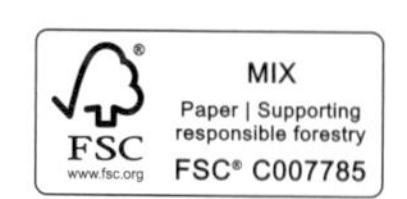

To all the students who came before, and
for all those who are to come.

✻

Contents

Figures

Tables

Images

Maps

Toolkit Exercises

How-To Guides

Abbreviations

ASEAN	Association of Southeast Asian Nations
AUKUS	Australia, United Kingdom, United States defence pact
BLM	Black Lives Matter
BRI	Belt and Road Initiative
BRICs	Brazil, Russia, India, China
BRICS	Brazil, Russia, India, China, South Africa
CCT	Conditional Cash Transfer
CEE	Central and Eastern European
CFCs	Chlorofluorocarbons
CFSP	Common Foreign and Security Policy
CO2	Carbon dioxide
COP	Conference of the Parties
DAC	Development Assistance Committee
DRC	Democratic Republic of the Congo
ECB	European Central Bank
ECSC	European Coal and Steel Community
EEC	European Economic Community
EU	European Union
FAO	Food and Agriculture Organization of the United Nations
FDI	Foreign Direct Investment
FSI	Fragile States Index
FTA	Free Trade Agreement
G7	Group of Seven
G20	Group of Twenty
GATT	General Agreement on Tariffs and Trade
GCR2P	Global Centre for the Responsibility to Protect
GDP	Gross Domestic Product
GNI	Gross National Income
GNP	Gross National Product
GVC	Global Value Chain
HDI	Human Development Index
IAEA	International Atomic Energy Agency
IBRD	International Bank for Reconstruction and Development
ICBM	Intercontinental ballistic missiles
ICISS	International Commission on Intervention and State Sovereignty
ICC	International Criminal Court
ICJ	International Court of Justice
IEA	International Energy Agency
ILO	International Labour Organization
IMF	International Monetary Fund
IO	International organization
IOM	International Organization for Migration
IPCC	Intergovernmental Panel on Climate Change
IPE	International Political Economy

ITU International Telecommunication Union

LDC Least Developed Country
LNG Liquefied Natural Gas

MAD Mutually Assured Destruction
MDGs Millennium Development Goals
MNE Multinational enterprise
MPA Marine protected areas
MPLA The Popular Movement for the Liberation of Angola

NATO North Atlantic Treaty Organization
NGO Non-governmental organization
NPT Treaty on the Non-Proliferation of Nuclear Weapons

ODA Official Development Assistance
OECD Organization for Economic Cooperation and Development
OHCHR Office of the High Commissioner for Human Rights

P5 Permanent Five
PCA Permanent Court of Arbitration
PKK Kurdistan Workers Party
PKO Peacekeeping operation
PMC Private military company
PPP Purchasing Power Parity
PRC People's Republic of China

R2P Responsibility to Protect
RFMO Regional Fisheries Management Organization
ROC Republic of China
RTA Regional Trade Agreement

SDGs Sustainable Development Goals
SEATO Southeast Asian Treaty Organization

TAN Transnational Advocacy Network
TOOLS Think Observe Organize Link Share
TPNW Treaty on the Prohibition of Nuclear Weapons

UAE United Arab Emirates
UDHR Universal Declaration of Human Rights
UK United Kingdom
UN United Nations
UNCTAD United Nations Conference on Trade and Development
UNDP United Nations Development Programme
UNEP United Nations Environment Programme
UNFCCC United Nations Framework Convention on Climate Change
UNGA United Nations General Assembly
UNIA Universal Negro Improvement Association
UNODA United Nations Office of Disarmament Affairs
UNSC United Nations Security Council
US United States [of America]
USSR Union of Socialist Soviet Republics

VNSA Violent non state actor
VOC Verenigde Oost-Indische Compagnie [United East Indies Company]

WHO World Health Organization
WMD Weapons of Mass Destruction
WTO World Trade Organization

Tour of the Book

Abstract

This introductory chapter is aimed at developing your understanding of the different perspectives that can shape your view, and by extension, understanding of the world in which you live. Your experience and outlook on the world around you provide your own unique starting point to the study of international politics. In this chapter you will start to consider how perceptions of the international system have largely been dominated by Europe and the West, looking first at how the world has itself been mapped and its evolution, before addressing depictions of a hierarchical world order including notions of First, Second and Third Worlds or global North and South, and how they may be challenged. The primary objective of this chapter, then, is to encourage you to consider not just your own experiences and global outlook, but how the study of international politics is itself shaped by oftentimes very different perspectives. The chapter goes on to describe international politics as a topic of study, why it matters, and how it is situated within wider disciplines. The chapter also introduces you to the 'toolkit' that will help guide your learning throughout the book to come, before outlining the three sections of the textbook to follow, focusing on the international system, the actors and issues in international politics.

Governance
The process and action by which decisions are made, managed and enforced within an organization or society.

◀ Key Terms
Highlight important terminology as it arises and explains it in accessible language.

Chapter Abstracts ▲
Provide an overview of the chapter, broken down into key ideas and questions we will consider.

---

1 Understanding the international system

HOW TO

APPROACH HISTORY IN YOUR POLITICAL RESEARCH

The events of the past inform the events of today, as surely as they will inform the events of tomorrow. How then can history help us in our own research? Here are just a few tips for how you might draw on lessons for the past in your international politics research.

Be reflective

History is everywhere and requires active reflection to understand its impacts on the 'now'. In international politics we tend to be concerned with history less from the perspective of understanding what happened and when, and more from the perspective of what history can teach us about the here and now. Always bear in mind that how we observe the lessons of the past can be highly subjective. As the adage goes, 'history is written by the victors'. Be *reflective* therefore of how history is written, and how the events we take as 'fact' may themselves have been interpreted. Remember that there may be different interpretations of the events, players and outcomes, and that other perspectives may have equal importance.

Think theory

When we come to draw on the lessons of the past to inform political research today, we have the benefit of theory to help guide and interpret our research. Realism (pg. 35–7), for example, views history as a cyclical process. Whether down to human nature, or the anarchic condition of the international system itself, by adopting a realist perspective we might assume that the world's history of competition and conflict is likely to repeat itself. If you are therefore looking to understand hegemony, or the balance of power of today's international system, realism advocates looking back at the past to find a suitable comparison. Marxism (pg. 52–5) similarly is a theory that draws on history to inform its assumptions of today's international system, advocating a materialist viewpoint which assumes that the history of all human societies has been shaped by socioeconomic forces. More critical theories, such as postcolonialism (pg. 55–8), also adopt historicism by looking to unpack the legacies and impacts of the past on today's societies. From these critical perspectives, history can be seen as a dynamic social process informing and influencing the international politics of today. When using theory to inform any historical research do just remember to be clear in the assumptions you are making, and why. You might also want to check out *How to – apply theory to your research and writing* (pg. 69) for more 'how to' tips on using theories to guide you.

Think sources

International history is a rich, thoroughly rewarding, avenue of research, whether you are interested in the specific foreign policy of one state, the politics around specific international issues, or the development and evolution of the international system itself. The benefit of studying history from an international politics perspective, moreover, is that source material can often be ample in supply, be that through libraries and archives, or via digital archival depositories (check out the Explore More boxes in this chapter for a few examples!) Do give thought though to the resources you are using to inform yourself of past events. Some general history websites can often be goldmines of information but be sure to fact-check to ensure that the resources you are using are reliable. Wherever possible always go *straight to source*. So rather than relying on someone else to tell you what, say the 1945 Yalta Conference Agreement (pg. 23) said, locate the actual document itself. This may be as simple as doing an internet or library search using the correct key words as primary source documentation is often readily available via public access archives (including online). Primary sources do also help you get closer to the history which can make a big difference to how well you understand the politics of today.

30

◀ How to Guides
Enable you to tackle different types of learning, research and assessment such as 'How to write a policy brief' and 'How to paraphrase theoretical discourse'. They are easy to follow and concise, making every aspect of the academic process accessible. Complementing the TOOLkit within each chapter, these guides provide the practical skills to implement your ideas.

Explore More

Discourse analysis is a research method often used by researchers of international politics to analyse the political meanings attributed to written and spoken texts. A discourse analysis would consider the context behind the text being analysed, analyse the structure of the speech, the cultural references being made, and the type of framing being employed.

As a simple discourse analysis exercise, look up the transcript from US President Donald Trump's Oval Office prime-time address of 8 January 2019 (scan the barcode for an easy way of locating this link).

When reading the transcript, ask yourself, what is the context behind this speech and how is this informing the language being used? What is the purpose or objective of the speech? What values, sentiments or identities are portrayed in the language being used, particularly as it concerns immigrants relative to US citizens? How does the speech portray the 'Other'?

By asking questions and unpacking the language we are researching, we can start to understand the political meanings informing such speech acts, as well as the relationships between the text itself and the wider context being analysed.

Scan the QR code for access to explore weblinks and more resources.

Explore More ▲
Directs you to additional reading materials, maps, further context and interactive quizzes. This broadens the scope of the book and allows you to conduct independent research related to key topics. Follow the barcode to access these and other resources at our accompanying website.

THE PEDAGOGICAL TOOLS

A methodology for approaching and analysing ideas

The following TOOLS are integrated throughout each chapter to guide your learning and build your analytic skills. At the end of every chapter, all of these TOOLS are combined in an exercise which will help you to approach a research question.

 THINK

As we touched upon earlier in this chapter, your own experience provides a foundational basis for learning (*Concrete Experience*). What you believe and what you know, are important to how you understand the world around you. Early in each chapter you will therefore find a **T**HINK box setting out some points and questions for your reflection. These questions are aimed at unpacking your own experiences, assumptions and beliefs and how they may shape your understanding of the subject material covered in that chapter. As you read through each chapter you can use the **T**HINK tool to reflect on your own experience and how the subject material relates to what you know, feel and believe.

◀ **Think**
questions are aimed at unpacking your experiences, assumptions and beliefs which frame your engagement with the topics at hand.

 OBSERVE

The next learning stage is *Reflective Observation* where you may look to make sense of your experience. The **O**BSERVE tool within each chapter and toolkit exercise encourages you to reflect on the variety of perspectives that can shape your understanding of the subject material. The **O**BSERVE tool is also especially important in considering more marginalized or critical perspectives within international politics, and which calls upon us as scholars to actively reflect on world views that critique more 'mainstream' assumptions and arguments. Reflection and observations also call upon you as a scholar to think not just about yourself, but who is involved in the issue itself, and why they might care. Observation thus represents that first important step towards understanding the politics at play, and in developing your critical analysis skills (pg.x).

◀ **Observe**
encourages you to reflect on a variety of perspectives that can shape your understanding. Observation represents the first important step towards understanding the politics at play.

 ORGANIZE

The next learning stage is *Abstract Conceptualization* where you are called on to assimilate and distil your reflective observations into a theory or concept. This requires you to **O**RGANIZE your thoughts, using logic and ideas rather than emotions or feelings to understand the topic you are studying. This stage of learning can often be the hardest to master. The **O**RGANIZE boxes throughout each chapter, and in the toolkit exercises, are therefore used in two key ways. First, the **O**RGANIZE tool is aimed at clarifying key concepts, and analytical and theoretical perspectives, or setting out key readings from the scholarship to help you reinforce your understanding. Second, the **O**RGANIZE boxes are used as signposts to help you make your own connections between the subject material being covered in that chapter, and the theory, concepts and analytical approaches discussed elsewhere in this book, along with some guiding questions to then help you organize your thinking.

◀ **Organize**
helps you to make direct connections between the subject material and the theories or concepts commonly utilised as analytical and explanatory tools. This enables you to organize your thoughts using logic and ideas rather than emotions or feelings.

 LINK

- *Consider*: As a former colony, the US has its own postcolonial legacy shaped not only by the British (whom the United States won independence from in 1783), but also by the French, Dutch, Italian, Spanish and Portuguese. Consider also that 574 Native American tribes live in the continental US and Alaska, and who are themselves subject to colonization. How might the United States' experience of colonialism have shaped its outlook on imperialism?
- *Explore*: In today's international system, the US has considerable power projection capability courtesy of its extensive network of military bases located around the world. See https://militarybases.com for more details on its base locations. Scan the barcode also to explore more about the rise (and fall?) of the US dollar as the world's reserve currency.
- *Connect*: Advocates of *Pax Americana* would suggest US military and economic influence has been a guarantor of international order and security since 1945. Is that influence evidence of the United States' hegemonic position in the world, or would you identify this as (neo-)imperialism at work?
- *Predict*: By 2050 what will the balance of power look like in our international system (pg. 20)? Would you predict a continued US economic and military hegemony or is decline inevitable?

◀ **Link**
encourages you to test your theories and make predictions about the real-world. They help to shape your understanding by encouraging you to consider the interests of all parties involved, and to set these in a wider context.

 SHARE

Communication is a key skill for any scholar of international politics to grasp. It is often a requirement of university courses that students not only construct an argument or position but be able to **S**HARE their case and communicate it in a clear and accessible way. At the end of each chapter, you will therefore find a 'How to' guide, with each guide encouraging you to communicate your knowledge in a meaningful way. These 'How to' guides address many of the key skills you will need as a scholar of international politics including 'how to identify quality sources', 'how to approach referencing', 'how to paraphrase', 'how to take a position' and 'how to develop critical analysis skills', for example. The **S**HARE feature of each toolkit exercise further provides guiding questions to help you address your research question, and which will signpost you to other relevant 'how to' guides in the book where you can find top tips on how to approach common politics assessment methods including essays, blogs, policy briefs, academic posters, oral presentations, literature reviews and reflective writing.

◀ **Share**
focuses on forming and communicating arguments, helping you to put ideas together coherently and convincingly. This prompt also points you to relevant 'How to' guides which can help with constructing different types of argument.

Online Learning and Teaching Resources

Accompanying this book is a full suite of supportive resources to help both students and lecturers get the most out of their learning and teaching.

Access the digital resources here: bloomsbury.pub/understanding-international-politics

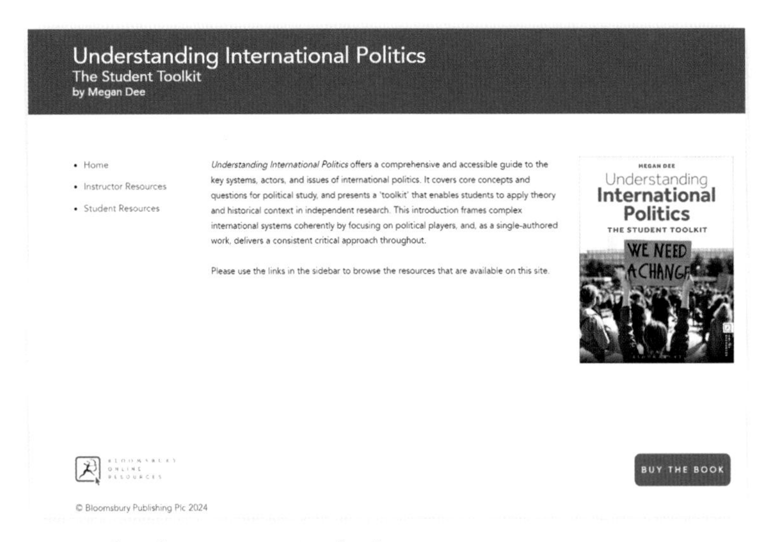

Resources for lecturers include:

- **Teaching preparation guide:** This manual provides detailed seminar notes and class discussion prompts for each chapter including some active learning activities such as role play and simulation-based exercises.
- **PowerPoint slides:** These contain key ideas from the chapter distilled into brief talking points, as well as selected illustrative material, for use in class.
- **Test bank:** This includes essay and revision questions for use in formative and summative assessments, which cover different levels of difficulty to use with a broad range of students.

Resources for students include:

- **Further reading materials:** This is a tailored list of chapter-by-chapter resources for students to explore and analyse independently, using and applying the book's TOOLS.

Part I

Understanding the international system

1 Your view of the world

Pexels / cottonbro studio

Abstract

This introductory chapter is aimed at developing your understanding of the different perspectives that can shape your view, and by extension, understanding of the world in which you live. Your experience and outlook on the world around you provide your own unique starting point to the study of international politics. In this chapter you will start to consider how perceptions of the international system have largely been dominated by Europe and the West, looking first at how the world has itself been mapped and its evolution, before addressing depictions of a hierarchical world order including notions of First, Second and Third Worlds or Global North and South, and how they may be challenged. The primary objective of this chapter, then, is to encourage you to consider not just your own experiences and global outlook, but how the study of international politics is itself shaped by oftentimes very different perspectives. The chapter goes on to describe international politics as a topic of study, why it matters, and how it is situated within wider disciplines. The chapter also introduces you to the 'toolkit' that will help guide your learning throughout the book to come, before outlining the three sections of the textbook to follow, focusing on the international system, the actors and issues in international politics.

ALL POLITICS STARTS WITH YOU

As someone approaching the study of international politics for the first time, it can be expected that you might feel some sense of excitement but also, potentially, foreboding. The excitement, of course, comes from grappling with a subject that is as interesting and diverse as any in academia can boast. We only need glance at our news feed to see international politics in action in a very real, oftentimes very pressing, way. We just need to see the reports of war, conflict and humanitarian disasters, to environmental concerns, issues relating to arms control or trade disputes to get a sense of the pertinence and constant topicality of the subject into which you now venture. International politics grapples with everything from conflict and competition to cooperation and collective action. From policy to strategy to power. All from the perspective of the international system itself – a global network of states that spans all the world's peoples and geographic territories. It is nevertheless that very scope that can also inspire some foreboding to those approaching it for the first time. After all, international politics grapples with topics as deep and wide as the world itself. Such a perspective can often prove overwhelming. Where should you even start?

Well, we start in fact with **you**.

If the art of politics is to recognize the competing views or visions of how things are (Wight 2006: 2), then the art of studying international politics is to recognize the many, often competing, visions of the world as it is, and the world as we want it to be. Before anyone can fully appreciate such differences of perspective involved in international politics, however, it is important to first reflect on your own view of the world. As Da Vinha (2019) suggests, individuals often generate their own geographic mental maps of the world around them, shaped by individual experience and perceptions, culture and identity. The questions any scholar of international politics should first ask themselves therefore include *What is my viewpoint or mental map of the world? How do I identify myself? How do my experiences influence my perspective of the world as it is, and the world as I want it to be?*

As an exercise, consider where you have been, whom you have spoken to, and the many ordinary activities you might have engaged in over the course of one day. As a hypothetical scenario say on this one day you take a drive to the supermarket. On the way you stop to fill up your car's tank with diesel and note that the cost has increased from last week. You meet with roadworks due to new cycling lanes being installed in your area. You get to the supermarket and find you must ask a shop assistant for help in tracking down an item you cannot find. Shopping in tow, you return home, listening now to the news on the radio which reports that world leaders are gathering at the United Nations (UN) to discuss the latest international crisis, and that the Foreign Minister or Secretary of State of your country is attending. Where in this scenario is the international politics?

In this seemingly innocuous series of activities, it can perhaps be easy to identify the radio report of world leaders meeting at the UN as the only international politics taking place. But look closer. The cost of fuel at the pump was by no means random. Instead, fuel prices are shaped by fluctuations in global energy prices, themselves shaped not only by market principles of supply and demand but by commodity prices that can be impacted by anything from natural disasters to political unrest in oil-producing countries. Do you have an opinion on the use of diesel fuel in cars? What is your viewpoint on where your fuel comes from or how secure your country's energy supply might appear?

Consider then the roadworks to install new cycling lanes. While likely actioned by your local authority/council, the decision to advance greener methods of travel has more likely than not been informed by global climate action efforts. Do you have an opinion on climate change? Do you think greener methods of travel facilitated at the local level can make a difference in addressing climate change globally? Finally reflect on our hypothetical supermarket. The assistant helping you locate your missing item could have been one of the 169 million migrant workers constituting nearly 5 per cent of the global labour force (ILO 2021). What is your viewpoint on immigration in your country? Have you ever considered your government's stance on this issue?

All politics starts with you because your experiences are what shape your opinions, assumptions and perceptions and therefore your own 'world view'. Believe it or not these perceptions are what will also continue to shape your scholarship of international politics.

If academia is a community of people concerned with the pursuit of research, education and scholarship, then your perspective and opinions matter to that community. You are now part of that community. Take a pause, therefore. Reflect. Get excited. What follows in this book are the first deliberate steps into a discipline that is intellectually challenging, exciting and thoroughly rewarding. One that will inspire your passion as well as your academic curiosity not only about international politics, but about the world in which we live.

THE WORLD IN WHICH WE LIVE

The world in which we live is occupied by roughly 7.8 billion people spread across a land area of around 148 million square kilometres. Take a moment to reflect on Map 1.1 of the World political map and you will see how land is carved up into a seemingly colourful patchwork of states, each with clearly demarcated borders, and each responsible for the peoples and territories within them. Yet maps themselves shape our understanding of the world around us. When reflecting on this map, what draws your eye? Think about the number of states you see or their relative size. Consider where state boundaries fall, sometimes along natural geographical lines like an ocean, a river or mountain range, other times though as perfectly straight lines as if drawn by a ruler on a page. Also consider that to map the world on to a flat piece of paper requires some distortion. This two-dimensional image ordered along clear lines of longitude and latitude is of course a three-dimensional sphere where straight lines are not necessarily so obvious. The relative size of states presented on the political map are also contorted by that necessity to straighten and flatten out the sphere. Land masses around the poles – such as North America, Antarctica and Russia – particularly tend to be over-exaggerated in terms of their relative size.

Mapping is an essential tool for viewing the world and for simplifying it. Yet it is also important to recognize that maps themselves shape our perceptions of relative size, importance and even dominance within the world around us. Taking a historical perspective of world mapping particularly highlights how the world has been distorted

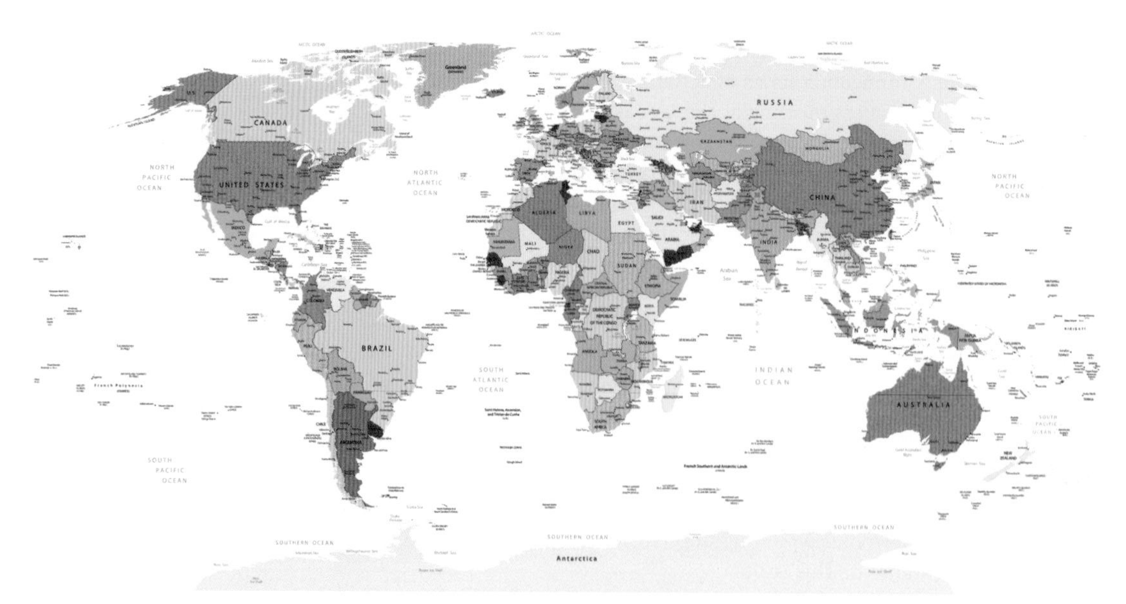

Map 1.1 World political map.
Source: Booka1/Getty Images.

over time as understandings of **cartography** – dominated as they were by European and American cartographers and map makers – evolved and changed. Take Map 1.2 by the Dutch map maker C. J. Visscher from the mid-17th century as an example. Observe the exaggerated size of the northern hemisphere relative to the south. The perceived importance of Europe and North America is also apparent in Visscher's visualization, with North America dominating the top left quadrant of the map, while South America is noticeably smaller. Europe too is presented as being roughly equal in scale to Russia and parts of Asia. Imperial connotations are also clearly apparent in the pictograms that encircle the map, again reflecting the perceptions and experiences shaping Visscher's outlook.

Cartography
The study and practice of map making.

While of course cartography has come a long way in capturing a truer image of the world 'as it is' since Visscher's day, the perceived dominance of the northern hemisphere over the south has nevertheless continued in the mental maps of many. Legacies of empire and colonialism continue to shape our understanding of the world around us. The idea of hierarchical order and a world divided along lines of power and dominance was noticeable during the Cold War, for example, where conceptualizations of First, Second and Third World dominated the political discourse of the day (Map 1.3).

Explore More

Want to know the true size of states and continents? Check out https://thetruesize.com

Scan the QR code for access to explore weblinks and more resources.

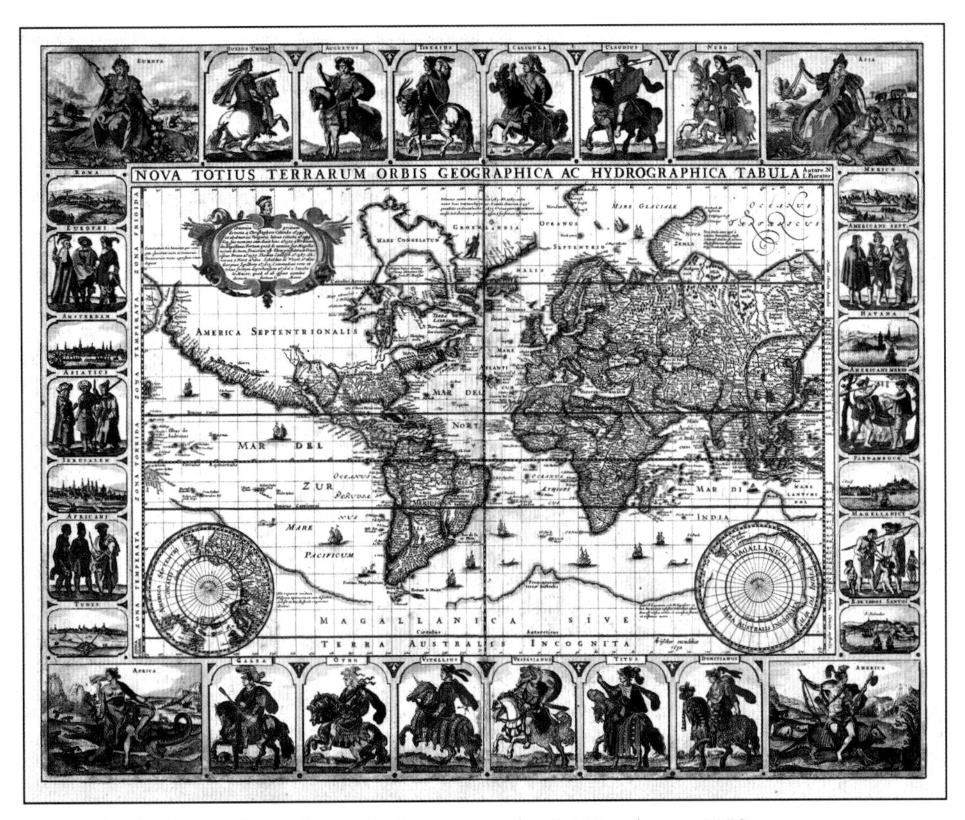

Map 1.2 World map from the mid-17th century by CJ Visscher *c.* 1652.
Source: Wikimedia Commons.

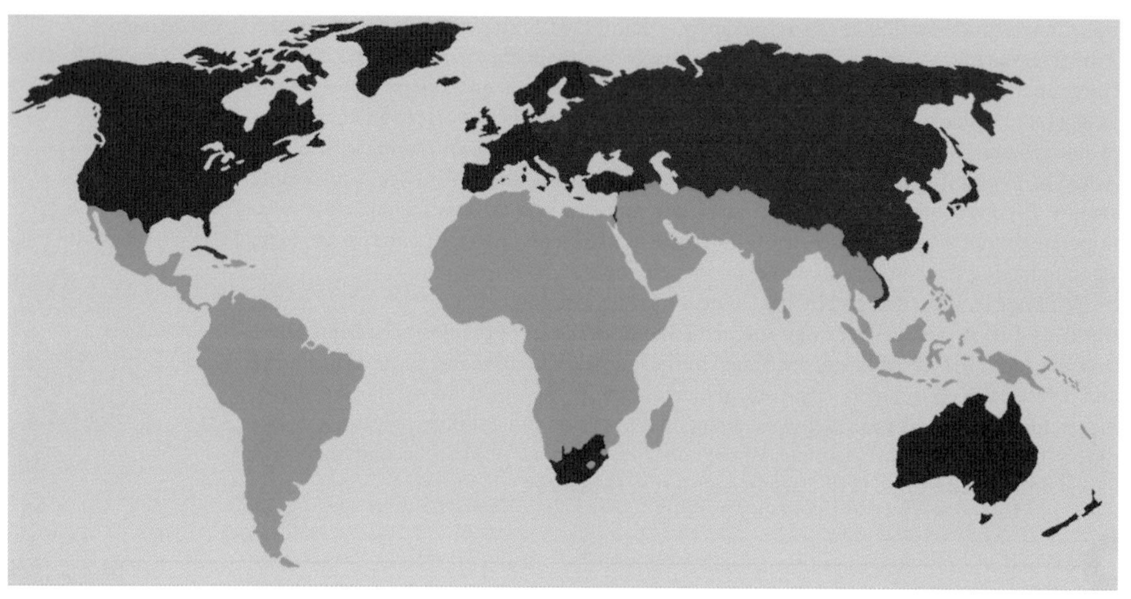

Map.1.3 World map depicting the First World in blue, Second World in red and Third World in green.
Source: Wikimedia Commons.

The division of the international system into Three Worlds can be traced in part to the French demographer, Alfred Sauvy, who first used the phrase 'Third World' in a paper written in 1952 entitled 'Three Worlds, One Planet'. In Sauvy's conceptualization, the 'First World' could be associated with the capitalist world, the 'Second World' with the communist world, and the 'Third World' with all the other countries that were non-aligned in the Cold War, and who were largely former colonies and developing countries. While perhaps less commonly used in the 21st century since the demise of communism and the fall of the Soviet Union, the *First World* continues in many respects to be used as shorthand for the advanced, industrialized, liberal democratic West or broader *Global North*, relative to the *Third World* of developing states, many of which are also identified as part of the *Global South*. Within such hierarchical depictions of a world divided by a dominant North and developing South, decolonization is of course a constant reminder. Parag Khanna (2018) makes the case that concepts such as Global North and Global South are simple rhetorical devices, yet they cannot truly be understood 'other than in the context of decolonization and post-decolonization'.

As we shall explore further in Chapter Two, the modern state system in which we now live has a long history of empire building, colonization and subsequent decolonization. History has a long reach, and the legacies of the past continue to influence perceptions, visualizations and narratives of hierarchy and dominance in how we visualize the world today. The study of international politics has equally been affected, having been dominated by Western perspectives that shaped much of what are presented as the earliest debates within the discipline. Decolonization is not then just the action of a state withdrawing from a former colony but must take on a wider meaning. Decolonizing our view of the world calls on us to actively reflect upon and challenge those ingrained mental maps that have been shaped by the colonial past, and with it, endemic racism. As new scholars to the study of international politics, be prepared therefore to challenge and really think beyond your own mental maps. Be prepared to question how the past informs the present, to question the power dynamics at play, to reflect on the voices that are marginalized or even silent, and to ask '*What do others think?*' and '*How might others perceive this?*' As we shall see in the following sections, the study of international politics will develop your skills in not just research and analysis, but critical reflection and argumentation also. Adopting a reflective practice now will serve you well as you make your jump into the discipline and discover more about the world views that ultimately shape it.

THE STUDY OF INTERNATIONAL POLITICS

International politics concerns the ideas, interests and institutions that frame the interactions of global actors and shape international outcomes. Where politics may be identified with the study of government – concerned with the activities of governing institutions, decision-making and power within countries – international politics can be identified with the study of **governance**, centring on the highest level of activity, decision-making and management within the international system itself. To study international politics is to learn about cooperation, contestation, competition and conflict within the international system, to discover the norms, laws and practices that shape the relationships between states and other non-state actors, and to explore the dynamics of power that determine actor behaviour and impact international outcomes. International politics scholarship requires you to understand the nature and make-up of the international system itself, the actors that make up its constituent parts, and the international issues that preoccupy much of their time.

Governance
The process and action by which decisions are made, managed and enforced within an organization or society.

An important point of note is that international politics operates in near constant overlap and proximity with international relations, international studies and world or global politics. In fact, the terms are now used almost interchangeably, with differences between them often seen as a point of semantics. Yet there is debate to be had over the distinctions between these terminologies – one that every university will take a position on when creating their degree programmes.

The first distinction is with regards the use of *international* or *global*. International relations and international politics both share the same proclivity towards the *international*. The reason for this is that reference to *international* tends to place the interaction of 'nations', and by extension the state, at the centre of the discipline. Adherents to international politics and international relations acknowledge a certain state-centrism to the world at large, considering the world in which we live as a system of states. The state thus remains fundamental as a unit of analysis and point of reference when understanding events and politics at the global level.

Newer references to *global* or even *world politics* by contrast have questioned the state-centrism of the international system, and certainly the role of the 'nation' if not necessarily the nation-state on the world stage. As the world has evolved and changed, modernization and **globalization** has, moreover, created a world more interconnected and interdependent than at any time in history. Such perspectives therefore question the dominant role of the state as a primary unit of analysis. Yet important to highlight is that both international and global perspectives recognize the rise of new and diverse non-state actors within the system – of multinational enterprises, non-governmental organizations, social movements and transnational advocacy networks, as well as violent non-state actors such as organized crime networks and terrorist organizations – all exerting new influences and new roles over a complex and interconnected international system.

Globalization
The spread of technology, products, information, services and people across national borders, establishing a more interconnected and interdependent global system.

The second distinction that fuels debate is between the words *relations*, *studies* or *politics*. The distinction here is less about 'who' matters and more to do with 'what' matters. Traditionally, *international relations* has tended to emphasize and even prioritize the relations between states themselves. Reference to *international studies* offers connotations of a discipline that moves beyond politics to capture all relations between international or global actors, thus addressing the non-political such as economic, religious, social or cultural relations. *Relations* and *studies* are also generally considered less adversarial terms than *politics* which can be perceived as a more competitive terminology. Prioritizing *politics* meanwhile places emphasis upon the political nature of actors and their behaviour at the global/international level across a wide myriad of issue areas. The focus on *politics* is, moreover, concerned with relationships of power, of governing and governance itself, and considers the more adversarial nature of such relationships. As a discipline, politics is also naturally interdisciplinary in nature. International politics therefore draws on a diverse range of subjects including, but not limited to, history, sociology, economics, business, management, psychology, etc.

While this debate may strike many as pedantic, the distinctions are in fact important to emphasize and reflect upon when commencing further study and research. For the purposes of this book, the term *international politics* is used. The book does adopt a certain state-centrism in its focus – because, arguably, states continue to be major players in international actions and interactions today. The book nevertheless gives careful attention to other non-state actors, to international and regional organizations, non-governmental organizations, multinational enterprises and violent non-state actors, for example. And it further emphasizes the politics at play within our international system, focusing on points of competition and contestation, but also cooperation between the actors within that system. Such an approach is not to the exclusion of *international relations* or *global politics* perspectives, but rather more as a middle ground between them.

A key point to highlight here is that debate itself is also academia's greatest attribute and healthiest component part. Understanding the academic, and even at times semantic, origins of the discipline you are entering is important in developing your understanding of scholarship and research. Debate moulds every academic discipline and, as we shall see when we turn to the debates that evolved and shaped the theoretical perspectives of international politics in Chapters Three and Four, our discipline is no exception.

As we discussed in the previous section, reflection is also a critical and necessary step in maintaining the health of our discipline, as is the ready acknowledgement that every scholar has their own perspective and 'mental maps' that shape what they think and write. Just as all politics starts with **you** and your experiences and views, the caveat follows that this book has also been shaped by its author's own experiences and world views. Conscious effort is made in the book to present a range of views and perspectives wherever possible, but more anglicized or Westernized perspectives may be evident at times. As you start to delve more deliberately into the chapters to come, therefore, reflect carefully. Consider the perspective being offered and question it. This book is not aimed at passive, but active learners, so think reflectively about what you are reading.

USING THE RIGHT TOOLS

A core aim of this book is that you not just read about international politics, but actively interact and engage with it. International politics is not a static subject. As international politics shifts and changes, so too does our study of it. This book is therefore written not just to inform, but to equip you with the tools you will need to undertake your own research and analysis into international politics itself. A key thread therefore running throughout all subsequent chapters of this book is an active learning *TOOLkit*, specifically developed to help you understand international politics by engaging directly with the subject material, digesting it, making connections, exploring further and developing your research and analytical skills at the same time.

The toolkit uses a phased approach to learning that builds on David Kolb's (1984) Learning Preference Model. Kolb argued that the process of learning comprises four stages: *Concrete Experience, Reflective Observation, Abstract Conceptualization* and *Active Experimentation*. According to Kolb, people tend not to use all four stages in their learning but prefer to concentrate on one or two of them. However, for learning to be at its most effective, all four stages need to be reached. The toolkit developed in this book has therefore been tailored to help you reach all four stages of learning for the materials covered in each chapter. To do this we use the acronym **TOOLS**, or **T**(hink) **O**(bserve) **O**(rganize) **L**(ink) and **S**(hare) – further detailed in the following sections. You will find these tools highlighted in boxes throughout each chapter. They are also used as a combined toolkit exercise at the end of each chapter to help you work through what you've learned, apply your knowledge and build up your understanding of international politics.

YOUR TOOLS

THINK

As we touched upon earlier in this chapter, your own experience provides a foundational basis for learning (*Concrete Experience*). What you believe and what you know, are important to how you understand the world around you. Early in each chapter you will therefore find a **T**HINK box setting out some points and questions for your reflection. These questions are aimed at unpacking your own experiences, assumptions and beliefs and how they may shape your understanding of the subject material covered in that chapter. As you read through each chapter you can use the **T**HINK tool to reflect on your own experience and how the subject material relates to what you know, feel and believe.

OBSERVE

The next learning stage is *Reflective Observation* where you may look to make sense of your experience. The **O**BSERVE tool within each chapter and toolkit exercise encourages you to reflect on the variety of perspectives that can shape your understanding of the subject material. The **O**BSERVE tool is also especially important in considering more marginalized or critical perspectives within international politics, and which calls upon us as scholars to actively reflect on world views that critique more 'mainstream' assumptions and arguments. Reflection and observations also call upon you as a scholar to think not just about yourself, but who is involved in the issue itself, and why they might care. Observation thus represents that first important step towards understanding the politics at play, and in developing your critical analysis skills (pg. 163).

ORGANIZE

The next learning stage is *Abstract Conceptualization* where you are called on to assimilate and distil your reflective observations into a theory or concept. This requires you to **O**RGANIZE your thoughts, using logic and ideas rather than emotions or feelings to understand the topic you are studying. This stage of learning can often be the hardest to master. The **O**RGANIZE boxes throughout each chapter, and in the toolkit exercises, are therefore used in two key ways. First, the **O**RGANIZE tool is aimed at clarifying key concepts, and analytical and theoretical perspectives, or setting out key readings from the scholarship to help you reinforce your understanding. Second, the **O**RGANIZE boxes are used as signposts to help you make your own connections between the subject material being covered in that chapter, and the theory, concepts and analytical approaches discussed elsewhere in this book, along with some guiding questions to then help you organize your thinking.

LINK

The final learning stage is *Active Experimentation* at which point you are looking to advance your knowledge, to test theories and make predictions about the real world. The **L**INK feature in each chapter and toolkit exercise then helps you to draw connections between what you know and think, what the scholarship can tell us, how theories or concepts can guide us, and what you can actively research to further hone your argument or position. Specifically, the **L**INK feature calls upon you to:

- *'Consider'* – points of reflection from that chapter and your knowledge from what you have read.
- *'Explore'* – to conduct your own independent research by actively looking beyond this book to further your knowledge and argument. This section also links to our companion website where you will find relevant news and analysis connected to that subject as a starting point for your research.
- *'Connect'* – makes specific connections between real-world examples and data and the theoretical connections already made, providing hints to enable you to make your own connections.
- *'Predict'* – encourages you to make your own informed predictions of what your research findings may mean to a real-world context in the future.

SHARE

Communication is a key skill for any scholar of international politics to grasp. It is often a requirement of university courses that students not only construct an argument or position but be able to **S**HARE their case and communicate it in a clear and accessible way. At the end of each chapter, you will therefore find a 'How to' guide, with each guide encouraging you to communicate your knowledge in a meaningful way. These 'How to' guides address many of the key skills you will need as a scholar of international politics including 'how to identify quality sources', 'how to approach referencing', 'how to paraphrase', 'how to take a position' and 'how to develop critical analysis skills', for example. The **S**HARE feature of each toolkit exercise further provides guiding questions to help you address your research question, and which will signpost you to other relevant 'how to' guides in the book where you can find top tips on how to approach common politics assessment methods including essays, blogs, policy briefs, academic posters, oral presentations, literature reviews and reflective writing.

OVERVIEW OF THE TEXTBOOK

In the chapters to follow you will be introduced to some of the theories, concepts, actors and issues within the study of international politics, providing an important foundation for you to then advance your research and scholarship in the discipline. To develop your understanding of international politics, the book is broken down into three main parts as follows:

Part I: Understanding the International System introduces you to the international system along with the various theories, concepts and levels of analysis we can utilize as scholars to understand, explain and critique international politics within that system. In Chapter Two you will therefore be introduced to the historical evolution of the international system, the seeming origins of the modern state system and the emergence of sovereignty as a key organizing principle, along with the impacts of imperialism, nationalism, war and the fall of empires on international politics both then and now.

In Chapter Three we then start to dig into the evolution of international politics as an academic discipline, and some of the theoretical foundations of how international politics came to be studied. In this chapter you will be introduced to realism and liberalism as popularized theoretical traditions within the discipline, enabling you to start developing your own theoretical toolkit for analysing, explaining and predicting behaviours, events and outcomes within international politics. Chapter Four further develops upon this theme, introducing you to a range of social and critical theoretical approaches including Marxism, postcolonialism, feminism and social constructivism. In Chapter Five you will refine your analytical toolkit yet further, by exploring the levels of analysis approach intended to help you finesse your understanding of how to use and apply different theories, consider where you should look for explanations, which actors and processes you then prioritize in your research and analysis, and how these choices start to shape your arguments. By the end of Part I therefore you will have a full arsenal of theoretical and analytical tools which you can draw upon in the subsequent chapters where our focus shifts towards international actors and issues.

In *Part II: Understanding the Actors*, our focus turns to the various different actors that we can consider when researching international politics. Chapter Six kicks off this section with a look at the state itself within international politics, addressing some of the complexities around sovereignty and statehood, and looking at statecraft and diplomacy, a state's foreign policy instruments, and how a state might exercise power. In Chapter Seven we then address the role of international organizations, looking at their evolution, membership and functions, with particular focus on the United Nations and its family of associated international organizations. Focus is also given in this chapter to how we might use theory to explain international cooperation through international organizations, as well as some of the common academic debates surrounding the agency, effectiveness and legitimacy of international organizations within international politics.

In Chapter Eight you will explore the emergence and spread of regional organizations within the international system. In this chapter you will discover more about the scope of regional organizations, their functions and membership, as well as particular insight into the European Union (EU) as one of the most integrated and institutionalized regional organizations in the world. The last chapter of this section then is Chapter Nine addressing Non-State Actors. This chapter captures a broad range of actors considered autonomous from the state within international politics, including those we might categorize as civil society actors, including non-governmental organizations, transnational advocacy networks and social movements. Focus also is given in this chapter to violent non-state actors, such as private military companies and terrorist organizations. The chapter also addresses multinational enterprises as non-state actors.

Armed with knowledge of the different actors within international politics, in *Part III: Understanding the Issues*, the book then introduces you to a range of different issues of importance within the study of international politics. Our first issues chapter is Chapter Ten in which we address two core topics of interest to international politics scholars – war and peace. In this chapter we discuss war and peace as a continuum of violence, conflict mediation and negotiation, and peace. You will be introduced to different types of warfare, how conflicts can be mediated, managed and negotiated truces kept, as well as different perspectives on what constitutes 'peace' within our international system. In Chapter Eleven these themes are developed as we consider security (and by extension, insecurity) as an issue within international politics. In this chapter you will learn some of the ways that we conceptualize security, including the different ways of understanding national security relative to human security. The chapter further shines a spotlight on nuclear weapons as a security concern within international politics today, addressing how we might observe nuclear weapons differently through national security versus human security lenses. The chapter also addresses other non-traditional security concerns including health security and cyber security.

In Chapter Twelve and Thirteen we then deep dive into issues commonly addressed by International Political Economy as a sub-discipline within international politics. In Chapter Twelve you will be introduced to Trade and Finance as key issues within the international economy, addressing the emergence of international economic organizations, the changing politics of international trade, trade wars, and the importance of currencies and foreign exchange. This chapter also addresses the emergence of cryptocurrencies and the contentions surrounding their use and regulation. Chapter Thirteen then focuses on issues of Equality and Development within international politics. In this chapter you will explore more about the marked inequalities within our international system, you will learn the different ways of conceptualizing development, including economic, human and sustainable development, as well as considering the politics of foreign aid.

In Chapter Fourteen our attention moves towards the related issues of Energy and the Environment within international politics. In this chapter you will address the increasing prevalence of energy politics on international agendas, much exacerbated by Russia's invasion of Ukraine in 2022, and the rising concern over energy security. Related to this, the chapter also unpacks the challenges associated with the use of fossil fuels for energy purposes and the growing environmental impacts this has generated for our climate. The chapter elaborates on energy and the environment as global commons, along with global efforts to try to tackle climate change. The chapter further addresses the international challenges associated with resource scarcity.

Our final two issues chapters then address Rights and Responsibility, and Race, Religion and Identity within international politics. Chapter Fifteen on Rights and Responsibility focuses on the distinctions between rights and duty, upon human rights, and international human rights law, and the debate over the universality of human rights. The chapter also tackles the development and challenges associated with humanitarian intervention within international politics, and the rights and responsibilities of states to not only defend the rights of their own citizens, but to intervene in other states where gross human rights violations occur.

Chapter Sixteen on Race, Religion and Identity then brings us back full circle to the reflections detailed in this introductory chapter where the focus is once again placed on you, your identities, your mental maps, your experiences and your perceptions. In this final chapter, discussion is given to two issues that have been marginalized and even silenced in the study of international politics, but which are becoming increasingly resurgent issues today, focusing first on race and racism within the study of international politics, before addressing the role of religion in international conflict and cooperation. The book concludes also with a reflection toolkit, asking, '*What does decolonization mean to me?*' thereby enabling you to critically and reflectively engage with the legacies of colonization and racism upon both the practice and study of international politics.

CONCLUSION

All politics starts with you. Are you ready? As you read on you will now have the chance to actively reflect, connect and research international politics. In addition to the book's toolkit, throughout the chapters to follow you will also find several 'Explore More' boxes integrated within the text. These Explore More boxes provide online resources that you can explore, investigating policy documents, position statements, reports, interactive maps and other tools that will help you take those first steps as an active researcher, going beyond these pages to undertake your own independent research and analysis.

Bear in mind also that this book is specifically geared towards active learning and to help you proactively engage and interact with theories, concepts, issues and actors at play within international politics. This book is not, nor should it be, the only resource you will utilize in your studies. When you read on therefore be prepared to explore further. You will also find many helpful resources at our companion website which you can access at bloomsbury.pub/understanding-international-politics or by scanning the barcode as you read on in the pages to follow.

Above all, be prepared to put your own 'mental maps' to the test, to challenge your assumptions, question what you 'know', and be ready to dig deeper. What follows in this book is not only the foundations of subject knowledge you will need to advance in your studies, but the tools that you yourself can use to become an independent researcher and scholar.

So let's start.

2 The evolution of the international system

Pexels / Suzy Hazelwood

Abstract

In this chapter you will develop your understanding of the historical context shaping our observations of international politics. The chapter focuses on the international system and how it has evolved over the past 500 years, addressing issues such as the nature and evolution of sovereignty, the emergence of statehood, the rise and fall of imperialism and colonization, Great Power competition and conflict and superpower contestation. In so doing, this chapter sets the stage for your analysis of contemporary international politics and the international system as it is today.

UNDERSTANDING THE INTERNATIONAL SYSTEM

In the last chapter we considered the world political map and how our own mental maps shape our perceptions of the world in which we live. When we look at the world political map (Map 1.1 pg. 4), we are essentially looking at the international system. A *system* can be understood as a network or assembly of parts that form a whole. *International* meanwhile refers to the involvement or interaction (*inter-*) of more than one country (*-national*). When we refer to the **international system**, therefore, we are referencing the entire global network or assembly of nations (states) that span the world's peoples and geographic territories.

International system The global network of states spanning the world's peoples and geographic territories.

A distinction must nevertheless be drawn here between the term **nation** and **state**. According to the 1933 *Montevideo Convention on the Rights and Duties of States*, a state, 'as a person of international law' should possess the following qualifications:

Nation
A large population that shares the same culture, history, traditions and language.

State
An independent political entity with clear geographic borders, territory and a defined people or community.

1. a permanent population
2. a defined territory
3. government and,
4. capacity to enter into relations with other states.

It does not necessarily follow that a nation equates to a state. As Benedict Anderson (1991) argued, a nation is an *imagined* political community. Yet translating a nation into a state (an independent political entity) can often be fraught with contestation and conflict. Consider the Kurdish nation as an example. The Kurds are a nation with an ethnic population of roughly 30 million people located in and around a region referred to as Kurdistan in the Middle East. Kurdistan is not a state, however. Kurdistan is a geographical region where the Kurdish people have historically been established, but that geographical region covers parts of Turkey, Iraq, Iran and Syria. The Kurdish population across each of these states have long fought for their political independence as a nation, yet have faced repression, disenfranchisement and bloodshed through many conflicts.

As we shall see as we go through this chapter, the evolution of the state as the main political unit within our international system has coincided with the emergence of nationalism as a doctrine, and the rise of nationhood. Often then when we refer to states in today's international system, we are referring to nation-states, that is, independent political entities representative of their respective nations. It is worth reflecting, however, on the distinctions between the *nation* as a people, a community or a body politic, and the *state* which makes up the institutions, laws and authority of a defined territory and people.

THE EVOLUTION OF THE INTERNATIONAL SYSTEM

The international system has changed dramatically in the last 500 years. The states that we identify on the world political map today have each formed and evolved over a long process spanning multiple wars, periods of peace, empires, colonization and decolonization. Even as recently as the end of the 20th century, the systemic shift that occurred with the collapse of the Soviet Union and the end of the Cold War saw the creation of thirty-four new states, the majority of which were formerly part of the Soviet Union. The world political map that we recognize today is therefore very different now from what it was even thirty to forty years ago, yet even more so when we look further back in history. In this section we explore the evolution of today's international system, looking first to the contested origins of the state system itself, to empires and colonization over the 18th to 19th centuries, to the rise of nationalism and the 20th century's world wars, Cold War and the process of decolonization.

Take a moment to reflect on the international history you have been taught, including the main topics and geographical areas of focus. In what ways do you think that historical perspective influences your view of the international system?

Prior to AD 1500 many societies around the world existed in relative isolation from one another. While most societies knew of those on their borders, entering relations with them whether through trade, or conflict, any international awareness was limited to a relatively small geographical area. Rather than one international system we might then consider the world prior to AD 1500 as multiple systems. During this period the world was not divided up by states as we recognize them today, but rather by empires, kingdoms and dynastic states, each with overlapping orders of authority. The Ming Dynasty – with a population of roughly 300 million people covering parts of modern-day China – was one of the most economically advanced empires on the planet. Peking (now Beijing) was the world's most populated city. By AD 1500, the Ottoman Empire had brought the Byzantine Empire to its end and was rapidly spreading into Northern Africa and the Balkans. In what is modern-day India, the Mughal Empire was forming, and would soon rule over much of subcontinental India, Pakistan, Afghanistan and Bangladesh. In the Americas, the Aztecs and Incas were the main empires in existence, with the Aztecs the dominant power.

Yet the story of the international system's evolution is most frequently told not from the perspective of the Ming Dynasty, Ottoman or Mughal Empires, nor from the view of the Aztecs, but rather from the perspective of the European powers. There are several reasons for this Eurocentric historical viewpoint. First, by the mid-15th century the **European Age of Discovery** had begun, with European kingdoms setting forth by sea to explore, trade with and, in time, conquer and settle lands far beyond their borders. Portugal was one of the first to undertake overseas exploration, travelling to the west coast of Africa, around the Cape of Good Hope and into the Indian Ocean. The Kingdom of Spain soon followed suit, conquering Granada in 1492, before Christopher Columbus set sail from Castile discovering the Caribbean and from there America. England, France and the Netherlands followed, first discovering, then exerting their dominance across the Americas, Africa and Asia. The story of the international system's history is therefore frequently told from the perspective of European imperialism – a point we shall return to in the following sections.

European Age of Discovery
A period in European history from the late 15th century to the mid-16th century in which the European powers undertook overseas exploration journeys, expanding their reach and eventual influence beyond Europe.

The second reason why there is often a Eurocentric focus when considering the origins and evolution of today's international system is that the modern state, and our understanding of an international system of states, is often traced to the end of the wars of religion in Europe. During the 16th and 17th centuries, Europe was made up of a complex network of empires, duchies, dynastic states and city-states. Overarching this complex network of overlapping authorities was the Holy Roman Empire, ruled by the Habsburg Dynasty spanning Spain, parts of the Netherlands, Germany, Austria and parts of modern-day Italy. This was a time of overlapping and intersecting layers of power and allegiance, where God and the Church were seen to have the highest authority, and where the struggle for power frequently reverberated around the ruling authority of the Catholic or Protestant Church. As the power of the Holy Roman Empire grew, so too did conflict as other powers sought to regain their influence and territories. For many historians of this era, war was considered a consequence of the Holy Roman Empire's quest for dominance over Europe. Principalities who resisted the authority of the Catholic Church, or who sought to balance the power of the Habsburgs, took up arms to protect their authority or defend their territories.

Wars were not always fought along clear religious lines, however. In the first half of the 16th century Catholic France regularly supported Protestant German princes in rebelling against the Habsburg Empire. From 1618 to 1648, during the Thirty Years War, Catholic France also supported the Protestant Dutch Republic and Sweden against the Habsburgs in what was one of Europe's longest and deadliest conflicts, with an estimated 8 million casualties. The Thirty Years War ended in the negotiation and signing of a series of Treaty-based agreements between the warring factions in the year 1648, commonly known as the **Peace of Westphalia**.

Peace of Westphalia
A collective term for the Treaties negotiated and signed by France, Sweden and the Holy Roman Empire in 1648 that brought an end to the Thirty Years War. The Peace of Westphalia is widely accredited for marking the origins of the modern state system.

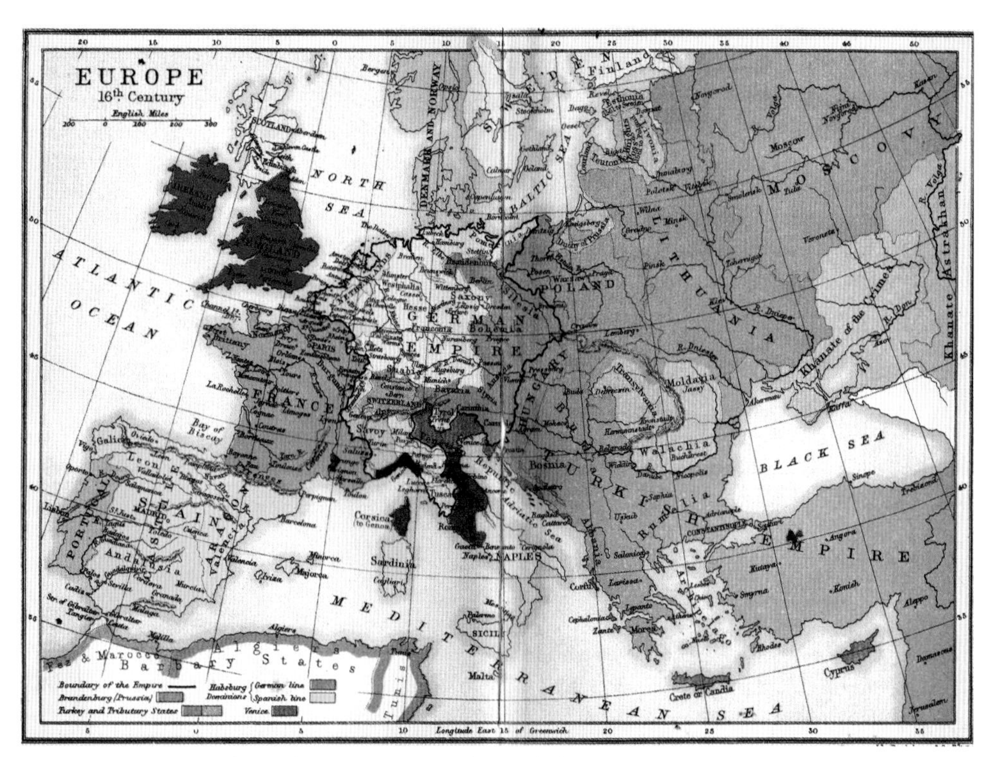

Map 2.1 Europe in the 16th century. Note the Habsburg Dynasty's dominions highlighted in yellow and dark green.

Source: Colin Waters/Alamy Stock Photo.

The Peace of Westphalia is considered significant for beginning the process of codifying sovereign territoriality, where specified geographical spaces or territories achieved political authority independent from any other higher authority. Specifically, the Peace of Westphalia began the process of recognizing the **sovereignty** of the member states of the Holy Roman Empire, empowering the 300 or so German princes who had been warring against the Catholic Church to gain certain religious freedoms while also enabling them to contract treaties with one another and with foreign powers. The Peace of Westphalia has consequently been acclaimed for making 'the territorial state the cornerstone of the modern state system' (Morgenthau 1985: 294), and as 'the peace [that] legitimized the ideas of sovereignty and dynastic autonomy from hierarchical control' (Holsti 1991: 39).

Sovereignty
The authority of a state to govern itself and to enter into relations with other states.

It should be noted, however, that the significance of the Peace of Westphalia as the point at which the modern state system first began is much debated. Hinsley (1967), for example, argued that Westphalia was largely concerned with formulating the theory of internal sovereignty (see next section) within the Holy Roman Empire, but that it was not until the 18th century that sovereignty itself became fully conceptualized and contextualized within and beyond Europe. Osiander (2001) takes this further in suggesting that the concept of sovereignty thought to have been derived in the Peace of Westphalia was largely a myth and that it was not until the 19th and 20th centuries that sovereignty truly came to be orientated as a defining principle of the modern state system.

Understanding sovereignty

While the origins of the modern state system are disputed, the principle of sovereignty itself is foundational to our understanding of the international system, and the role of the state within it. Sovereignty has two core dimensions – *internal* and *external*. First, as was developed in the Peace of Westphalia, sovereignty relates to internal hierarchy within a society. In 1576 Jean Bodin wrote in the *Six Books of the Republic* that power and authority should be concentrated in a sovereign (a King) who alone would possess monopoly on the use of force over a people and territory. Less than a hundred years later, Thomas Hobbes writing in *Leviathan* (1651) further advanced the argument for establishing sovereignty around a theory of political obligation. Sovereignty, Hobbes claimed, is a social contract between a sovereign who promises to protect their subjects and their subjects who promise to obey. *Internal* sovereignty can therefore be understood as the belief of authority by a sovereign (government, monarch, ruler) over a people and territory.

Internal sovereignty
The belief of authority by a sovereign over a defined people and territory, including authority over a territory's law and order, and monopoly over the use of force.

Applied to the state, **internal sovereignty** therefore assumes that the state has:

1. a clearly defined people and territory
2. authority (that is a recognized hierarchy) over the law and order of that territory
3. monopoly and control over the use of force in which to uphold laws and defend its people

Yet, as Hobbes also identified, while it was possible to achieve peace within a defined territory courtesy of the internal hierarchy established between sovereign and people, beyond these sovereign borders, a 'state of nature' prevailed. Between states there is no overriding authority to maintain law and order. The international system is therefore without authority. It is **anarchic**. The *external* dimension of sovereignty therefore recognizes external independence. Like the German princes seeking to cede control from the Holy Roman Empire, the sovereign state is considered independent from external interference.

Anarchy
The absence of authority. Often used to refer to the condition of the international system.

External sovereignty
The belief of independence by a sovereign from external interference.

Applied to the state, **external sovereignty** therefore assumes that the state is:

1. Free from the external interference of other authorities or powers.
2. Independent in determining its own interests.
3. Equal to other sovereign territories, possessing the same rights and duties as any other state

What is important to highlight is that sovereignty fundamentally concerns understandings of legitimate authority and control (Krasner 1982). As F. H. Hinsley (1967: 242) states, 'Men do not wield or submit to sovereignty. They wield or submit to authority of power ... Although we speak of it as something concrete that may be lost or acquired, eroded or increased, sovereignty is not a fact. It is an assumption about authority ...' When we refer therefore to sovereignty and the evolution of the international system, we are ultimately referring to an evolution of derived authority across territories and peoples around the world. As we shall also see in the next sections, how sovereignty has come to rest upon the seemingly 'fixed' world political map of the nearly 200 sovereign states we identify today, has ebbed and flowed across several centuries of exploration, colonization, nationalism and war.

Imperialism
The policy or practice of extending power and dominion of a state through direct territorial acquisition or indirect control over the political or economic life of other areas.

Colony
A country or territory under full or partial control of another country and occupied by settlers from that country.

Colonialism
A direct form of imperialism that sees an imperial power establish colonies in territories beyond their own sovereign borders.

Imperialism's rise

During the 17th, 18th and 19th centuries, one of the defining characteristics of the international system was that of **imperialism**, as European powers began to compete for control over most of the rest of the world, establishing **colonies** in the Americas, Africa, Asia and Oceania. Imperialism is the policy or practice of extending power and dominion of a state through *direct* territorial acquisitions (**colonialism**) or *indirect* control over the political or economic life of other areas. Imperialism therefore sees the extension of a state's authority and influence (sovereignty) over new territories.

Imperialism was driven not only by the quest for domination but by the policy of **mercantilism** which associated the power of the state with the pursuit of wealth. During this period of international history, national economic policies were driven by the need to augment the power of the state relative to others. Trade was a key driving force in the pursuit of national wealth and, as Carr (2021: 5) identified, 'the only way for a nation to expand its markets and therefore its wealth was to capture them from some other nation'.

Mercantilism Widely thought to be the dominant economic policy of the 18th and 19th centuries. Mercantilism is an economic policy intended to maximize the exports and minimize the imports of an economy, advocating the use of protectionist measures to augment a state's economic power at the expense of rival economies.

One prominent example of imperialism's mercantilist roots can be found in the Dutch East India Company (also called the United East Indies Company or *Verenigde Oost-Indische Compagnie* VOC). The VOC was founded by the Dutch Republic in 1602 to protect and project Dutch trade interests in the Indian Ocean. The VOC became a core instrument of Dutch imperial control and was granted a charter for a trade monopoly in the Indies, with the rights to conclude treaties, wage war, strike its own coins and establish colonies. The VOC subsequently dominated trade routes between the Atlantic and Pacific Oceans. The VOC presents a particularly interesting example therefore of how both *direct* and *indirect* imperial control could be exerted through a combination of colonization and trade monopolization. Incidentally, the VOC also provides one of the first true examples of a multinational enterprise (MNE) (see Chapter Nine).

Where empires spread, international trade followed. With each new colony established, however, indigenous peoples would be either systematically wiped out, enslaved or brought into subjugation to the colonizer. From AD 1600 the slave trade began to boom as colonies spread throughout Africa and Asia, selling captive men, women and children to Europeans, and then on to America, often being traded for other 'commodities' such as molasses or rum (pg. 206). Between 1640 and 1807,[1] the British Empire was estimated to have transported 3.1 million Africans (of whom 2.7 million arrived) to colonies in the Caribbean, North and South America and other countries (UK National Archives 2022).

By the later end of the 19th century, imperial competition between the European powers had reached a pinnacle with the colonization of Africa. The 'Scramble for Africa', also called the 'Partition' or 'Conquest' of Africa took place during the period 1881 to 1914. During this period, European powers occupied the continent and attempted to colonize it. Prior to 1881, only 10 per cent of the African continent was directly controlled by Europe. By the year 1914 around 90 per cent of Africa was under European rule with only Ethiopia and Liberia free of colonial rule.

Explore More

The origins of the British Empire can be traced back to as early as 1497 when England first established an overseas colony in Newfoundland. While the British Empire is widely considered to have ended by around the 1960s when the majority of the UK's colonies had become independent sovereign states, its formal end may be better marked in 1997 when the British government returned Hong Kong to Chinese control. The UK still has fourteen overseas territories to this day, each former crown colonies. You can explore more about the UK's foreign and colonial history, including original records relating to the transatlantic slave trade with an online register of enslaved people and slave owners, by visiting www.nationalarchives.gov.uk.

Scan the QR code for access to explore weblinks and more resources.

[1] On 25 March 1807 Britain passed the Abolition of the Slave Trade Act.

OBSERVE

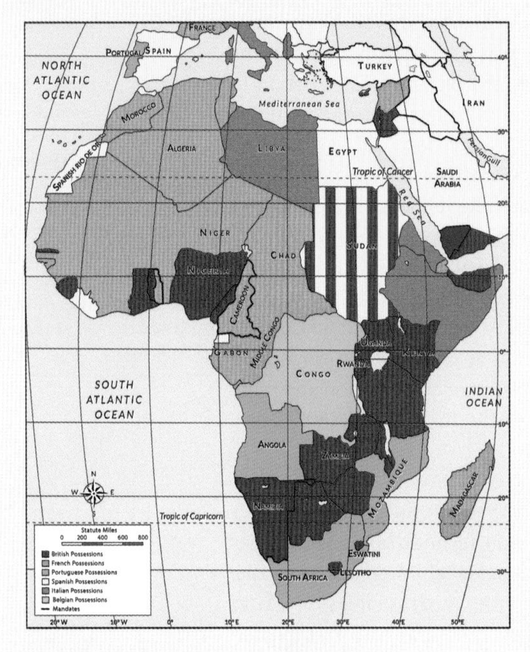

Map 2.2 Political map of Africa after the 'Scramble for Africa'.

Map 2.3 Political map of Africa today.

The key on the left-hand map reads: red: 'British Possessions', orange: 'French Possessions', green: 'Portuguese Possessions'; yellow: 'Spanish Possessions', purple: 'Italian Possessions' and blue 'Belgian Possessions'

In 1884 German Chancellor, Otto von Bismarck, hosted the Berlin Conference on the Congo (or West Africa Conference). The conference, attended by thirteen European states, the US and the Ottoman Empire, established many of the borders that carved up the African continent during the subsequent 'Scramble for Africa' and which continue to exist today. The territorial boundaries were determined on the somewhat patchwork exploration of the continent by European explorers, and based on their knowledge of rivers, mountain ranges, latitude and longitude. In some cases, lines were literally drawn on the map. No African representatives attended the conference. Little consideration was given to how the territorial divides would impact local populations, even when borders divided tribes, broke established trade routes, or neglected historical and cultural sensitivities. The artificial division of Africa's territories at the Berlin conference has had lasting effects.

As our discussion so far reflects, imperialism cannot be understood solely in terms of economics or the settling of new colonies, but fundamentally as a relationship of domination and difference. As new colonies were established around the world, and the slave trade boomed, race also became a defining difference between colonizer and colonized (Chapter Sixteen). Imperialism was grounded on a belief of racial superiority, with the European Age of Discovery underwritten by white supremacy. As Europe's empires rose to prominence, settling and then subjugating Africa, Asia, the Caribbean and Americas, the international system during this period of history must be understood as a system divided by geographical and racial difference between dominators and the dominated – a point we will continue to return to throughout the course of this book.

ORGANIZE

Image 2.1 An illustration from *Puck* magazine entitled 'From the Cape to Cairo' c.1902. The strapline to the illustration reads 'Though the process be costly, the road of progress must be cut'.

Source: Keppler, Udo J., 1872–1956, Library of Congress.

Reflect on this illustration published in *Puck* magazine in 1902. The British Empire – depicted as Britannia – carries a large white banner labelled Civilization with British soldiers and colonists behind her, advancing on the 'natives', one carrying a flag labelled Barbarism. The 'natives' here are depicted dark-skinned and bare-chested, and with only spears and shields. Several men are shown fallen, unable to rise. The British Army and colonists meanwhile are all white-skinned and depicted fully clothed and carrying guns or axes, exuding both force and order.

What do you think this cartoon reveals about imperialism and colonization as related, yet distinct, concepts?

Nationalism meets Great Power conflict and cooperation

While imperialism continued to shape the international system through the spread of European colonies and international trade routes, important changes were also starting to occur within Europe which would continue to shape the international system over the next few centuries. During the 18th and 19th centuries the rights of the sovereign (embodied by emperors, kings, princes and other ruling elites) were met with growing resistance from an increasingly mobilized and organized 'people'. While in the early modern period mercantilism primarily drove the interests of sovereign rulers, by the 18th century it was common people that were to increasingly become the focal point for how the sovereign state should derive its authority.

Rousseau was among the first to reject the idea that sovereignty should reside in a personal sovereign (monarch) or ruling class, and who identified that a nation was embodied in its people. Such principles were to spark both the French and American revolutions. In 1783 the United States of America declared its independence from Britain following the War of Independence (or American Revolution) and became its own sovereign nation. The French Revolution, which began in 1789 and ended in the late 1790s with the rise of Napoleon Bonaparte, also witnessed the rise of the 'third estate', the rejection of absolute monarchy, the advocation of republicanism, and marked the beginnings of democratization of the modern nation-state.

Napoleon went on to become both First Consul of the French Republic and French Emperor, leading France into a series of wars that established the first French Empire spanning much of continental Europe. As we shall explore further in Chapter Seven when we look at international organizations, it was following Napoleon's defeat and surrender in May 1814 that the European powers first began to institutionalize multilateral diplomacy (pg. 109). The 1814–15 Congress of Vienna instituted a series of dialogues that sought to establish a long-term peace plan for Europe through the restoration and resizing of state boundaries to establish a **balance of power**. The **Concert of Europe** which stemmed from the Congress of Vienna proved particularly successful as a cooperative mechanism that facilitated relative peace between the European powers over much of the 19th century.

Over the course of the 19th century, **nationalism** also became an increasingly potent force within European societies. Several new states formed under nationalist doctrines, including Greece (1830), Belgium (1831), Italy (1861), and Romania, Serbia and Montenegro (1878). Nationalism also shaped the reunification of Germany in 1871, a move that subsequently altered the balance of power and created new **great power** competition on the continent.

By 1914 great power competition within Europe had reached fever pitch. Alliance-building between the great powers after the reunification of Germany resulted in a Europe divided between the *Triple Alliance* (Germany, Austria-Hungary and Italy) and the *Triple Entente* (France, Britain and Russia). Heightened tensions between the two blocs were driven by the Triple Entente's concerns over German **hegemonic** ambitions and mistrust over its military intentions. The spark that then ignited World War One came on 28 June 1914 when Archduke Franz Ferdinand, heir to the Austro-Hungarian throne, and his wife were assassinated by a Bosnian terrorist with possible ties to the Serbian government. From that spark followed a series of ultimatums, military mobilizations and declarations of war between the members of the *Triple Alliance* and *Triple Entente*. World War One, or the 'Great War', thus began four years of largely trench-based warfare that left 8.5 million soldiers dead, 21 million more wounded, plus several million civilians dead or wounded.

It was in the aftermath of World War One that much of the dominant story of our academic discipline's own origins were forged (see Chapter Three). During this period, states began to implement and institutionalize cooperative mechanisms in an effort to achieve lasting peace. Prominent amongst these international efforts was the formation of the **League of Nations** intended to serve as a general association of nations and a longer-term institutional framework for states to be able to air their grievances and, through dialogue, prevent any return to war.

Over the 1920s the League was successful in facilitating international cooperation on issues such as the return of prisoners of war, the management of refugees, combatting slavery, preventing malaria and leprosy, and tackling the drugs trade. Yet as a conflict mediator and preventer, the League of Nations proved ineffective. Faced with a highly

Balance of power
Where competitor states within a system possess roughly equivalent material power capabilities.

Concert of Europe
A consensus between Europe's great powers to maintain their sovereign territoriality and maintain Europe's balance of power.

Nationalism
A political ideology advancing the objective of political independence for a given nation.

Great power
A sovereign state recognized to have advanced material capabilities and influence within the international system.

Hegemony
The position of being the dominant state in a system, be that regional or global.

League of Nations
An international organization established in 1920 to facilitate international peace, and disbanded in 1946 with the establishment of the United Nations.

volatile European continent after World War One, along with the rise of fascist dictatorships in Italy, Germany and Japan, the League soon found itself both divided and ignored.

By 1939 Europe was once again on the brink of war. German Chancellor, Adolf Hitler, intent on the goal of reasserting the German *'Aryan'* race to prominence, and of extending *'Lebensraum'* (living space) for the German people, sent troops to occupy Austria in 1938 and Czechoslovakia in 1939. On 1 September 1939, Germany, aligned with the Soviet Union, invaded Poland. Two days later Britain and France, who had previously guaranteed Poland military support in the face of military aggression, declared war on Germany.

By late 1941 the United States and Japan had entered the war. A year earlier, in 1940, Japan, already at war with China, had occupied French Indochina. With plans to then strike British, Dutch and US territories across Southeast Asia, on the morning of 7 December 1941 177 Japanese Imperial aircraft attacked the US airbase at Pearl Harbor on the island of Oahu in Hawaii. The same day, the US formally declared war against Japan. After Pearl Harbor, Japan went on to invade the Philippines which was then under US control (see Toolkit at the end of this chapter). The combined US-Philippines army was defeated by Japan by April 1942, but the war continued to play out across the islands through US and Philippine resistance efforts.

By 8 May 1945, Germany formally surrendered. While Allied forces had liberated the Philippines from Japanese control in 1944 through a naval invasion, war in the Pacific nevertheless continued. Seeking a swift end to the fighting, and in an effort to force Japan to surrender, on 6 August 1945 the United States dropped an atomic bomb on the Japanese city of Hiroshima, followed three days later by the bombing of Nagasaki (pg. 195). On 2 September 1945, World War Two came to its official close as Japan issued its formal surrender to the US. As we address in greater detail in Chapter Eleven, this first use of atomic weapons in 1945 not only brought World War Two to an abrupt close but went on to fundamentally alter the global security environment and balance of power within the international system.

Cold War and empires ending

As we saw in the previous section, a popular telling of international history over the period 1648 to 1945 highlights the importance of sovereignty, empire, nationalism, and cooperation and conflict between the great powers, particularly in Europe. After 1945 many of these characteristics have continued to inform our understanding of the international system. Yet, in sharp contrast to the previous few centuries, the period from 1945 to the early 1990s was to be dominated not by the European great powers and empire building, but by the United States and the Soviet Union, along with the steady process of decline and then disintegration of empires around the world.

With Europe crippled by the disruption and destruction of two world wars and now focused on rebuilding and integration (pg. 134), the main focal points for political contestation within the international system centred on the sole remaining **superpowers**: the US and USSR. The great power conflict that had led to two world wars was therefore replaced by superpower competition that held at its epicentre a nuclear arms race, and which, as we saw in Chapter One, pitted the democratic 'West' against a communist 'East' and created an international system seemingly divided into First, Second and Third Worlds (Map 1.2 pg. 5).

Superpower
A powerful state with advanced material capabilities possessing a global influence and dominance within the international system. A term commonly used during the post-World War Two and Cold War eras to refer to the United States and Soviet Union.

The origins of the Cold War can in part be dated to 1917 and the Russian Revolution, which saw the Bolsheviks establish the Union of Soviet Socialist Republics (USSR). During World War Two, the Soviet Union, led by Joseph Stalin, formed an uneasy alliance with the United States and United Kingdom. It was during the final year of World War Two that the Soviet Union, US and UK met in Crimea to negotiate the Yalta Conference Agreement. The Yalta Agreement was significant for several reasons. It set out several outcomes for when the Allies would win the war, including the objective for a United Nations conference to be held in the US, the terms of reparation, how to do deal with war criminals, and agreeing the terms of dealing with Japan, as well as for the Liberation of Europe.

Specifically, the Yalta Agreement enshrined 'the right of all people to choose the form of government under which they will live – the restoration of sovereign rights and self-government to those peoples'. The agreement also stated that any interim governmental authorities established in newly liberated states would be 'broadly representative of all democratic elements in the population and pledged to the earliest possible establishment through free elections to Governments responses to the will of the people' (Yalta Conference Agreement 1945).

When World War Two came to its end, however, the Yalta Conference Agreement was only partially implemented. In February 1946, Stalin, in his first radio address to the USSR following Germany and Japan's surrender, detailed how World War Two both tested and proved communism's victory, and stated that imperialism and capitalism were the enemies of communism. That same month, US Diplomat George Keenan sent an 8,000-word telegram to the US Department of State outlining his views of the Soviet Union. Amid the first few lines of this document – referred to as the 'Long Telegram' – Keenan expressed that 'in the long run there can be no permanent peaceful coexistence' with the USSR (Keenan 1946).

In March 1946 in his famous 'Iron Curtain' speech delivered in the US, UK Prime Minister Winston Churchill further outlined the underlying mistrust between the West and Soviet Union born out of Stalin's failure to uphold the terms of the Yalta Conference by ensuring free elections in Nazi-freed Poland, Czechoslovakia, Hungary, Romania and Bulgaria. Instead, communist governments had been established in these countries, backed by Moscow. As Churchill stated, 'this is not the Liberated Europe we fought to build. Nor is it one which contains the essentials of permanent peace' (Churchill 1946).

By 2 March 1947 in an address to the US Senate and House of Representatives, later to be known as the Truman Doctrine, US President Harry Truman announced that the United States would be compelled to protect free peoples from totalitarian regimes that, 'by direct or indirect aggression, undermine the foundations of international peace and hence the security of the United States' (Truman Doctrine 1947).

Containment
A foreign policy strategy pursued by the United States during the Cold War that aimed to contain Soviet influence through isolation thereby preventing the further spread of communism.

While there is no obvious start date of the Cold War, the Truman Doctrine is widely recognized to be the start of the US foreign policy of **containment** against the spread of communism and Soviet influence. The Cold War was so named due not only to the severe chill in relations between the US and USSR during the next forty years, but for the fact that, despite several close calls, no direct military conflict ensued between the

Explore More

You can really make international history come to life through research. Interested in reading the actual agreed texts from the Yalta Conference, Stalin's 1946 speech stating that imperialism and capitalism are enemies of communism, or Churchill's 'Iron Curtain' speech? Check out https://digitalarchive.wilsoncenter.org whose *Cold War International History Project* boasts one of the world's best digital archives of Cold War texts.

Ever wondered what Cold War propaganda looked like? Check out https://coldwar.unc.edu for a *Visual Guide to the Cold War.*

Scan the QR code for access to explore weblinks and more resources.

two superpowers. Rather, from the 1950s through to 1991 when the USSR collapsed, Cold War relations between the two superpowers were largely characterized by a nuclear arms race which maintained a state of **deterrence** courtesy of the doctrine of **Mutually Assured Destruction**. The Cold War was also characterized by pronounced competition between the US and USSR within the United Nations, as well as between the Western NATO defensive security alliance, and the Soviet Warsaw Pact (pg. 129). Competition between the two superpowers further extended into a space race as both the US and USSR sought to extend their influence and show their pre-eminence by being the first to land on the Moon.

While the Cold War can be considered a period of comparative stability for the international system between 1945 and 1991, particularly after the turbulent years of the early 20th century, it is only when we look beyond the dominant Eurocentric historical telling of this period that we start to see that the Cold War was neither cold nor entirely stable. Important to highlight from this period of international history is that the Cold War was not only characterized by numerous **proxy wars** fought with US and Soviet backing, but by intensive **decolonization** as anti-colonial revolts, coups, wars and independence shook the long-established empires of the 18th and 19th centuries.

With European states still in recovery after World War Two, and with many colonies still partially cut off from their colonial governors, many colonies took the opportunity to exert their sovereign independence. Indonesia and Vietnam were the first to proclaim independence from Dutch and French imperial rule in 1945. India quickly followed, negotiating its independence from the British Empire in 1947, and with it, the creation of Pakistan. Other colonial territories also gained their independence in this period such as Laos, Cambodia, the Maldives, Singapore, Tunisia, Kenya, Ghana and Guinea. In Africa, decolonization spread quickly. What began with Egypt's declaration of independence from the British Empire in 1922, then accelerated across the continent from the 1950s onwards. By 1977, fifty-four African countries had gained their independence from Europe's colonial powers.

Independence, while a watershed moment for many nations in gaining their sovereignty from colonial rule, was also challenging for many postcolonial states who were left with economic difficulties, continuing ethnic tensions and international pressures. As the European powers declined, power struggles ensued. An example of this can be seen in Angola. Angola declared its independence from Portugal in April 1974, yet from 1975 to 2002 Angola faced civil war shaped by internal power struggles and a proxy war involving the US, South Africa, Cuba and the USSR.

While conflict marred the newly gained independence for several postcolonial states like Angola, decolonization also signified a time of increasing collaboration and international organization between many postcolonial states. In 1955 a meeting of twenty-nine newly independent Asian and African states was held at Bandung in Indonesia. The Bandung Conference (pg. 269) was concerned both with the perceived US and Soviet dominance of the international system, and particularly over Asia, as well as by concerns of Western colonialism. The Bandung Conference consensus document subsequently condemned colonialism, promoted the principles of the United Nations Charter (pg. 114), and advocated several core principles for the conference parties' relations with one another, including:

1. mutual respect,
2. territorial integrity and sovereignty,
3. non-aggression,
4. non-interference in the internal affairs of others,
5. equality and mutual benefit,
6. and peaceful coexistence

Deterrence
A foreign policy strategy that aims to maintain peace by persuading enemies that they will receive significant punishment or retaliation if they attack first. Deterrence is based on the logic that threat of the use of force will deter or dissuade others from acting.

Mutually Assured Destruction (MAD)
A principle of deterrence founded on the logic that a nuclear attack by one nuclear-armed state against another would result in immediate counterattack resulting in the mutual destruction of both states.

Proxy war
A war that is instigated or supported by a major power or powers yet fought by other smaller countries or parties on their behalf.

Decolonization
The process of a state or empire withdrawing from a former colony, leaving it independent.

LINK

Image 2.2
A group of Cuban soldiers alongside soldiers from the Popular Movement for the Liberation of Angola (MPLA) on patrol in Luanda, southern Angola *c.* February 1988.

Source: Pascal Guyot/ Getty Images.

Consider

The Popular Movement for the Liberation of Angola (MPLA) formed from the Angolan Communist Party. During the Angolan Civil War (1975–2002) Cuba sent thousands of troops to support the Soviet-backed MPLA. By 1985 approximately 36,000 Cuban military personnel were located in Angola serving in Cuban brigades (CIA 1985).

Explore

Scan the barcode to find out more about the Angolan Civil War, the warring factions, and how they were each supported by other powers. Follow the links to find out more about decolonization as a violent process.

Connect

The 'Scramble for Africa', which saw nearly the entire African continent come under colonial rule from 1870 to 1914, was reversed in just half that time through decolonization between 1950 and 1977. Decolonization was highly destabilizing for some states, however, resulting in civil unrest. In Angola, when Portugal withdrew in 1975, tensions between three different factions, previously united in their anti-colonial protest, then went to war. Angola's civil war subsequently became a proxy war, as other powers, influenced by the respective ideologies of the warring factions, intervened by providing military support and finance.

Predict

Is decolonization always a violent process? What examples can you find of other postcolonial states that suffered from civil and proxy wars during this period of international history? What examples can you identify of states who experienced more peaceful processes of decolonization?

While Africa-Asia interstate cooperation became rather infrequent after Bandung, the principles advanced at the conference nevertheless continued to bear fruit. In 1961 the Non-Aligned Movement (NAM) was initiated on the principles of the Bandung Conference. The NAM was formed as a group of non-aligned states who were not part of any collective defence alliance such as NATO (pg. 129) or who had no bilateral security agreements with one of the superpowers. The NAM was also deliberately formed to give a collective voice to developing countries, and to ensure that they had a means of advancing their own agenda within international affairs. Today the NAM makes up the largest political grouping in the United Nations, with 120 member states predominantly from Africa, Asia and the Americas, representing nearly two-thirds of the UN's membership, and 55 per cent of the world's population.

The process of decolonization fundamentally redrew the world political map. Yet decolonization is not only a process. A **postcolonial** legacy also remains. The demise of empires and imperialism is also subject to debate. For example, **neo-imperialism** has emerged as a critique of political power in today's international system. Neo-imperialism has been used to describe the foreign policy strategy of numerous states since the decline of Europe's empires in the 20th century. In contrast to the imperialism of the 18th and 19th centuries – which saw empires combine both direct and indirect controls over territories around the world – the neo-imperialism of the 21st century instead emphasizes the indirect controls exerted by either former colonial powers, or by great powers such as the US, over other states largely through economic dependency – a point we shall advance in the toolkit exercise at the end of this chapter.

Postcolonialism
Understood as both the political, cultural and economic condition of former colonies, and a theoretical approach concerned with colonial history and its legacy upon the present.

Neo-imperialism
The dominance of a state or group of states over weaker states, largely through indirect means such as economic, cultural or political dependency. Closely related, and at times used synonymously, with the term neo-colonialism.

CONCLUSION

As this chapter has reflected upon, the international system has undergone a considerable evolution in the past 500 years. The world has shifted from a system of kingdoms, empires and dynastic states with loose and decentralized orders of authority, to an international system where sovereign states make up the primary units, each with their own clearly demarcated borders and territory. While the world has changed dramatically since the turn of the 21st century, looking back over five centuries' worth of history also shows us how far the world has come. From Westphalia to imperialism, nationalism and world wars, to nuclear arms races and decolonization. And yet international politics never sits still, and new issues are now presenting themselves, with new topics for research and debate. In the following chapters you will get to grips with some of the competing perspectives that shape our understanding of the world in which we live, and of the theory that can provide us with important tools for explaining, critiquing and predicting international politics itself. Before turning to the next chapters, however, why not apply your knowledge from this chapter by trying the following toolkit exercise which asks, *'Is the United States an imperial power?'*

TOOLKIT

Is the United States an imperial power?

THINK

- Reflect on your own mental map of the United States, your knowledge of its history and your perceptions of the role that it plays in international politics. How significant do you perceive the US as a power in today's international system?

OBSERVE

Image 2.3 'School begins', an illustration by Louis Dalrymple published in US-based *Puck* magazine c. 1898. The cartoon shows 'Uncle Sam' lecturing children labelled Philippines, Hawaii, Puerto Rico and Cuba.

Source: Wikimedia Commons.

- Observe the caricatures and stereotypes in this image, including the writing on the blackboard and above the door. Observe also the Native American depicted sitting apart by the door with his textbook upside down.
- During the Spanish-American War of 1898, the US acquired territories in the western Pacific and South America. Cuba and the Philippines gained their independence from the US in 1902 and 1946 respectively, although Hawaii and Puerto Rico remain under US authority.
- After World War Two the United States became the uncontested leader of the Western liberal democratic world. The period after 1945 through to the end of the Cold War (and arguably even beyond into the 21st century) is often described as the *Pax Americana*. This terminology has both imperial and hegemonic connotations largely due to its connection to the *Pax Romana* and *Pax Britannica* which were periods in international history where first the Roman Empire and then British Empire held hegemonic positions within the international system courtesy of their size and influence.

ORGANIZE

- Imperialism is the policy or practice of extending a state's power and dominion through direct territorial acquisition and/or indirect control over the political or economic life of other areas. During the Cold War the term 'dollar imperialism' was coined by the Soviet Union to refer to the United States' economic policies which were creating a European dependence, thereby consolidating American influence in Europe. Claims of dollar imperialism also continue to be used to describe the rise of the US dollar as the world's strongest and most popular 'reserve currency' (that is, the currency that is most widely accepted for trade throughout the world).
- Neo-imperialism is a relatively new concept focusing less on imperialism as *direct* control over other territories (i.e. colonialism), but more upon the *indirect* controls that powerful states exert over weaker ones, for example through economic dependence.
- Mercantilism was a hallmark of imperialism in the 18th and 19th centuries which saw the advancement of policies to protect a state's wealth, while enhancing their export potential over other rivals. While there was a general retreat from mercantilist economic policy over the latter half of the 20th century, US President Trump's 'America First' strategy from 2016 to 2021 involved the introduction of trade protection measures, and the aggressive pursuit of 'trade wars' against America's main economic competitors, namely China and the EU (pg. 213).

LINK

- *Consider*: As a former colony, the US has its own postcolonial legacy shaped not only by the British (whom the United States won independence from in 1783), but also by the French, Dutch, Italian, Spanish and Portuguese. Consider also that 574 Native American tribes live in the continental US and Alaska, and who are themselves subject to colonization. How might the United States' experience of colonialism have shaped its outlook on imperialism?
- *Explore*: In today's international system, the US has considerable power projection capability courtesy of its extensive network of military bases located around the world. See https://militarybases.com for more details on its base locations. Scan the barcode also to explore more about the rise (and fall?) of the US dollar as the world's reserve currency.
- *Connect*: Advocates of *Pax Americana* would suggest US military and economic influence has been a guarantor of international order and security since 1945. Is that influence evidence of the United States' hegemonic position in the world, or would you identify this as (neo-)imperialism at work?
- *Predict*: By 2050 what will the balance of power look like in our international system (pg. 20)? Would you predict a continued US economic and military hegemony or is decline inevitable?

SHARE

- Answer the question *'Is the United States an imperial power?'*

  This question encourages you to reflect on not only the historical context of imperialism and the US but the US in contemporary international politics. You can also address the question from different angles. Be clear about which concepts best help you answer the question and construct your argument. How do you understand imperialism and neo-imperialism? Do you think US imperialism applies historically, in a contemporary context, or both? Reflect on whether you might focus primarily on the US's power within the international system, or a more state-level perspective that considers imperial legacies within the US or upon former colonies. Are there any real-world examples or data you might utilize to reinforce your argument? For some pointers on conducting historical research check out *How to – approach history in your political research* (pg. 30). You may also want to look at *How to – take a position* (pg. 144).

HOW TO

APPROACH HISTORY IN YOUR POLITICAL RESEARCH

The events of the past inform the events of today, as surely as they will inform the events of tomorrow. How then can history help us in our own research? Here are just a few tips for how you might draw on lessons for the past in your international politics research.

Be reflective

History is everywhere and requires active reflection to understand its impacts on the 'now'. In international politics we tend to be concerned with history less from the perspective of understanding what happened and when, and more from the perspective of what history can teach us about the here and now. Always bear in mind that how we observe the lessons of the past can be highly subjective. As the adage goes, 'history is written by the victors'. Be *reflective* therefore of how history is written, and how the events we take as 'fact' may themselves have been interpreted. Remember that there may be different interpretations of the events, players and outcomes, and that other perspectives may have equal importance.

Think theory

When we come to draw on the lessons of the past to inform political research today, we have the benefit of theory to help guide and interpret our research. Realism (pg. 35–7), for example, views history as a cyclical process. Whether down to human nature, or the anarchic condition of the international system itself, by adopting a realist perspective we might assume that the world's history of competition and conflict is likely to repeat itself. If you are therefore looking to understand hegemony, or the balance of power of today's international system, realism advocates looking back at the past to find a suitable comparison. Marxism (pg. 52–5) similarly is a theory that draws on history to inform its assumptions of today's international system, advocating a materialist viewpoint which assumes that the history of all human societies has been shaped by socioeconomic forces. More critical theories, such as postcolonialism (pg. 55–8), also adopt historicism by looking to unpack the legacies and impacts of the past on today's societies. From these critical perspectives, history can be seen as a dynamic social process informing and influencing the international politics of today. When using theory to inform any historical research do just remember to be clear in the assumptions you are making, and why. You might also want to check out *How to – apply theory to your research and writing* (pg. 69) for more 'how to' tips on using theories to guide you.

Think sources

International history is a rich, thoroughly rewarding, avenue of research, whether you are interested in the specific foreign policy of one state, the politics around specific international issues, or the development and evolution of the international system itself. The benefit of studying history from an international politics perspective, moreover, is that source material can often be ample in supply, be that through libraries and archives, or via digital archival depositories (check out the Explore More boxes in this chapter for a few examples!) Do give thought though to the resources you are using to inform yourself of past events. Some general history websites can often be goldmines of information but be sure to fact-check to ensure that the resources you are using are reliable. Wherever possible always go *straight to source.* So rather than relying on someone else to tell you what, say the 1945 Yalta Conference Agreement (pg. 23) said, locate the actual document itself. This may be as simple as doing an internet or library search using the correct key words as primary source documentation is often readily available via public access archives (including online). Primary sources do also help you get closer to the history which can make a big difference to how well you understand the politics of today.

Think relevance

Researching history may at times feel a little like falling into a never-ending hole. International history is vast and therefore your research 'field' can become a little daunting when you start to take a backward look. This need not be an overly daunting task, however. Rather, be clear in the parameters you are setting for yourself and your research from the outset. What is the timeline you are concerned with? What historical events might you prioritize? Keep your research *relevant*. Use the history to inform the present. Like pulling on a thread, you may find your research expands as new history is revealed to you. But always keep your original research parameters in mind, not least in recalling *why* you are researching history for answers in the first place. This will help you maintain a clear focus on the now while also exploring the events of the past.

3 Theoretical foundations to the study of international politics

Unsplash / Janko Ferlič

Abstract

In this chapter you will start to explore some of the theoretical foundations to the study of international politics. We look first at how theory can be utilized as an explanatory and interpretive tool in your research. From there we consider some of the disputed history of the origins of our discipline, before focusing on the two theoretical approaches often considered prominent in shaping its evolution. The chapter then sets out to introduce realism and liberalism as theoretical approaches that you might utilize in your own research, addressing their competing assumptions and propositions, along with some of the 'neo' variants. In so doing, this chapter lays an important foundation in building your theoretical knowledge and understanding of international politics; foundations which we then continue to develop in Chapter Four where more social and critical theoretical approaches are then introduced.

THEORY AS AN EXPLANATORY AND INTERPRETIVE TOOL

In Chapter One we saw that the art of studying international politics is to recognize the many, often competing, visions of the world as it is, and the world as we want it to be. Our own views of the world often will determine our politics. Yet as a scholar of international politics you are tasked with developing a critical reflexivity over the assumptions and propositions that shape not just your own, but the many different and competing views of the world. The key to developing that art is to build a strong foundation in the theories that can provide explanatory and interpretive tools to guide your research and analysis of international politics. Theory is first and foremost a toolkit; it provides a set of principles and a framework for analysis and explanation premised on assumptions and propositions.

Theories of international politics are ultimately concerned with **understanding, explaining, critiquing** and **predicting** events within our international system. Some of the more foundational questions which theories of international politics seek to provide answers for might include:

Understanding
Developing insight and judgement on what something means.

Explaining
The capacity to reveal and describe actions, events or workings.

Critiquing
Providing detailed assessment and evaluation of something.

Predicting
Utilizing your knowledge and experience to determine probable consequences or actions in the future.

1. Why do states go to war?
2. Why do states uphold international law (and why do they break it)?
3. Is enduring peace possible?
4. What conditions are necessary to establish international order and security?

Theories can provide a powerful tool in explaining the world around us, but it should be made clear that no one theory can explain everything. Because all theory is derived from abstraction, no theory can fully explain every nuance or ambiguity within the complex world in which we live. Theories are also based on assumptions, be that about human nature, a world view or the prioritization of specific topics of analysis. Because of this our own individual perceptions and world views – our mental maps – as scholars invariably shape the theories we both favour in our research and the theories we tend to ignore. What is therefore helpful as a scholar new to the discipline of international politics is to forearm yourself with a knowledge arsenal covering a variety of different theoretical approaches. From there you can more reflexively determine which theory or theories you will seek to utilize in your own research and analysis, and why you are doing so.

This chapter sets out some of these theoretical foundations by introducing you to two theories – realism and liberalism – often addressed as dominant in the origins and evolution of international politics as an academic discipline, and which remain important theoretical lenses for your toolkit. In the next chapter you will then be introduced to other critical and social theories that have challenged realism and liberalism's assumptions and propositions, and their dominance in the discipline. To begin let us first clarify some core concepts to help you when entering the fray of theoretical discourse.

ONTOLOGY, METHODOLOGY AND EPISTEMOLOGY

Some of the major distinguishing features of theoretical debate within international politics can be identified as ontological, methodological and epistemological. **Ontology** is concerned with what *is*, the nature and relations of being. As a field of study, ontology considers concepts such as existence, being and reality. As will be shown in the next section, a popular narrative within the study of international politics has been of the discipline's earliest debate centring on the nature and reality of the world 'as it is'.

Ontology
The study of what is, the nature and relations of being.

Methodology meanwhile is concerned with the methods and principles used in research or study. Our interest in methodology stems from the principles we apply to theory and research. For example, is state behaviour best explained through scientific principles of assumed rational decision-making, or should philosophical or sociological principles grounded in the study of human nature and society apply? As we shall see later in this chapter, theoretical approaches in the study of international politics have also evolved through methodological debate, and its gradual advancement of political science during the latter half of the 20th century.

Methodology
A system of methods and principles used in research or study.

A third distinguishing feature of theoretical debate within international politics is concerned with **epistemology** relating to the nature, origin and limits of knowledge. Epistemology calls on us to consider not just 'what we know' but *why we know it*. As we shall address when we take a closer look at the emergence of critical and social theories

Epistemology
The study of the nature, origin and limits of knowledge.

in Chapter Four, epistemological debate has opened up the discipline in recent years by calling on its scholars to critically reflect on the very assumptions that have shaped theoretical knowledge since the discipline first emerged just over a century ago. As we turn then to consider different theoretical approaches and their assumptions, we shall continue to reflect upon the ontology, methodology and epistemology at play.

THE ORIGINS OF A DISCIPLINE

Our discipline has a complicated history that draws from many different subjects and backgrounds. A popularized part-myth follows that international politics was a discipline born in a single act (Acharya 2021: 305) in 1919 when the world's first *Department of International Politics* was established at the University College of Wales, Aberystwyth, along with the academic post of *Woodrow Wilson Chair of International Politics*. The part-myth follows that after the Armistice of World War One in 1918, relative peace returned to continental Europe and beyond. US President Woodrow Wilson's fourteen-point plan to bring about the cessation of armed conflict and establish a long-term peace was being actioned in part, not least with the creation of the League of Nations which was established in January 1920 (pg. 22). Supported by a £20,000 endowment from Lord David Davies of Llandinam (1880–1944), the *Woodrow Wilson Chair of International Politics* post was created both to honour the memory of the university's fallen students during World War One, and to facilitate 'the study of those related problems of law and politics, of ethics and economics, which are raised by the prospect of a League of Nations and for the truer understanding of civilization other than our own' (Aberystwyth University 2023).

Yet, as Acharya (2021) critiques, the discipline's foundations were not born 'out of nothing' but have instead been shaped by multiple spaces, including both colonial and postcolonial worlds. Vitalis argues in his study *White World Order, Black Power Politics: The Birth of American International Relations* (2015) that in the early decades of the 20th century in the United States, the study of international relations in fact meant the study of race relations, with race subjection being the issue that preoccupied the first self-identified professors of international relations in the 1910s and 1920s. For Vitalis, along with many other disciplinary historians and critical scholars, the narrative that has shaped our discipline has been dominated by a racially white world view, to the suppression of minority and subjugated voices. As you will see as we focus upon the theoretical discourse that shaped the dominant telling of our discipline's foundations and evolution, race and race relations were soon to become a minority view (a point we deliberately revisit in Chapter Sixteen). As new scholars to the discipline it is therefore important to not only understand the narratives that have shaped – and indeed dominated – the theoretical underpinnings of the discipline, but to critically reflect on the perspectives that have also been neglected. It is also for this reason that our 'toolkit' feature **O**BSERVE used throughout this book deliberately highlights racial, postcolonial and other critical views in encouraging you to actively reflect on other perspectives and often ignored viewpoints.

The interwar years

A dominant narrative of the evolution of international politics as an academic discipline is that it was shaped by a first 'great debate' that took place in the 1920s and 1930s between those who may be identified as *realists* – that is, those who believed that the reality of the world around us is one inherently driven by power politics and competition between states – and *liberals*, who saw the catastrophic events of World War One as an incentive to strive for peace through the means of modernization, democracy, international organizations and economic interdependence. Largely driven by classical political philosophy and beliefs about human nature, the academic debate during this interwar year period is thought to have hinged upon questions over the inevitability of war, the merits and demerits of military disarmament, and the prospects for lasting peace. If great power competition and the quest for military hegemony had created the conditions for World War One, what were the prospects for overcoming great power politics, achieving disarmament and establishing legal frameworks for peace?

THINK

Do you think peace and progress are possible among states, or are the pursuit of power and competition more likely? How might that view shape your understanding of international politics and the research you undertake?

Influenced by classical liberal philosophers such as Immanuel Kant, Thomas Jefferson, James Madison and John Locke, liberal thinkers in the early 20th century began to consolidate liberal theory, centred upon the approach called **liberal idealism**. For example, in 1909 Norman Angell wrote *Europe's Optical Illusion* (later renamed *The Great Illusion*) in which he highlighted the futility and costliness of war and advanced the thesis that modernization and economic interdependence between states would advance the goals of peace. Woodrow Wilson's own staunch advocacy of liberal ideals further advanced the cause of peace after World War One. Wilson's liberal idealism was premised on the logic of peace being born through the promotion of liberal democracy and through international organizations to oversee peaceful relations between states. As with classical liberal philosophy, therefore, liberal idealism developed as a school of thought that assumed the inherent goodness of human nature. The assumption followed that those states, governed as they are expected to be, by rational men (and women), will seek to cooperate with one another in international affairs. While liberalism does not claim that war would be completely eradicated, liberal idealism assumed that peace would prevail where a harmony of interests would become manifest, where democracy and education flourished, and where international organizations were established to foster peaceful relations between states.

Liberal idealism
A school of thought grounded in liberal political philosophy that assumes human nature is good, that international cooperation advances mutual welfare, and that progress and modernization within the international system are possible.

The launch of the League of Nations in 1920 can also be identified as a point of advancement for liberal idealism, whereby the cause of peace through democracy promotion, cooperation, modernization and progress was trumpeted. This was, in turn, followed by international treaties such as the 1925 **Locarno Pact** and the **Kellogg-Briand Treaty** in 1928 which sought to abolish war. For liberal thinkers, it was such advances in international organization and law that would set the example for peace. Arthur Ponsonby, for example, argued that the resolute disarmament of all states would eventually set the example that would make the abolition of war possible (Ponsonby 1928: 232).

Locarno Pact
A series of treaties signed between Germany, France, Belgium, Great Britain and Italy to mutually guarantee peace in Western Europe. The Pact was initialled in Locarno, Switzerland on 16 October 1925.

Yet for other statesmen turned scholars such as Philip Kerr (1928) (see also pg. 281), followed later by E. H. Carr, the view advanced by such liberal idealism was branded 'utopian', premised in part on a misunderstanding of the realities and nature of the international system, and shaped by a perspective built on what the world 'ought to be' rather than the world 'as it is'. Kerr defined these two schools of debate as being between [liberal] 'idealists' and what he categorized as 'practical people' [realists]. He stated:

Kellogg-Briand Treaty
A General Treaty for Renunciation of War as an Instrument of National Policy. The Pact was initiated by French Foreign Minister Aristide Briand, to establish a bilateral non-aggression pact with the United States, before becoming a multilateral treaty.

> On the one side we find the idealists, people who are disgusted at the injustice and violence which seem continuously to dominate the world and who vigorously demand that the nations should immediately abolish war and substitute it for a process of settlement by reason and justice. On the other side we find the practical people, men and women who, while not at all unsympathetic to the general ideal of peace, see clearly the hard facts of the world in which we live, and dislike lifting their

heads above the clouds lest they should also take their feet off the ground of national security. (Kerr 1928: 361)

In sharp contrast to liberalism's emphasis on, for example, Kant's ideals of *Perpetual Peace*, realist thought instead drew on the philosophies of Thucydides, Niccolò Machiavelli and Thomas Hobbes. According to classical realist thought, human nature is inherently egoistic. Humankind both fears death and exerts power over others to achieve personal gain. It is only the rule of law and fear of punishment that keeps humankind in order. Thomas Hobbes, for example, argued that in a state of nature where there is no sovereign to maintain order and security, life is, *'solitary, poor, nasty, brutish, and short'*. For this reason, international politics is assumed to be driven by self-interest, and concerns over national security, and where the most powerful dominate.

For classical realist thinkers like Philip Kerr, national security concerns also made it impossible for states to disarm. Efforts such as the Kellogg-Briand Pact were judged both idealistic and unrealistic (Image 3.1). As Kerr stated, the international system comprised states that are 'self-centred, sensitive, ambitious and quarrelsome entities' (Kerr 1928: 366) which meant it was in every state's national interest to possess armaments for security and defence. E. H. Carr mirrored many of these same points, emphasizing international politics as a struggle for power. Writing over the 1930s, in his book *The Twenty Years Crisis: 1919–1939* – published in fact in the same year as World War Two then broke out – Carr advanced a more 'realistic' understanding of international politics as the struggle between conflicting interests and desires.

Image 3.1 An American anti-pacifist cartoon from 1928 on the need for an adequate US naval force to back the Kellogg-Briand Pact.

Source: GRANGER – Historical Picture Archive/Alamy.

While the outbreak of World War Two appeared to prove Carr's critique of liberal idealism correct, the discourse shaping realism and liberalism did not stop there. In 1948 Hans Morgenthau went on to publish his seminal *Politics Among Nations: The Struggle for Power and Peace*. Morgenthau advanced classical realism as a theory of international politics. He argued that human nature drove men, and by extension the state, to seek to dominate each other. Fear, insecurity and the aspiration for power thus motivate state behaviour. Morgenthau further argued that military disarmament is impossible because 'Men do not fight because they have arms. They have arms because they deem it necessary to fight' (Morgenthau 1948 [1985]). Speaking also to what had become an increasing liberal preoccupation over the 1940s to establish **world government** as a means of establishing world peace and prevent nuclear annihilation, Morgenthau claimed that while world government could create the conditions for disarmament and peace, the chances of ever establishing and maintaining one were negligible.

World government
The idea that all humankind is governed by one common worldwide political authority.

English School
A theory of international politics that acknowledges that states are the primary actors within the international system but argues that shared interests and institutions creates an international society of states where peaceful co-existence is possible.

Explore More

Realism is often referenced as the oldest theory of international politics as realist logics can be traced throughout historical discourse. For example, in the 5th century BC Thucydides wrote the *History of the Peloponnesian Wars*. In his *Melian Dialogue*, Thucydides relates the discourse between the invading Athenians and the islanders of Melos who, despite their neutrality, had been sieged by Athens and expected to surrender and pay tribute. In that dialogue Thucydides cites the now much popularized realist statement that '*the strong do what they can, and the weak suffer what they must*'. You can read the full text of this short Dialogue at www.sophia-project.org/classical-philosophy.html

Scan the QR code for access to explore weblinks and more resources.

OBSERVE

According to Hollis and Smith (1990), there are at least two sides to every story in international politics. The debate between realists and liberal idealists seems to epitomize this with two competing world views, and two stories to tell in explaining the chances for peace and the inevitability of war.

Yet consider how our perspectives can be shaped by the perspectives *not* told. Much of the reason why realism and liberalism are treated as 'dominant' or 'mainstream' in our discipline today is because the popularized narrative of our discipline prioritized them. Yet these theories and the debate itself can now be critiqued, not only for neglecting a wider discourse, shaped by other disciplines such as history, philosophy or race studies, but for their studious neglect of other perspectives as well. The realist vs idealist discourse was noticeably blinkered, for example, in addressing imperialism and race (Chapter Sixteen), as well as gender and class (Chapter Four).

The emergence of the 'neos'

Over the course of the 1960s and 1970s, scholars continued to develop theoretical approaches for viewing the international system. Hedley Bull, a key thinker within the **English School**, advanced the concept of **international society** which, he argued, exists among states who share common interests, values and institutions. In his *Anarchical*

International society
An English School construct which observes the societal nature of interstate relations, and the conception that states are bound by common rules, shared values and interests.

International order
A set of common rules, norms and institutions that govern the relationships between states.

Liberal international order
A model of international order built on liberal democratic values, rules and norms, and overseen by international organizations. Commonly associated with the post-1945 international order.

Positivism
A methodological and philosophical approach to knowledge that assumes that the only real knowledge is scientific knowledge that can be tested and verified. In political science, positivist approaches are commonly associated with inductive, hypothesis-testing methods of enquiry.

Structure
Referring to something that exists independent of actors, but which also shapes the behaviour of actors.

Structural realism
The name commonly associated with Waltz's *Theory of International Po*litics due to his emphasis on the structure of the international system as a determinant of state behaviour.

Internal balancing
The tactic that sees states develop their military, economic and technological capabilities to match or surpass rival states.

External balancing
The tactic that sees states form alliances with other more powerful states to deter attack from stronger rivals.

Society: A Study of Order in World Politics, published in 1977, Bull further advanced that **international order** is itself established within international society where common interests, rules and institutions are in place. The concept of international order has since been developed further, with particular emphasis on the **liberal international order** which emerged during the post-World War Two period through the US-sponsored creation of rules-based international institutions, and by the advancement of economic liberalism and liberal democracy.

Over the course of the 1970s and 1980s, theoretical discourse within international politics also began to take a new turn. During the interwar years, early debates had been observed largely amongst lawyers, philosophers, former diplomats and historians. After World War Two, however, the discipline rapidly spread, particularly within the United States where the government and public foundations provided support for a more scientific focus on 'International Relations' (pg. 7). Over the course of the Cold War, a new generation of international politics scholars emerged trained less in philosophy, history or the Classics, but now in economics, mathematics and in the political, social and natural sciences. Increasing focus was given to **positivism** and the favouring of inductive, rigorous, hypothesis-testing methods as new modes of enquiry.

Neorealism

A key thinker often highlighted during this period was Kenneth Waltz. Challenging the classical realism of Morgenthau and his emphasis on human nature as a motivator for state behaviour, Waltz claimed that the **structure** of the international system itself was a key determinant in shaping how states behaved. Waltz's *Theory of International Politics* is now widely accredited as the main political thought behind **structural realism**. For structural realists, the very fact that the structure of the international system is anarchic (pg. 18) and therefore without an overarching authority to maintain law and order between states, means that states must seek to defend themselves, prioritizing their own national security and seeking to balance power against those they judge to be a threat.

States will seek to balance power through two methods – *internal* and *external balancing*. **Internal balancing** is where a state seeks to enhance its military and economic capabilities to match rival states. There are frequent examples of internal balancing behaviours littered across international history, particularly in the form of arms races, as we saw in Chapter Two with the example of the US and USSR. **External balancing** meanwhile occurs where a state builds alliances with other more powerful states to deter attack from stronger rivals. Again, as we saw in Chapter Two, the events leading up to World Wars One and Two, and during the Cold War, provide several historical examples of external balancing behaviours with alliances being forged to counterbalance other rival blocs – the Triple Alliance and the Entente Cordiale (pg. 22), for example, or NATO and the Warsaw Pact (pg. 25). Contemporary examples of balancing behaviour may also be identified, for example, in the Australia, UK and US trilateral defence pact or AUKUS, announced in September 2021 (pg. 69).

Within the realist school, **neorealism** became a collective terminology in referring to the various new realist theoretical approaches that were developing in this time. Structural realism, for example, can also be identified with **defensive neorealism** due to the emphasis Waltz placed on states seeking to defend themselves by maximizing their security through establishing a balance of power. **Offensive neorealism** is another 'neo' variant, developed by John Mearsheimer at the turn of the 21st century. In contrast to Waltz, Mearsheimer argued that while the anarchic structure of the international system does motivate states to find security in a balance of power, states still cannot trust others to maintain that balance. Because of this mistrust, states are motivated to continue to maximize their power so that they become the strongest state in the system. While neorealist approaches thus equally recognize the importance of the anarchic structure of the international system as a determinant for state behaviour, emphasizing the competitive nature of international politics due to the international self-help system, where they have differed is over the question of *how much power* states should seek to secure themselves.

For offensive neorealists, *power maximization* is the only way to achieve security within the international system. A state must therefore continue to maximize its power by advancing its military, technological and economic capabilities, until it clearly surpasses its competitors. Other states may seek to advance their own power, but a hegemon – that is, the most powerful state within the system (pg. 22) – secures its position by always maintaining a marked lead in its power capabilities. Defensive neorealism, meanwhile, advances the argument that states seek to *maximize their security*. Order and security are best achieved within the international system when a balance of power is achieved between two or more superpowers who then take on the responsibility for maintaining global order and security. We will pick up this debate again in Chapter Five when we address the concepts of power and polarity within the international system.

Neorealism
The collective term for the positivist theoretical approaches developed in the realist school, distinguished from more classical approaches that favoured philosophical explanations for state behaviour premised on human nature.

Defensive neorealism
The theory that states seek to maximize their security by establishing a balance of power.

Offensive neorealism
The theory that states would seek to maximize their power to ensure their security.

Neoliberalism

While realism did much to advance the positivist turn in theorizing international politics during the later parts of the 20th century, classical liberalism also underwent its own evolution during this period. Like neorealism, neoliberalism has also become something of a collective terminology to refer to the various new theoretical approaches that emerged within the liberal school of thought over the 1970s and 1980s (Figure 3.1). For liberal thinkers during this period, US hegemony after World War Two was seen to establish a seemingly stable liberal international order, built on international organizations, liberal democracy and international trade. Globalization was also advancing and connecting the

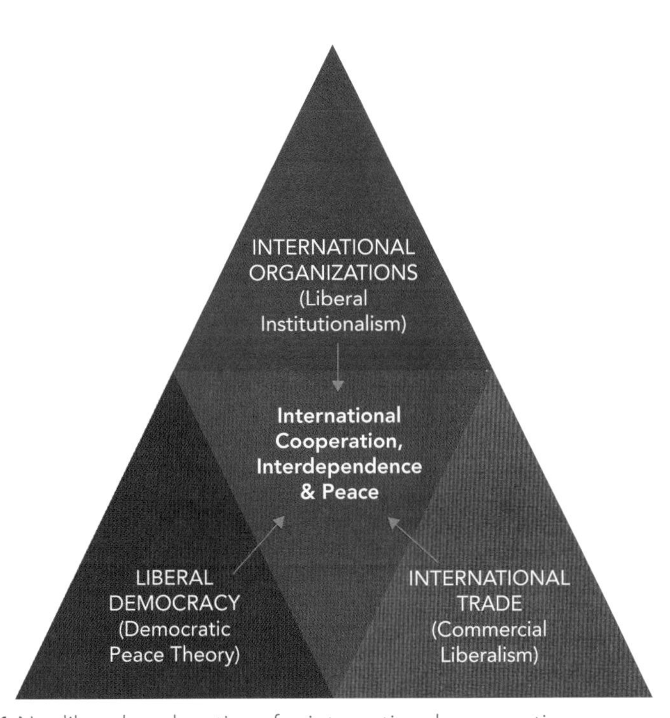

Figure 3.1 Neoliberal explanations for international cooperation

world through trade and technology. One 'neoliberal' variant that then emerged during this period was **commercial liberalism.** Advanced by Thomas Friedman, commercial liberalism argues that free trade and economic interdependence are pacifying forces and essential to peace building. Related therefore to Norman Angell's arguments from 1909 that war is costly, commercial liberalism considers trade as a form of state power, and free trade flows between countries as a precursor to peaceful and prosperous relations.

Commercial liberalism A neoliberal theory that argues that free trade and economic interdependence will act as pacifiers.

Another related 'neo' variant is **liberal institutionalism**. This theory is commonly associated with Robert Keohane and Joseph Nye who, when writing in the 1970s and 1980s, advanced the idea that within the international system, states are inextricably connected through multiple complex channels, and that cooperation within international institutions facilitates peaceful relations. Specifically, liberal institutionalism assumes that international organizations and international law facilitate international cooperation and dispute resolution.

Liberal institutionalism A neoliberal theory that argues that the growth of international institutions and the advancement of international law create conditions for international cooperation.

While agreeing with neorealist assumptions that the international system is anarchic and that states are the primary actors within that system, Keohane and Nye also advanced the argument that **complex interdependence** exists within and between states which generates conditions for cooperation and peaceful interaction. In so doing neoliberalism also challenges the realist emphasis on states being the only actors that matter within the international system, as well as the idea that national security is the sole priority issue for states within international politics. Rather, neoliberal thinkers such as Keohane and Nye argue that national agendas can shift and evolve, and that economics as well as other forms of interdependence will create linkages between states that bring about an eventual decline in military force as a foreign policy tool.

Complex interdependence The idea that states and their fortunes are inextricably linked together through multiple channels.

Another neoliberal variant we can identify is **democratic peace theory** which argues that liberal democracy is itself a conductor for peace within the international system. Democratic peace theory argues that liberal democratic states behave differently to other states. In sharp contrast to neorealism which tends to ignore the internal political make-up within states, democratic peace theory makes the case that a state's system of government impacts its international outlook and affects its behaviour within the international system. Democratic governments are, in turn, believed to mitigate against international conflict because, within democratic societies, governments are held accountable by educated citizens who do not want to see war conducted in their name. Democratic peace theory therefore assumes that democratic states do not go to war with other democracies. While liberal states may therefore be involved in conflict with non-liberal states, they will be less inclined to enter conflict with other liberal states. This, in turn, leads to the construction of **zones of peace** which, democratic peace theorists suggest, are identifiable in Europe, North America and Australasia where conflict between liberal states is now considered highly improbable.

Democratic peace theory A neoliberal theory that argues that liberal democracy is itself a conductor for peace within the international system.

Zones of peace Geographical areas made up of liberal democracies who are at peace with one another.

ORGANIZE

Both realism and liberalism are considered predictive theories in so far as they can help us make certain judgements about how states might behave in the future, based on the assumptions and propositions that the theories are grounded on. Therefore, where liberalism might predict a future that sees the peaceful spread of liberal democracies, free trade and interdependence within our international system, realism would predict a future that sees a competitive system that is highly conflict-prone.

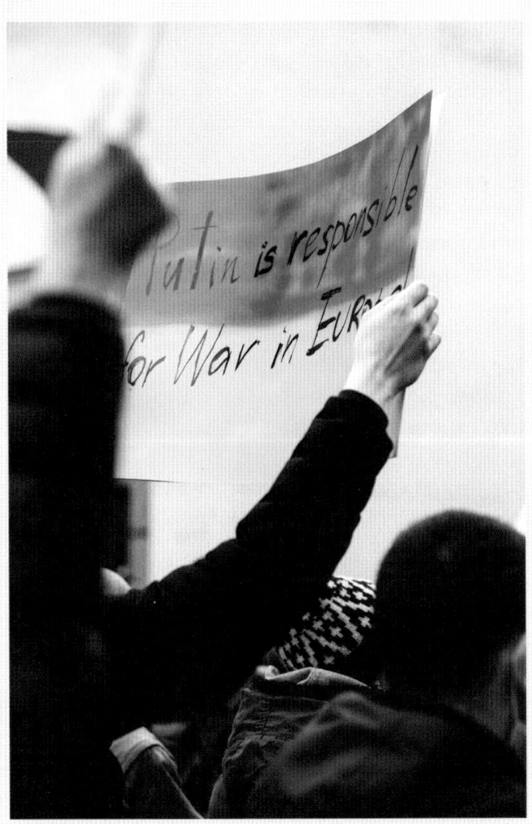

Interestingly both realist and liberal scholars have partially predicted the events that have transpired in Ukraine. John Mearsheimer, for example, predicted that NATO's expansion into Eastern Europe would provoke Russia into more aggressive actions in the region, because as a great power, Russia must maximize its power, keeping Ukraine within its sphere of influence and deterring any efforts Ukraine makes towards NATO and the West. Francis Fukuyama also predicted that the democratization of Russia and Ukraine would first be 'preceded by a painful process of national separation, one that will not be accomplished quickly or without bloodshed' (Fukuyama 1992). That prediction has in part been proven correct, although the true democratization of both Ukraine and Russia remains to be seen.

Image 3.2 A protester holds a sign saying 'Putin is responsible for War in Europe'. Since Russia's invasion of Ukraine the European 'zone of peace' has become increasingly insecure.

Source: Markus Spiske/Pexels.

SUMMARIZING REALISM AND LIBERALISM

So far in this chapter we have considered the disputed origins of our discipline, the theoretical 'great debate' that has largely dominated the theoretical narrative of the discipline's evolution and introduced you to realism and liberalism and their various strands. Because these are theories that you can start to utilize in your own research and analysis, in this section you will find a summary comparative of the main theoretical assumptions and propositions of both realism and liberalism, alongside their respective strengths and weaknesses detailed in Tables 3.1 and 3.2. We will revisit these toolboxes as we progress through the chapters to follow.

Realism summary toolbox

Realism makes several assumptions about human nature, the international system and what motivates state behaviour that can inform your research and analysis of international politics. These assumptions are summarized as follows:

1. Human nature is inherently egoistic. Within individual states, man's natural tendency to pursue his own selfish ambitions is moderated, and order and security maintained,

courtesy of the authority of a sovereign ruler (monarch or government). Within international politics, however, the international system is anarchic, and it is that lack of overarching authority above the state that is the main determinant (and constraint) of state behaviour. In this anarchic system, states must rely on **self-help**. And as Morgenthau claimed, such a self-help system will always make peace elusive.
2. States are the primary actors in the international system. Realist theorizing of international politics therefore focuses its core energies on the actions and interactions of the state, and especially the most powerful states. Other actors are considered marginal to that core state-centric focus.
3. States are unitary actors. Realists do not look inside the state for causes of state behaviour. The emphasis is not therefore on sub-level government, or bureaucratic politics within the state.
4. States are rational actors. States therefore make their decisions based on the rational calculation of costs and benefits.
5. Within an anarchic self-help international system, states will be principally concerned with the pursuit and defence of national security. The international system is inherently competitive, with no overarching authority to maintain order and security between states. Security is therefore a central problem in international politics.

Self-help
The inability to call on others for support or aid. Typically associated with the anarchic condition of the international system.

Taking these assumptions into consideration, the realist tradition within international politics then advances the following theoretical propositions to explain state behaviour, security and conflict within the international system:

1. Due to the competitive nature of the international system, states will care deeply about relative gains, that is, a preoccupation with doing better than their competitors.
2. International politics is a **zero-sum game**. As states are rational actors they will pursue and uphold their own national interests, even if that is at the expense of other states within the system.
3. States can never be sure of other states' intentions. The anarchic condition of the international system, coupled with the assumption that states are preoccupied with their own national security, creates an environment of uncertainty and mistrust.
4. Mistrust creates a **security dilemma.** A security dilemma exists where a state, seeking to build up its military power for defensive purposes, finds its actions construed as an aggressive move by other states, who in turn start to build up their military power to compensate.
5. As states are concerned primarily with their own security in a self-help system, states will seek to either build a balance of power or seek to maximize their power so that they are the most powerful state in the system.

Zero-sum game
A situation where whatever is gained by one side or actor is lost by another.

Security dilemma
Where a state, seeking to build up its military power for defensive purposes, finds its actions construed as aggressive by other states, who in turn start to build up their military power to compensate.

Table 3.1 Realism's strengths and weaknesses

Strengths	Weaknesses
• grasps competitive nature of international politics • recognizes importance of power and self-help that limit cooperation • highlights relevance of the system's structure that compels states to pursue their own security/interests	• narrow focus on national security • neglects the more cooperative nature of international politics • overlooks how international and domestic actors can affect state behaviour • bypasses the role that international organizations, norms, rules and laws can play in shaping state behaviour

Liberalism summary toolbox

Like realism, liberalism is a theoretical tradition premised on assumptions about human nature, the international system and state behaviour. Like realism, liberalism assumes that the structure of the international system is anarchic. Also, like realism, liberalism assumes that states are rational actors, and that they are the main actors in the international system. In contrast to realism, however, liberalism's main assumptions include:

1. Human nature is inherently good and presupposed to seek cooperation with others. By extension, liberalism assumes that while the international system is anarchic, states can mitigate the negative impacts of anarchy through international cooperation.
2. States are the main actors in the international system, but other actors play important roles. Liberalism therefore considers the role of non-state actors such as multinational enterprises or international organizations which both create and deepen interdependence between states.
3. States are concerned with national security, but security is not the only national interest that states seek to pursue or defend. Liberalism assumes that states will pursue economic interests particularly, looking to build reciprocal and trusting relationships with other states through free trade.
4. Through free trade, states will become economically interdependent upon one another. The liberal assumption follows that complex interdependence between states will pacify them as war would prove too costly.
5. The internal political make-up of a state and its governing institutions matter in explaining state behaviour. Democracies are assumed to be more prone to the pursuit of peace than non-democratic regimes.

Building then on liberalism's main theoretical assumptions, several liberal propositions can also be identified in helping to explain state behaviour, cooperation and progress within international politics:

1. It is in the state's self-interest to cooperate with others. States will seek to pursue a harmony of interests with other states within the international system because international politics is a **non-zero-sum game**.
2. States are concerned with **absolute gains** for themselves and those they cooperate with.
3. While conflict may not be completely eradicated, war is by no means inevitable within the international system. Through cooperation and modernization progress can be made.
4. While states will continue to look to pursue and defend their national security, this will be achieved through international organizations. States will therefore seek to work with others to achieve **collective security**.
5. Peace is achievable through the spread of democracy, free trade and international organizations.

For reflection and summation Table 3.3 further compares realism and liberalism's main theoretical contributions.

Non-zero-sum game
A situation where there is a net benefit to the system based on the interactions of the sides or actors involved.

Absolute gains
Concerning the collective gains that states can achieve by working together within the international system.

Collective security
Cooperation among states to achieve security through collective means.

Table 3.2 Liberalism's strengths and weaknesses

Strengths	Weaknesses
• grasps cooperative nature of international politics • recognizes importance of both national and international organizations in shaping state behaviour • highlights interdependence that develops between states, particularly through free trade and economics	• struggles to explain the conflictual nature of international politics, including when cooperative efforts fail • tends to bypass the link between power and global order and security • overlooks how illiberal states rise to influence and shape international politics

LINK

Consider

Do you find yourself agreeing with realism and/or liberalism's viewpoint of international politics? Which assumptions and propositions do you think are most valid?

Explore

Dig deeper into your favoured theoretical perspective by exploring Conversations with History at www.uctv.tv/cwh which offers a wealth of video interviews including with realist and liberal scholars such as Kenneth Waltz, John Mearsheimer, Stephen Walt, Robert Keohane, Francis Fukuyama, etc.

Connect

It can help to view theories as lenses that offer different views on the world (Smith 2021). Each theory can help you interpret, explain or predict certain aspects of international politics, but they can also have their blind spots and weaknesses. Tang (2013), for example, suggests that no one theory can be valid across all times, but that theories like realism and liberalism can be found helpful through different phases of history. Remember also that our own mental maps and perspectives shape the theories we favour or ignore.

Predict

Do you think the international system in 2050 will have more or less conflict? Apply the theoretical lenses offered by either realism or liberalism to help you answer this question. What critique would you expect the other approach to offer?

Scan the QR code for access to explore weblinks and more resources.

CONCLUSION

In this chapter you have addressed some of the theoretical foundations that underpin the study of international politics, focusing on how theory can help us understand, explain, critique and predict, and introducing you to two theories that have been prominent in the popularized narratives of our discipline since the interwar years. Realism and liberalism continue to provide important lenses for scholars of international politics, often now through their various 'neo' guises, with their respective assumptions and propositions continuing to shape our understanding of international politics. While neither theory can help us explain every aspect of international politics nor, as we shall see in the next chapter, should their respective assumptions be taken for granted, they do provide researchers of international politics an important foundation for explaining the behaviour of states within our international system. In the following chapter you will continue to advance your knowledge arsenal of theoretical approaches within international politics by considering the rise of critical and social theories. Before turning to the next chapter, however, take a moment to reflect on what you have learned about realism and liberalism by trying your hand at the following toolkit exercise.

Table 3.3 Comparing realism and liberalism's theoretical assumptions and propositions

	Realism	Liberalism
Human Nature	Human nature is inherently egoistic, fearful of death, and prone to use power over others to advance personal gain.	Human nature is inherently good. Humankind seeks to work with others for the advancement of mutual welfare.
The International System	The international system is anarchic. It is a self-help system.	The international system is anarchic. International organizations nevertheless provide forums for dialogue and foster closer interdependence between states.
The State as Actor	The state is the main actor in international politics.	The state is the main actor in international politics, though other actors also play an important role, such as MNEs or international organizations.
	States are rational actors.	States are rational actors.
	States are unitary actors. Internal political make-up of states matters only in so far as it impacts state power and material capabilities.	Internal political make-up of states matters. Democracies and better educated societies generate the best conditions for peace.
Motivation for State Behaviour	States will pursue their national interests.	States will pursue a harmony of interests.
	Power competition will mean states pursue relative gains.	Mutual interdependence and international cooperation will mean states pursue absolute gains.
	States are motivated to preserve their national security above all things.	States are motivated by more than just national security interests.
Prospects of International Conflict	Conflict is inevitable due to human nature and the anarchic condition of the international system.	Conflict may not be eradicated, but it can be mitigated through international cooperation, the spread of democracy and free trade, and pursuit of collective security through international organizations.
Prospects of International Peace	Peace is fleeting, history showcases that progress is only ever marginal.	Peace is possible, progress can be made.

TOOLKIT

Does a self-help international system mean states are concerned with relative gains?

THINK

- Reflect on your own personality. Are you naturally competitive or collaborative? How much do you care about the gains of others relative to your own?
- Consider this scenario. You live in a country with no government to uphold order and security, and where you have only yourself to rely upon for survival. How much would you now care about your gains relative to others?

OBSERVE

Image 3.3 Flags fly outside the Palais des Nations in Geneva. The building was originally built for the League of Nations in the 1930s, but became a headquarters for the United Nations in 1946.

Source: Mathias Reding/Unsplash.

- In the 1940s debate grew over the prospects of world government (pg. 37) and its necessity in preventing nuclear annihilation. In 1947 Albert Einstein wrote of how world government was the only solution to atomic war, even if that were a 'limited' world government focused primarily on maintaining security.
- While world government never materialized, since 1945 numerous regional and international organizations have emerged to facilitate greater international cooperation between sovereign states. The United Nations, formed in 1945, has near-universal membership and remit. Yet states remain the primary actors within the UN, with the UN serving more in the role of 'convenor' than government.
- Regional free trade agreements have also seen a decade-on-decade growth since the 1990s, with over 500 agreements in place around the world (pg. 133). International organizations, globalization and economic and cultural interconnectedness between states have thus become hallmarks of a liberal international order where capitalism, free trade and democracy are often considered dominant forces. Whereas the anarchic condition of the system would suggest a self-help environment, debate continues as to whether such an environment necessarily breeds a competitive or collaborative outlook in states.

ORGANIZE

- Realism suggests that states are principally concerned with relative gains. A state feels secure when it makes gains relative to others, and insecure when other states gain more than it does. Remind yourself of the realist assumptions about the characteristics of the international system (pg. 42). According to realist scholars, states must pay attention to their relative capabilities and strengths, particularly in terms of military and economic capability and resources. This focus on relative gains makes cooperation with other states difficult because international politics is seen as a zero-sum game.
- Liberalism suggests that states are concerned with absolute gains. From this perspective, the state is primarily interested in assessing its own benefits, regardless of what others gain at the same time. Reflect again on liberal assumptions about the international system, and the prospects for international cooperation (pg. 43). How might international organizations, such as the UN, facilitate absolute gains?

LINK

- *Consider*: Much of the debate between realism and liberal idealism in the 1920s and 1930s centred on the prospects of military disarmament and efforts to abolish war. What lessons do you think you might draw from that debate in understanding the competitive vs collaborative nature of states within the international system today?
- *Explore*: Explore how mutual benefits might be achieved in international politics. Consider, for example, the European Union's priorities and actions and the achievements it is accredited with at https://european-union.europa.eu (see also Chapter Eight) or the prospects of tackling climate change through international cooperation at the United Nations by visiting https://unfccc.int (see also Chapter Fourteen).
- *Connect*: For a state to be concerned only with relative gains suggests a state that is inherently concerned with its power, position and survival in the international system. Does international order and national security alone determine whether states will pursue relative or absolute gains?
- *Predict*: What are the chances of establishing a world government to advance world peace? What would need to change to achieve this?

Scan the QR code for access to explore weblinks and more resources.

SHARE

- Answer the question 'Does a self-help international system mean states are concerned with relative gains?'

  What key theoretical points will help you develop your argument in answering this question? What examples might you draw upon to support your case? For some helpful tips see *How to – Paraphrase theoretical discourse in your politics writing* on pg. 48. See also *How to – approach an international politics essay* for tips on tackling this question as an essay (pg. 182).

HOW TO

PARAPHRASE THEORETICAL DISCOURSE IN YOUR POLITICS WRITING

In most international politics courses, whether at introductory level or in more advanced study, you will be expected to communicate in writing your knowledge and understanding of a theory or theories of international politics. Take, for example, the toolkit question in the last section. This could be an essay or exam question and, in answering it, you would need to be able to demonstrate not just knowledge, but informed opinion about theory. There is a challenge in how best to use theoretical discourse in your writing, not least how you should go about essentially reiterating already well-used concepts and phrases commonly used in theory in a way that is still your own work. Universities have stringent academic integrity and misconduct policies, and plagiarism is not only unacceptable, but severely punishable. Plagiarism can be identified where someone has repeated sections of text from another source without due reference. Milder forms of plagiarism can also be identified, however, where there is evidence of the extensive use of quotations in an essay, as this may be seen as a failure to use your own words.

The key to overcoming this challenge then is to develop the art of *paraphrasing*. To paraphrase is to rewrite or restate an original source in your own words. To paraphrase effectively in your academic writing, you need to have a good understanding of the original source being restated. References must still always be included when paraphrasing. Good referencing is important in showing transparency in your research and writing, but how you restate someone else's words, and then reference correctly, takes some practice. Below then are just a few top tips in paraphrasing theoretical discourse.

Be a good note-taker

When reading other people's work take notes and be diligent in recording where a particular point or phrase came from. When paraphrasing it is better to write from your own notes and reflections of original source material, rather than lifting material straight from the book or article (Godfrey 2018: 63). Paraphrasing from your own notes also ensures that you are already starting to draw upon your own words and reflections to present your point. Take the following example of paraphrasing using this book:

Original Source

In 1948 Hans Morgenthau went on to publish his seminal *Politics among Nations: The Struggle for Power and Peace*. Morgenthau advanced classical realism as a theory of international politics. He argued that human nature drove men, and by extension the state, to seek to dominate each other. Fear, insecurity and the aspiration for power thus motivate state behaviour. Morgenthau further argued that military disarmament is impossible because 'Men do not fight because they have arms. They have arms because they deem it necessary to fight' (Morgenthau 1948 [1985]). (Dee 2024: 37)

Own Notes

From Dee, M. (2024). Understanding International Politics: The Student Toolkit pg. 37.

Morgenthau furthered the study of classical realism in international politics after WWII. He believed that it was human nature to fear death and to dominate others – this is associated with classical realism which sees human nature as a factor shaping state behaviour.

In the international system states are driven by fear, insecurity and power.

Morgenthau (1948–1985 edition) Politics among Nations: The Struggle for Peace and Power – important early work in realist theory *track down in library*.

Essay paraphrase

Classical realist thinkers like Hans Morgenthau argued that human nature was a driver of state behaviour due to fear, insecurity and the quest for power (Dee 2024: 37). In the title of his influential book, Morgenthau (1948) suggested that the politics among nations would be a 'Struggle for Peace and Power'.

Know your material

Familiarity with a subject breeds confidence. The more you familiarize yourself with theory, the greater your confidence will be in communicating that knowledge to others. Understanding your subject material will make it easier for you to communicate with confidence, and to paraphrase using your own words. When writing about theory particularly, you also need to know the commonly used words or phrases that you *cannot change*. Considering realism, for example, you would not look to put quotation marks or seek to amend commonly used words such as *relative gains* or *self-help, balance of power or security dilemma*. These are commonly understood concepts and key words in realist thinking. What is important is how you present those concepts or key words so that you are not just lifting statements made by another author directly from source.

The 3 Rs: Rephrase, Reorder and Reference

When paraphrasing in your theoretical writing, think about 'the 3 'Rs': *Rephrase, Reorder and Reference*. You should be looking to utilize your own phraseology and sentence structure to present information, and then also include in-text citations (pg. 126) to the original source material that you are drawing from. Take the following as an example again drawn from this book:

Paraphrasing using the 3Rs

"After World War Two, theoretical discourse within international politics began to refocus on positivist approaches (Dee 2024: 38). As Dee (2024: 38) states, while the interwar years saw debate centred on history, philosophy and law, enquiry soon shifted towards the social sciences."

As this example shows, the paraphrase shows a *reordering* of the sentence structure from the original source, as well as a *rephrasing* of certain words and phrases (while maintaining key words that cannot be changed like positivism). The paraphrase also includes *references* in the form of in-text citations to show and signpost to the original source, thereby reflecting transparency (see also *How to – approach referencing* on pg. 126).

Only quote something when it adds something

It can be easy to just quote the words of someone else when trying to present information in an essay but, when used too much, direct quoting can also signal a lack of understanding or laziness. When discussing theory – which tends not to change and where the same principles can be written about time and again – the desire to just quote someone else is especially strong. As a rule, always avoid direct quotes of material that you can easily communicate in your own words. And only use direct quotes when what the author is saying really adds something to your own argument.

4 Critical and social theoretical approaches in international politics

Unsplash / Dan Dimmock

Abstract

This chapter continues to develop your understanding of the different theoretical approaches commonly used in the study of international politics. The chapter first addresses the ongoing evolution of theoretical debate and scholarship within international politics. From there, the chapter introduces you to several commonly utilized critical and social theoretical traditions within international politics, including Marxism, postcolonialism, feminism and constructivism. By the end of this chapter, you will have a familiarity with the different theoretical assumptions and propositions that have shaped these theories, and an awareness of the major strengths and weaknesses of using each approach in your own research and analysis.

AN EVOLVING THEORETICAL DEBATE

In Chapter Three we saw how the study and academic discourse surrounding international politics has evolved through multiple spaces and perspectives. The popularized narrative (or myth according to more critical views) (pg. 34. Acharya 2021) follows that our discipline was founded during the interwar years and consolidated during the Cold War. Much of that narrative is built upon an understanding of several **great debates.** The first and second great debates we covered in the last chapter with the first centred on realism and liberal idealism in the interwar years, and the second addressing the subsequent evolution of realism and liberalism into more 'modern' positivist theories, grounded in the social sciences (pg. 37–8). By the 1980s and 1990s, however, the theoretical discourse undertook

Great debates
A popularized narrative which suggests that international politics evolved as a discipline through major theoretical discursive moments.

several new evolutions. A third great debate has been commonly associated with the discourse between realist, liberal and Marxist scholars oriented towards international political economy and inequalities within the international system. A fourth great debate is also commonly attributed to the respective merits of new **post-positivist** approaches relative to the more mainstream positivism of neorealism and neoliberalism.

During this period several social and critical theoretical approaches began to become more commonplace as theoretical approaches within international politics. These theoretical approaches sought to critique realism and liberalism, being not only disillusioned with the paradigmatic dominance of both traditions, but also seeing their limitations in explaining the transformation of the international system towards the end of the Cold War.

Writing in 1981, critical theorist Robert Cox made the case that theory had two purposes giving rise to two distinct types of theory within international politics – **problem-solving theory** and **critical theory**. Realism and liberalism – particularly their neo-variants – were both considered problem-solving theories in so far as they assumed that the reality of the international system is objective and therefore possible to research, explain and potentially problem-solve through positivist lenses. Critical theorists, however, assume that knowledge is subjective. Our own perspectives shape and shift our understanding of reality, and knowledge must be assumed to have multiple and diverse viewpoints.

According to Cox, problem-solving theories not only take for granted the institutions and social power relations at the heart of international politics, but also reinforce them. Concepts such as sovereignty, anarchy, capitalism, democracy, hegemony and security, for example, are considered by problem-solving theories as 'known' – simple conceptual assumptions that set the scientific parameters for explaining problems within international politics. Critical theoretical approaches, however, deliberately reflect on these concepts and consider the underlying power structures that they may be grounded upon. Specifically, critical theorists set out to shine a light on structures and relations of power within international politics and to offer alternatives for 'feasible transformations of the existing world' (Cox 1981: 90). Critical theory has gone on to become increasingly prevalent in international politics scholarship, with its epistemological logics (pg. 33) seen within several theoretical traditions, from Marxism to feminism to postcolonialism and beyond.

Social theories have similarly built upon post-positivist logics to challenge the assumptions of realism and liberalism and to offer alternative means to explain and interpret the world around us. Social constructivism was first introduced as a theoretical approach within international politics by Nicholas Onuf in 1989[1] and then advanced by Alexander Wendt with his seminal 1992 article 'Anarchy is What States Make of It'. As we shall see later in this chapter, constructivism challenges liberal and realist assumptions by highlighting that the international system is a social realm and emphasizes how norms and identities matter in shaping state behaviour. Constructivism has since gone on to become widely utilized within international politics scholarship, to the point of being recognized as another 'mainstream' theoretical approach within the discipline (Adler 2013).

Of course, the story of our discipline and its evolution is far more complex and multifaceted than the great debates narrative suggests. Yet we can also see that the discipline has evolved and advanced through its theoretical discourse. The seemingly dominant strand of scholarship focused on realist and liberal ontological and methodological approaches to the study of international politics over the latter half of the 20th century was by no means isolated, but is joined by a far broader array of global and theoretical perspectives that also call on us to question our assumptions of what we know as researchers. This diversity of approaches greatly enriches our discipline and provides scholars of international politics a far wider set of intellectual tools for our analysis.

Post-positivism
A methodological and philosophical approach to knowledge that critiques and amends positivist assumptions that the only knowledge is scientific knowledge (*pg. 38*). Post-positivism concerns the social and historical meanings embedded within international politics.

Problem-solving theory
A typically positivist theoretical approach that takes existing social and power relationships as given and focuses on solving problems within the world at large.

Critical theory
A theoretical approach that critiques existing social and power relationships, and associated scientific assumptions, calling them into question and presenting alternatives for transforming the existing world.

[1] Social constructivism's origins are in fact traced back to sociological scholarship. See Adler (2013) for a useful overview of constructivism's evolution.

THINK

An inscription on the Social Science Research Building at the University of Chicago states 'If you cannot measure it, your knowledge is meagre and unsatisfactory'. Do you agree with that statement? Is something only *known* if it is first tested and verified? What do you see as the respective merits of positivist and post-positivist approaches in theorizing international politics?

In the following sections we shall consider some of these different critical and social theoretical approaches, including Marxism, postcolonialism, feminism and constructivism. In each section you will then also find a summary toolbox outlining the main assumptions and propositions for each theoretical approach, enabling you to then draw upon these theories in your own research and analysis. The chapter concludes then with a comparative table detailing all the theories we have addressed in both Chapters Three and Four. These theories will significantly add to your knowledge arsenal when it comes to researching, explaining and critiquing international politics, and we will continue to revisit them as we go on throughout the book.

MARXISM

Marxism is a broad theoretical church within the study of international politics. While originally centred upon the political philosophy of Karl Marx, Marxism as a theoretical tradition has evolved across numerous branches over the 19th and 20th centuries. While often discredited by more mainstream theoretical schools within international politics for being overly centred on **materialist** explanations for action and behaviour within the international system, we may identify several contributions that Marxism has made to the way we theorize and understand the politics of the world around us.

First and foremost, Marxism provides a critical lens for observing and explaining socioeconomics, globalization (pg. 7), **capitalism** and inequalities in the distribution of production and wealth over time. Writing in the 1840s, Karl Marx and Friedrich Engels argued that capitalist globalization was not only a historically particular economic system, but that capitalism was transforming the international system to such an extent that the major fault lines were not between states, but between the two dominant classes: the ruling bourgeoisie who control production within states, and an increasingly transnational working proletariat who make up society's labour force. Because capitalism creates class inequalities and class struggle, Marxism suggests that societal change can only come through revolution. For Marx and Engels, a transnational proletariat would spread the values of Enlightenment, such as liberty, equality and fraternity, and would rise up against the exploitation and oppression of the bourgeoisie. **Communism** would then replace a global capitalist economy.

Marxism has further inspired more critical theoretical approaches within international politics. 'Western Marxism' is a strand of Marxism traced to the establishment of the **Frankfurt School** in the 1920s and to the works of Italian Marxist Antonio Gramsci around the same time. Western Marxism stood apart from the organized working class and revolutionary actions of Eastern Europe's communist political parties. The Frankfurt School was an intellectual and philosophically driven institution, dedicated to the advancement of socio-political research and epistemological advancements,

Materialism
Primarily concerned with the objective reality of the material world. In Marxist scholarship, materialism is often associated with how societies are organized around material forces and needs, with particular emphasis on production and labour.

Capitalism
An economic system in which wealth is privately owned, and the economy is ordered around market principles of supply and demand, competition and the acquisition of profit.

Communism
An economic system built on community ownership of the means of production, and where wealth is distributed according to ability and need.

Frankfurt School
A school of socio-political research and epistemology centred originally on the Institute of Social Research in Frankfurt in the 1920s, with key thinkers such as Theodor Adorno, Max Horkheimer, Herbert Marcuse, and later Jurgen Habermas and Walter Benjamin.

which observed that the construction of knowledge was itself a purposive social action. Knowledge, therefore, was seen as a historical and social construct, shaped by the same economic and political forces as any other social activity. That epistemology continues to shape critical theory today.

The works of Antonio Gramsci meanwhile helped to shape Marxism into an international theory. Imprisoned by Mussolini's fascist government for the last 11 years of his life, Gramsci wrote prolifically on Marxist theory as well as critical and educational theory during this time. His prison notebooks included his theory of **cultural hegemony** which Gramsci used to explain how the ruling capitalist class both establish and maintain control over society through subtle forms of political power based not on coercion but consent. Drawn to the question of why communist and socialist revolutions had *not* occurred within capitalist societies, Gramsci argued that capitalism had become deeply rooted due to the spread of a hegemonic culture that reflected the values and norms of the ruling classes. Hegemonic power had therefore become entrenched through popular culture that spread a social vision appealing to the interests of all, making subordinate groups more likely to consent to the power of dominant groups and the maintenance of the status quo. For Gramsci, it was only by questioning that dominant order that people would come to question capitalism.

Cultural hegemony Domination or control through ideological or cultural means. Where the values and interests of the ruling class become the status quo and accepted cultural norm.

Gramsci's writing, and his theory of cultural hegemony, went on to inspire Cox's critical theory of global order, challenging him to question how theories themselves are embedded in frameworks of values and interests. As Cox stated, 'theory is always *for* someone and *for* some purpose' (Cox 1981). In the Gramscian view, theoretical assumptions and propositions cannot be assumed as neutral, but are rather shaped by pre-existing power structures and identities. Critical theory therefore calls upon us to question those pre-existing power structures and challenge the cultural hegemony which shapes our perceptions of the world around us.

While the end of the Cold War and collapse of communism did diminish Marxism's place as a prominent paradigm within the study of international politics, Marxist explanations, particularly in the Gramscian tradition, continue to offer an important critical socioeconomic perspective on capitalism and our international system. During the 1970s and 1980s when debate shifted towards questions of global wealth, production and inequality within the international system, Marxism provided one such critical lens. While neoliberalism had already emerged as a dominant theoretical approach in the study and practice of international political economy (pg. 204–6), neoliberalism's focus on wealth and development also brought with it questions of global inequality, poverty and development, particularly from the perspective of the least developed countries or 'Third World'. In contrast to neoliberalism's claims that the least developed countries would eventually start to modernize and progress as developed countries, the experience of the Third World suggested a more perpetual state of *under*development that capitalism could not easily overcome. Marxist scholars emphasized these social hierarchies and dependencies within the international system, setting out to challenge the assumed dominance of realist and liberal perspectives within international politics.

Dependency theory, for example, advanced during this period courtesy of several Latin American scholars such as Brazilian economist and sociologist Ruy Mauro Marini, developing on the works of Argentinian economist Raúl Prebisch. Dependency theory set out to explain global socioeconomic inequality and the inherent dependency of the least developed nations on the wealthier states in the Global North. Dependency theory argues that the global political and economic order has evolved into an exploitative relationship between the rich developed countries (the 'core') and the poor underdeveloped countries (the 'periphery'). According to dependency theory, imperialism exacerbated the peripheral position of underdeveloped nations within world markets. As colonies were established to provide cheap labour and essential raw materials for their respective empires, they became structurally dependent; never developing the productive capacity to develop high-value products that would enable them to compete in global markets.

While the connections between Marxism and dependency theory have been contested (Chilcote 1981), the concept of dependency has frequently been utilized by Marxist scholars and is thought to have stimulated Marxist analyses of development and underdevelopment within international political economy, a point we shall revisit in Chapters Twelve and Thirteen.

Image 4.1 Dependency in action? Around 70 per cent of the world's cobalt supply – a core material used in rechargeable batteries – is mined in the Democratic Republic of Congo (DRC). Yet many of the DRC's cobalt and copper mining and processing facilities – such as this facility in Lualaba Province – are owned by large multinational enterprises located in the industrialized Global North.

Source: Per-Anders Pettersson/Getty Images.

Even with decolonization, economic dependencies between the rich core and poor periphery remain. Dependency theorists, such as André Gunder Frank, argued that underdevelopment in former colonies across Latin America is due to imperial powers exploiting the labour and resources of these former colonies. Developing countries continue to supply cheap labour and raw materials to the core countries, lacking the capability to develop their own high-value products, while the core continues to exploit those resources to advance their own competitive advantage on the world stage. As Frank therefore argues, 'economic development and underdevelopment are the opposite faces of the same coin' (Frank 1967: 9), with imperialism largely responsible for integrating states into a global capitalist system in which Europe or the United States is the metropolitan centre (1967: 6).

Marxism summary toolbox

As we did with realism and liberalism in Chapter Three, in this toolbox section you will find a summary of Marxism's main theoretical assumptions and propositions, alongside its respective strengths and weaknesses detailed in Table 4.1.

We can identify the following Marxist assumptions as relevant for the study of international politics:

1. The social world is material therefore economics is a primary driver of politics both in the domestic and international sphere.
2. Capitalism is a historically particular type of international order.
3. The main actors within international politics are socioeconomic actors. Marxism considers the power and prevalence of multinational businesses alongside that of the state, with the state established primarily to serve capitalist interests.
4. International capitalism is inherently flawed due to the class inequalities between the ruling bourgeoisie and the working proletariat.
5. Change is possible in international politics through revolution which will then bring an end to class inequality.

Taking Marxism's assumptions into consideration, we can in turn identify several Marxist theoretical propositions which can inform our understanding, explanation and critique of international politics:

1. Economics and politics are inextricably interlinked, as attested by the history of imperialism where states aggressively pursued foreign policies that advance their own wealth at the expense of others.
2. Ruling elites will advance and protect capitalism and the firms, institutions and banks that support the capitalist system.
3. An increasingly transnationalized proletariat will spread their ideals of liberty, equality and fraternity, thereby resisting oppression, poverty and exploitation.
4. Capitalism will only be sustained through co-option and consensus of elite values among subordinate groups within society, thereby advancing their cultural hegemony.
5. Within international politics, former colonizer states, whose ruling elites have prospered most from capitalism, will continue to advance and protect their capitalist interests at the expense of exploitative relationships with former colonized states in the periphery.

Table 4.1 Marxism's strengths and weaknesses

Strengths	Weaknesses
• addresses the importance of economic and materialist forces within international politics • provides a critical lens for explaining inequality within the international system • adopts a historical perspective to researching and understanding socioconomic forces in the international system	• adopts a narrow focus on materialist explanations within international politics to the potential neglect of other variables • neglects to account for broader benefits of capitalism, globalization and a more connected world

POSTCOLONIALISM

Another theory that has grown in prominence within the study of international politics is postcolonialism. Just as dependency theory evolved from scholarship in the Global South with a focus on economic dependency, postcolonialism places its specific emphasis on Third World perspectives in the narrative of international politics. A key point of focus for postcolonial scholars is the central role that colonialism has had on both colonized and colonizer societies and the relationships between them. Like other critical theories, postcolonialism is interested in offering a fuller narrative of international politics, one which highlights the dominance of Western perspectives.

Postcolonialism emerged originally from literary studies, and particularly from the works of Edward Said whose analysis of Western literary sources highlighted the discursive link between Western imperialism and culture and portrayals of the Eastern world – a link Said theorized as **orientalism**. Said highlighted not only Europe's cultural domination, but also how Western literature had produced an 'othering' effect in which Westerners were depicted as 'rational, peaceful, liberal, [and] logical' (Said 1995: 49) compared to those outside the West who were identified as 'irrational, degenerate, primitive, mystical, suspicious, sexually depraved and so on' (Kapoor 2002: 650). Such othering – or 'worlding' as Spivak (1985) addresses – continues to be highlighted by postcolonial scholars in international politics today. For example, postcolonialism highlighted how Arab and Muslim men have been portrayed as 'terrorists' in Western narratives of the War on Terror (pg. 155). The concept of the 'Third World' is another example of discursive 'othering' that distinguishes former colonies from the 'First World'. In the debate around immigration (pg. 229–32), othering is also highlighted where governments seek to defend anti-immigration policies (pg. 282).

Orientalism
A critical concept developed by Edward Said to highlight how Eastern cultures are 'othered' by the West through stereotypical, racist or sexualized narratives.

Whereas dependency theorists highlight the structural economic and developmental inequalities between former colonized and colonizer, postcolonial theorists emphasize the discursive and cultural dimensions of power and inbuilt hierarchy within the international system. Postcolonialism specifically draws attention to how other theories of international politics neglect colonialism, as well as questions of race and ethnicity, gender and class. Postcolonial scholars draw attention to those power hierarchies and the legacies of imperialism and colonialism within non-Western societies.

Explore More

Discourse analysis is a research method often used by researchers of international politics to analyse the political meanings attributed to written and spoken texts. A discourse analysis would consider the context behind the text being analysed, analyse the structure of the speech, the cultural references being made, and the type of framing being employed.

As a simple discourse analysis exercise, look up the transcript from US President Donald Trump's Oval Office prime-time address of 8 January 2019 (scan the barcode for an easy way of locating this link).

When reading the transcript, ask yourself, what is the context behind this speech and how is this informing the language being used? What is the purpose or objective of the speech? What values, sentiments or identities are portrayed in the language being used, particularly as it concerns immigrants relative to US citizens? How does the speech portray the 'Other'?

By asking questions and unpacking the language we are researching, we can start to understand the political meanings informing such speech acts, as well as the relationships between the text itself and the wider context being analysed.

Scan the QR code for access to explore weblinks and more resources.

Much as Said focused on literature, such as novels, travel writings, opera and the media, postcolonial studies today pay special attention to how **discourses** within international politics are constructed to reflect power, difference and 'othering'. For example, postcolonial scholars highlight how the Western view of sovereignty is very different to that of the Global South. As discussed in Chapter Two, a Western (predominantly former colonizer) perspective of sovereignty is that of a principle universally accepted, and which makes near sacrosanct the fundamental principle of external non-interference. Yet, the lived experience of numerous states in the global South (many of which are former colonies), has been of Western powers not only imposing sovereignty and their territorial boundaries upon them, but of also directly interfering in their domestic affairs, whether through proxy wars during the Cold War (pg. 25), humanitarian or peacekeeping missions since the 1990s (pg. 270), or through political conditionality linked to aid and development assistance (pg. 236).

Discourse
Things that are said or written down that reveal or help us better understand how meanings are produced.

Postcolonial scholars highlight how the dominant story of international politics, and the evolution of the international system, has been told principally from the perspective of Europe and America, much to the neglect of Third World perspectives. Yet the view from the South can often tell a very different story. Recall that, for the Third World, the narrative of the Cold War was not that of a 'long peace' and a stable bipolar world order as depicted by scholars in the West. Rather the Cold War was, for many parts of the Global South, a time of conflict, war and instability, and where the process of decolonization was rapidly under way (see Biswas 2021). Postcolonial scholars aim therefore to emphasize the multiple and overlapping worlds and subsequent narratives that make up international politics, and the need to broaden our historical awareness to recognize the various histories that shape the world around us.

Postcolonialism has nevertheless been critiqued for providing more of an alternative version of history rather than strictly a theory useful to the study of international politics (Young 1990). It has also been criticized for homogenizing the concept of colonialism such that postcolonialism can be seen as a way to organize the experience of 'more than three quarters of the people living in the world' (Ashcroft et al. 1989: 1 cited in Gandhi 1998: 166). However, as Nair (2017) deftly highlights, postcolonialism in fact brings together 'a deep concern with histories of colonialism and imperialism, how these are carried through the present – and how inequalities and oppressions embedded in race, class and gender relations on a global scale matter for our understanding' of international politics (Nair 2017). Postcolonialism therefore offers us an important critical lens to question established theoretical and historical assumptions, identify alternative perspectives, and draw upon discourse as a specific tool in our research of international politics.

Postcolonialism Summary Toolbox

In using postcolonialism in your own scholarship, you can identify the following main assumptions concerning the study and practice of international politics:

1. Colonialism plays a central role in international politics.
2. The colonial encounter impacts not only colonized and colonizer societies, but the ongoing relationship between the two.
3. Mainstream narratives of international politics, including how international politics is studied, are dominated by Euro-American stories and perspectives.
4. A global hierarchy exists in which the First World dominates, and Third World perspectives are subordinated.

Drawing then upon postcolonialism's assumptions, we can also identify the following propositions in advancing our research and analysis:

1. Colonialism's legacy is one of long-term damage on both the colonizer and colonized.
2. Western cultural discourses of non-Western cultures are often stereotyped and racialized, producing an 'othering' effect.
3. Postcolonialism proposes that discourse matters in shaping identities as well as relationships of power within international politics.
4. The Third World is not subordinate or sidelined in international politics, but an active agent within international politics.

Table 4.2 Postcolonialism's strengths and weaknesses

Strengths	Weaknesses
• addresses the importance of colonialism and the Third World within international politics • provides a critical lens for explaining colonial, decolonial and postcolonial legacies • adopts a discourse perspective to researching and understanding colonial narratives in international politics	• critiqued as an alternative history of international politics rather than being a theory of international politics • critiqued for homogenizing the concept of colonialism • adopts a narrow focus on colonial explanations to the potential neglect of other variables

FEMINISM

Feminism is a theoretical tradition that also emerged within the study of international politics during the wider post-positivist and critical turn during the 1980s and 1990s. Feminism places its emphasis upon gender as an analytical and empirical category of study within international politics. Specifically, feminist theorizing shifts the study of international politics away from interstate relations and on to marginalized peoples, particularly highlighting the marginalization of women and broader gender inequalities within global power structures. As Reinharz identifies, feminist research is aimed at 'making the invisible visible, bringing women's lives to the center, rendering the trivial important, putting the spotlight on women as competent actors, and understanding women as subjects rather than objects' (Reinharz 1992: 248). Sjoberg and Tickner (2013: 174) suggest that a key question facing feminists when commencing research in international politics is 'Where are the women?' Feminism therefore applies 'gendered lenses' to what, why and how we study international politics.

Feminist scholars recognize that human beings have religions, cultures and identities which are highly fluid social constructs (Tickner 2002: 342). The actions and interactions of humankind cannot, therefore, be studied as if they are inanimate, unchanging objects (Sjoberg and Tickner 2013). Where we are to theorize international politics, feminist scholars argue the need for reflexivity over the knowledge claims and assumptions that shape our understanding of the world around us, and an openness to challenge those assumptions. Feminism therefore emphasizes the implications of gender for different issues in international politics, but also offers a feminist critique of those traditional assumptions and propositions that have dominated theories of international politics (most of which have been developed by men), and to expose the gender biases within them.

Feminist research in international politics is broad-ranging and multifaceted, but can also be identified by different aspects of feminism. *Empirical feminism* is concerned with

ORGANIZE

Image 4.2 Women take to the streets of Kabul to protest in September 2021 after the Taliban announced their new all-male interim government.

Source: Marcus Yam/Contributor/Getty Images.

In a 2002 analysis of the 9/11 terrorist attacks against the United States, feminist scholar J. Ann Tickner showcased the gendering of images and discourses both within the discipline of international politics and within the public discourse surrounding the events of 9/11. Tickner identified how, during times of war, gendering images saw men placed in the role of *warriors*, and women in the role of *victims* (Tickner 2002). In the days following 9/11 Tickner highlighted that the only time women appeared in the US media was to show Afghan women wearing full burqas, portrayed in the role of victims to extremist Muslim jihadists and the Taliban, while women reporters also disappeared from the pages of newspapers and TV screens (Tickner 2002: 335). Yet, as this image of women protesting in Kabul nearly twenty years after Tickner's article highlights, the history of Afghan women is not always that of victimhood.

Reflecting political commitment to gender emancipation, Tickner went on to offer 'alternative models of masculinity', outlining several lessons to be learned for a post-9/11 era that ensured women were not subordinated through gendered discourses surrounding war, religion or culture (Tickner 2002).

revealing the gendered dimensions within international politics, revealing real-world practical insights into the role of women in diverse issue areas such as in theatres of war (Enloe 2010; Kronsell 2012), political economy (Rai and Waylen 2013), or migration (Chin 2013). *Analytical feminism* seeks to deconstruct fundamental theoretical constructs within international politics (True 2022), highlighting the dominant masculinity inherent in many of our discipline's key constructs such as sovereignty, war or security (Enloe 2014). *Normative feminism*, meanwhile, is concerned with generating a 'normative agenda for global change' (True 2022: 156). In this regard, feminism offers clear overlaps with critical theory in so far as it aims to critique more traditional theoretical approaches, presents a reflective epistemological lens on to the world, and offers alternative conceptualizations of power and relationships within international politics. Feminist scholars, in fact, make an explicit normative commitment to gender emancipation and the transformation of unequal power relationships (Sjoberg and Tickner 2013: 174). Feminist research, moreover, offers normative guidelines for action within international politics, such as in the adoption of ethical approaches to peacekeeping (Robinson 2019), gendering diplomacy and international negotiation (Aggestam and Towns 2018), and theorizing feminist foreign policy (Aggestam, Bergman Rosamond and Kronsell 2020).

Explore More

Since 2014, states such as Sweden, Canada, Mexico and Spain have sought to adopt Feminist Foreign Policies. According to the *Centre for Feminist Foreign Policy*, Feminist Foreign Policy, or FFP, 'is a political framework centred around the wellbeing of marginalized people and invokes processes of self-reflection regarding foreign policy's hierarchical global systems'. Several other states have also announced their intentions to pursue a more feminist approach in their external relations. You can explore FFP further at centreforfeministforeignpolicy.org.

Scan the QR code for access to explore weblinks and more resources.

Feminism summary toolbox

Much like critical theory, feminism stands apart by explicitly critiquing and challenging the very assumptions that have shaped theory-building efforts within international politics. The premise of critical theory is to challenge objective knowledge assumptions, not create them. Yet even within critical perspectives we can identify certain methodological assumptions that inform their perspective on theorizing and researching international politics. Feminism's assumptions can therefore be summarized as follows:

1. Our own perspectives shape and shift our understanding of reality.
2. Knowledge must be assumed to have multiple and diverse different viewpoints.
3. Mainstream 'problem-solving' theories both take for granted and subsequently reinforce existing social and power relationships within the international system.
4. Existing orders include marginalized peoples, yet mainstream theories fail to account for those in the global political margins.
5. Relationships and relational power matter in international politics.

In critiquing the assumptions of more mainstream 'problem-solving' theories such as realism and liberalism, for example, feminism has advanced research and analysis across numerous fields of enquiry within international politics. From that research we can identify the following areas of focus in advancing feminism's propositions:

1. Feminism proposes a political commitment to emancipatory politics. Research should be oriented therefore towards the global political margins.

2. Aware of the subjectivity of knowledge, feminism proposes self-reflexivity over how knowledge is situated within a particular context. For this reason, feminist research is often geared towards reflective critiques of hegemonic Western masculine logics and the gender assumptions that influence conceptualizations of war, security and power.
3. Recognizing the inequalities of power within the international system, feminism works to highlight existing power inequalities, and to offer alternative conceptualizations for the advancement of all.

Table 4.3 Feminism's strengths and weaknesses

Strengths	Weaknesses
• offers a gendered lens to researching and understanding international politics • shines a light on power hierarchies, emphasizing those in the political margins • explores knowledge claims and seeks alternative conceptualizations of dominant narratives within international politics	• adopts a narrow focus on gendered explanations within international politics to the potential neglect of other explanations • critiqued by problem-solving theorists for being too interpretivist and subjective

CONSTRUCTIVISM

In the last few sections, we have seen how theoretical discourses within the study of international politics began to challenge the positivist liberal and realist traditions and heralded in more post-positivist and critical theoretical approaches. Another key theoretical tradition to emerge during this period was social constructivism. Like the other theories we have addressed so far in this chapter, constructivism also arose as a deliberate critique to neorealism and neoliberalism and the assumptions they made. Whereas neorealist and neoliberal scholars assumed that the international system was a strategic realm in which states acted as pre-constituted, atomistic, self-interested and, above all, rational decision-makers, constructivism directly challenged those assumptions.

Specifically, constructivism offers an approach to the research and analysis of international politics that assumes that the international system is a social realm in which beliefs, **norms**, values and identities play a fundamental role in the construction of social reality. Constructivism therefore adopts the ontological perspective of the social world as 'intersubjectively and collectively meaningful structures and processes' (Adler 2013: 121).

Norm
A common standard of what is considered acceptable or appropriate behaviour.

To understand this, consider for a moment the idea of 'self'. As we discussed in Chapter One, your view of the world is shaped by your own 'self', that is your experiences, your beliefs, your values. The mental maps we forge in our minds of the world 'out there' also shape our understanding of those we might consider as 'other'. These foundational understandings of who we are relative to others are shaped directly by our experiences and the meanings we attribute to them. Similarly, socially constructed meanings also matter in international politics, as the world in which we live is forged and shaped by the meanings attributed to the structures and processes within it. For constructivist scholars, the world in which we live is not therefore some abstract, objective structure as observed by neorealist and neoliberal perspectives. Rather the world in which we live is an interactive process with embedded social meanings. The actors within our international system also have **agency** to make their own choices. According to Wendt (1987), agents possess three specific capacities: a theoretical understanding of their activities, reflexive monitoring and the potential to adapt their behaviour, and the capacity to make decisions. Agents

Agency
Having the capacity to act.

within international politics – be that states, firms, other non-state actors or individuals alike – in turn make their decisions based on their experiences, history and the meanings they attribute to the social world around them.

Constructivism arose principally with the concern of explaining change and transitions, such as the transition from the Cold War to the post-Cold War era, or from conflict to cooperation. For constructivist scholars, realism and liberalism struggled to explain some of the transformations that were taking place within the international system towards the end of the 20th century. Constructivism set out to offer new insights into the changes that were taking place by placing special focus on the social forces and interactions motivating state behaviour, such as how moral, ethical and normative considerations shape state interests and their relations with others. According to constructivist scholars, states are not simply strategic actors who think rationally, but are social entities. State interests are not therefore pre-determined by the anarchic structure of the international system but are socially constructed through processes of social interaction and constituted by norms, values, ideas, beliefs and identities.

For constructivist scholars such as March and Olsen (1998) theories such as neorealism and neoliberalism focused also too heavily on what they described as a **logic of consequences,** which assumes that self-interested actors are thought to be concerned solely with the consequences of their actions. Constructivist approaches instead highlight the **logic of appropriateness,** whereby actors are thought to be shaped by an awareness of appropriate behaviour, shaped by ideas, values and social interactions. Within international politics, states and other actors are thought to become socialized to following certain social norms and rules.

Logic of consequences The logic that states, as rational actors, are motivated by a consequentialist view of international politics, whereby there is a logical and rational consequence to every action.

Logic of appropriateness The logic that states, as social actors, are motivated by their awareness of what is considered appropriate behaviour within international politics.

Constructivist empirical research is therefore commonly geared towards understanding how norms are constructed, as well as how common rules, identities, institutions and practices have the potential to shape and even change action and behaviour within international politics. Consider, for example, why states decide *not* to develop nuclear weapons, or why the international community used sanctions against South Africa during apartheid. As constructivist scholars highlight, these actions can be explained through analysis of the norms that shape state behaviour, such as the norm of non-proliferation (Rublee 2009) and racial equality (Klotz 2018).

Constructivism summary toolbox

When utilizing constructivism in research and analysis, we can identify the following key constructivist assumptions:

1. The international system is a social realm. The international system may be anarchic, but anarchy is considered a process rather than a structure of the international system. Anarchy then is 'what states make of it' (Wendt 1992), not an ordering principle that dictates state behaviour.
2. Actors within the international system are social entities whose identities inform their interests which in turn shape their actions.
3. State interests are not pre-determined but fluid and socially constructed.
4. Norms matter in international politics, providing standards of appropriate behaviour that shape the actions and interactions of actors within the international system.

Taking these assumptions into consideration, the following constructivist propositions can also help you in your research:

1. Explanations for change within international politics are embedded within historical context and social reality. Material factors alone cannot explain change within

international politics, but rather how material and ideational factors combine to influence different outcomes.

2. Actors within international politics do not just 'act' but rather 'interact' with others. All decisions within international politics are shaped by social reality and imbued with meaning.
3. Agency is a key point of examination in international politics research.
4. Practices, norms, values, morals, institutions and identities are imbued with social meaning and determine appropriate standards of behaviour in international politics. Explaining why states behave the way they do therefore requires analysis of the meanings attributed to the world around us, and how this shapes different possibilities and outcomes within international politics.

Table 4.4 Constructivism's strengths and weaknesses

Strengths	Weaknesses
• offers explanation for change in international politics • accounts for international politics as a social realm • highlights social- and agency-oriented perspectives • emphasizes the role that norms and identities have in shaping state behaviour	• struggles to account for when states ignore norms or do act out of rational self-interest

Consider

Why do states abide by international norms? And why do they then stop? In 1985 the Democratic People's Republic of North Korea (DPRK) joined the Treaty on the Non-Proliferation of Nuclear Weapons (NPT) (pg. 193) as a non-nuclear-weapon state, agreeing to abide by the codified global norm of nuclear non-proliferation, thereby confirming its commitment not to develop nuclear weapons. In 2003, however, the DPRK withdrew from the NPT and began to proactively pursue a nuclear weapons programme. The DPRK is today a nuclear-weapon state.

Explore

Find out more about norm dynamics and how to research them by looking up these journal articles:

- Finnemore, M. and K. Sikkink (1998), 'International norm dynamics and political change', *International Organization*, 52(4): 887–917.
- Björkdahl, A. (2002), 'Norms in international relations: Some conceptual and methodological reflections', *Cambridge Review of International Affairs*, 15(1): 9–23.

Scan the barcode also for useful links concerning the DPRK and the norm of non-proliferation.

Connect

From a realist perspective, states are self-interested, rational actors motivated by a logic of consequences. From the constructivist perspective, however, states are social actors, shaped and influenced by social interactions and a logic of appropriateness. Whereas realists would suggest that states abide by norms and rules only when it is in their rational self-interest to do so, constructivists argue that they do so out of a social understanding and awareness of what constitutes appropriate behaviour. Reflect again on the question 'Why do states abide by international norms?' How might a realist and constructivist each address this question? What are the limitations of these theories in addressing this question with specific reference to the DPRK example?

Predict

Might other states follow the DPRK's example and develop their own nuclear weapons programme, or will the global norm concerning non-proliferation be upheld?

COMPARING THEORETICAL APPROACHES IN INTERNATIONAL POLITICS

In the last sections we have seen how critical and social theories have emerged and developed within the study of international politics. These critical and social theories call on us to reflect upon the ontological, methodological and epistemological assumptions of theory, and serve as important alternatives to the more positivist theoretical approaches presented by realism and liberalism. In Table 4.5 you will find a comparative breakdown of the major assumptions and propositions advanced by all six of the theoretical traditions we have covered so far in this book. As highlighted in the last chapter, it is helpful to adopt a reflective approach when considering the theoretical assumptions and propositions presented by these different approaches because, as scholars and researchers of international politics, it is important to understand the competing theoretical perspectives at play. These theoretical approaches can then be utilized as tools to explain and interpret the world around us.

CONCLUSION

In this chapter we have considered several critical and social theories that emerged as alternatives to the assumptions of realist and liberal approaches, and which greatly add to our toolkit for understanding, explaining and critiquing international politics. In the chapter we have particularly considered the epistemological features of more critical and social theories, such as Marxism, postcolonialism, feminism and constructivism, and how we should treat knowledge itself when theorizing international politics. Are we, as researchers of international politics, a part of what we research, or are we separate from it? Do we adopt objective lenses when researching the world 'out there'? Or do we start by questioning those lenses and thinking about the assumptions that shape our knowledge and, by extension, our understanding? These are not questions you need to have answers to immediately, but which any scholar and researcher of international politics should be prepared to reflect on at some stage. You can kick-start that reflection by turning your hand now to the following toolkit exercise which asks, *'Does identity shape state behaviour in international politics?'* In the next chapter you will continue to fine-tune your understanding by thinking about how to 'pitch' these different theoretical approaches across different levels of analysis.

Table 4.5 Comparing theoretical approaches in international politics

	Realism	Liberalism	Marxism	Feminism	Postcolonialism	Constructivism
Issues/ concepts of focus:	Conflict Power Anarchy	Cooperation International organizations Free trade Democracy	Capitalism Imperialism Dependency Cultural hegemony	Gender	Colonial legacies Third World	Change Norms Identity Agency
On the interna-tional system:	The international system is anarchic. It is a self-help system.	The international system is anarchic. International organizations nevertheless provide forums for dialogue and foster closer interdependence between states.	The international system is an international capitalist system.	The international system is gender-hierarchical. Emphasizes people and activities, more than the international system itself.	The international system is a hierarchical order. Emphasis on Global North and Global South.	The international system is a social realm. Anarchy is what states make of it.
On actors:	The state is the main actor in international politics. States are rational actors. States are unitary actors.	The state is the main actor in international politics, though other actors play important roles, such as MNEs or international organizations. States are rational actors. Internal political make-up of states matters. Democracies and better educated societies generate the best conditions for peace.	The main actors in international politics are socioeconomic actors. Dependency theory highlights core vs. periphery states in a hierarchical economic relationship within an international capitalist system.	Highlights the role of women within international politics, along with other marginalized peoples overlooked by more mainstream theoretical perspectives.	The Third World should be recognized as an active agent within international politics. Third World views have been neglected by the dominant Euro-American story of international politics.	States are important actors within international politics but not the sole actors. Non-state actors, including civil society, NGOs, etc. also play an important role and can exert their own agency.

	Realism	Liberalism	Marxism	Feminism	Postcolonialism	Constructivism
Useful works:	Morgenthau (1948) Waltz (1979; 1990) Mearsheimer (2001) Walt (1999) Lebow (2003)	Keohane (1984) Oye (1986) Russett and Oneal (2003) Rousseau (2005) Milner and Moravcsik (2009)	Cox and Sinclair (1996) Brewer (1990) Wood (2003) Anievas (2010) Bieler and Morton (2018)	Enloe (2014) Tickner (2001) True (2003) Peterson and Runyan (2013) Sjoberg (2013)	Said (1995) Chowdhry and Nair (2002) Krishna (2009) Sajed (2013) Phạm and Shilliam (2016)	Onuf (1989) Finnemore (1996) Wendt (1992; 1999) Fierke and Jørgensen (2001) Hoyoon Jung (2019)
Useful for:	Explaining why states compete with one another	Explaining why states cooperate	Explaining socioeconomic inequality	Explaining the role of gender in international politics Reconstructing discourses in a gender-neutral way	Explaining impacts of colonialism in international politics Offering Third World narratives	Explaining change within international politics Highlighting social and agency-oriented perspectives
Weaker for:	Explaining why states cooperate	Explaining why states compete	Explaining non-economic/ capitalist issues within international politics	Explaining variables other than those seen through gendered lenses	Explaining variables other than those seen through colonial lenses	Explaining why states ignore norms, or if states do act upon rational/ strategic logics.

TOOLKIT

Does identity shape state behaviour in international politics?

THINK

- As an individual how do you identify yourself? How does that identity shape the way you think and act?

OBSERVE

Image 4.3 World leaders interact at the G7 meeting in Quebec, Canada in 2018. Seated is US President Donald Trump. German Chancellor Angela Merkel (C) and French President Emmanuel Macron lean in against the table while Japanese Prime Minister Shinzo Abe looks on with his arms folded.

Source: Handout/Getty Images.

- What identities do you think are playing out in this scene from the 2018 G7 Summit?
- Do states have identities?

ORGANIZE

- Theories like neorealism or neoliberalism highlight that states are the primary actors in international politics and that their interests are pre-determined by the anarchic structure of the system. Because the international system is considered a strategic realm where state behaviour is shaped by calculations relating to power, economics and interests, social identities are not considered a salient feature when determining state interests. As positivist theoretical approaches, neorealism and neoliberalism would also challenge the extent to which identity can be measured as a discernible or verifiable variable influencing state behaviour in international politics.
- Critical theoretical approaches highlight the importance of people when understanding international politics. Postcolonialism would also reflect on the discursive production of identity within international politics, and how colonialism might have impacted the identities of both colonizer and colonized states in today's international system. What identities do you think feminism would emphasize (pg. 58–60)?
- Constructivism also emphasizes that identity and norms are crucial to understanding why states act the way they do. Constructivists are interested in how identities are formed, how they change and how they impact the actions and interactions of different actors.

LINK

- *Consider*: In 2018 New Zealand's Prime Minister Jacinda Ardern made history by being the first female world leader to take her baby on to the floor of the UN General Assembly. Speaking after the event, Ardern made the point that just 5 per cent of world leaders are women, and highlighted the limited number of young leaders in international politics as well (*The Guardian* 2018)
- *Explore*: Explore how youth or gendered identities might shape international politics. Look up the Pew Research Centre www.pewresearch.org who conducted a 2017 study into gendered representations in national office, or check out *The Atlantic's* 2016 article on 'The "myth" of Female Foreign Policy' at www.theatlantic.com.
- *Connect*: In what way might a head of state's age, race, religion, class or gender influence their foreign policy? What other variables need to be taken into consideration in determining what motivates state behaviour?
- *Predict*: Would more female or young heads of state make a difference to international politics?

Scan the QR code for access to explore weblinks and more resources.

SHARE

- Answer the question, '*Does identity shape state behaviour in international politics?*'

  What theory/theories and examples will help you construct your argument? What real-world examples or case study might you utilize to reinforce your argument? This question encourages you to really apply your knowledge of theory, so check out *How to – apply theory to your research and writing* (pg. 69).

HOW TO

APPLY THEORY TO YOUR RESEARCH AND WRITING

Research designs in international politics tend to fall into two camps – positivist or interpretive (Lamont 2022). Positivist research will often start with an observable 'problem' within international politics and then utilize theory to explain and offer plausible explanation – akin therefore to Cox's terminology of problem-solving theory (pg. 51). **Interpretive research**, meanwhile, can be associated with post-positivist theoretical approaches and is often linked to critical or social theories in international politics. Interpretive research will often start with a more ontological 'problem' that seeks to interpret and understand meanings within international politics. Understanding these different approaches is a useful starting point in undertaking your own research and analysis of problems within international politics, as each approach requires you to adopt a stance not only on *how* you will research (*methodology*), but also on the *ontological* and *epistemological* theoretical perspectives of the problem you are interested in.

Background on AUKUS

AUKUS is a defence pact between Australia, the United Kingdom and the United States launched on 15 September 2021. The trilateral cooperation pact provides UK and US support to Australia in the development of its own nuclear-powered submarines, enabling Australia to join an elite club of just seven states in the world with this capability. The Pact noticeably enhances Western military presence in the Indo-Pacific and has been seen as a means of countering a growing Chinese naval presence within the region. China's Premier Xi Jinping subsequently renounced AUKUS as a reversion to 'Cold War mentality and ideological prejudice', calling the agreement 'extremely irresponsible'. New Zealand also responded to the Pact by announcing that it would ban Australia's submarines from its waters, in line with existing policy on the presence of nuclear-powered

Interpretive research
Research oriented towards how meanings are derived and performed, and which sees the researcher and the social world as interconnected.

Image 4.4 Australian Prime Minister Anthony Albanese (left), US President Joe Biden (centre) and British Prime Minister Rishi Sunak (right) take questions during a press conference following an AUKUS trilateral meeting in San Diego in March 2023.

Source: Anadolu Agency/Contributor/Getty Images.

submarines and their support of nuclear non-proliferation norms. The pact caused further controversy for France, who had been working in partnership with Australia to develop twelve diesel-powered submarines. France's Foreign Minister Le Drian referred to AUKUS as a 'stab in the back', calling out Australia's betrayal of French trust in pursuing private talks with the US and UK, and stating that it was 'unacceptable behaviour between friends and allies'. France went on to cancel its regular bilateral defence talks with the UK and recalled its ambassadors in Canberra and Washington in diplomatic response to the pact.

Let's consider the positivist and interpretive research that could be conducted around the decision by Australia to enter a defence pact with the United States and United Kingdom.

A positivist question might be: *'Why did Australia sign a defence pact with the UK and US (AUKUS) in September 2021?'*

An interpretive question might be: *'Why did the French Foreign Minister state that AUKUS was unacceptable behaviour for allies and partners?'*

In both cases you can identify a problem or puzzle, but each question requires the application of a different **theoretical framework.** Choosing which theory or theories to draw upon in your theoretical framework is all part of developing your academic judgement – remembering that no one theory can explain everything so adopting a toolkit approach can be useful when approaching your research problem. Here then are some tips on approaching a theoretical framework, drawing again on our **TOOLS**.

THINK [What do I want to explain?]

An important starting point for any scholar of international politics is for you to think about what you are seeking to explain. Take the two questions we've just outlined concerning AUKUS as an example. Both questions are 'why' questions which require you to offer explanation and argument. Both questions also outline 'problems' but the first sets up a positivist problem, while the second sets out an interpretive problem. The first question identifies the problem or puzzle of trying to *explain the motivation for state behaviour*: namely, why Australia would choose to ally with the US and the UK to the obvious chagrin of not only France but China. The second question seeks to *explain how state behaviour is perceived by allies*: namely how 'unacceptable behaviour' has been interpreted by France in the case of AUKUS. Condensing your problem into a clear point of focus – what you ultimately want to explain – better enables you to determine which theory or theories you then draw upon for your analysis.

OBSERVE [What are the different theoretical perspectives?]

The next step in developing your theoretical framework is to consider the different theoretical perspectives that could be utilized in explaining or interpreting your problem. In the case of our AUKUS research questions, you could draw on any number of the theoretical traditions outlined in Chapters Three and Four of this book, but it helps to consider which theory or theories you think would have the greatest **explanatory power**, and which may be poorly suited to your problem. Realism may be particularly well suited to explaining the state motivations behind AUKUS, while constructivism could be a ripe avenue for explaining why France deemed AUKUS to be 'unacceptable behaviour'. Marxism, meanwhile, may struggle to offer obvious explanation for either question unless you explicitly turned the focus of your enquiry on to more socioeconomic factors. The key is to think through and observe the different theoretical perspectives you could use and start to focus in on the theory or theories you find most useful. This step is also very important in demonstrating critical reflection of your problem – something we will revisit in *How to – develop critical analysis skills* (pg. 161).

Theoretical framework
A written structure that identifies and justifies which theory or theories will be applied within a research study.

Explanatory power
The ability of a hypothesis, theory or variable to explain a subject matter effectively. A variable with high explanatory power has a high level of accuracy and detail in showcasing a clear and justifiable causal relationship to the subject being explained.

ORGANIZE [What theoretical assumptions and propositions can I draw upon?]

Having determined which theory or theories have the best explanatory power in helping you to explain your problem, the next step is to organize your thinking so that you clearly and logically set out those theoretical assumptions and propositions that will make up your theoretical framework. In addressing the question *'Why did Australia sign a defence pact with the UK and US (AUKUS) in September 2021?'*, you may look to highlight realism's assumptions about the international system being a self-help system, and that security is a central problem of international politics. You would also look to flag neorealist propositions about states seeking to balance power through internal and external balancing behaviours. Key concepts for developing in this realist theoretical framework would therefore relate to the balance of power, relative gains and the security dilemma.

In addressing the question *'Why did the French Foreign Minister state that AUKUS was unacceptable behaviour for allies and partners?'*, you may in turn look to highlight constructivism's assumptions and propositions about the international system being a social realm where state behaviour is seen to be motivated by norms and values, not just strategic rational decision-making. A key concept for development in this constructivist framework would therefore relate to norms and the logic of appropriateness.

LINK and SHARE [How do I develop the theoretical framework in my writing?]

By this stage of your planning, you should have a clear idea of your problem, the different theoretical perspectives at play, and a good sense of which theory or theories offer best explanatory power. Now you are looking to link your knowledge of the problem and the theoretical perspectives and to share them in a meaningful way. To achieve this, you would first set out your theoretical framework – see also *How to – approach an international politics essay* (pg. 182).

A good theoretical framework discusses and evaluates the relevant theories to your problem, showing your engagement with the scholarship around the theories themselves, and defining any key concepts that may be useful to your subsequent analysis. The theoretical framework would also clearly and methodically present the theoretical assumptions and propositions that you mean to guide the subsequent analysis of your problem.

Some theoretical frameworks may be longer than others – for example, a theoretical framework may make up an entire chapter of your longer research dissertation, while for a short essay it would only represent one to two paragraphs. The main thing is that the theoretical framework sets out the guiding theoretical principles that will shape analysis of your real-world problem and help you to interpret your results in a meaningful and convincing way.

Whichever theoretical framework you adopt, remember theory is there to help you make connections and explain something, but it also there for you to reflect on and critique. A theoretical framework can be a guide you use to set up your analysis and the issues you chose to prioritize, but it can also serve as a means of testing and critiquing theoretical assumptions. If you get to the end of your analysis and find strong evidence in favour of one theory or another, then state as much in your findings. If you find a theoretical assumption is unverifiable from your analysis, state this also. Applying, testing and critiquing theory is what enables the theoretical discourse within international politics to grow and evolve, so get involved!

5 Refining your toolkit: The levels of analysis

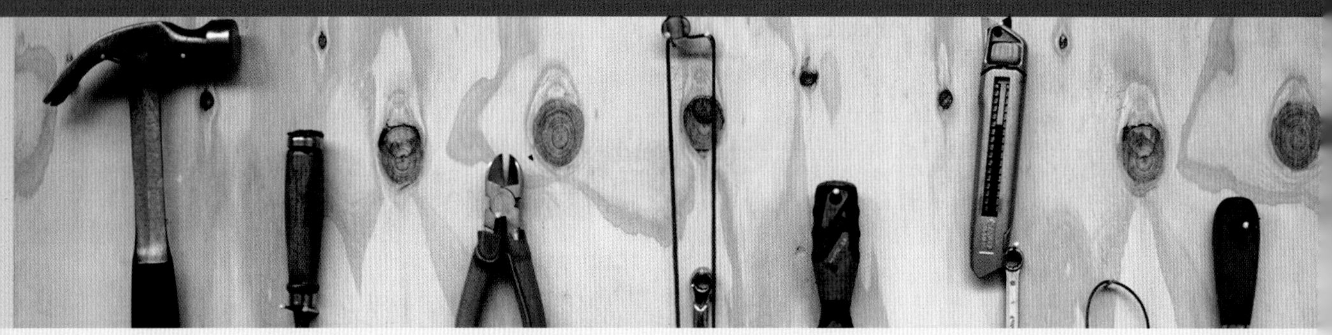

Unsplash / Katie Rodriguez

Abstract

This chapter is aimed at further developing your researcher toolkit. Advancing your knowledge of the theoretical approaches covered in the last two chapters, this chapter introduces you to the levels of analysis – a common analytical device used within international politics scholarship. The chapter details each of the levels of analysis including the international level, state level and individual level, enabling you to reflect on where you should look for explanations, which actors and processes you will prioritize in your research, and how this then shapes your argument. The chapter concludes with a combined toolkit exercise and 'how to' guide for you to apply the levels of analysis approach yourself, asking the question, *'Why did the UK vote to leave the European Union?'*

REFINING YOUR TOOLKIT

In the previous chapters you were introduced to several different theoretical approaches used in international politics research and scholarship. In the last chapter's 'how to' guide (pg. 70–1) we also addressed how you might apply theory to your research and writing, outlining how to work through different theoretical perspectives, and to consider which theory or theories have more or less explanatory power. As we have already seen, no one theory can explain everything in international politics. But as we develop an understanding of the different theoretical approaches and their assumptions and propositions, these tools can then be used to understand, analyse, critique and explain events, issues, processes and the behaviour and interactions of different actors at work within international politics. As you read on in this book, you will notice these theories being used as tools to guide you towards explanation and critique, as well as to showcase competing views around some of the common debates within our subject. The aim of this chapter, however, is to help you finesse your understanding of how to use and apply these tools by considering where you should look for explanations, which actors and processes you then prioritize in your research and analysis, and how these choices start to shape your arguments.

To achieve this, the chapter introduces you to the levels of analysis approach, a commonly used analytical tool within international politics scholarship, which enables you to undertake analysis by looking at different levels or categories, including the *international* level, the *state* level and the *individual* level of analysis. In the following sections the levels of analysis will be discussed in turn, providing opportunity for you to revise your knowledge of the theoretical perspectives we've discussed so far, consider how they apply to each level, and how you in turn might utilize them when undertaking your own research. The chapter concludes with a combined toolkit exercise and 'how to' guide for you to conduct your own levels of analysis approach in addressing the question '*Why did the UK vote to leave the European Union?*'

In media commentary of international politics, states can often be discussed as if they are individual actors with personalities and emotions i.e. 'Russia fumes after Finland and Sweden push for NATO membership' (CBS News 2022). From this perspective states are treated as unitary actors. We tend not to look much closer, say at the state's internal structures, leaders or citizenry.

Other times, commentary refers to governments as actors, i.e. 'Kremlin says U.S.-supplied tanks will "burn" in Ukraine' (Reuters 2023). The onus then is placed on the internal machine of state and the bureaucracy that serves as its governing institution.

Other times, however, commentary addresses individual state leaders i.e. 'Putin warns of hitting "new targets" if Kyiv gets new missiles' (Al Jazeera 2022c). Emphasis then is placed on the individual leader, distinct from national institutions, or the wider population.

Think about how you describe states in your own discussions. Are there any implicit assumptions that you are making about the state as an actor in your own narratives?

THE LEVELS OF ANALYSIS

The levels of analysis are an analytical approach originally developed by Kenneth Waltz (pg. 38) in his work, *Man, the State and War* (1959), as a means of examining different levels of explanation for international conflict. These levels include the *international level* (the system of states), the *state level* (the internal structure and processes of the state), and the *individual level* (the attitudes, decisions and influence of people themselves). As scholars of international politics, we can often favour one of these levels in our own observations, which then shapes which theories we choose to draw upon, and the explanations we offer in any research and analysis. Yet as Waltz (1959: 5) highlights, 'where one begins his explanation of events makes a difference'. The levels of analysis approach then is a means by which you can start to examine your assumptions, consider your research choices and make informed decisions about the theoretical tools you want to draw upon in any analysis.

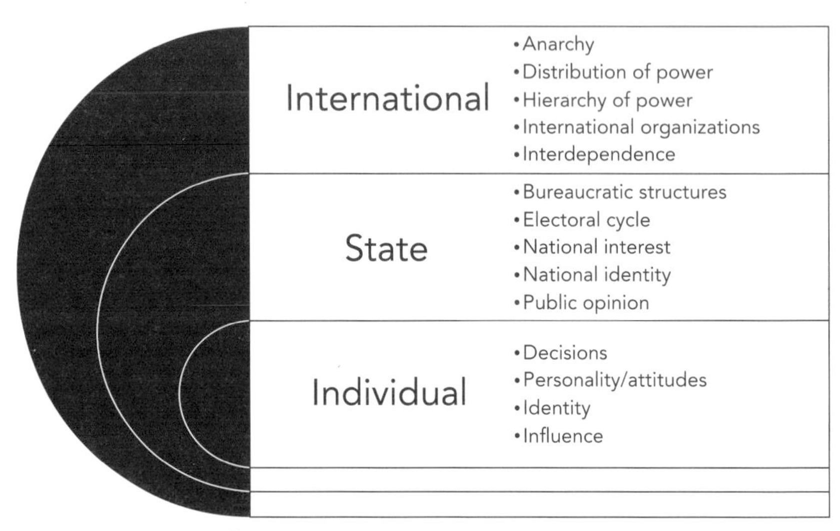

Figure 5.1 The levels of analysis

Important to highlight before moving on to detail each of the levels – summarized in Figure 5.1 – is that the levels of analysis tool is not without its limitations. One limitation we must reflect upon is that the levels of analysis approach originates from realist scholarship, therefore the levels of analysis do invariably favour the state as a primary unit of analysis within international politics. Yet as we shall see as we move into the next chapters, international and regional organizations, multinational enterprises, violent non-state actors and civil society actors all play a prominent role in international politics. To address this, some scholars add additional levels to their analysis such as the regional or sub-national level. For example, Buzan and Little (2000) utilize five levels of analysis including international systems, sub-systems (groups of units such as regional organizations), units (entities composed of various sub-groups such as organizations and communities), subunits (such as bureaucracies, lobbies), and individuals. Others, like Singer (1960: 453), however, highlight that 'while other groups, classes, or levels of human organization may influence the course of events, they can do so only by acting upon and influencing the state itself'. In the following sections you will notice that there is a certain state-centrism in the discussion of each level of analysis. However, a deliberately broad lens is adopted to enable you to observe not only the importance of the state within international politics, but also the variety of different actors and their respective influences upon the actors and processes we are analysing.

Another limitation we can identify of the levels of analysis approach is that it has tended to be utilized more by problem-solving theoretical approaches (pg. 51), thereby treating the reality of the international system objectively and the concepts we use to analyse each level as 'known' facts to be accepted rather than reflected upon. Thus, the international system often tends to be addressed as a pre-existing structure, sovereign states as primary units, and the individuals within it as rational actors who serve the national interest of the state. Critical theoretical approaches, however, call on us to question the acceptance of such pre-existing structures, and the constructs used to analyse them. In the following sections, discussion is therefore given to critical observations of the levels of analysis themselves, enabling you to reflect on different viewpoints and how you can draw upon them in applying the levels of analysis in your own research.

A further limitation we might identify of the levels of analysis approach is that it can cause us to compartmentalize our analysis into isolated levels of explanation, neglecting that some explanations may overlap or combine, and that real-world international politics does not always fit neatly into analytical categories. A risk also follows that 'the firmness with which a person is wedded to one image [level] colors his interpretation of the others' (Waltz 1959: 226), and that we then pursue overly narrow conceptualizations of cause and effect within international politics. This can also make it harder to locate explanations and outcomes within international politics when they relate to transnational actors autonomous of the state as a unit of analysis, such as MNEs (pg. 156–60) or global civil society (pg. 148). International politics is also highly complex and the levels of analysis approach cannot capture every nuance. What the level of analysis approach does provide, however, is an analytical construct to help you sort and arrange that complexity, all the while being mindful of the limitations it can present.

Important also to highlight is, as Buzan and Little (2000: 69) state, 'levels are simply referents for where explanations and outcomes are located. They are not sources of explanation in themselves.' As you read on in this chapter, therefore, look to use the levels to help you sort through different explanations, reflect on different theoretical perspectives, consider your own assumptions, and start to arrange your thinking.

THE INTERNATIONAL LEVEL

At the international level of analysis our interest is primarily oriented towards the international system (pg. 14) and how its various structures and characteristics can shape the action and interaction of actors within it. As with any system, the international system is formed of various parts – or units. Much like in biology where we consider an ecosystem as the interaction of the various organisms within it, in international politics, we consider the international system as the network, relationships and interactions of the various actors that form its constituent parts, particularly where that concerns states. Many of the theoretical traditions we have addressed so far pay attention to the system level when developing their assumptions and propositions. For example, we have seen that anarchy – the absence of any overarching authority above the state itself – has been considered a fundamental characteristic of the contemporary international system (pg. 18). Neorealism particularly emphasizes how anarchy creates a self-help system. States, acting out of self-interest, amid a climate of uncertainty, mistrust and fear (pg. 42), will then act to defend their national security and advance their national interests. Anarchy then becomes a key characteristic explaining why states compete with one another and why states go to war.

Waltz's structural realism especially prioritizes the international system as an explanatory variable in international politics, stressing how the distribution of power – or **polarity** – of the international system explains state behaviour. For Waltz, for example, *bipolarity* is the most stable form of international system because within a bipolar system there exist two equally balanced centres of power that maintain global order and security. The Cold War is often highlighted as an exemplar of bipolarity with power distributed relatively equally between two superpowers (pg. 23) – the US and the Soviet Union. During the Cold War, the logic of deterrence, coupled with the principle of mutually assured destruction associated with the use of nuclear weapons, ensured that the two superpowers never formally went to war. The Cold War then was about sustaining the balance of power by thwarting any effort by the other superpower to achieve any technological, military, economic or political superiority. For the majority of other states, foreign policy was then predominantly geared towards alliance-building and sustaining good relations with one or other superpower.

Polarity
The distribution or number of centres of power that exist within the international system.

In contrast, other realist scholars suggest that a unipolar system, in which there exists only one centre of power, is the safest and most stable. Wohlforth (1999: 9), for example, argues that unipolarity is where one state has 'capabilities too great to be counterbalanced' by any other state in the system, and with many acclaiming the United States' 'unipolar moment' upon the decline and eventual demise of the Soviet Union (Krauthammer 1990). Wohlforth further argued that unipolarity is the most durable and peaceful world order because it reduces the likelihood of hegemonic rivalry from other states. As no other state can challenge a **hyperpower** in a unipolar system, other states may instead focus less on competing with them and more on enjoying the benefits of peace and security that the hegemon (pg. 22) oversees.

Hyperpower
A term based on the French *hyperpuissance* coined in the late 1990s with reference to the status of the United States as the only power with superior military and economic dominance within the international system, which no other state could rival.

Hegemonic stability theory
The theory that international stability can be achieved where one hegemon is willing and able to lead others, and act in a way that will ensure a prosperous peace.

These arguments link also to **hegemonic stability theory** which states that the international system will remain stable where there is one hegemon to dominate it and maintain stability – a theory related to the concepts of *Pax Britannica* and *Pax Americana* and the relative peace that was established within the international systems during the 19th century (led by Britain), and the post-World War Two era (led by the United States) (pg. 23–5).

Where most neorealist scholars tend to agree is on the relative instability of a *multipolar* system, where there exist multiple centres of power, and where states must cooperate and compete in shifting patterns and alliances. In a multipolar world there are multiple great powers, along with rising powers who seek to join the great power ranks. According to Waltz (1979: 131), joining the great power ranks demands that a state rank highly in terms of:

- Size of population
- Resource endowment
- Economic capability
- Military strength
- Political stability and competence.

Great powers are also thought to possess special responsibilities in so far as they have the most powerful material, and particularly military, capabilities within the international system (Bull 1980). For Waltz (1979) particularly, great powers possess the greatest interest in the stability of the international system and thus the greatest stake in upholding order and stability. Morgenthau (1978: 24) also reflected on the 'foremost responsibility' of the United States after World War Two. Neoliberal approaches also align in this regard by highlighting that great powers are willing to take on special responsibilities, particularly where it concerns the management of international order and security. Neoliberal approaches, however, go further in suggesting that great powers take on special responsibilities to maintain the legitimacy of an international order in which they themselves have a dominant position (Ikenberry 2017).

Returning to the structural realist perspective, the presence of multiple great powers within the international system – that is a multipolar system – is not only found to shape the responsibilities of the great powers themselves but is characterized by uncertainty and competition. In a multipolar world the distribution of power makes it difficult for states to assess the behaviour of others which can result in miscalculations. It is also harder for states to form alliances, with alliance formation likely to be fleeting and issue-specific and with greater potential for conflict. Persistent competitiveness is also thought to characterize the relations between the great powers themselves, as states will pursue foreign policies that aim to weaken their competitors, while enhancing their own relative power capabilities. Table 5.1 summarizes the different characteristics of uni-, bi- and multipolar systems.

It should be noted that such structural approaches are heavily critiqued for adopting too reductionist a view of the international system itself as a source of explanation for

Table 5.1 Characteristics of unipolar, bipolar and multipolar systems

	Unipolarity	Bipolarity	Multipolarity
Number of 'poles'	One centre of power (hyperpower)	Two centres of power (superpowers)	Three or more centres of power (great powers)
Characteristics	Hegemonic stability *Pax Americana* *Pax Britannica*	Balance of power Deterrence	Uncertainty Competition Miscalculation
Time periods	19th century; late 20th century – early 21st century	Mid–late 20th century	Late 19th century – mid-20th century; 21st century

state behaviour (Buzan and Little 2000). Feminist scholars, for example, typically reject structural realism (True 2022: 152). Adopting such a structurally narrow lens is found to not only discount the nuances of international politics – not least in terms of gender hierarchy (Sjoberg 2013) – but of the other international actors and interactions at work within that system.

Liberal theoretical perspectives, for example, also highlight that interdependence (pg. 40) is a characteristic of the international system and an important point of focus for analysing international politics. From the liberal perspective, the liberal international order (pg. 38) emerged because of closer interdependence between states. Economic development (pg. 225), the international economy (pg. 205) and the growth of international and regional organizations have served as structures for the interaction of states along with a wide variety of non-state actors within the international system. Processes of economic connectivity, free trade and the lowering of barriers to trade, alongside the growth of diplomacy, and multilateralism have therefore become hallmarks of the liberal international system, facilitating freedom of movement and exchange, as well as enhanced opportunity for dialogue, cooperation and bargaining. Collective action has therefore become feasible within the international system because of the interconnectedness and interdependence between the units within it. This perspective further chimes with Buzan and Little (2000: 69–70) who suggest that while '[s]ome organizations (the UN), structures (the global market), and processes (international law) operate at the system level', other sub-systemic regional organizations can also be distinguished 'by the particular nature or intensity of their interactions/interdependence with each other'.

Constructivists also emphasize the importance of social interaction and relationships within the international system. Because the international system is considered a social realm (pg. 62), states do not just operate according to rational logics based on cost–benefit calculations, risk assessments or fear. States develop social relationships, they interact frequently through international organizations, and they interact through dialogue. In essence, 'anarchy is what states make of it' (Wendt 1992). Socially constructed national identities shape national interests and impact state behaviour. Over time, shared international norms, values and identities become socially constructed, further impacting what states deem to be appropriate behaviour (pg. 62). Thus, common understandings of concepts, standards, norms and practices – from anything such as sovereignty and power to human rights and sustainable development – become embedded over time within the international system through frequent dialogue, the development of social relationships and social learning.

OBSERVE

Source: Pool / Getty Images.

Image 5.1 During the 2017 G20 Finance Ministers meeting in Kurhaus, Baden-Baden, Germany. Ministers and Central Bank Governors met for a High-Level Symposium entitled 'Global Economic Governance in a Multipolar World'. The G20 was formed in 1999 as a forum for the Finance Ministers and Central Bank Governors among the world's top 20 economic powers but was elevated to Leaders' Level in 2009 after the Global Financial Crisis. Today the G20 is considered the 'premier forum for international economic cooperation' and itself a signal to the emerging multipolarity within our international system.

During the 2000s the rising economic prominence of Brazil, Russia, India, China and South Africa (BRICS) caused many to question whether we were witnessing the emergence of a multipolar system. Since the 2010s references to a 'multipolar world' have become increasingly commonplace. Multipolarity has become embedded in international discourses, as seen in this image from the G20 Finance Ministers meeting in 2017. Its meaning – that the distribution of power in the international system is divided between multiple great powers – is then treated as an assumed fact about the international system.

Yet, when we reflect on the concept of polarity and multipolarity from a critical perspective, we can see that what is 'known' is largely shaped by a dominant realist strand of thinking about power and the international system. Rather than accepting that the international system is multipolar, critical theory challenges us to question why this has become a presumed knowledge, and to look at the power claims behind it. It also calls upon us to ask on whose terms multipolarity is being enacted, and who is being neglected in turn (Dietz et al. 2011). Postcolonialism further stresses the 'othering' that presumptions of multipolarity can generate; that of a world divided between 'us' – the powerful economic centres, and 'them' – the weak others. From a critical perspective we are therefore encouraged as researchers to enquire further of these discourses of power, how they shape our understanding of the 'international system', and how we utilize such discourse in our own research and analysis.

Critical theoretical approaches further critique what is 'known' about the international system, and the distribution of power within it, at the international level of analysis. Postcolonialism stresses the legacy of imperialism as an international system and the extent to which colonialism has continued to foster a hierarchy of power within contemporary international politics, signposting to the 'othering' which shapes discourses within international politics, and which serve to delineate a hierarchy of different systems such as Global North and South, or Western and Third World. Dependency theorists also emphasize how the international system is characterized by a hierarchy of economic power and dependency between the wealthy industrialized core and the poor developing periphery. From a critical perspective, therefore, we can start to challenge the very notion of there being any one single international system, but rather an array of multiple overlapping systems that are constructed and shaped both by legacies of the past and discourses of power, hegemony, and hierarchy.

THE STATE LEVEL

In the last section we addressed the various characteristics of the international system that we can draw upon to offer explanation and critique of international politics, and how these can be supported through engagement with the theoretical tools we have been developing. A second level of analysis that we can then utilize is the state level of analysis. In Chapter Two we observed that the sovereign state has become the main organizing unit by which peoples and territories within the international system are ordered. As we saw in the last section, however, while the state features as a primary unit of analysis in the international level of analysis, it also tends to be treated as a unitary actor. Observed from the international level of analysis, we can see that the state is acting because we can recognize the cause and effect of its actions relative to the wider system, but the internal functioning, interests and identity of the state itself is not an object of our enquiry. At the state level of analysis, however, our focus deliberately shifts to the internal structures and processes of the state itself for explanation of why it acts as it does. Our concern then moves to consider the government and bureaucratic structures of the state, who is in power, and how national interests and identities are formed.

When approaching the state level of analysis, an important first reflection that we must make is that states are not unitary actors, but are complex bureaucracies, comprising a web of ministries, departments, chambers, committees and other institutions and agencies that serve as its primary governing structures. Some states operate as a system of multi-level governance where power is devolved or federalized to the sub-state level, adding further complexity to how it functions. At the state level of analysis, how the state then operates as a bureaucratic structure, how it makes decisions, and the processes that influence its national interest and subsequent foreign policy, are all sources of explanation for why that state behaves the way it does.

From the liberal theoretical perspective, the internal political make-up of a state is assumed to matter a great deal in shaping its behaviour in the international system. Democratic states are thought to operate in a structure of checks and balances. Governing institutions check and balance each other, while the citizenry holds them accountable through regular elections. Politicians also serve as representatives of the people; therefore, their decisions are held to account by the people that they serve. Democratic peace theory (pg. 40), by extension, argues that liberal democratic states are more likely to enjoy peaceful relations with other democratic states. Democratic peace theorists further signpost to there being greater likelihood of intrastate civil wars, as well as conflicts between democratic and **authoritarian** states, than between liberal democratic states.

Authoritarianism
A political system where power is concentrated in a leader or political elite and whose authority is strictly enforced, often at the expense of individual freedoms.

When we adopt a state level of analysis, we can observe that elections and national electoral cycles are important factors explaining a state's governing structures and subsequent policies. In democratic states it is – typically – the political party who wins the majority vote in an election that may then form a government and start to enter into relations with other states. But there is no one-size-fits-all electoral system in democracies. Some states have multi-party systems where no one party can win a majority, requiring that a government coalition is formed, potentially impacting the government's foreign policy preferences, as well as its cohesion and effectiveness in implementing them. Some states operate a two-party system with clearly defined foreign policy stances between the two parties. For example, the United States' foreign policy can fluctuate markedly between Republican and Democratic Administrations. By way of example, consider that, under a Democratic Administration (2009–16), the US both negotiated and signed the 2015 Paris Climate Agreement to reduce global greenhouse gases and provide climate finance to developing countries (pg. 252). Under the Republican Administration (2016–21), however, the US formally withdrew from the Paris Climate Agreement – a move that was then reversed by the incoming Democratic Administration in 2021.

ORGANIZE

Electoral cycles and changes in government administrations can impact even long-standing foreign policy positions. Consider that in 2022 Sweden abandoned its long-held feminist foreign policy (pg. 60) and reversed its long-standing opposition to NATO membership (pg. 131–2).

While at the international level of analysis we might attribute this sea change in Swedish foreign policy to Russia's invasion of Ukraine. At the state level, we can observe that Sweden's feminist foreign policy was launched by a left-leaning coalition government in 2014. The radical shift in Sweden's foreign policy in 2022 was announced just days following a national election and the formation of a new right-leaning coalition government.

This in turn highlights the importance of domestic politics in shaping a state's national interest and how effectively it can pursue those interests in its relations with other states. Putnam (1988) argued that in international negotiations where states seek to find common ground where there are competing or conflictual interests, two games are ultimately being played out. The first game is being played at the international level between the state's negotiators and their foreign counterparts. The state therefore advances its national interests by seeking to find a negotiated outcome with other states. The second game, however, is being played at the domestic level for each state. At the domestic level the government must not only ensure that any negotiated agreement meets the demands of their national interest but will also receive sufficient political support to be signed and ratified. According to Putnam, it is only where an international negotiation results in domestic benefits for the respective states that any deal can ultimately be adopted. We can particularly observe the significance of the domestic level in the context of international trade negotiations, where a negotiated deal is found to negatively impact certain industries or sectors within the national economy. Thus, domestic constituencies and the politics within a state's governing structures matter to how that state can advance its national interests within the international system.

Role theory
A theoretical approach that uses roles to identify and explain the relationship between actors within the international system. Role theory focuses both on how national roles are conceived (*ego*), and how they are perceived by others (*alter*). Roles played by states might include revisionist power, status quo player, non-aligned, great power, leader, defender, mediator, etc.

At the state level of analysis, constructivism would also highlight that a state's national interest is not determined simply by bargaining, bureaucracy and two-level games. Rather, a state's national interests are socially constructed over time, and are directly informed by a state's national identity. **Role theory**, for example, highlights how a state's foreign policy can be driven by the different national role conceptions that states conceive for themselves, drawing upon their national identities, norms and ideas. Constructivists also reflect on the importance of how states perceive their international status. For example, when the UK public voted to leave the European Union in 2016, scholarship examined the UK's national identity, its national role conceptions and how the UK government used Brexit to bolster a perceived decline in its global status while championing a vision of 'Global Britain' (HM Government 2021; Blagden 2019; Daddow 2019; Beasley, Kaarbo and Oppermann 2020; Oppermann, Beasley and Kaarbo 2021; Hill 2023). Feminist scholarship has also shown how a state's social identity has gendered dimensions (True 2022: 152–3). A state's reputational status, for example, might be influenced by whether, and to what extent, it achieves gender equality, or delivers on international gender norms (Krook and True 2012; Towns 2011).

We can also observe that public opinion can influence a government's perceptions of the national interest and the policies they then seek to advance. Politicians are expected to represent the views of their domestic constituencies because they may be rejected at the next election if they do not. But elections are an imperfect gauge of public opinion, and public attitudes themselves can often vary considerably across issue areas. For this reason, public-opinion polling has become a regular activity for many states as the political elite seek to keep abreast of public attitudes across different issues. The media has also become an important medium for shaping public opinion, reporting on the activities of governments, as well as determining what and how issues within international affairs should be reported. Constructivist approaches particularly highlight the importance of these shared narratives, and the role that the media can play in 'framing' how events are perceived and interpreted by the public, and how seriously the political elite then takes them (Cross 2017).

At the state level of analysis, we can also observe how civil society and businesses now also play an important role in trying to shape and influence national political agendas, including through lobbying and by agenda-setting (pg. 149–50). Critical perspectives further highlight the importance of civil society, not only in holding governments accountable, but as agents of change, capable of shaping discourses, championing human rights and advocating social justice. The rise of social movements has particularly highlighted the importance of mass publics in shaping both public opinion and national and international agendas – a point we shall return to in Chapter Nine.

Explore More

Public-opinion polling offers an important – if at times somewhat controversial – method for understanding people's views. Polling is considered both important and necessary for governments to be able to understand the wishes of the people they represent, along with the issues that they care about. Yet opinion polls are often questioned for their accuracy, validity and bias, with doubts then raised over the questions being asked, who the respondents were, and the sampling method applied. The Pew Research Centre offers a short online course explaining how public-opinion polling works – available online: www.pewresearch.org. You may also want to explore Politico's *Europe Poll of Polls*. Available online: www.politico.eu, which includes daily updates on polling conducted across Europe. Scan the barcode also for links to other polling data and analysis from around the world.

Scan the QR code for access to explore weblinks and more resources.

THE INDIVIDUAL LEVEL

So far in this chapter we have considered some of the characteristics or variables that we can focus upon at the state and international levels to help explain processes, behaviours and outcomes within international politics. In this section we consider a third level of analysis that we can utilize in our research. At the individual level of analysis, we address the individuals that shape and make decisions in international politics. Our attention therefore turns away from the system of states, or the structure and processes of the state itself, in offering explanation or critique, to focus instead on people.

At the individual level of analysis, we are often interested in those in high political office, such as heads of state or international organizations. But the individual level of analysis also enables us to focus on other individuals as well – individuals such as those private citizens who have been prominent in raising awareness or directly influencing specific issues within international politics. For social and critical theoretical approaches particularly, the individual level of analysis is especially important as it is through human experience, perceptions and choices, as well as the interactions between people, that knowledge is constructed, and social realities created. From a post-positivist perspective (pg. 50), international politics is not some object to be tested and explained but a subjective realm where people matter – both in the actions and interactions being observed, and in the research and analysis itself. We ourselves are not separate from the events we are researching, therefore we as individual researchers are also important when constructing knowledge and shaping understandings of international politics.

When approaching the individual level of analysis we can address many different characteristics of the individual, but typically we will be concerned with the nature, traits, personality, experiences and, ultimately, decisions that individuals make. Consider that who decides what and when are often foundational to understanding an event, process or policy. All policies are themselves a product of decisions about what to do (and not do), and how to do it (Peterson and Bomberg 1999: 4). The capacity to decide in international politics, moreover, resides solely with individuals, therefore the individual level of analysis enables us to shine a light directly on to those people.

As we observed in Chapter Three, both classical realism and classical liberalism took human nature as a starting point when developing their assumptions and propositions. Classical realism's assumptions that human nature is naturally egoistic, selfish and mistrustful thus translated into the proposition that states themselves are driven by the selfish pursuit of national interest and the necessity for national security. Classical liberalism by contrast assumed that human nature was inherently good, naturally social and inclined towards cooperation and progress. Thus, states themselves were observed to follow the same traits.

At the individual level of analysis, we can similarly observe how some national leaders can exhibit certain realist and liberal traits in their own leadership styles, particularly as it concerns their attitudes towards foreign policy. To demonstrate this, let's return to the example of the US and the Paris Climate Agreement. We could argue that the United States' position towards the Paris Climate Agreement was driven by the attitudes of its individual presidents. President Obama (2009 to 2016) was seen to personally champion internationalism, collective action and was progressive in addressing climate change – all traits typically linked with a liberal attitude. By contrast President Trump (2016 to 2021) was seen to favour a 'strongman' (Rachman 2016; Bremmer 2018) style of leadership, championing 'America First', pursuing a trade war against the United States' economic rivals (pg. 213), advancing aggressive anti-immigration policies (pg. 281), and retreating from multiple international agreements – all traits we might associate more with realism. We can also observe that President Biden (2021–) – formerly vice president to President Obama – made rejoining the Paris Agreement a personal campaign promise, and symbolically made it one of his first executive orders upon taking office.

Individual identity can also be a powerful influencing factor, and an important explanatory tool in international politics. For feminist scholars particularly, gender is considered a fundamental identifier. In international politics scholarship, much attention has therefore been paid to gendered dynamics, be that oriented towards the number of female leaders in high political office (Vinas 2014), focusing on the individual leadership style of specific leaders (Yoder 2020), or comparing and critiquing gendered personality traits associated with female leaders (see Schramm and Stark 2020). Gendered dynamics are also considered important in the roles played by individual peacekeepers and mediators in conflict situations (Azizah, Maksum and Hidayahtulloh 2020; Scheuermann and Zürn 2020).

As well as their identity, a leader's personal style, and the social relationships they foster, can also be important in shaping their attitudes and approach to a state's foreign policy. For example, returning to the example of AUKUS discussed in the last chapter (pg. 69–70) we can observe that Australia's then Prime Minister Scott Morrison had a close relationship with then UK Prime Minister Johnson, to the point of being caricatured as the 'ScoMo-BoJo bromance' (van Leeuwen 2021). According to media commentary, 'the personal relationship between Morrison and Johnson – two populist conservative politicians – came into play' (Parker et al. 2021) in the AUKUS talks. We can therefore identify how individual personalities, relationships and decisions can be looked to as sources of explanation in international politics.

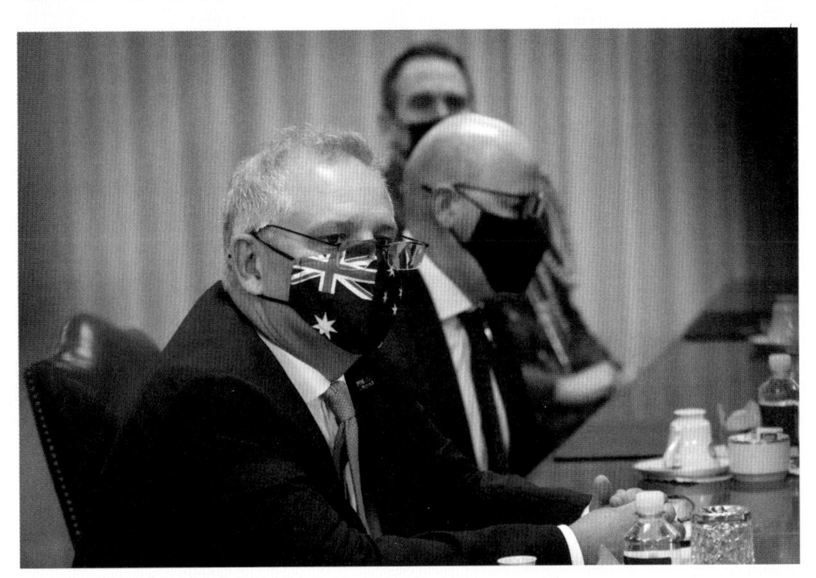

Image 5.2 Then Australian Prime Minister Scott Morrison attends a meeting at the Pentagon in Arlington, USA in September 2021. The week previously Australia, the UK and USA announced a new trilateral security pact (AUKUS), enabling Australia to develop nuclear-powered submarines.

Source: Drew Angerer / Getty Images.

Consider

In the last chapter's 'How to' guide we considered the case of the Australia, UK, US defence pact (AUKUS) announced in September 2021. Reflect again on the background to AUKUS section (pg. 69–71) and consider the question, *'Why did Australia join a defence pact with the UK and the US (AUKUS)?'*

Explore

We can look for answers to this question by using a levels-of-analysis approach. Scan the barcode to access commentary and analysis of the AUKUS deal.

Connect

A levels-of-analysis approach enables us to look for different sources of explanation at different levels, as follows:

International level of analysis

At the international level our analysis is directed towards the system itself, to the rising power of China, and its growing influence over the Indo-Pacific region (pg. 129). An emerging multipolarity and China's growing influence in the region can also be observed as a cause of concern for Australia. Australia has not only experienced rapidly deteriorating relations with China (its largest trading partner), but is considered an ally of the US and the 'U.S.-led global order' (Schuman 2021). From a structural realist perspective multipolarity is assumed to be unstable, uncertain and competitive. Alliances will therefore form to counterbalance those states that are perceived to be the greatest threat. AUKUS then may be identified as a rational response by Australia to 'counter Chinese aggression in the Asia-Pacific' (Groch 2023). We can also observe that AUKUS amplifies Australia's interdependence with the UK and US, with Australia gaining access to nuclear-power technology – considered the United States' 'most closely guarded secrets' (Groch 2023) – and bolstering its status among an elite club of only seven states in the world with nuclear-powered submarines.

State level of analysis

At the state level our analysis turns to Australia itself, including its national interest, identity, bureaucratic structures, electoral cycle and public opinion. One source of explanation may be the domestic perception within Australia that China presents a threat. For example, national opinion polling conducted in 2021 and 2022 showed that more than six in ten Australians believed China's foreign policy poses a critical threat to Australia's vital interest (Lowy Institute 2022a), and 52 per cent of those polled also believed AUKUS would make Australia safer (Lowy Institute 2022b). We can also identify that AUKUS had received broadly bipartisan support within Australia's main political parties in the Federal Parliament and Government (Groch 2023) which has enabled the Pact to progress despite a change of government administration after the May 2022 Australian national elections.

Individual level of analysis

At the individual level our analysis may then focus on Australia's individual heads of state. AUKUS was signed by Australia's former Prime Minister Scott Morrison (pictured) in September 2021, and then progressed by Prime Minister Anthony Albanese when he was elected in May 2022. From the individual level of analysis, we might particularly look to the decisions that Morrison took in negotiating the deal, his personal leadership style as well as his attitudes to foreign policy and how this shaped his approach to AUKUS. For some, the fact that AUKUS was negotiated in secret and then announced with great fanfare – resulting also in a diplomatic fallout with the French (pg. 69) – carried 'Morrison's individual branding' and the 'hallmarks' of his own personal leadership style and approach to foreign policy (Grattan 2021). AUKUS has further been described as Prime Minister Morrison's 'most significant legacy' (Grattan 2021); a legacy that has seen Australia's reputation elevated in the region and its 'neutralist, non-aligned approach to Australian foreign policy ... dead in the water' (Downer 2023).

Predict

Each level of analysis provides referent points for different sources of explanation as to why Australia joined the UK and the US in the AUKUS pact. What other sources of explanation do you think need to be considered in each level of analysis? How would you then answer the question *'Why did Australia join the UK and US in the AUKUS defence pact?'* (see also *How to – take a position* on pg. 144)

More than just considering how the decisions of individuals in high public office shape international politics, we can also observe how private citizens can come to influence and shape the world around us. Consider, for example, the many millions of individuals around the world who sign petitions, attend rallies and join social media campaigns. Each of these individuals is active within international politics, and each is shaped by their identities, attitudes and experiences. Consider also that even the individual activist can have an inordinate impact on international politics. The 'Greta Thunberg effect', for example, was a phrase coined in specific reference to the impact that youth climate activist Greta Thunberg had, not only in mobilizing a global movement against climate change, but for her ability to hold national and international leaders accountable (*The Guardian* 2019).

The Greta Thunberg effect in turn highlights how popular figures can raise awareness, influence public opinion and shape the issues that those in high public office then come to care about. Consider that when religious leaders such as Pope Francis, the Head of the Catholic Church, or the Dalai Lama, the Head of Tibetan Buddhism, speak, they command the attention of a global audience (pg. 286). Billionaires, such as Jeff Bezos, Elon Musk and Richard Branson have considerable public followings on social media. In the early 2020s they also had collateral to finance a new private space race that advanced space exploration while launching the frontier of space tourism.

Businessmen, along with film and TV celebrities, are also individuals with the public eye upon them and who, when they speak, have a large following. The growth of **celebrity humanitarianism** highlights a phenomenon that has grown to new heights since the turn of the 21st century. Many celebrities have used their public profile to raise awareness of humanitarian crises around the world, and to push for change. Well-known business leaders, including, for example, George Soros and Bill Gates, also funnel large sums of money into philanthropic humanitarian assistance projects.

Celebrity humanitarianism
A form of advocacy by celebrities who utilize their profile and influence to raise awareness and/or funds for humanitarian crises or problems.

Image 5.3 Greta Thunberg speaks to a press conference at the European Parliament in 2019.

Source: Wikimedia Commons.

Explore More

In 2021 Budabin and Richey published *Batman Saves the Congo* with Minnesota University Press. The book investigates the role of the Eastern Congo Initiative – www.easterncongo.org – founded by celebrity Ben Affleck to help Congolese development by giving grants to community organizations. According to Budabin and Richey (2021), Affleck possessed convening power as a celebrity, and was therefore capable of bringing together strategic partners, including big businesses, to advance a business-based model that provided grants to community organizations in the Congo. While innovative in its capacity to raise awareness, funding and elite support, Budabin and Richey (2021) have also critiqued the impact of the Eastern Congo Initiative, highlighting it as an example of how celebrity interventionism can disrupt economic development in a country, reinforcing private over public solutions, and constitutes a 'worrying trend of unaccountable elite leadership in North-South relations.'

Scan the QR code for access to explore weblinks and more resources.

For some critical scholars, however, the rise of celebrity humanitarianism has given rise to concern. On the one hand celebrities can raise awareness and inject funding into causes, reaching communities that government or agency-funded projects cannot reach, or have been neglected. Yet, studies have also highlighted how celebrity humanitarianism can be unaccountable and may even prove disruptive of development practices and politics within a country (Budabin and Richey 2021). Some highlight celebrity humanitarianism as an exercise for 'White Saviours' (Cole 2012), while others see it less as philanthropy and altruism and more as a means to promote the celebrity brand while legitimizing inequality and neoliberal capitalism (Kapoor 2013).

Critical scholars do not just emphasize the influence of the celebrity. Critical scholars also observe that all individuals are key actors in international politics as all individuals shape ideas and inform knowledge. Your perceptions, experiences and attitudes also play an important part in shaping knowledge, legitimizing ideas and challenging or reinforcing power structures. Our own individual decisions as researchers and observers of international politics are therefore part of the process of knowledge creation and evolution. Take a moment, therefore, before moving on through this book to reflect on the importance of the individual, and your own subjective involvement in international politics as an active researcher and scholar. Your decisions, your analyses, your arguments – they are all now part of that discussion.

CONCLUSION

In this chapter we have considered the levels of analysis as an analytical construct that enables you to 'pitch' different theoretical perspectives and their assumptions and propositions across different categories for analysis, critique and explanation. In reflecting on the *international*, *state* and *individual* levels of analysis in turn, we have been able to identify some of the various characteristics, issues and sources of explanation that we can start to focus upon when researching any given issue, event, actor or topic within international politics. How you apply these levels will of course be contingent upon the academic choices you yourself will make as an independent scholar. In the following combined toolkit and 'how to' guide, you can start to test out some of these skills, and refine your knowledge further. You will also continue to advance your knowledge and apply your toolkit as you move on through this book.

 **TOOLKIT**

Why did the UK vote to leave the European Union?

THINK

- Your own closeness or distance to an issue or event in international politics can shape which level of analysis and sources of explanation you might look to prioritize. What was your personal experience or observations of Brexit (if any)? How do you think your own awareness or distance from Brexit might shape the tools you will utilize in your research?

OBSERVE

Image 5.4 During the Brexit referendum in 2016, sovereignty protection, border control and immigration became core issues. For the Leave Campaign, the UK's membership of the EU was directly linked to voters' fears of uncontrollable immigration and insecurity, and the necessity to 'take back control'.
Source: Carl Court/Getty Images.

- During the Brexit referendum the British people were asked, 'Should the UK leave the European Union, or remain within it?' The campaign that shaped the referendum vote was highly polarizing, dividing political parties and voters between Remain and Leave camps. On 23 June 2016 the UK public narrowly voted 51.9 per cent Leave to 48.1 per cent Remain.

ORGANIZE

- When looking at some of the scholarship around Brexit, we can identify various explanations for why Brexit happened. The levels of analysis approach can help you to filter them, for example:
- At the *international level* of analysis, we might reflect on the UK's history as an imperial power. Scholars have, for example, highlighted the importance of the 'Anglosphere' and the legacy

of empire in shaping the UK's perceived global status, and its subsequent pursuit of Brexit to regain lost influence (Bell and Vucetic 2019).

- At the *state level* of analysis, scholars have highlighted the influence of national identity and national role conceptions in shaping UK Euroscepticism and a desire to enhance its global status separate from the EU (pg. 81; see also Carl, Dennison and Evans 2018). Scholars also emphasize the importance of the UK's domestic constituency and public opinion (Richards and Diamond 2019), as well as positive leader images of UK Prime Minister Boris Johnson as being highly influential among voters and were found to enhance the likelihood of voting to exit the EU (Clarke, Goodwin and Whiteley 2017).
- At the *individual level* of analysis, scholars have highlighted the influence of leader image (pg. 83), as well as the failings of successive British leaders during Brexit (Atkins and Gaffney 2020).
- Reflect again on Figure 5.1 (pg. 74), what other variables do you think might be relevant in explaining why the UK voted to leave the EU?

LINK

- *Consider*: While the Brexit vote was tight, few were prepared for the result (Cohn 2016). Many voters were undecided, making it difficult to rely on public polling. Despite being a domestic popular vote, the impact of the Brexit referendum and the subsequent decision to leave the EU, not only sent shock waves around the world, but fundamentally altered both British and EU politics. For the UK particularly, Brexit has resulted in political and electoral upheaval – including five prime ministers in six years – a complete reorientation of its laws, policies and regulations, and a global strategic reorientation (HM Government 2021).
- *Explore*: Scan the barcode for some useful weblinks providing a timeline, as well as research and analysis of the UK's withdrawal from the EU.
- *Connect*: Waltz emphasized that where we begin our explanation of events in international politics makes a difference (pg. 73). Reflect again on what you know about Brexit – you can also use the *Explore* links to familiarize yourself with what happened and when. What actors, issues, concepts or theories stand out to you as a starting point for explanation? Will you focus on sources of explanation within the international system? What was happening at the state level that stands out to you? Perhaps your interest is in the individuals or identities involved? Do particular concepts strike you as important – for example, anarchy (pg. 18), sovereignty (pg. 17–18), othering (pg. 56) or status (pg. 81)?
- *Predict*: Depending on *why* you think Brexit happened, do you think it likely that other EU member states will exit the EU (pg. 140–1)? This is an opportunity for you to reflect on the wider implications of your argument, and the extent to which it may help us to understand other events in international politics.

SHARE

- Answer the question '*Why did the UK vote to leave the European Union?*'

  Using a levels of analysis approach can be a useful tool for answering big questions like this where there may be multiple, even times competing, explanations. There are different ways you might use the levels of analysis approach, however. Three ways to use this approach are outlined in the 'How To' guide on the next page.

HOW TO

USE THE LEVELS OF ANALYSIS APPROACH

1. As a research strategy

The levels of analysis can be used as an analytical tool to help you work through the different explanations that *could* be presented in your work, before settling on the area you feel warrants more careful research and analysis. Adopting this approach means you can first work through the different levels and where possible explanations might lie. From there you can start to refine your choices, reflect upon your assumptions, and then use your background research to justify which avenue you want to pursue in your own research. You can also use your background research to inform any critical discussion you subsequently introduce when writing up your work, enabling you to highlight competing perspectives and clarify why you rejected them (see *How to – develop critical analysis skills* pg. 163).

2. As a literature review strategy

You can consider using the levels of analysis as a means of sorting and organizing your reading of the existing scholarship around an issue. When reading around your topic you could look to categorize which level or levels of analysis other scholars tend to speak to. Ask yourself when reading around the literature if the focus is on international, state or individual levels of analysis, or the extent to which any of these levels are more neglected than others (see also *How to – approach a literature review* pg. 202).

3. As a framework of analysis

You can also utilize the levels of analysis as an **analytical framework**. An analytical framework is a useful visual tool for explaining how you organized and sorted your analysis. In this case you utilize the levels of analysis as an explicit framework for structuring and writing up your analysis. As an analytical framework the levels of analysis enable you to showcase the complexity of an issue, offer competing or complementary explanations, and to present an informed argument of what explanation or explanations you find most persuasive (see also *How to – take a position* pg. 144).

Analytical framework
A framework that enables a researcher to visually present how an analysis has been sorted and conducted.

Part II

Understanding the actors

6 The state

Pexels / Darya Sannikova

Abstract

In this chapter you will be introduced to the state as an actor within today's international system. First, the state is discussed as an independent political entity, revisiting its evolution and characteristics as the main organizing unit for peoples and territories across the globe. The chapter then focuses on the state as a foreign policy actor, addressing its various foreign policy tools, statecraft and diplomacy, before considering how states exercise different types of power. From there the chapter introduces you to the debate about when and why states are considered fragile or 'failed'. The chapter concludes with a toolkit exercise addressing the question, *'Is Taiwan a sovereign state?'*

INTRODUCING THE STATE

As we did in Chapter One, let's begin by looking at the world political map – Map 6.1. Consider the map and its patchwork of colours, each colour representing one of the nearly 200 sovereign states in our world today. Consider the geography that divides continents and defines the landscape of each region. Think about the borders that signify the territorial boundaries of each state and how they have each been shaped by their geography, culture, ethnicity, language and the legacies of empire. Consider that within each state exists not only a defined territory, but a specified people or peoples who may be relatively homogeneous in their national language, ethnicity and culture (e.g. France, Germany or Japan), or diverse multinational states (e.g. Bolivia, Canada, Belgium, South Africa, India or Indonesia).

Map 6.1 World Political Map.
Source: Booka1/Getty Images.

In Chapter Two we also discussed the emergence of the modern state system, and how the sovereign state became the main organizing unit of peoples and territories across the globe. We addressed how revolution and nationalism shaped the evolution of the modern state, with the people becoming the focal point for how the sovereign state derived its authority. We have also seen how the state has come to embody both *internal sovereignty* of a defined people and territory, and *external sovereignty* (pg. 18) through its autonomy from outside interference.

Consider again that, according to the 1933 Montevideo Convention on the Rights and Duties of States (pg. 15), a state possesses the following qualifications:

- a permanent population
- a defined territory
- government and
- the capacity to enter into relations with other states.

Going further, another common conceptualization provided by the German economist, philosopher and sociologist Max Weber (1864–1920), is that the state is 'a compulsory political organization with continuous operations ... in so far as its administrative staff successfully upholds the claim to the monopoly of the legitimate use of physical force in the enforcement of its order' (Weber 1925/1978: 54 cited in Hay and Lister 2006: 8). From both these qualifications and Weber's conceptualization we can then identify several important characteristics of the state.

First, the state is a political organization with continuous operations. That is, a state possesses a system of **government**, such as an **autocracy**, **democracy** or **oligarchy**, with an administrative staff whose role and responsibility is to oversee the ongoing administrative and legal order of a territory and its population.

Second, the state has the legitimate right to use or authorize the use of physical force within a territory and over its population. As Weber highlights, the state has 'monopoly

Government
A group of people who have the authority to govern the affairs of the state.

Autocracy
A system of government in which supreme power is held by one person or polity. Can include forms of absolute monarchy or dictatorships.

Democracy
Meaning 'rule of the people'. A system of government where the citizens elect representatives to governing bodies for fixed terms of office.

Oligarchy
Meaning 'rule of the few'. A system of government where power is held by a small number of people such as the nobility, wealthy, religious or military leaders.

over the legitimate use of physical force in the enforcement of its order'. The state's government therefore has both the responsibility and legitimacy to maintain order and security within the state. It is also worth noting that since the rise of the **welfare state** after World War Two, the characterization of the state has further advanced to encompass the state's responsibility not only for the security of its people, but also for their welfare (Holsti 1995: 97).

Welfare state
A state in which the government undertakes to protect the health and wellbeing of its citizens, providing for the financial and social needs of the poorest.

Statehood
Constituting a state. The status of being recognized as an independent sovereign state.

Third, states have the capacity to enter into relations with other states. A state's government is therefore recognized as the legitimate representative of that people and territory and can enter into foreign and diplomatic relations with other governments.

While these characteristics of **statehood** may strike you as obvious, the determination of what constitutes a state remains heavily contested within the social and political sciences, including within international politics. In part that contestation comes down to a question of recognition. According to the declarative theory of statehood, a state is recognized as an independent political entity when it *declares* itself to be an independent state. The constitutive theory of statehood, however, argues that a state must first receive recognition as an independent political entity by others before it is formally acknowledged as such.

THINK

Weber's conceptualization of the state emphasizes the legitimacy of the state to use physical force to uphold order and security within its territory. Reflect on your own understanding of the legitimacy of government. Does the system of government within a state shape how you perceive the state's legitimacy to use physical force to uphold order and security? When, and under what conditions, do you think the use of force by a government over its people is legitimate and justified? What would make such use of force *illegitimate*? You may also want to flick forward to find out more about the responsibility of the state by looking at Chapter Fifteen on Rights and Responsibility.

Explore More

Why not test your country geography and flag knowledge by trying your hand at some of the quizzes at www.sporcle.com. There are numerous quizzes you can choose from, like the 'Country Triangles' quiz or search for 'Countries of …' and select a region to test your knowledge. NB. When you take the countries of the world quiz, note how many countries it lists!

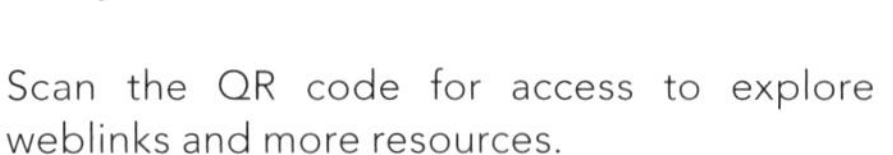

Scan the QR code for access to explore weblinks and more resources.

Consider then this question. How many independent sovereign states are there in the world today? If you were to do an internet search of this question you would likely return a variety of different answers. By various counts there are 193, 195, 196 or 197 independent sovereign states in our international system today. Yet, as with all things in international politics, the reason for these disputed numbers comes down to competing perspectives, criteria and definitions.

We can agree that there are currently 193 member states of the United Nations (UN). That means that 193 states have met, upon acceptance, the UN's requirement of membership as 'peace-loving states which accept the obligations contained in the present [UN] Charter' (UN 1945: Art IV). They have therefore each been recommended for UN membership by the UN Security Council and accepted for membership by the UN General Assembly. As members of the UN these 193 states are therefore formally and legally recognized as states and may enter into diplomatic relations with one another.

Two other political entities – the Holy See and Palestine – also have permanent observer status within the UN. The Holy See is the universal government of the Catholic Church and oversees the Vatican City State (pg. 286), which is a sovereign territory of just 0.44 square kilometres. Palestine is officially the State of Palestine, but Palestine's application for full membership of the UN in 2011 was rejected on the grounds that it lacked effective government and was not 'peace-loving' in accordance with Article 4 of the UN Charter. Together with the UN's 193 full members, the Holy See and Palestine bring the official tally to 195 states.

Kosovo is another independent political entity, widely considered a **de facto state**, having declared its independence from Serbia in 2008. But despite receiving recognition from over 100 UN members, Kosovo is only partially recognized as a sovereign state. Taiwan, similarly, is only partially recognized. In 1971 the UN passed a resolution recognizing the People's Republic of China (PRC) as the only legitimate representative of China to the UN. Since then, Taiwan (also named the Republic of China or ROC) has pushed for its recognition as a sovereign state, gaining support from several UN members, but remains mostly unrecognized due to China's wider influence and resistance to Taiwan's claim to sovereignty (see also the Toolkit exercise at the end of this chapter).

De facto state
Separatist state-like entities with political autonomy over a people and territory, but who lack international legal status.

OBSERVE

Image 6.1 Former US Secretary of State Hillary Clinton (seated R) and then Kosovar President Atifete Jahjaga (seated L) sign a US–Kosovo Agreement at the White House in 2011.

Source: KAREN BLEIER/Getty Images.

In this image, then US Secretary of State Clinton and Kosovar President Jahjaga sign the US–Kosovo Agreement on the Protection and Preservation of Certain Cultural Properties. Note how Kosovar flags hang together with the US flag adding further symbolism to an image which resonates of America's recognition of Kosovo as an independent sovereign state. Kosovo has been treated as a de facto state since separating from Serbia in 2008, but does not receive universal recognition. Kosovo therefore 'displays accoutrements of statehood except for international legal status' (Florea 2014: 788).

Kosovo's case is important to highlight because while sovereign states are considered central actors in international politics, 'they are not the sole units worthy of systematic inquiry' (Florea 2014). While theoretical approaches to international politics typically prioritize the state as the primary (oftentimes sole) unit of analysis (see Chapter Three), we must observe that states themselves are contested actors, and that political authority in contemporary international politics is often divided between both state and non-state actors. The sovereign state does not therefore have monopoly over political authority or political order within the international system.

THE STATE AS AN ACTOR

While there is contestation over what constitutes statehood, particularly where it concerns state recognition and legitimacy, what we must acknowledge is that states have considerable capacity to act within international politics. Governments of recognized states can enter into diplomatic relations with other states. States can be members of international and regional organizations and enter into **bilateral** or **multilateral** agreements with other states. States can declare war on one another, determine whether, or to what extent, they will uphold international laws and agreements, and have authority and responsibility for how their peoples and territories are managed, cared for and protected. States can determine the scope of their external action, whether or not they will be isolated from some in the international system, while pursuing alliances with others, or the extent to which they will seek to persuade or coerce others. For a state to 'act', it must not only possess the characteristics discussed in the last section, but also have the will and capacity to behave actively and deliberately in relation to other actors in the international system.

Bilateral
Between two parties, typically used in reference to two states.

Multilateral
Between three or more parties, typically used in reference to multiple states.

Governments have agency within international politics, but their actions can also be shaped, and even limited, by international politics. In a globalized, interconnected world, government decision-making concerning their own domestic policies can have impacts far beyond their own borders, much as international events, international organizations and international laws can have direct impacts on governments and domestic actions within their own borders. As scholars of international politics, we must also be mindful of this.

Consider, for example, the events of the Covid-19 pandemic. Covid-19 highlighted how governments can be impacted by international events and international organizations. As Covid-19 spread, the World Health Organization's (WHO) classification of the virus as a pandemic in March 2020 and its guidance that all countries 'detect, test, treat, isolate, trace, and mobilize their people in the response' (WHO 2020) was followed by over 100 countries who implemented partial or full national lockdowns, and instigated national detect, test and trace policies.

Yet Covid-19 also highlights the impacts of domestic policies on international politics. What began with the Wuhan Municipal Health Commission in China issuing a media statement concerning the discovery of an unknown pneumonic virus on 31 December 2019, soon became a national crisis which saw the Chinese government impose its first lockdown. By 30 January 2020 the WHO had declared Covid-19 a global emergency and by March 2020 a pandemic. Considerable attention has since been paid to domestic public health policies around the world, not least for the Chinese government, whose decisions leading up to and after the identification of the virus have received extensive scrutiny by other states and international organizations.

We can further observe a state's **foreign policy** as a crucial 'hinge' between understanding a state's domestic public politics, policy and processes, and its activities within international politics (Hill 2003: 23). According to Morin and Paquin (2018), foreign policy can be understood as 'a set of actions or rules governing the actions of an independent political authority deployed in the international environment' (Morin and Paquin 2018). As

Foreign policy
The objectives and actions that determine a state's interactions with other actors in the international system.

they highlight, foreign policy is the action of an *independent political authority* because foreign policy is typically reserved to sovereign states. A state's government is therefore 'the legal custodian of [that] state's sovereignty' and represents the state's international personality (Morin and Paquin 2018).

STATECRAFT AND DIPLOMACY

As the previous section highlighted, states and their governments are unique in possessing legitimate sovereign authority to conduct foreign policy. How the state manages and strategizes its relations with other states, however, is the focal point of **statecraft**, relating to the art and skill of managing government affairs within international politics. Statecraft is focused primarily on planning and strategy. For a government to action its foreign policy it must first strategize how it will achieve its goals and objectives within the international system. A government's statecraft is also linked to how effectively it can manage the resources the state has at its disposal as a foreign policy actor.

Statecraft
The art of planning and strategizing a state's foreign policy in pursuit or defence of its national interests.

Governments have a variety of positive and negative instruments they can utilize in their foreign policy to advance or defend their state's interests with other states – see Table 6.1. Positive foreign policy tools might include, for example, the offer of a reciprocal trade agreement, the granting of favourable market access, or recognition of a state's diplomats. Negative foreign policy tools might include the use of economic sanctions, the withdrawal of foreign direct investment (FDI) or aid, the removal of diplomats, or, at its most extreme, the use of force. Statecraft, then, is the strategic determination of the most effective use of these foreign policy instruments to advance a state's national interests.

Diplomacy meanwhile addresses how states action their statecraft. The distinction between statecraft and diplomacy is subtle. According to former US diplomat Chas Freeman (1997), '[s]tatecraft is concerned with the application of power of the state to other states and peoples. Diplomacy applies this power by persuasive measures short of war' (Freeman 1997: ix). While statecraft is therefore concerned with planning how the state will interact with other states, diplomats are at the front line in executing that plan.

Diplomacy
The profession and activity of representing a state's national interests abroad.

Diplomats are officials appointed to serve their national government's interests abroad. Diplomats not only represent their government's interests to foreign governments but are also responsible for initiating and facilitating agreements between them. Because of the unique role diplomats play in representing their state's interests and promoting friendly relations with other states, diplomacy is also commonly associated with **international negotiation**. International negotiation in fact makes up a significant proportion of interstate relations, although it has tended to be under-studied in international politics. Negotiation, however, is a critical function of diplomacy, particularly as a process of conflict mediation (pg. 176) and dispute resolution. Negotiation can facilitate cooperation where there are conflicting interests between states and can cover anything from reciprocal trade agreements to peace and security pacts. Also consider that, without international negotiation, no international organization, international law or international agreement would exist. International negotiation should therefore not be underestimated as an important function of interstate diplomacy and of international politics more broadly.

International negotiation
The process of negotiating agreement between states. May involve two (bilateral) or more (multilateral) parties.

Diplomats are appointed to serve as their state's official representative to a designated foreign country or international organization. Once appointed by their national government, they must then also be accredited by the foreign government in the state in which they will serve. This is because diplomatic relations between states can only take place by mutual consent. States are also at liberty to refuse accreditation to another state's diplomat(s) and can also retract accreditation by declaring individual diplomats **persona non grata**. Diplomatic accreditation and removal or refusal to grant accreditation are also frequently utilized instruments of a state's foreign policy (Table 6.1).

Persona non grata
Meaning 'unwelcome person'. A formal status applied by a host country to foreign diplomats or other persons to signal that they are no longer welcome in the country. Those who are persona non grata will either be recalled by their own government, or forcibly deported by the host country.

Table 6.1 Foreign policy instruments

	Positive tools	Negative tools
Economic	Improved market access	Restricting market access
	Increasing FDI	Decreasing or removing FDI
	Providing development aid	Withholding development aid
	Extending loans	Calling in or delaying loans
	Lifting or reducing sanctions	Applying sanctions
	Lifting a boycott (ban on imports)	Instituting a boycott
	Lifting an embargo (ban on exports)	Instituting an embargo
Diplomatic	Diplomatic accreditation	Removal or refusal to grant diplomatic accreditation (*persona non grata*)
	Establishing/upgrading diplomatic relations	Downgrading/removing diplomatic relations
Military	Providing military aid	Removal of military aid
	Military base location	Military base relocation
		Threat of the use of force
		Use of force

Source: adapted from Smith (2014)

Political dialogue
A diplomatic relationship between states that fosters regular political meetings between their governments in an effort to strengthen ties between them.

Cooperation agreement
A formal political agreement between states signifying their intent to cooperate across specified policy fields, often including economic cooperation.

Strategic partnership
A formal political partnership between states signifying their intent to work together on strategic points of common interest, often including security dimensions.

Diplomacy can also be used as a foreign policy tool by either enhancing and deepening diplomatic relations, or by downgrading diplomatic relations between states. **Political dialogue** is a typical first stage of diplomatic cooperation that sees states establish and strengthen their political, economic and cultural ties through regular bilateral meetings. In time, political dialogue may deepen to become a **cooperation agreement** in which states formalize their cooperation within or across specific policy fields. In some cases, and increasingly commonplace in today's international politics, states will seek to consolidate their relationship as a **strategic partnership**. Strategic partnerships signify a special relationship between states, identifying them as strategic allies and partners that share common political and economic bonds, and usually with a common security dimension as well. China, for example, has around seventy strategic partners around the world, India around twenty. The United States has sixty formal strategic partners and another forty or so informal partnerships or 'strategic dialogues'. As a foreign policy instrument, therefore, these forms of diplomatic relationships can be used to foster closer cooperation between states. They can, however, also be used to signal diplomatic concern about a partner state, for example, by failing to renew a cooperation agreement, or downgrading a relationship status.

EXERCISING STATE POWER

In Table 6.1 we saw the various foreign policy instruments that a state may exercise within the international system. How a state utilizes those instruments, however, can also be a means by which it exercises power in international politics. As Freeman highlighted, '[s]tatecraft is concerned with the *application of power* of the state to other states and peoples. Diplomacy *applies this power* by persuasive measures short of war' (Freeman 1997:

ix *emphasis added*). Yet, while all independent states can be considered equal in terms of possessing internal and external sovereignty, they are vastly unequal when it comes to their size, resources, economic capability, military strength and competence. For example, as Waltz suggests, for states to join the ranks of the great powers requires that they possess the greatest resources, capabilities and strengths (pg. 76).

Within international politics, power can nevertheless be understood in different ways. A state can exercise power by exerting influence over others. A state may, though, also be considered a power because of the material capabilities it possesses. As you will see by any cursory glance at the world political map, there are considerable disparities between states with regards to their size and geography. Historically, land and people have been essential ingredients for traditionally agrarian-based societies to sustain themselves and generate greater wealth. The larger a state's territories and population, the more material capabilities – and thus power resources – it has at its disposal.

It is no coincidence, for example, that the United States, a state of just over 9.5 million square kilometres and 331 million people, geographically separated from other powerful states, surrounded by peaceful neighbours, with a diverse climate and terrain well suited to agriculture and forestry and rich in natural resources, with a good infrastructure and access to two oceans, is also the richest nation in the world. Nor is it a coincidence that today, the US, as the world's richest nation, is also the world's strongest military power. Compare the US then to any one of the fifty states classified by the World Bank as 'small states', such as the small island state of Nauru located in the Southwest Pacific Ocean. Nauru is but 20 square kilometres in land area with a population of around 10,000 people. With a tropical climate, but poor soil quality and no lakes or rivers, Nauru must import nearly all of its food, water and manufactured goods from abroad, yet with its closest neighbour some 300 kilometres away. In this comparison we can see that while the government of the United States may have the resources and capability to draw upon its statecraft and diplomacy to action any one of the foreign policy instruments outlined in Table 6.1, the government of Nauru may be rather more constrained. The disparities between states in terms of their overall geography, size, population, resources and wealth, therefore, make for marked inequalities in their relative material capabilities within international politics – a point that realists particularly emphasize in their assumptions concerning who the great powers are and the balance of power within the international system (pg. 77).

Adopting a more critical lens, we may observe how the legacies of imperialism and colonialism have also greatly exacerbated the inequality between states with regards to their relative material capabilities and power within international politics. As we saw in Chapter Four – and develop further in Chapter Thirteen when we focus on Equality and Development as issues within international politics – former colonies are frequently characterized by their *under*development, relative to industrialized states in the Global North. Dependency theorists particularly emphasize the continued dependency that former colonies have upon their former colonizers. For critical scholars, therefore, the legacy of colonialism is most apparent when addressing the power imbalance within international politics, and those structures which reinforce the hegemonic power (pg. 22) of advanced industrialized states, at the expense of smaller and weaker developing states.

We can also observe that states can exercise their power through different means and strategies. A government may exercise **hard power** when it seeks to influence others by threatening or rewarding them using the foreign policy instruments at its disposal. Understanding the use of hard power is not dissimilar to the metaphor of the donkey: to get the donkey to move, you either beat it with the stick or reward it with a carrot. Similarly, hard power is exercised as a 'carrot' when a state utilizes any one of the positive foreign policy tools outlined in Table 6.1 to influence another state or states to act a certain way, and as a 'stick' when utilizing any one of the negative tools that coerce them into action.

Hard power
The exercise of power through command and coercion, typically exercised through direct military and economic means.

Smart power
The exercise of power through both hard and soft means.

What is distinctive about hard power is that it is premised exclusively on using a state's material power resources to command others – whether by punishment or incentive. Neorealists, who advance the idea that power is sourced principally from a state's own material capabilities, such as the size of its armed forces, economy, population, technological advancement and geography, place particular emphasis on hard power tactics within international politics. A state may then only wield power over others where it possesses sufficient material capabilities to influence others.

Soft power
The exercise of power through co-option, attraction and persuasion, typically exercised through indirect cultural, diplomatic and political means.

States can also choose to exercise **soft power** through co-option and persuasion. Whereas hard power is sourced through a state's material capabilities, exercised through coercion or command, soft power is sourced in the state's culture, political values and its global standing. As Nye (1990: 182) reflects, 'if a state can make its power legitimate in the eyes of others, it will encounter less resistance to its wishes'. Where a state has a culture that is attractive to others, political norms and values that others are willing to follow, and institutions that are perceived favourably by others, that state will more easily be able to influence others. Soft power can also be exercised in a state's use of the positive foreign policy instruments outlined in Table 6.1, particularly instruments such as granting foreign aid, cancelling foreign debts, or granting another state non-reciprocal market access. In this way, soft power becomes a persuasive, but not commanding or coercive, mechanism of influence for states to use in their relations with others. Soft power, then, can be understood as a more indirect form of power relative to hard power, being based more on power by attraction, example and ideals.

ORGANIZE

Since the Cold War there has been ongoing debate about the changing nature of power within the international system. Within that debate, soft power has been portrayed as the more effective means of exercising power 'with' others, rather than over them. In the early 2000s the debate about the changing nature of power was further informed by a shift towards the term **smart power**, now popularized by governments and academia alike. Smart power is associated with the combination and 'smart' use of both hard and soft power which complement and reinforce one another. See also:

- Nye, J. (2008), *The Powers to Lead*, Oxford: Oxford University Press.
- Gallarotti, G. M. (2015). 'Smart power: Definitions, importance, and effectiveness', *Journal of Strategic Studies*, 3: 245–281.

Reflect again on the discussion about great powers and polarity within the international system in the last chapter (pg. 75–6). While great power is in part about a state's special responsibilities and duties, it primarily concerns its relative material power capability, and how it exercises and projects that power beyond its borders. How would you associate the use of hard power, soft power or smart power with today's great powers? Are there examples of powerful states in today's international system that you think prioritizes one or other of these forms of power?

FAILED AND FRAGILE STATES

In the chapter so far, we have considered the state as an actor, addressing its foreign policy, statecraft and diplomacy, and the exercise of state power – all of which assume that the state, as an independent political entity, has the capacity to actively and deliberately enter into relations with others in the international system. However, since the 1990s, growing attention has been paid not only to de facto states (pg. 95), but also to what are identified as 'failed' and 'fragile' states within international politics. The categorization of 'failed state' first started to be used within academic and policy circles during the 1990s when the proliferation of civil conflicts in the post-Cold War period placed a new emphasis on the challenges stemming from states whose governing institutions were fragmenting, and who were struggling with economic recession, development and domestic security conditions.

Yet understanding what constitutes a failed state is ambiguous. For some scholars, state failure is associated with state instability (Goldstone 2008), for others it is the loss of political order and the monopoly over the use of force within a defined territory (Bates 2008). Others still see state failure as primarily a development problem, determined by a state's extreme weaknesses in its economic policies, institutions and governance (Chauvet and Collier 2008). The criteria by which a state is judged to have 'failed' are therefore diverse, but which, in broad terms, relate to 'the complete collapse of state authority' (Iqbal and Starr 2015: 12), and therefore the collapse of *internal sovereignty*.

Since the early 2000s, the term 'fragile state' has also entered the common lexicon of international politics, particularly among international donors, agencies and government departments focused on development, humanitarian assistance and peacebuilding. The World Bank, for example, identifies its Low-Income Countries Under Stress (LICUS) as 'fragile', in so far as they are 'characterized by a debilitating combination of weak governance, policies and institutions' (World Bank, cited in Iqbal and Starr 2015). According to the Organization for Economic Cooperation and Development (OECD) and the UK's former Department of International Development,[1] a fragile state is when 'the government cannot or will not deliver core functions to the majority of its people, including the poor' (UK DfID 2009: 2). The Fragile States Index offers further development on the concept, highlighting that the most common attributes of state fragility may include:

- The loss of physical control of its territory or a monopoly on the legitimate use of force.
- The erosion of legitimate authority to make collective decisions.
- An inability to provide reasonable public services.
- The inability to interact with other states as a full member of the international community (Fragile States Index 2018).

Explore More

The Fragile States Index (FSI) assesses the risks and vulnerabilities faced by 179 countries based on twelve cohesion, economic, political and social indicators of state fragility. In 2022, for example, the FSI identified that Yemen and Somalia were the top two most fragile states in the world. The FSI is also useful in showing changes to a state's fragility over time. Note that in the FSI 2021 analysis, the country found to have had the largest year-on-year worsening in their total fragility score was the United States, while the country with the biggest improvement was also one of the world's youngest states – Timor-Leste. You can explore the FSI's most recent data using their interactive world map at https://fragilestatesindex.org.

Scan the QR code for access to explore weblinks and more resources.

Critical scholars would suggest, however, that the seemingly prescriptive use of the terms 'failed' and 'fragile' state follow a dominant liberal security model (pg. 195), and cannot therefore be dissociated from Western political narratives on security and development. Critical scholars in fact highlight that the political labelling of failed and fragile states

[1]Now part of the Foreign, Commonwealth and Development Office (FCDO).

provides Western states with the grounds 'to justify forms of political interference in the internal affairs of war-torn or poor countries' (Nay 2013: 330). Failed states are also seen as a preoccupation of the Western world concerning the Global South, where conflicts, humanitarian crises and instability are reframed as state failure – building on a presumed link between state failure and terrorism – to justify accessing or increasing military and financial Western resources to that state (Bøås and Jennings 2007). Bøås and Jennings (2007) particularly highlight that branding states as 'failed' is inherently political, and only occurs when the security interests of Western states are directly threatened.

Afghanistan provides one striking case of a state that has been identified as fragile or failed on numerous occasions dating back half a century. Afghanistan was first described as a failed state in 1978 (Iqbal and Starr 2015) when a communist coup, followed by Soviet invasion, led to the eventual collapse of centralized government and war between guerrilla fighters, or *mujahideen*, and Soviet forces that left about 1 million Afghan citizens dead. By 1992, the then Soviet-backed government in Afghanistan, led by Mohammad Najibullah, crumbled once again, leaving the state in turmoil and President Najibullah in hiding. By 1995 the **Taliban** had taken over territory in southern Afghanistan, promising to restore order and security to the region by establishing an Islamic Emirate of Afghanistan. Within a few years the Taliban controlled most of the country, although only three other states officially recognized the Taliban as the government of Afghanistan.

Taliban
A militant Islamic fundamentalist political movement whose goal is to establish Afghanistan as an Islamic State. The Taliban controlled Afghanistan between 1995 and 2001 and retook control in 2021.

Some years later, in November 2001, the Taliban was then removed from power by the US-led invasion *Operation Enduring Freedom*. While the Taliban had controlled Afghanistan for several years, the invasion followed just one month after the 9/11 terrorist attacks by **Al Qaeda** against the United States (pg. 169), with strikes directly targeting the Taliban as well as identified Al Qaeda locations within the country. By the summer of 2002 a transitional government had been established in Afghanistan under the leadership of President Hamid Karzai, who remained in power – with support from NATO-led peacekeeping forces – until 2014 when he was replaced following democratic elections.

Al Qaeda
A militant Islamic fundamentalist group, founded by Osama bin Laden in the late 1980s, responsible for numerous terror attacks against the United States, the deadliest of which included the 9/11 attacks that resulted in nearly 3,000 deaths.

US and NATO forces remained in Afghanistan for two decades, providing peacekeeping, reconstruction and humanitarian support to the people of Afghanistan. While US military involvement in the country had started to decrease by the late 2010s, in 2021, shortly before the 20th anniversary of the 9/11 terrorist attacks, the US government announced its intention to withdraw all US troops from Afghanistan. Within weeks of the announcement, and the commencement of US troop withdrawal, the Taliban managed to retake control of the country. Afghanistan's elected President Ghani fled, and Afghanistan was once again thrown into a state of turmoil.

At the time of writing, no state has recognized the Taliban as the official government of Afghanistan. When the Taliban retook control in 2021, Afghanistan's state and private assets abroad were frozen. Financial aid for Afghanistan, including loans and development assistance, were also reduced by individual states and international organizations. The Afghan economy subsequently floundered, as salaries went unpaid, basic services went unprovided, and prices rose. A UN report published in October 2021 stated that 'the combined shocks of drought, conflict, Covid-19 and an economic crisis in Afghanistan, have left more than half the population – [that's 22.8 million people] – facing a record level of acute hunger' (UN 2021a). The report went on to state that 'Afghanistan is now among the world's worst humanitarian crises' (UN 2021a). Afghanistan's 'fragility', therefore, continues to present a pressing problem, not least for the people of Afghanistan.

CONCLUSION

The aim of this chapter has been to introduce you to the state as an actor within international politics. A key aim has been to help you develop your understanding of what the state can do – how it can act, how it can exercise power, and the foreign policy instruments at its disposal – as well as to reflect on the disparities that exist among states where it concerns their relative power. The chapter has also highlighted how statehood – and the principle of sovereignty itself – remains a contested concept in international politics. You can develop your understanding of the contested nature of sovereignty and the state within international politics by trying your hand now at the following toolkit exercise asking, *'Is Taiwan a sovereign state?'*

LINK

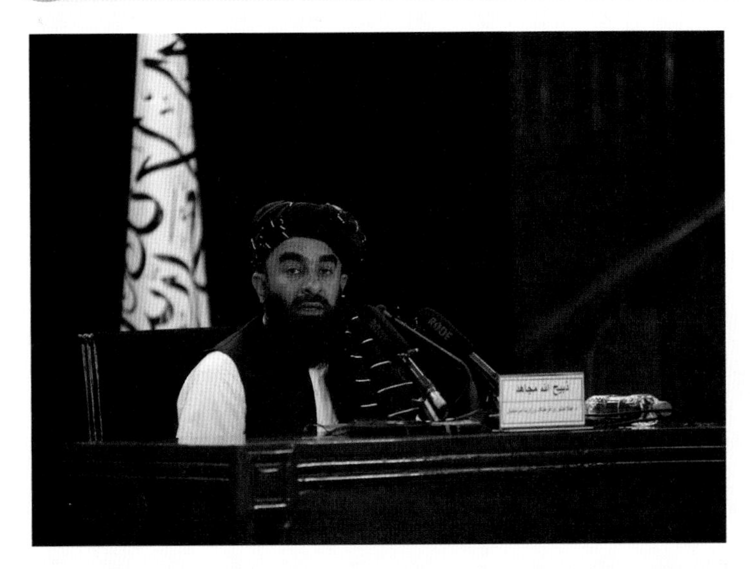

Image 6.2 A Taliban spokesman speaks during a press conference in Kabul, Afghanistan on 21 September 2021 in which new ministers of the Taliban's interim government were announced. The press conference was held five weeks after the Taliban took power in Afghanistan, and just three weeks after US Armed Forces had completed their withdrawal from the country.

Source: Anadolu Agency/Getty Images.

Consider

Is Afghanistan a failed or fragile state today?

Explore

Afghanistan has had a difficult history that has been frequently shaped by interventions from foreign powers. You can explore the timeline of the US intervention in Afghanistan at www.cfr.org. You may also want to explore the link between failed states and terrorism. Writing in 2008 James Piazza published a study showing empirical evidence that states with 'chronic state failures' are statistically more likely to host terrorist groups or be targets for terrorist attacks, see James A. Piazza (2008), 'Incubators of terror: Do failed and failing states promote transnational terrorism?', *International Studies Quarterly*, 52(3): 469–488.

Connect

Consider the Fragile States Index criteria for identifying a 'fragile' state on pg. 101. Do you think Afghanistan qualifies as a fragile state based on these criteria? Why might Afghanistan be labelled a 'failed' state from a critical perspective? Do you agree with that labelling?

Predict

If the Taliban is recognized as the official government of Afghanistan by other states, how might that impact its labelling as a 'failed' or 'fragile' state? Does the legitimacy of a state's government impact its perceived failure by other states in the international system, or is it stability that matters most?

Scan the QR code for access to explore weblinks and more resources.

TOOLKIT

Is Taiwan a sovereign state?

THINK

- During the 1949 Chinese Civil War, the incumbent government of the Republic of China (ROC) was forced to retreat from mainland China, declaring Taipei on the island of Taiwan their temporary capital. Since then, the ROC has governed Taiwan as a democratic state. The Chinese Communist Party then established the People's Republic of China (PRC) with Beijing as China's capital. While the ROC government in Taipei identifies itself as a sovereign and independent state, the PRC government in Beijing staunchly defends a 'One China' policy that considers Taiwan inviolable Chinese territory with the PRC its legitimate government.
- Who do you think is the legitimate government of China? Should Taiwan be considered a distinct sovereign entity separate from China or do you see it as part of China? Why?

OBSERVE

Image 6.3 Taiwan's flag flies as Taiwan's National Honour Guard stand on parade during National Day celebrations in Taipei, held each year on 10 October.

Source: Bloomberg/Getty Images.

- Taiwan has its own flag, a constitution, elected government and its own armed forces. On 10 October, there is an annual holiday in Taiwan marking the anniversary of the Wuchang Uprising which led to the collapse of the Qing dynasty in China and the subsequent establishment of the ROC government in 1912. The day before the 2021 National Day celebrations commenced in Taipei, PRC President Xi gave a statement in which he vowed to achieve 'peaceful reunification' with Taiwan. The PRC views Taiwan as its twenty-third province and has stated that any formal declaration of Taiwanese independence would constitute an act of war.
- China frequently undertakes military exercises around the Taiwan Strait – a 180km-stretch of water separating Taiwan from China – to exert PRC sovereignty and warn Taiwan not to formally declare its independence. The Taiwanese military is, however, heavily supported by arms provided, in large part, by the United States courtesy of the 1979 US–Taiwan Relations Act which sets out the US policy to 'provide Taiwan with arms of a defensive character'. The Act acknowledges the 'governing authorities of Taiwan' (rather than explicitly mentioning the ROC). The Act is nevertheless significant in enshrining the unofficial relationship between the US and Taiwan, and as a deterrent to China using force against Taiwan.

ORGANIZE

- Taiwan was ranked 21st out of 142 countries in the Global Firepower Index in 2022, indicating its thriving military capabilities. Taiwan is also the world's fifteenth largest merchandize exporter and a recognized leader in information and communication technology. Since 2013 Taiwan has established economic cooperation agreements with countries such as New Zealand and Singapore, establishing its credentials as an important regional economic player. Taiwan also has 214 missions located in foreign countries around the world, though only twenty-one are considered formal embassies in those states that do recognize Taiwan's statehood. How do you think these capabilities relate to the foreign policy instruments outlined in Table 6.1 (pg. 98)? What foreign policy instruments can Taiwan exercise as a form of *hard power* or *soft power* (pg. 99–100)?
- Reflect again on the characteristics of a state, the related principles of *internal* and *external sovereignty* (pg. 17–18) as well as the concept of de facto state (pg. 95) as discussed in this chapter. Does Taiwan meet the criteria of statehood as set out in the Montevideo Convention on the Rights and Duties of the State (pg. 15)?
- Taiwan has repeatedly claimed that it need not make any declaration of independence from China as it is already an independent state. To what extent does Taiwan meet the criteria for either *declarative or constitutive statehood* (pg. 94)?

LINK

- *Consider*: A state cannot obtain recognition by the UN until the state first applies, the UN Security Council then recommends the state for membership, and the UN General Assembly votes in its favour. To get a membership application past the UN Security Council, however, requires support from nine of the fifteen members and must ensure that none of the five permanent members of the Council (which includes China) vote against the application. The PRC has blocked every effort to accept Taiwan as either a member or observer of the UN or its related institutions and agencies.
- *Explore*: Explore more about the scope of Taiwan's government, particularly its Ministry of Foreign Affairs and Consular activities at www.taiwan.gov.tw.
- *Connect*: The PRC refuses to have diplomatic relations with any state that recognizes the ROC, therefore Taiwan's formal recognition as a sovereign state by others has been limited to a small few (i.e. Costa Rica, Nauru, Jamaica and Tuvalu). However, fifty-nine countries, the EU, and China's two quasi-dependent territories, Hong Kong and Macau, have established unofficial diplomatic relations with Taiwan. To what extent do you think formal diplomatic recognition therefore matters to Taiwan's statehood?
- *Predict*: What do you think might happen if the United States were to formally recognize Taiwan as a sovereign state?

Scan the QR code for access to explore weblinks and more resources.

SHARE

- Answer the question 'Is Taiwan a sovereign state?'

  If you were to approach this as an essay question, what do you think your argument will be? What concepts or theory discussed in this chapter could you draw upon to support and justify your argument? Consider how you will structure your argument and present your case. You may want to look at *How to – approach an international politics essay* (pg. 182) to help you with this.

HOW TO

IDENTIFY QUALITY SOURCES

You need to be able to draw upon quality sources to inform your academic research and writing. As a student you are expected to read a broad range of relevant literature and research, and understand, evaluate and critique it. As international politics research is often fast-moving, addressing contemporary events or issues, you are also likely to draw upon quite a diverse array of source material including not only academic journals and books, but grey literature (pg. 202), as well as media coverage and blogs, much of which is found on the internet. With any internet-based research, however, you need to learn how to filter out the reliable from the less reliable so that your research and writing is not then misinformed, or wrong.

Sources come in a variety of formats, each with varying degrees of quality as academic materials. As a rule, most of the material you can find through your university library will be considered 'reliable'. Most journal articles and academic books go through a rigorous double-blind peer review process and tend to form the mainstay of the academic scholarship around most topics in international politics. Engaging with journal articles and academic books listed in your course reading list is required of course, but you always want to demonstrate that you are exploring further and proactively seeking out sources that enrich and inform your research and writing. Table 6.2 offers a breakdown of possible sources you may locate in your international politics research, and some tips on their respective quality and utility.

Triangulation
Ensuring the credibility and validity of your research findings by checking against other source materials or research methods.

Explore More

Check out this useful three-minute YouTube video which lists five top tips for evaluating the information you find on the internet in your academic research: https://youtu.be/S5NSMX7IlcU

Scan the QR code for access to explore weblinks and more resources.

Table 6.2 Identifying quality sources in your research

Source	Quality	Utility for international politics research
Journal articles and academic books	High	Essential and forms the mainstay of academic research. *See also How to* – approach *a literature review* (pg. 201). Be aware that academic research can take a long time to work through the review and publication process so journal articles and books may not be as useful as other sources for providing up-to-the-minute insight into contemporary international politics.
Grey literature (i.e. reports, research and positions not formally published in books/ journals)	Medium-High	A great resource in international politics research, especially where it concerns engagement with government positions or accessing research provided by international organizations or think tanks. Be mindful though that grey literature tends not to go through as rigorous a review process as published academic works so some fact checking or triangulation with other sources can be beneficial. Grey literature has its benefits, however, in being timelier than most published academic works.
Media reporting	Medium	Excellent for keeping your finger on the pulse of contemporary international politics, as well as for discourse or content analyses where media framing is part of your research design. Be mindful though of the quality of reporting – newspaper broadsheets tend to be more reliable than tabloids for example – as well as the nationality of the reporting company as this can skew the perspective being offered.
Current affairs magazines	Medium	There are many weekly or monthly magazines dedicated to international politics coverage which provide a rich resource for up-to-date events and analysis. As with media reporting, though, be mindful of any biases that may filter through to the analysis.
General knowledge websites	Low	There are numerous websites in existence that are dedicated to general knowledge. Some are developed by experts, but most are informed by information gleaned from other websites and have not gone through a rigorous proofing or review process. While these websites can be useful in providing you with some knowledge, always fact check before relying on these sources as materials in your academic writing. Above all, triangulate to ensure that the source materials you are drawing upon are informed and accurate.
Essay writing websites	Very low – to be avoided	There are now multitudes of websites dedicated to helping students with essay writing and which post past essays written by students. Using such websites in your research and writing is very high risk and should be avoided. Materials on these websites are unchecked and unreliable. To cite them would be noted by your marker as indicative of your lack of understanding, and using them without reference would be seen as academic misconduct (pg. 48).

7 International organizations

Pexels / Niklas Jeromin

Abstract

Since 1945, international organizations (IOs) have become a prominent presence within international politics. In this chapter you will be introduced to IOs, addressing what they are, their purpose and their function in facilitating interstate dialogue, generating collective action and arbitrating interstate disputes. The chapter begins with a brief introduction of IOs, looking at the history of how they have developed and spread since the 19th century, and some of their common features, before considering how different theories address why IOs form and spread. The chapter then turns a spotlight on the United Nations (UN) and its 'family' of other IOs, agencies and programmes that have emanated from it. Finally, the chapter introduces you to some of the academic debates that have surrounded IOs in recent years, particularly concerning their authority to act, effectiveness and legitimacy. The chapter culminates in a toolkit exercise for you to apply your knowledge, asking, *'How feasible is UN Security Council reform?'*

INTRODUCING INTERNATIONAL ORGANIZATIONS

In the last chapter we looked at the state as an actor and power in international politics. As we saw, over the evolution of the modern state system, the sovereign state has become the main organizing unit for nations around the world. Yet, we must also acknowledge that, in contemporary international politics, states neither act nor interact in a vacuum. Most states are not isolated from one another but are closely interconnected through economic, social and political links. From the 19th century, states began to interact through international conferences and engaged in diplomacy to overcome common challenges. After the Napoleonic Wars, the 1814–15 Congress of Vienna initiated the Concert of Europe aimed at facilitating mutual consultation and dialogue among Europe's great powers (pg. 22). The Concert of Europe in fact marks one of the earliest examples of multilateral diplomacy, highlighting the benefits of mutual consultation and coordination between states within Europe. The Concert of Europe is also often accredited with sustaining relative peace in Europe for much of the 19th century. Yet, the rise of nationalism and great power competition across Europe leading up to World Wars One and Two also highlighted the challenge of sustaining multilateralism where competing hegemonic interests prevail.

THINK

Multilateralism is the process by which three or more states work together to pursue common interests and collective action (pg. 111). In today's lexicon, multilateralism is often used to denote the process of interaction among the majority of states within the international system, with particular emphasis placed on international organizations as an important focal point for multilateral decision-making.

What issues do you think are best served through multilateralism in today's international system? What do you think are some of the main challenges facing multilateral decision-making?

An international organization (IO) is defined as an entity established by formal political agreement to perform specific tasks for its member states. The 19th century witnessed a growth in new international transboundary issues associated with the spread of international trade and migration, democratization, and due to advancements in telecommunications, industry and technology. It was during this period that the first formal institutionalized mechanisms for interstate interaction were established with the birth of IOs. The very first IO – the International Telegraphic Union – was established in 1865. The ITU was designed to manage the first international telegraph networks and to address the transboundary challenge of cross-border communication after the first transatlantic telegraph cable was laid in 1858. Prior to this, each state had its own telegraph rules, standards and operating systems. Where lines crossed national borders, telegraphs had to be stopped and translated into the system used by that specific state. To overcome that problem, representatives of twenty states came together in Paris. The result was the International Telegraph Convention, the first international agreement to standardize telegraph equipment, set uniform operating instructions, and agree common international tariff and accounting rules among the participating states. Delegates at the Paris conference also agreed to the creation of the International Telegraphic Union to supervise and oversee the Convention. Today the renamed International Telecommunication Union (ITU) is an agency within the United Nations (UN) overseeing all global communications networks. All 193 UN member states are members of the ITU. They are served by a General-Secretariat, located in the ITU's headquarters in Geneva, who manage the ITU's administrative and financial activities. The ITU is subsequently the longest serving IO in existence.

Following the launch of the ITU in 1865, states continued to develop more formal mechanisms for interstate interaction, across a wider array of issue areas. What began with international organizations (IOs) formed to address non-political, technical transboundary arrangements between states, then spread to IOs formed for the purposes of dispute resolution and arbitration. In 1899 the first of the International Peace Conferences, also known as the Hague Conventions, not only established the formal rules of war (pg. 171), but also established a Permanent Court of Arbitration (PCA). The PCA continues to this day as an IO providing dispute resolution services to its 122 states, or 'contracting parties'.

By 1919/20 the League of Nations had also been founded – the first IO of its kind established with the express purpose of maintaining world peace (pg. 22). The League of Nations established three permanent organs – the *Council* (made up of a select number of permanent and non-permanent member states, who took most of the major decisions), the *Assembly* (which met annually with each member of the League given one vote), and a *Secretariat* (serving as a permanent civil service for the League). In addition, the League included a Permanent Court of International Justice, which oversaw cases and delivered advisory opinions for the League's member states. The League also established the International Labour Organization (ILO) which included government ministers and workers from each of the member states.

As we saw in Chapter Two, the League of Nations was dissolved in 1946 being replaced by the UN. The same organs developed by the League were then also replicated in the organization of the UN such as the UN Security Council, the UN General Assembly, and the UN General-Secretary and Secretariat. The Permanent Court of International Justice was also reborn as the International Court of Justice (ICJ), while the ILO continues in operation to this day. We shall revisit the UN's permanent organs a little later in this chapter.

Gender parity
The proportional and equal inclusion of women in decision-making positions within an organization.

OBSERVE

Image 7.1 The first session of the League of Nations in Geneva, 15 November 1920. The League grew from forty-two original members to sixty-three before it was dissolved in 1946. According to Article 5 of the Covenant of the League of Nations, in both the League's Assembly (here pictured) and Council, decisions required the agreement of all members represented at the meeting, with the exception of procedural matters which could be decided by a majority vote.

Source: Getty Images / Hulton Archive

In this image delegates to the first League of Nations Assembly meet. Note the predominantly male, white faces among the delegates. Very few women were in fact involved in state diplomacy when the League of Nations was formed, although the League did permit women to serve in an equal capacity with men. In 1922 only six of the 177 delegates to the League were women (a number that remained stagnant even when the United Nations (UN) was formed in 1945, when only eight of the 800 delegates at the conference were women). Today, representation of women within the UN system has seen considerable progress, although it is noted that **gender parity** has not yet been reached within the

UN's Secretariat. At the time of writing, women continue to remain under-represented in the highest paid UN leadership and senior management positions, while being over-represented in more junior levels within the organization (UN 2017a).

The League of Nations was also formed at a time of increasing anti-colonial unrest around the world, the decline of Europe's empires and the push towards national self-determination. While colonized nations had been able to participate at earlier international organizations, including the ITU, the Covenant of the League of Nations explicitly outlined that *any self-governing State, Dominion or Colony* could become a member. Several British colonies were original contracting parties to the League, and were treated as autonomous members, including Canada, Australia, South Africa, New Zealand and India. Two other British colonies – Ireland and Egypt – also later joined. Other colonies, however, were treated as mandated territories. Article 22 of the League's Covenant granted authorization to member nations to govern former German and Turkish colonies following their defeat in World War One. Several African and Asian colonies were also judged unready to govern themselves, with their administration then distributed among the Allied powers (pg. 284).

Since 1945, there has been significant proliferation of both international organizations (IOs) and non-governmental organizations (NGOs) (Chapter Nine) within international politics. IOs are distinctive from NGOs, however, being established specifically by and for national governments, whereas NGOs are autonomous of governments. As states serve as their members, IOs are also often referred to as *intergovernmental* organizations. IOs are also distinctive from other multilateral groupings of states, such as the **Group of 7 (G7)**, for example, which serve as informal institutions for mutual consultation through **summitry** rather than being formal organizations.

IOs are also distinctive in that states may voluntarily join them but, in so doing, then commit to abide by the rules and standards of that IO. As we saw in Chapter Six, while all sovereign states may apply to join the UN, they must still agree to abide by the principles set out in the UN Charter and have their membership approved by the UN Security Council and General Assembly. Other more thematic IOs, such as the World Trade Organization (pg. 211–12), also require that states adhere to specific terms of accession before they are admitted. Membership of an IO will also typically involve costs, such as contributing to the organization's budget which is used to cover the costs of the IO's headquarters, permanent staff and various functions. IOs usually include some form of bureaucratic structure, such as a Secretariat, to oversee the IO's operation. Dependent upon their scope and remit, IOs can design, implement and oversee various activities as agreed by its members. In so doing, IOs provide an important mechanism for implementing **collective action** across a wide range of issue areas within international politics. The common features of IOs are summarized in Table 7.1.

As we proceed with this chapter, we shall also see that today's IOs do reflect many of the same characteristics of the early cooperative efforts of the 19th and early 20th centuries. Specifically:

1. Like the Concert of Europe, IOs today continue to facilitate mutual consultation among states. Like the Concert of Europe, though, IOs can also be restrained by the interests of the great powers.
2. Like the original International Telegraphic Union, IOs continue to offer non-political, functional and specialized services on behalf of their member states.
3. And, like the Permanent Court of Arbitration (PCA) and Permanent International Court of Justice, IOs today continue to provide legal oversight over international treaties and agreements, as well as providing an important mechanism for arbitration and international dispute resolution.

Group of 7
An intergovernmental forum whose members include the world's seven largest and most advanced liberal democratic economies including Canada, France, Germany, Italy, Japan, the UK and the USA. The EU also participates in the G7 as an enumerated member.

Summitry
The use of summits or conferences for international discussion, negotiation and agreement.

Collective action
Actions agreed collectively by states to overcome a common problem.

Table 7.1 Common features of international organizations

	Common Feature
Scope/Function	Determined by international treaty, constitution or charter
	May be universal in scope, thematic or technical
Operation	Decision-making by states, participating in a dedicated Council, Assembly and/or other executive or ministerial body
	Supported by a secretariat who provide the IOs' bureaucratic, technical or other specialized functions
	Budget funded primarily by member states
	Has a headquarters, permanent staff and logo
Membership	Universal (inclusive) or restricted (exclusive) as determined by the original treaty. Membership criteria nevertheless apply.
	States are principal members, though other IOs and non-state actors may participate as observers
	Membership is voluntary

THEORIZING INTERNATIONAL ORGANIZATIONS

The creation, proliferation and longevity of international organizations (IOs) within international politics has long focused the attention of scholars of international politics. Much as security studies (Chapter Eleven) or international political economy (Chapter Twelve) are considered sub-disciplines within international politics, international organization is also an area of dedicated academic interest and debate. Foundational to that discourse have been the competing ontologies (pg. 33.) about whether international cooperation is feasible in an anarchic international system, whether IOs can be effective at facilitating collective action, and the extent to which IOs can help establish global order and peace.

As we saw in Chapter Three, realism and liberalism markedly differ in their assumptions about interstate cooperation and peace (pg. 41–3). Neorealism and neoliberalism also disagree over the extent to which IOs can mitigate the anarchic condition and establish order and peace within the international system. According to the liberal tradition, states are not solely motivated by security concerns, but by a harmony of interests and the mutual benefits that can be gained by working with others. Neoliberal scholars especially highlight the combined merits of liberal democracy, international trade and IOs in establishing international cooperation and peace. The League of Nations particularly triumphed these liberal values and committed its contracting parties to promote international cooperation and to achieve international peace and security.

Rule of law
A philosophy or principle of governance in which all people, institutions and governments are accountable to the same public laws, equally enforced and independently adjudicated.

While the League was ultimately unable to prevent the events that led to World War Two, the principles it enshrined lived on in the UN Charter, and the notion of a liberal international order (pg. 38) that emerged in the post-World War Two era. The subsequent spread of IOs during the latter half of the 20th century further consolidated this liberal international order, with new IOs enshrining liberal values, such as upholding the **rule of law**, respecting human rights or promoting fundamental freedoms. From a liberal perspective, therefore, IOs chart a pathway to peace. IOs are therefore found to constitute essential forums for interstate collaboration, cooperation and problem-solving.

Scholars within the realist tradition, by contrast, emphasize how, whether due to human nature or the anarchic condition of the international system, international competition and conflict are more prevalent than cooperation between states. From the neorealist perspective, power is a key feature of international politics, therefore any effort to establish IOs can only succeed if the great powers are involved, and their interests are directly served. While neorealist scholars have struggled to explain why IOs then spread to such an extent after World War Two, or why states will readily comply with international agreements, conventions and laws, even where it may not serve their immediate national interests, they have provided ample discourse on how power politics is itself a central feature of IOs in international politics.

For neorealism, IOs are considered instruments of their member states, and which particularly serve the interests of the great powers. For example, under the terms of the UN Charter, the USA, Russia, China, the UK and France (the P5) are granted special rights. The P5 are each permanent members of the UN Security Council, and each have a right of veto. Decisions on any substantive issues within the UN Security Council (UNSC) requires not only an affirmative vote by nine members, but consent by each of the P5. The P5 therefore have significant power to block decisions within the UNSC in accordance with their own national interests. Similarly, within the International Monetary Fund (IMF) – an international organization established following the 1944 Bretton Woods Conference hosted by the United States (pg. 211–12) – weighted voting shares grant greater voting power to the largest financial contributors. The United States has the greatest voting share within the IMF, being its largest financial contributor, which can give the US considerable power over the IO's decisions. For this reason, neorealists highlight how IOs are just tools for the great powers who can then exert their power to push or block change in accordance with their special interests. As a result, IOs are presented as limited forums, beneficial in serving some state interests, but unlikely to deliver meaningful collective action due to the mistrust and conflicting interests between them.

Functionalism
The theory that states will cooperate over specific functional issues where it means overcoming common problems and pursuing common interests. Functionalism assumes that international cooperation over technical or bureaucratic issues can then be extended to other policy areas over time.

ORGANIZE

Reflect again on the summary toolbox outlining the assumptions and propositions that shape realist and liberal theoretical approaches in international politics in Chapter Three (pg. 41–4), paying particular attention to the concepts of *relative gain* and *absolute gain*, *zero-sum game* and *non-zero sum game*. How might realist and liberal approaches be used to answer the following questions?:

- Why do states establish international organizations?
- Why do states comply with the rules, conventions and agreements established through international organizations?

Reflect also on the limitations of both realist and liberal approaches in addressing these questions. What other social and critical theories might you draw upon to further inform your answers?

Other theoretical lenses have also been developed specifically to address the emergence and growth of IOs. David Mitrany, who developed the theory of **functionalism**, used the experience of wartime cooperation in shipping, and the lessons of the League of Nations, to argue that states would establish IOs, run by bureaucrats and technical experts, that would each perform functionally specific activities aimed at solving common international problems. Where there was a particular need for interstate cooperation, addressing a specific transnational problem – such as disease control, for example – IOs would provide the functional response. The functional nature of IOs further meant that states would be largely shielded from the politicization and power politics that Mitrany found to have hindered international cooperation and the effectiveness of the League of Nations. Mitrany believed that, over time, states could come to cede greater authority to IOs who would provide a system for 'working peace'.

Ernst Haas developed further on Mitrany's arguments, reflecting on the difficulty of trying to keep technical and political issues separate. Haas advanced the theory of neofunctionalism (see pg. 139) suggesting that where IOs made progress in more technical and economic issues, states would come to see the benefits of cooperating across more issues areas, creating a process called 'spillover'. Where states learned to cooperate and see progress in technical and economic policy fields, they would then be more likely to extend that cooperation into more politically sensitive policy fields, such as security – a point we shall revisit in the next chapter when we address the integration of regional organizations and the case of the European Union.

THE UNITED NATIONS

So far in this chapter we have addressed how international organizations (IO) evolved, their function, membership and operations, and some of the different theoretical perspectives concerning why IOs are created. In this section we shall turn a spotlight on to the largest universal IO within today's international system – the United Nations (UN). The foundational treaty of the UN – the UN Charter – was agreed and signed on 26 June 1945 at the UN Conference on International Organization held in San Francisco. The Charter was based on proposals by the United States, the UK, the Soviet Union and China and was originally signed by representatives from fifty countries. The UN Charter committed its members to develop 'friendly relations among nations based on respect for the principle of *equal rights* and *self-determination of peoples* and to take other appropriate measures to strengthen *universal peace*' (UN 1945: Art 1(2) *emphasis added).* The preamble to the UN Charter specifically mentions the need 'to save succeeding generations from the scourge of war', and the commitment by its members:

1. to practise tolerance and live together in peace with one another as good neighbours,
2. to unite their strength to maintain international peace and security,
3. to ensure that armed force should not be used, save in the common interest, and
4. to promote the economic and social advancement of all people (UN 1945).

The UN officially came into existence on 24 October 1945. The principal organs of the UN include the UN General Assembly (UNGA), the UN Security Council (UNSC), the Economic and Social Council, the UN Secretariat, the International Court of Justice (ICJ) and the Trusteeship Council, with each organ serving a specific function – detailed in Table 7.2.

Since 1945 the UN has evolved extensively beyond these original six organs into a 'family' of IOs, agencies and funds with headquarters around the world. As its membership grew, expanding from an original fifty members to what are now 193 member states, so too did the UN's remit and operations. Through a process of **emanation**, the UN has now developed an extensive network of connected IOs, programmes and funds, all coming under the umbrella of its primary organs – see Figure 7.1. Most of the 'specialized agencies' established by the UN are themselves IOs, such as the World Health Organization (WHO), the World Bank and the International Monetary Fund (IMF), to name a few. Other older IOs have also been subsumed into the UN family such as the ITU and ILO.

Emanation
A process referring to the creation of new international organizations, agencies and programmes by another international organization.

Table 7.2 The functions and operation of the UN's principal organs

UN principal organ	Function and operation
UN General Assembly	• Main deliberative forum of the UN • All UN members attend meetings and can vote on resolutions • All members are equal regardless of size/power (1 member = 1 vote) • Meets annually in full session or for ad hoc emergency sessions • Main work achieved through committees with more limited membership, each focused on specific issues: 1st Committee (security), 2nd Committee (economics/finance), 3rd (social, humanitarian and cultural issues), 4th (special political and decolonization affairs), 5th (administration and budget) and 6th (legal)
UN Security Council	• Primary responsibility for maintaining international peace and security • Restricted membership comprising five permanent members (US, Russia, China, UK and France) and ten non-permanent members elected for a two-year term. • Agreement requires nine votes to pass; P5 each have a veto, however, creating a high threshold for consensus • Meets whenever peace is threatened • Authority to investigate disputes, dispatch a mission, appoint special envoys, issue ceasefire directives, dispatch military observers or peacekeeping forces, apply economic sanctions, arms embargoes, financial penalties or travel restrictions, severe diplomatic relations, order a blockade, or authorize collective military action
UN Secretariat	• Carries out the day-to-day work of the UN as mandated by the other main organs • Provides administrative and technical support for all UN activities • Headed by the UN Secretary-General who is the UN's chief administrative officer as well as the public face of the IO • Secretary-General appointed by the UNGA, on the recommendation of the UNSC for a five-year term, which can be rolled over
Economic and Social Council	• Coordinates the economic and social work of the UN and its family of organizations • Made up of fifty-four members, elected by the UNGA for three-year terms • Meets throughout the year as a main forum, supported also by issue-specific commissions and five regional commissions
International Court of Justice	• The main judicial organ of the UN, intended to settle legal disputes submitted by member states in accordance with international law • States participate in proceedings voluntarily, but are then obligated to comply with the Court's decision • Composed of fifteen judges elected to nine-year terms of office by the UNGA and UNSC • Located in The Hague, Netherlands
Trusteeship Council	• Intended to provide international supervision for selected territories in preparing them for self-government or independence • Established by the UN Charter to address the work of phased decolonization begun under the League of Nations • Suspended operations in 1994

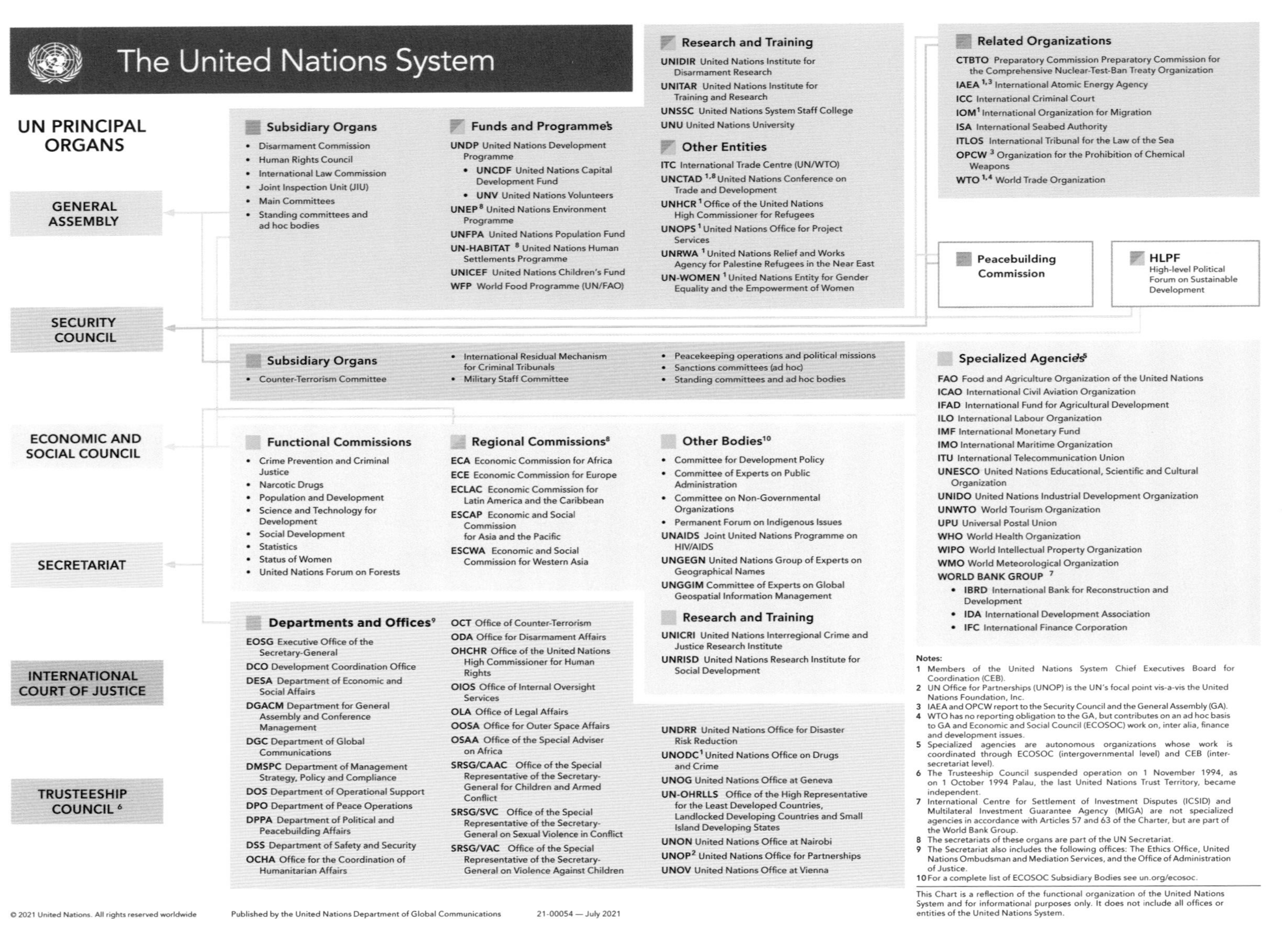

Figure 7.1 The United Nations System Chart, by the Department of Global Communications ©2022. Reprinted with the permission of the United Nations

Other IOs are also closely related to the UN, although not directly within the UN family, such as the World Trade Organization (WTO) and the International Atomic Energy Agency (IAEA). Unlike the UN's specialized agencies, these related IOs were created through separate intergovernmental pathways and have their own distinct arrangements for cooperation and collaboration with the UN. They can therefore be understood more as cousins rather than immediate family members to the UN.

As Figure 7.1 suggests, the UN has a vast scale of activity, to the extent that there are very few issues within international politics that the UN is not, in some way, involved in. In broad terms, however, the work of the UN is typically addressed across three main pillars: peace and security, development and human rights. These three pillars are integrated across all UN activities. For example, in 2017 the UN General Assembly and UN Security Council adopted a set of comprehensive and far-reaching resolutions intended to set a new agenda for delivering **sustainable peace**. The sustainable peace agenda overarches all three pillars of the UN by pursuing coordinated activities 'aimed at preventing the outbreak, escalation, continuation and recurrence of violence'; a task now advanced by the entire UN system rather than being limited to specific UN organs or agencies (UN 2017b).

Across all areas of its activity, **international law** is also a primary concern of the UN. Under the UN Charter, a key goal of the UN is 'to establish conditions under which justice and respect for the obligations arising from treaties and sources of international law can be maintained' (UN 1945). The rule of law is considered a foundation of the UN, as an essential liberal value underpinning peace and stability. UN member states are expected to abide by the UN Charter as well as the wider body of international law. The Secretary-General of the UN is the depository of more than 560 multilateral treaties, conventions and agreements that make up a considerable body of international law. Many multilateral conventions are pioneered and negotiated by the UN General Assembly, as well as intergovernmental treaty bodies associated with the UN, providing legal frameworks and standards addressing a wide range of topics such as disarmament, terrorism, the environment, migration and human rights.

Sustainable peace
A comprehensive, multi-sectoral and inclusive process in building, strengthening and sustaining peace, where peace is understood holistically and not just as the absence of war. Also referred to as 'positive' peace.

International law
A body of rules established by custom, convention or treaty that control or affect the rights of states and their relations with one another

Explore More

In 2020 the UN marked its 75th anniversary by launching a global consultation to ask people about their hopes and fears for the future, about priorities for recovering from Covid-19, and how the public perceived the role of the UN. Over 1 million people responded, with 60 per cent of respondents stating they believed the UN had made the world a better place, and 75 per cent saying they thought the UN was 'essential' for tackling the challenges the world faces. Find out more by visiting www.un.org/un75. The UN75 consultation and report subsequently fed into the UN Secretary-General's *Our Common Agenda* report, published in September 2021, which set out twelve key proposals that the UN would seek to action. Among them was the proposal to 'upgrade' the UN itself. Find out more about the proposals by reading the report at www.un.org.

Scan the QR code for access to explore weblinks and more resources.

As well as being a depository, the UN facilitates the negotiation of international laws and their codification, and passes judgement on disputes between states where international law is in question. The International Court of Justice (ICJ) – or 'World Court' – is the primary UN organ for settling disputes between states, and has considered over 170 cases since 1946, particularly addressing interstate disputes where sovereignty is in question such as over land and maritime boundaries (pg. 247). Important to note that the ICJ is a court open only to states and to certain organs and institutions of the UN system. The ICJ does not therefore try individuals or participate in criminal proceedings, which are typically addressed through other courts, such as the International Criminal Court (pg. 265–7) which is separate from the UN family.

Supporting the UN's various activities is a Secretariat and permanent staff who are, in turn, paid for by an annual budget – of around $3 billion – provided from regular financial contributions by UN member states. Determining how much each state pays is premised on a precise formula, called a 'scale of assessment', which requires that the wealthiest states – those with the highest gross national income (GNI) and thus largest share of the global economy – pay the most. The United States is the largest contributor, paying 22 per cent of the UN's regular budget, followed by China (12 per cent), Japan (8.5 per cent), Germany (6 per cent), the UK (4.6 per cent), France (4.4 per cent), Italy (3.3 per cent), Canada (2.7 per cent) and Australia and South Korea (both on 2.2 per cent) as the top ten contributors.

The UN has faced a recurring budget challenge, however, as not all UN member states pay on time, and in the amount specified. In recent years, the UN has experienced several severe budget crises, with many states habitually late in paying their dues, while others do not pay at all. In 2019, for example, the United States did not pay its annual contribution to the UN budget, after already being in arrears for outstanding payments from previous UN budgets – including the separate UN peacekeeping budget. The Trump Administration at the time was openly sceptical of the benefits of the UN, calling into question the United States' financial contributions to the UN and several other IOs. As a result, the UN experienced a severe financial crisis because of unpaid dues, with some programmes being starved of the finances needed to operate (*Washington Post* 2019).

DEBATING IOS: AUTHORITY, EFFECTIVENESS AND LEGITIMACY

As the controversy surrounding the UN's budget highlights, the UN can often present a subject of both censure and acclaim within international politics. For some the UN is a beacon of international cooperation, a critical forum for multilateral dialogue and negotiation, a bastion of international law, and the foundation to a liberal international order that established order and stability following two world wars. For others, however, the UN is a source of discontent – an IO that costs too much, spends too much, delivers too little or oversteps its authority. At the heart of these contrasting perspectives exist several enduring debates concerning the authority, effectiveness and legitimacy of IOs within international politics.

Are IOs actors or agents?

An underlying question concerning any scholarship of international organizations (IOs) is whether IOs can be considered actors within international politics, or simply agents of the states who formed them and make up their membership. This relates to questions of sovereignty within the international system and how much authority sovereign states retain or cede to IOs. Over the past three-quarters of a century, IOs have not only grown in number but have also become increasingly institutionalized. The bureaucratic structures within IOs, and the number of permanent staff that they employ, have increased. The UN, for example, which is the largest IO in the world, has offices in 193 countries and employs around 37,000 people. With this bureaucratizing effect, debate has followed as to whether IOs are taking on increasing capacity and authority to act within international politics. This complements a long-standing debate within our discipline about whether actors other than states (should) have agency within international politics. Are IOs taking on more control from states, and exerting greater authority over transboundary international issues, or are they mere agents given limited authority to act by states?

One way of addressing this question is to use the **principal-agent model** which argues that states (the *principals*) are the primary actors in international politics, but use IOs as *agents* to act on their collective behalf. States therefore authorize IOs to act for them in performing specific tasks. For example, the IAEA is authorized by its members to collect information on whether states meet their obligations to control the uses of nuclear energy. The WHO is authorized by its members to design and execute specific policies and programmes designed to respond to health emergencies, to promote health and to expand universal health coverage. The WTO meanwhile is authorized by its members to agree, oversee and enforce the rules of the multilateral trading system.

Principal-agent model
A theory of international organization which argues that states (the principals) give powers to international organizations (the agent) to act on their behalf. In this model, states remain the primary actors, while IOs are simply their agents.

According to the principal-agent model, principals agree to give IOs capacity to act on their behalf primarily for reasons of efficacy. By offsetting certain tasks to an IO, states can benefit from the IO's specialism in specific functions, reducing transaction costs and locking in other states to the process. Establishing an IO and working through it then is a rational cost–benefit calculation to which states remain in control. While IOs therefore have the expertise and authority to act in performing delegated functions, the principals must still create that authority and continue to retain control over the agent's remit and parameters. Any independence then exerted by the IO are constrained by the parameters established by states themselves.

A competing argument, however, suggests that IOs are capable of autonomous action beyond the delegated authority stipulated by their member states. For example, it was the UN and its family of IOs who defined 'refugee' as a new category of actor within international politics. It was the UN who linked poverty with development goals, and the UN who promoted human rights as a new priority issue for global actors (Barnett and Finnemore 1999: 699). Constructivists particularly highlight the unintended consequences of IOs, and their capacity to exercise power beyond the efficiency goals set out by their creators. IOs 'create actors, specify responsibilities and authority among them, and define the work these actors should do, giving it meaning and normative value. Even when they lack material resources, IOs exercise power as they constitute and construct the social world' (Barnett and Finnemore 1999: 700).

The **organizational culture approach** particularly highlights how authority is conferred on IOs, courtesy of their expertise, and independence as bureaucracies. Each IO has its own organizational culture; the permanent staff who supply the IO's administrative and technical functions, but who also promulgate the IO's expertise. An IO's staff is largely impartial as they are not appointed by states but hired by the IO to serve the IO's primary functions. As they serve the interest of the IO, staff will advance the IO, prioritizing its effectiveness and advancing its principles. States will often then defer to IOs, not only for impartial opinion but for their considerable technical expertise. Through this impartiality and expertise, IOs can then shape and define agendas. They can establish new norms or practices. And they can enhance the legitimacy of activities and outcomes within international politics because of the legal and moral authority associated with them.

Organizational culture approach
A theory of international organization which argues that the organizational culture of an international organization shapes its capability to act in international politics.

Are IOs effective?

Another related debate is the extent to which IOs are effective at fulfilling their various functions and tackling transboundary global challenges. When the League of Nations was established, Woodrow Wilson (1919) declared that '[i]t is a definite guarantee of peace. It is a definite guarantee by word against aggression ... It is a league that can be used for cooperation in any international matter.' Yet, as we know, the *guarantee* of peace

Image 7.2 Mothers participate in the launch of the world's first malaria vaccine pilot programme in Gisambai, Kenya in March 2023. The pilot programme has been led and coordinated by the World Health Organization with vaccines rolled out to 1.2 million children in Kenya, Ghana and Malawi.

Source: YASUYOSHI CHIBA/Getty Images.

Wilson attributed to the League was unfounded. How we determine the effectiveness of IOs ultimately depends upon our expectations about their respective functions, and the assumptions we make concerning their autonomy and authority to act relative to sovereign states within the international system.

Consider the example of the World Health Organization (WHO). The WHO was established as a UN agency in 1948 for the specific purpose of promoting health, keeping the world safe and to serve the vulnerable. According to its constitution, among the WHO's primary functions are the tasks of directing and coordinating international health work, establishing and maintaining effective collaboration with the UN and its other agencies, providing administrative and technical services, as well as providing research, information, counsel and assistance in the field of health. Also, according to the WHO's constitution, it is national governments who have responsibility for the health of their peoples.

The WHO has had many success stories – such as its contribution to the eradication of smallpox in the 1980s, its worldwide immunization programmes, and its ongoing efforts to tackle HIV and malaria (Image 7.2). Yet the WHO is also heavily criticized when international health emergencies arise. In 2014 the WHO was criticized for its slow response time, poor leadership, weak management and other operational failings during the Ebola crisis. During the Covid-19 pandemic, the WHO was also criticized for its response time in alerting people to the pandemic and over its expert advice to states in how to respond to the crisis, particularly in the early stages of the crisis. When determining the WHO's effectiveness, however, different perspectives must be considered. On the one hand the WHO has been ineffective in meeting some of its functions associated with health emergencies. Yet, on the other, states too must take responsibility for their own national responsiveness and ultimate responsibilities as health providers for their own citizens (pg. 94).

Explore More

You can discover more about the governance and constitution of the World Health Organization (WHO) at www.who.int. In May 2021 *The Independent Panel for Pandemic Preparedness and Response* released its report 'Covid-19: Make it the Last Pandemic' in which the panel highlighted the failures, gaps and delays in preparedness and response to the crisis. Highlighted failures were identified of the WHO itself – concerning its speed of response particularly – but also of states who failed to then take appropriate measures to halt the spread of the virus. You can read the report at https://theindependentpanel.org.

Scan the QR code for access to explore weblinks and more resources.

Are IOs legitimate?

Another debate to be aware of when considering IOs and their function within international politics concerns their legitimacy. According to Tallberg and Zürn (2019: 585), political legitimacy is defined as 'beliefs within a given constituency or other relevant audience that a political institution's exercise of authority is appropriate'. Legitimacy directly stems from the perception among governments and their publics that an IO's authority is being appropriately exercised. When an IO acts in international politics, the question not only follows as to whether it was effective, but whether its actions were legitimate. When an IO has perceived legitimacy, it is considered more relevant to states, its actions are seen as justified, and states are more likely to comply with its standards, rules and norms. Where an IO loses legitimacy in the eyes of governments and citizens, the IO become less relevant, non-compliance becomes more commonplace, and its actions are deemed less justified.

The UN has long been seen as a legitimizing force within international politics. With its near-universal membership, concern for international peace and security, advocacy of international law and the rule of law, and the fact that its decisions are made either by consensus or majoritarian vote, when the UN 'acts' in the international system, those actions are generally considered to be legitimate and justified, particularly where it concerns the use of force. Consider that when the United States and the United Kingdom invaded Iraq in 2003, their actions were roundly condemned by other governments around the world as 'illegitimate' because no UN Security Council (UNSC) resolution had been passed to support the invasion. Yet when the US and the UK, among others, conducted military air strikes against Libya in 2011, the actions were judged 'legitimate' because a UNSC resolution had been agreed and the air strikes were therefore deemed justified.

Yet while the UN – and particularly the UNSC – is widely looked to as a legitimizer of the use of force in international politics, the UNSC has also experienced an ongoing crisis of legitimacy. During the Cold War, that crisis of legitimacy was due to veto paralysis (Morris and Wheeler 2007) that meant the UNSC was left impotent to address any major security crisis because the US and the USSR would veto any decisions that negatively affected their own national interests, or directly or inadvertently aided the interests of their opponent. The crisis of legitimacy has nevertheless continued into the 21st century and stems primarily from two sources.

First, the UNSC continues to be dominated by a select handful of UN members, and its decisions continue to be shaped by the interests of the P5, particularly with regards their right of veto. The UNSC's legitimacy has therefore been questioned due to its membership and procedures which give unfair distinction to a minority of states, favoured when the UN was first formed. As former UN Secretary-General Kofi Annan stated, '[t]he council's present makeup reflects the world of 1945, not that of the twenty-first century' (Annan 2005).

Second, the UNSC's legitimacy is questioned over its performance and the extent to which it fulfils its function under the UN Charter, and not just the interests of its more powerful member states. As Frederking and Patane (2017) state, '[i]f the UNSC legitimately pursues international peace and security, then the most devastating conflicts should dominate its agenda. If the UNSC is legitimate, then the veto powers should uphold their end of the global social contract established by the UN Charter and determine its agenda by the intrinsic nature of the conflicts'. Yet history tells us that the UNSC has not always acted when the worst conflicts arise (pg. 271–2), calling its legitimacy into question.

The UN system – and particularly the UNSC – has subsequently been subject to ongoing reform discussions – not least since its 75th anniversary – a topic we shall return to in the toolkit exercise at the end of this chapter.

LINK

Image 7.3 Skulls of genocide victims at the Ntarama Church memorial in Rwanda. In spring 1994 hundreds of thousands of ethnic Tutsi and moderate Hutus were murdered by extremist Hutus. Considered one of the darkest moments in its history, the UN did nothing to stop the slaughter.

Source: Scott Chacon/Wikimedia Commons.

Consider

In 1993 the UNSC authorized a peacekeeping mission to Rwanda. It was not a military mission, but intended to oversee a ceasefire between the Hutu and Tutsi populations, help humanitarian aid deliveries and contribute to the security of the capital, Kigali. UN forces pulled out, however, after ten Belgian soldiers were killed, leaving the Tutsi population unprotected. The UNSC then failed to recognize – or acknowledge – the signals that genocide was possible within the country. In just 100 days, almost 1 million Rwandans were slaughtered.

Explore

Twenty years after the Rwandan genocide, the UNSC acknowledged that a failure of 'political will' led to the UN's failures to act in 1994. Read more about this at www.un.org. You may also want to check out Chapter Fifteen for more discussion on the events that unfolded in Rwanda and the UN's response.

Connect

How effective was the UNSC as the UN organ with 'primary responsibility to maintain international peace and security' in Rwanda's case? Consider also the UNSC as an agent or actor (pg. 118–9). Whose responsibility was it to protect the Tutsis?

Predict

Can the UNSC legitimately intervene in every conflict in the future? What would prevent the UNSC from intervening?

Scan the QR code for access to explore weblinks and more resources.

CONCLUSION

As key takeaways from this chapter we can highlight that international organizations (IO) are formed with three distinct purposes. They are forums and mechanisms for mutual consultation between states, advancing diplomacy and dialogue as a means of establishing order and stability. IOs are technical problem-solvers, aimed at overcoming collective transboundary problems. And IOs are legal mechanisms, serving as forums for arbitration and advice when disputes arise between states. Yet, underlying every IO remain tensions concerning their authority, effectiveness and legitimacy to act in an international system where sovereignty remains resided in the nation-state. We shall continue to develop on these takeaways in the following chapters in this section, particularly in the next chapter where we consider the proliferation of regional organizations, and the related issues surrounding sovereignty pooling and integration. For now, though, why not try out the following toolkit exercise and develop your knowledge further by addressing the question, *'How feasible is UNSC reform?'*

TOOLKIT

How feasible is UNSC reform?

THINK

- In a 2022 UN General Assembly debate on reforming the UN Security Council, the Iranian representative stated that the 'veto is not a right, but rather a privilege unfairly granted to some member states in violation of the United Nations Charter' (UN 2022a). What do you think of this statement? In what ways might the veto power of the P5 members of the UNSC be considered a violation of the UN Charter?

OBSERVE

Image 7.4 Ukrainian President Zelensky addresses the UN Security Council during a meeting on 5 April 2022. During the address Zelensky challenged the United Nations to either 'act immediately' or 'dissolve yourself altogether' in response to Russian atrocities against the people of Ukraine following their invasion in February 2022.

Source: TIMOTHY A. CLARY/ Getty Images.

- In 2005 the UN Secretary-General Kofi Annan (2005) issued a report entitled *In Larger Freedom* setting out the call for far-reaching comprehensive reform of the UN, including the UN Security Council (UNSC). Debate soon followed, with various blocs of countries working for reform. Among them were the G4 nations who campaigned to increase UNSC membership to twenty-five states, including six new permanent members (Brazil, Japan, Germany and India, plus two African countries – likely South Africa and Nigeria), and an additional three non-permanent seats. Other proposals focused on creating new permanent seats for each region. The push for reform diminished again towards the 2010s but once again entered the limelight following Russia's invasion of Ukraine in 2022, and the fact that Russia's veto power has largely hamstrung the UNSC from taking any cohesive and deliberate action.
- To mark the UN's 75th anniversary, the UN General Assembly passed a resolution which made direct reference to 'upgrade' the United Nations and reiterated the 'call for reforms of three of the principal organs of the United Nations'. The resolution went on to state that '[w]e commit to instil new life in the discussions on the reform of the Security Council' (UN 2020: 4).

- The 2021 *Our Common Agenda* Report (pg. 117) also reaffirmed that for the UN to be more effective, it must develop new capabilities that 'promote agility, integration and cohesion across the [UN] system'; a process that the UN Secretary-General observed would be part of a wider transformation towards a United Nations '2.0' (UN 2021b: 75-76).

ORGANIZE

- Revisit the UNSC decision-making procedures on pg. 115. What would be required for the UNSC to approve any reform proposal?
- Reflect on the different theoretical perspectives that explain why IOs were formed and then spread (pg. 112–4). What would be the realist, liberal and functional arguments for upgrading the UN? How might these logics explain reforming the UN Security Council specifically?
- The *Our Common Agenda* report also details the need for the UNSC to be more inclusive, legitimate and 'representative of the 21st century, such as through enlargement, including better representation for Africa' (UN 2020: 77). Revisit the critical theoretical approaches outlined in Chapter Four, particularly postcolonialism. How might you analyse the discourse from a postcolonial viewpoint?

LINK

- *Consider*: The UNSC has already been reformed once. In 1963 the UNSC increased its membership from eleven to fifteen members.
- *Connect*: Advocates for UNSC reform highlight how increased representation and democratization of the UNSC would enhance its legitimacy. What do you think more members could mean for UNSC effectiveness?
- *Explore*: Find out more about some of the different proposals for UNSC reform at https://ourworld.unu.edu. Explore the article 'Will Ukraine's Tragedy Spur UN Security Council Reform?' Available online: www.project-syndicate.org. You may also be interested to read the 2022 UNGA debate on Security Council Reform Available online: https://press.un.org.
- *Predict*: What do you think the prospects are for UNSC reform in the 2020s?

Scan the QR code for access to explore weblinks and more resources.

SHARE

- Answer the question *'How feasible is UNSC reform?'*

  What sources might you draw upon to inform your argument to this question? Remember to be careful in how you are referencing those sources (see *How to – identify quality sources* pg. 106 and *How to – approach referencing* pg. 126). Reflect also on how you can utilize different theories to set up your key points and argument – see *How to – apply theory to your research and writing* (pg. 69), and be sure to adopt a clear position as well (see *How to – take a position* (pg. 144) for some tips and advice).

HOW TO

APPROACH REFERENCING

Referencing is essential for your academic writing. As a student you are expected to actively engage with the scholarship around your topic and to showcase that engagement in your assessed works. It can take practice to become proficient in different referencing styles and approaches but mastering the art of referencing early is important. Referencing helps evidence your research and engagement with the scholarship. Referencing also adds transparency to your writing, ensuring your sources are acknowledged and can also be identified and traced by others. As we saw in *How to – paraphrase theoretical discourse in your politics writing* (pg. 48), it is also important that you reference to help avoid charges of **plagiarism**. It is also considered poor academic practice to submit assessment which lacks or has inadequate referencing. The following are five top tips for how to approach referencing in your academic work.

Check the referencing style

Many university departments adopt a preference on the referencing style they expect students to use in their written work. Others may be more flexible and give you the choice. Be sure to check this though so that you are meeting referencing guidelines in your assessed work. In international politics, scholarship referencing styles might include, for example, Harvard, Chicago, Vancouver, APA, MHRA, OSCOLA or MLA styles (to name a few). Some of these styles even have different variants unique to specific universities. Whichever style you are expected to adopt by your department, bear in mind that each has its own specific style of citing references, both in the text and for listing all of your references in full. Your university library should have guides to help you learn how to use your referencing style in specific terms. Be assured, learning a referencing style is a little like riding a bike – while a challenge to get going, it soon becomes second nature.

In-text citations

An important element of any academic writing is **citations**. Citations allow you to clearly show your engagement with the scholarship, and your transparency in showing where ideas, arguments and data are drawn from within the main body of your text. Be aware that referencing styles will vary with regards to how in-text citations are listed. For example, some are based on an author-date system (Harvard), others a numerical system (Vancouver) and others a notes and bibliography system (MHRA). For example:

Author-date style:
According to Dee (2024: pg. 126) it is important to cite sources to show transparency in your academic writing. Many universities use preferred referencing styles (Dee 2024: 126).

> The full text of the source is then listed in alphabetical order (author surname first) in the references list at the end of the paper.

Numerical style:
According to Dee (1) it is important to cite sources to show transparency in your academic writing. Many universities use preferred referencing styles (2).

> The full text of the source is then listed in numerical order in the references list at the end of the paper.

Plagiarism
The practice of taking someone else's work or ideas and passing them off as your own.

Citation
Acknowledgement to specific materials in your work that have come from another source.

Notes and bibliography style:
According to Dee[1] it is important to cite sources to show transparency in your academic writing. Many universities use preferred referencing styles.[2]

The full text of the source is then listed in a footnote. If the same reference occurs again, it is subsequently abbreviated.

To ibid or not to ibid?

Some referencing styles, particularly those which adopt a numerical or notes and bibliography approach, permit the use of *ibid* when referring to a source more than once. Ibid is short for *ibidem* which is Latin for 'in the same place'. Ibid should only be used in specific circumstances, however. *First*, your referencing style must allow its use. Author-date styles like Harvard referencing do not use it so be sure to check this when you are learning the particulars of your referencing style. *Second*, where use of ibid is permitted, be sure you only include it when referring to the next consecutive reference in a list after an earlier reference to the same work (see footnotes by way of example).

Reference list or bibliography?

Be aware that there can be a difference between a reference list and a bibliography. Typically, a reference list includes a list at the end of your paper detailing all those sources actually cited in the body of your text. A bibliography by contrast lists all the sources you have consulted in writing your paper, including any you may not have cited directly. You should receive instruction from your course coordinator or programme lead as to the practice to adopt for listing your sources but, if in doubt, just check.

Software to help

There are various referencing software packages out there that can help you compile and manage the references you are using. Most will also work in conjunction with your word processing package enabling you to automatically format your citations and references list to a preferred referencing style. Examples include RefWorks, Endnote, Mendeley, Zotero, etc. Your university library may be able to help direct you to the best software to use. Bear in mind though that these softwares are only fully effective when used for noting and storing your source material as well, so are less useful where you take handwritten notes of your readings and noted references.

---

[1]Megan Dee (2024), *Understanding International Politics: The Student Toolkit,* London: Bloomsbury, p. 126.
[2]Ibid., p. 126.

8 Regional organizations

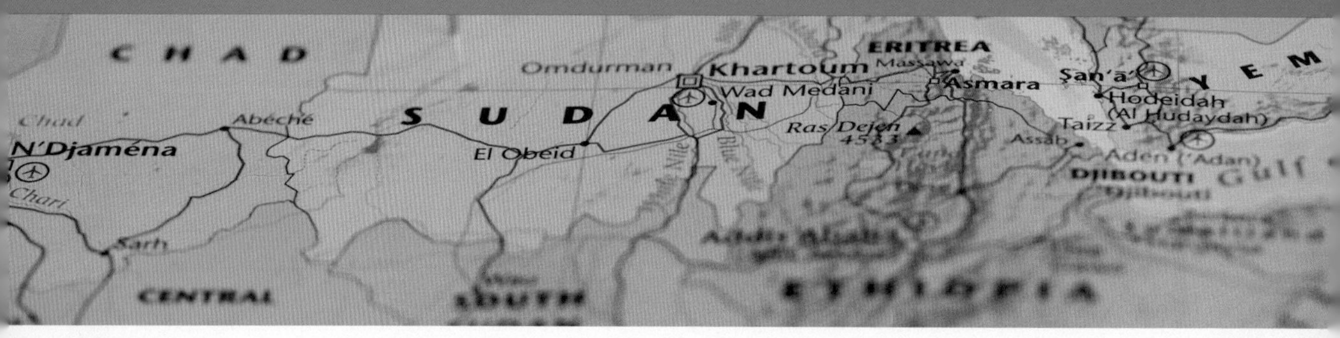

Pexels / Lara Jameson

Abstract

In this chapter you will discover more about the increasing importance of regionalism within international politics, and how regional organizations emerged and spread. The chapter focuses on efforts by states to maximize their regional security, promote human rights and democracy, and achieve collective gains through economic cooperation. Today, regional organizations make up a vast, increasingly dense, network of geographical blocs spanning multiple and overlapping policy fields. The chapter further shines a spotlight on the European Union, one of the most integrated and institutionalized regional organizations in the world. From there we consider the debate around the willingness of states to not only cooperate but integrate within regional organizations, addressing some of the differences between the EU, ASEAN and African Union. The chapter concludes with a toolkit exercise asking, '*Was the Battle of Marawi a turning point for the ASEAN-way?*'

Regionalism
A process by which states within a specified region work together to facilitate ongoing coordination and cooperation within political, security and/or economic policy fields, typically through the creation of regional organizations.

UNDERSTANDING REGIONAL ORGANIZATIONS

As we saw in the last chapter, the end of World War Two saw a noticeable leap forward in states' collective action (pg. 111) to develop international organizations that could deter and prevent a repeat of the destruction and bloodshed of the first half of the 20th century. The newly emerging liberal international order (see pg. 38) not only created the United Nations (UN) and its family of international organizations, programmes and agencies, but also saw a marked increase in **regionalism**.

THINK

Regions can be contested and evolving constructs, built on competing interpretations and mental maps (pg. 3). The Indo-Pacific, for example, is a highly contested regional construct (Das 2019), broadly spanning the connected space between the Indian and Pacific Oceans. While the strategic importance of the Indo-Pacific region has been recognized by the likes of the United States (who renamed the US Pacific Command the Indo-Pacific Command in 2018), the United Kingdom (who has emphasized its strategic 'tilt' to the region since 2021), and China (courtesy of its Belt and Road Initiative pg. 207), the region remains a fluid and contested space.

What mental maps do you have of the region(s) in which you in live? What regions would you identify as contested in the world today?

Regionalism is the process by which states within a specified region actively coordinate their activities across political, security and economic policy fields. It is important to emphasize, however, that a region can be very broadly defined. Understanding where a region starts and finishes can often be subjective. **Regions** are social constructs (pg. 61–3), determined not simply by geography, but by identities shaped through culture, religion, colonialism, economics, history and politics. Regions may be understood as continental, as in the case of Europe, but can also be subcontinental, or even transcontinental – consider the Middle East and Eurasia, respectively. A common denominator within a region, however, is that there is some association and relationship between the states, whether that be geographical, normative, cultural or economic. Regionalism can also be understood as a process of multilateralism (pg. 109) within a given region, often leading to the creation of **regional organizations** which are specifically designed to facilitate the ongoing coordination and cooperation among states.

Region
A geographical area with geographical, normative, cultural or economic association between the states. Regions may be subcontinental (Middle East), continental (Europe), or transcontinental (Eurasia) in nature.

Regional organization
International organizations whose members include three or more states from within a specified region.

The growth of regionalism in the second half of the 20th century was not only inspired by the desire to achieve peace and prosperity among states at both global and regional levels. It was further fuelled by ideological divisions that dominated international politics during this period. The start of the Cold War incited many countries to align within regional blocs either led, or supported, by the United States or the Soviet Union. This division along ideological lines was particularly pronounced in the emergence of new regional organizations focused on security and defence. The North Atlantic Treaty Organization (NATO) when it was formed in 1949 included member states from across a broadly conceived North Atlantic region, encompassing the United States and Canada, but also ten Western European democracies. By contrast the Warsaw Pact, formed in 1955, was made up of the Soviet Union, alongside seven other Central and Eastern European (CEE) socialist republics. Similarly, regionalism was also occurring in other policy fields, including with the formation of the European Economic Community (later European Union) in 1957, formed originally of Belgium, France, Germany, Italy, Luxembourg and the Netherlands, all of whom were like-minded liberal democracies, and all NATO members.

Regionalism was also growing in Latin America, the Caribbean and Pacific, Africa, the Middle East and Southeast Asia, with the creation of numerous regional organizations including, for example:

- The Arab League (1945)
- The Organization of African Unity (1963) (later the African Union)
- The Association of Southeast Asian Nations (ASEAN) (1967)
- The Andean Community of Nations (1969)
- The Caribbean Community (1973)
- The Latin American Integration Association (1980).

OBSERVE

Image 8.1 Delegates at a meeting of the Southeast Asia Treaty Organization (SEATO) in Manila, Philippines in 1966.

Source: Wikimedia Commons.

The Association of Southeast Asian Nations (ASEAN) was not the first regional organization established in Southeast Asia. The Southeast Asia Treaty Organization (SEATO), established in 1955, was a US-backed counterpart to NATO. Its members included the US, France, the UK, Australia, New Zealand and Pakistan, with only the Philippines and Thailand from Southeast Asia itself, although Vietnam, Laos and Cambodia were granted observer status. SEATO's close ties to the United States were nevertheless viewed with some suspicion by others in the region, particularly Indonesia who was host to the Bandung Conference (pg. 25–6) and was deeply cautious of neo-imperial entrapment by either the Americans or Soviets (Clark 2011: 293-4). Two other regional organizations were also established in the 1960s including the Association of Southeast Asia (ASA) in 1961 and MAPHILINDO in 1968 – both of which were short-lived and soon dissolved.

ASEAN's foundations must therefore be observed not only in the context of the regional organizations that went before it, but also the ideological battleground during the Cold War. Colonial and anti-imperial legacies must also be observed as crucial in shaping the approach of newly independent states towards regional cooperation. According to one postcolonial scholar, 'a large part of the common glue that brought the countries of ASEAN together in the first place was not a shared history or culture but rather a shared need to govern newly independent and often fragile states, many of whom were still traumatized by the colonial encounter' (Clark 2011: 296).

The multiplying of regional organizations in the decades after World War Two has further resulted in a dense network of multiple and overlapping regional organization memberships. Consider, for example, that Turkey has close regional connections both to Europe and Asia. In terms of regional organization membership, therefore, Turkey is a member of the Economic Cooperation Council, The Asia Cooperation Dialogue, the Organization for Security and Cooperation in Europe, the Council of Europe, the Black Sea Economic Cooperation, the South-East European Cooperation Process, and NATO. Since 1987 Turkey has also been negotiating its accession to the European Union. Another interesting example is the United Kingdom, who is a member of the Organization for Security and Cooperation in Europe, the Council of Europe, NATO, the British-Irish Council and the Commonwealth of Nations. In 2019 the UK also exited the European Union (pg. 87–8) – setting an unusual precedent for reverse regionalism in the case of the EU – a topic we shall revisit later in the chapter. For now, let us turn to consider the function of regional organizations and some of the thematic issues that they address.

THE FUNCTION OF REGIONAL ORGANIZATIONS

As we have discussed so far, regional organizations must be considered as a process of regionalism. Regional organizations are established as a process of multilateral coordination by states within a region, and are intended to facilitate their ongoing coordination and cooperation. Much like international organizations, regional organizations are also established as formal institutions, typically with a headquarters, permanent staff and logo. Like international organizations, membership of regional organizations are also principally states, although membership then typically is restricted to states within the defined region that the organization represents rather than being universal (Table 7.1 pg. 112).

Like international organizations, regional organizations also have a defined scope or function, as set out in an international treaty, constitution or charter. The main function of regional organizations will, of course, differ on a case-by-case basis, with many regional organizations often having multiple purposes. In general terms, however, we can identify three broad thematic issues behind the creation of regional organizations: *security, economics* and *politics*.

Some regional organizations are created to further regional coordination on a relatively narrow set of issues within one thematic issue area – such as NATO which is oriented specifically to security. Other regional organizations, however, have broader remits that span all three thematic issues, including, for example, the African Union, ASEAN or EU. It is also important to identify that while some regional organizations were originally created to further regional cooperation within one thematic issue, **scope expansion** can also occur over time which extends the regional organization's scope across new themes. Such forms of scope expansion can also create overlaps with other existing regional security and political organizations, further adding to regionalism's complexity. Let's then take a closer look at some examples of regional security, economic and political organizations.

Scope expansion
The process by which the original scope of a regional organization within one policy field is expanded to include additional policy fields.

Defensive alliance
A form of military alliance whereby allies promise to aid one another in the case of attack.

Collective defence
The principle that an attack against one ally is an attack against all allies. The principle of collective defence is one enshrined in Article 5 of the Washington Treaty that founded the North Atlantic Treaty Organization.

Security regional organizations

Regional organizations formed primarily for security purposes were especially prominent in the first wave of regionalism after World War Two. The first regional security organization to form was NATO, established in April 1949. NATO was formed as a **defensive alliance** for the North Atlantic region, modelled on a principle of **collective defence,** where member states committed to defend each other in the case of attack. According to Article 5 of NATO's founding treaty, the North Atlantic Treaty (or more commonly, the Washington Treaty), NATO members 'agree that an armed attack against one or more of them in Europe or North America shall be considered an attack against them all'.

Since 1949, NATO's remit has consistently remained one dedicated to security and defence. While NATO has seen periods of expansion, both in terms of its enlargement, and even in the scope of its activity, the organization has always remained a security alliance first and foremost. Formed originally with twelve member states, at the time of writing NATO has undergone nine rounds of enlargement and now has thirty-one member states with Finland joining the alliance in 2023. These successive rounds of enlargement have largely tracked wider geopolitical developments in the North Atlantic region over the course of the Cold War and into the post-Cold War period. The first three rounds of NATO enlargement took place during the Cold War, bringing Greece, Turkey, West Germany and Spain into the alliance. With the end of the Cold War, however, successive NATO enlargements brought in the former Soviet, now newly democratic Central and Eastern European states. Since 2008, NATO has further redirected its enlargement focus to the Western Balkans, as well as opening the door for future membership to countries like Georgia and Ukraine.

With successive enlargements, NATO has also undergone an evolution and expansion of its security remit, moving beyond a more traditional military focus, to address a far broader range of non-traditional security domains as well (pg. 190–1). While, as a defensive alliance, NATO's primary objective remains to deliver collective defence to its member states in the case of attack, NATO has also enhanced its capacity to respond to a growing range of threats, including terrorism and cyberattack, hybrid warfare and even space security.

Explore More

The 1949 Washington Treaty that founded NATO is fourteen articles long. Despite NATO's longevity and enlargement, the original treaty has never had to be amended, as each NATO member can apply the text of the treaty in accordance with their own capabilities and circumstances. You can explore the treaty text by visiting www.nato.int

Scan the QR code for access to explore weblinks and more resources.

ORGANIZE

Liberalism emphasizes that states join regional security organizations to enhance their collective defence, peace and prosperity by working collectively with others in their region. Social constructivism meanwhile would emphasize the shared identity, norms and perceptions of threat among states within a region, and the socialization which takes place within regional security organizations.

Neorealism in contrast suggests that regional organizations emerged to counterbalance existing power structures. The creation of NATO in 1949 as a defensive alliance built, according to the first NATO Secretary General Lord Ismay, to 'keep the Russians out, the Americans in, and the Germans down', is often thought to reflect this realist logic, as does the fact that, six years later, the Soviet Union created the Warsaw Pact to balance against NATO.

Reflect again on neorealism's assumptions about balancing behaviours (pg. 38). How well do you think this logic explains the creation of regional security organizations? How well do you think this logic helps to explain why NATO continued to enlarge and evolve after the collapse of the Soviet Union?

Other examples of security-based regional organizations include the Organization for Security and Cooperation in Europe (OSCE). The OSCE in fact includes fifty-seven member states across North America, Europe and Asia, and is one of the world's largest regional security organizations. Initially launched as the Conference for Security and Cooperation in Europe as a form for dialogue and negotiation between the East and West in the early 1970s, by 1994 it had evolved and institutionalized into the OSCE which continues to this day.

Further examples of regional organizations with a security remit include ASEAN and the African Union. Although both organizations include economic and political remits, both address the promotion of regional peace and stability as one of their core aims and purposes. The African Union's Constitutive Act of July 2000, for example, highlights that the aim of the African Union is to 'promote peace, security and stability on the continent', alongside other aims such as defending the sovereignty, territorial integrity and independence of member states, promoting democratic principles, human and people's rights, and sustainable development. The African Union further aims to ensure the coordination and harmonization of policies between existing and future Regional Economic Communities across the continent, a theme to which we now turn.

Economic regional organizations

While security was a prominent issue driving the emergence of new regional organizations after World War Two, this was soon to give way to a groundswell of new regional organizations focused primarily on economics. Regional economic organizations emerged with the primary function of enhancing economic cooperation between states, including through the establishment of economic dialogue and partnership mechanisms, free trade areas and common markets. The European Union's earliest predecessor, the European Coal and Steel Community, formed in 1952, is an early example of a regional economic organization. Later examples also include the South Asian Association for Regional Cooperation (1985), the Asia Pacific Economic Cooperation (1989), the Central European Initiative (1989), the Arab Maghreb Union (1989), the Central America Integrations System (1991), the South African Development Community (1992), the North American Free Trade Agreement (1994), the Common Market for Eastern and Southern Africa (1994), the Central African Economic and Monetary Community (1998), the Community of Sahel-Saharan States (1998), and the East African Community (1999).

Since the end of the Cold War, regional economic organizations have also continued to evolve as states have sought to tap into the prospects for collective gain through regional trade agreements (RTAs) and the creation of regional trade blocs (pg. 214). This increase is especially evidenced in the decade-on-decade growth of RTAs in force since the 1950s, increasing from just two in 1958, to eighty-two by 2000, rising again to 212 in 2010, and 313 RTAs in 2020 (WTO 2023a). In fact, according to the World Trade Organization, at the time of writing, only three countries in the world were *not* involved in RTAs – Mauritania, Somalia and South Sudan (WTO 2023a).

Political regional organizations

Regional organizations also formed with the specific objective of furthering regional political cooperation around shared values. For example, one of the first regional political organizations to form was the League of Arab States; a loose collaborative alliance among twenty-two Arab countries based on a shared culture and historical experience. The Arab League's Charter, signed on 22 March 1945, set out its 'view to strengthen the close relations and numerous ties which bind the Arab States' through close cooperation on economic and financial matters, communications, cultural matters, issues relating to nationality, social welfare matters and health matters. Since its formation, the Arab League continues to coordinate across a variety of political issues and has played a particularly active role on issues such as Palestinian statehood (pg. 95).

Another example of a regional political organization can be found in the Council of Europe (pg. 265) which was formed in 1949 with the aim of furthering democracy in Europe and advancing common values around respect for human rights and the rule of law. The Council of Europe today has forty-six members. Every member of the organization agrees to not only strengthen human rights but are themselves subject also to independent monitoring mechanisms to ensure their own compliance. All members must, for example, have abolished the death penalty. The Council of Europe also advocates values including non-discrimination, freedom of speech, gender equality, protection of children's rights and cultural diversity. Noticeably, the Council of Europe excluded Russia from the organization in March 2022 after twenty-six years of membership due to its invasion of Ukraine (Council of Europe 2022).

SPOTLIGHT ON THE EUROPEAN UNION

In this section we turn a spotlight on a regional organization that has undergone extensive evolution, enlargement and scope expansion since its formation in 1957 – the European Union (EU). Originally conceived as the European Economic Coal and Steel Community in the aftermath of World War Two, before forming as the European Economic Community, the now EU has become one of the most integrated and institutionalized forms of regional organization in the world.

Origins of the EU

As we have already discussed in this chapter, an increasing push towards regionalism after World War Two saw a marked growth in regional organizations around the globe during the latter half of the 20th century. Yet perhaps one of the most extraordinary pushes towards regionalism was being played out in Europe itself in the very ruins of the war. Having been enemies at the very epicentre of both World Wars One and Two, France and (West) Germany were to become two of the first European states to make tentative steps towards not just cooperation but economic integration through the creation of a regional organization.

On 9 May 1950, the French Foreign Minister Robert Schuman presented his plan to bring coal and steel production under a High Authority. Coal was a primary energy source in Europe at that time, while steel was fundamental to industry. Both coal and steel production were not only vital commodities for economic development and recovery from the war but were also essential resources for conducting warfare again in the future. With French concerns that Germany could once again use its coal and steel industries to claim dominance in the region, the Schuman Plan sought to 'lock in' Germany's coal and steel production to a common community. Federalist in orientation, the Schuman Plan favoured **supranationalism** whereby sovereign control over coal and steel production would be pooled, with decisions taken by a High Authority rather than controlled nationally by the states themselves.

Supranationalism
The principle and process whereby interests transcend national boundaries and authorized decision-making is made above (*supra*) the state level.

The Schuman Plan led to the European Coal and Steel Community (ECSC), which was created two years later in 1952. The ECSC had six members: Belgium, France, Germany, Italy, Luxembourg and the Netherlands, later known as the 'EC-6'. While the ECSC may be identified as the first regional economic organization to form in Europe after World

War Two, we can see that its creation was driven not simply by economic purposes, but by political and security concerns as well.

The EC-6 also sought to establish a European Defence Community around the same time. The European Defence Community's Treaty of Paris had also been signed in 1952 with the purpose of establishing a Pan-European defence force and to act as a counterbalance to the Soviet Union. In sharp contrast to NATO, which had been formed as a defensive alliance where individual member states maintained sovereign authority over their own armed forces, the European Defence Community was modelled on a supranational form of governance, where member states would pool their armed forces to create a common European defensive force. The European Defence Community nevertheless failed to gain political support and, in 1954, was rejected by the French Parliament.

From 1954 the EC-6 focused their energies specifically upon economic regionalism. Building upon the success of the ECSC which had created a common market with a common governance structure over coal and steel production, the EC-6 sought to further the scope of the common market across a far broader economic remit and to harmonize their national commercial and economic policies. In March 1957, the EC-6 signed the Treaties of Rome establishing both the European Economic Community (EEC) and the European Atomic Energy Community (Euratom).

Over the next decade, the EEC became a fully functioning customs union covering all trade in goods, with a common external tariff and quotas being imposed on all goods entering the Community. The development of the EEC's Common Commercial Policy (CCP) in the 1960s further reinforced the EEC's goals of harmonious development of economic activities and closer relations between the states belonging to the EEC. The common market not only tackled restrictions to trade within the EEC, but the Common Commercial Policy ensured that the EEC negotiated as one bloc in all trade negotiations with other countries, establishing the EEC as a single, powerful, economic actor on the world stage.

An evolving Union

As we have considered so far and will return to a little later in this chapter, cooperation and even integration among states within regional organizations can often result in a process of scope expansion, or spillover, where the benefits of cooperating in one policy field starts to highlight the benefits of cooperating in others. Yet the evolution of the EEC, and the spillover that occurred later in the 20th century, did not always run smoothly. During the 1960s the new EEC struggled to expand its scope of operation beyond the creation of a customs union, largely due to French reticence towards supranationalism. The EEC was modelled on the institutions formed under the ECSC, including a European Commission (to replace the ECSC High Authority) to represent Community interests, a Council of Ministers to represent member state national interests, and a European Parliament to represent the citizens. In 1961, however, France set out its plans for a rival political community. The *Fouchet Plans* were an effort by French President Charles de Gaulle to alter the balance of institutional power within Western Europe, away from the supranational institutions of the EEC, and towards a looser, intergovernmental approach based on cooperation between sovereign states.

It was only after De Gaulle left office in 1969 that the EEC began to take substantive steps forward in expanding its scope of operations. During the 1970s European Political Cooperation (EPC) emerged which saw the EEC members begin to coordinate and consult one another over their respective foreign policies. In 1973 the EEC also saw its first round of enlargement, as the EC-6 were joined by Denmark, Ireland and the United Kingdom. By 1979 citizens from across the now EC-9 were, for the first time, given the vote to directly elect members of the European Parliament. In 1981 Greece became the EEC's tenth member, followed by Portugal and Spain in 1986.

By 1993 the Treaty on European Union (TEU or 'Maastricht Treaty') entered into force, formally creating the European Union as a successor to the EEC. The Maastricht Treaty established the EU's Common Foreign and Security Policy (CFSP) requiring EU member states to coordinate on all matters concerning foreign and security policy and to achieve common positions in EU external action. By 1999 the EU went on to launch a European Security and Defence Policy where EU member states reaffirmed their willingness to develop 'capabilities for autonomous action, backed up by credible military forces'. By 2003, the EU had launched its first European Security Strategy and conducted its first military mission – *EUFOR Concordia* in the former Yugoslavian Republic of Macedonia. Then, in 2004, the EU underwent a 'big bang' enlargement, accepting ten new member states from Central and Eastern Europe and Malta.

By 2007 the EU member states agreed the Treaty on the Functioning of the European Union (TFEU or 'Lisbon Treaty') which not only gave the EU full legal personality but offered clearer clarification on the powers of the Union itself. Specifically, the TFEU specifies four types of **competence**: *exclusive competence* where the EU legislates and member states implement; *shared competence*, where member states can legislate and adopt legally binding measures, but only if the EU has not done so; *supporting competence*, where the EU may support, coordinate or supplement the actions of the member states; and *special competence* where the EU may take measures to ensure that EU countries coordinate their economic, social and employment policies at EU level, and which also captures the EU's special arrangements around its common foreign, security and defence policies.

Competence
The capacity of the EU to act within a given policy field. Under the EU treaties the EU member states agree to confer certain competences on the EU who can then act on their behalf, for example, in trade policy making.

Table 8.1 shows the full scope of EU and EU member state activities by level of competence. As this table showcases, while the EU has considerable power to legislate in the realm of economic, trade and monetary policy, in most policy fields, the EU shares legislative power with its member states or must play a supporting role to member states' own national legislations. Thus, while we can see that the EU has evolved considerably as a regional organization spanning economic, political and security fields – to the extent that there is no policy field in which the EU does not take an interest – the EU is still a highly variable actor in terms of its competence to act across all policies.

Explore More

The European Union has evolved to such an extent that it has become a prominent presence within international politics. Since 2010 the EU has even developed certain qualities of 'statehood' such as having a quasi-Foreign Minister, in the form of the EU High Representative for Foreign Policy and Security Affairs, a diplomatic service in the form of its External Action Service (EEAS) and with some 140 EU delegations and offices around the world. While the EU struggles to present itself as a coordinated actor in some areas of its Common Foreign and Security Policy, on matters of trade, development and the environment, for example, the EU is often identified as a leading global actor and influencer. To find out more about the EU's external relations check out the European Union External Action Service at https://eeas.europa.eu.

Scan the QR code for access to explore weblinks and more resources.

Table 8.1 The EU's levels of competence by policy field

Exclusive Competence	Shared Competence	Supporting Competence	Special Competence
• Customs union • Competition • Monetary policy (Euro Area) • Conservation of marine biological resources under the Common Fisheries Policy • Common commercial policy • Conclusion of international agreements under certain conditions	• Internal market • Social policy • Economic, social and territorial cohesion (regional policy) • Agriculture and Fisheries (except conservation of marine biological resources) • Environment • Consumer protection • Transport • Trans-European networks • Energy • Area of freedom, security and justice • Shared safety concerns in public health matters • Research, technological development, space • Development cooperation and humanitarian aid	• Protection and improvement of human health • Industry • Culture • Tourism • Education, vocational training, youth and sport • Civil protection • Administrative cooperation	• Economic, social and employment policies • Common foreign and security policy • Common defence and security policy

Then, 2007 also saw Bulgaria and Romania join the EU and, in 2013, Croatia became the EU's twenty-eighth member. EU enlargement had been on pause since 2013, although several states in the EU's eastern and south-eastern neighbourhood are considered candidate countries for EU accession including Albania, Bosnia and Herzegovina, Montenegro, North Macedonia, Serbia and Turkey. Since the Russo-Ukraine war in 2022, Ukraine and Moldova are also now candidate countries for EU membership (Map 8.1), while Georgia and Kosovo (pg. 95–6) are considered potential candidates. The EU has therefore generated 'ever closer Union' for its expanding membership, while remaining highly attractive to those states on its borders. Despite this, in 2016 the EU was also rocked by the UK's referendum decision supporting the UK's withdrawal from the EU (pg. 87–8). On 1 January 2021, the UK became the first EU member state to activate its right to withdraw from the Union, bringing the EU's total membership down to twenty-seven member states.

COOPERATION OR INTEGRATION – HOW FAR WILL STATES GO?

As the example of the EU particularly showcases, a core question we might ask when researching regionalism and regional organizations is, *To what extent* will *states not only cooperate, but in fact integrate within regional organizations?* As we discussed in Chapter Three, the question of international cooperation, and the extent to which states will work together in pursuit of common and shared goals within the international system,

Map 8.1 A map of Europe in 2023 depicting the EU's member states (blue), candidate states (pale pink), potential candidates (yellow) and former member (grey blue stripes). Countries depicted in purple are members of the European Economic Area (EEA), a regional trade agreement that includes all EU member states, plus Iceland and Norway. Countries within the yellow borders are part of the EU's passport-free travel zone, the Schengen Area.

Source: Wikimedia Commons.

remains an enduring, even foundational, question to the discipline of international politics itself. Yet, when addressed from the regional perspective, where regional cooperation has intensified and institutionalized and regional organizations like the EU highlight increasing **sovereignty pooling** and **integration**, this question becomes even more pertinent.

The willingness of states to not just cooperate but in fact integrate at the regional level can be explained through a variety of theoretical lenses. **Federalism**, for example, emphasizes that integration is a solution to the anarchic condition of the international system. If sovereignty and the pursuit of national self-interest is the cause of conflict in the international system, then the creation of international federations can facilitate peace and cooperation through states pooling sovereignty to the federal level. Decisions taken within international federations of states would be in the interests of the collective, rather than favouring national self-interest. Jean Monnet, the author of the Schuman Plan which created the ECSC as the forerunner to the EEC, was himself a staunch advocate of European federalism.

Another theoretical perspective which can help us to explain why states might pursue integration is **liberal intergovernmentalism**. In 1993 Andrew Moravcsik published *The Choice for Europe* which argued that while EU member states have their own distinctive national preferences, they choose to bargain with one another at the European level. Decisions taken at the European level are then a reflection of the relative power of the member states and that bargaining process. Decisions to then pool sovereignty to the supranational level are also a rational choice made by states keen to increase the credibility of their mutual commitments, and to ensure compliance by others.

Another theoretical perspective which has also gained ground in European integration studies is **neofunctionalism**. Ernst Haas (pg. 114) theorized that the creation of supranational European institutions would lead to further political spillover as, over time, more competences would fall to the EU through a transfer of demands, expectations and even loyalties from the national to European level. From the neofunctional perspective, therefore, integration within regional organizations is a natural and logical process as states observe the functional benefits of pooling their sovereignty and ceding competence to the supranational level across more and more issues.

As we saw in Table 8.1, while the EU does have highly variable competence to act in international politics, it also stands markedly apart as a unique form of regional organization with supranational as well as intergovernmental capabilities. The aim of 'ever closer union' is also enshrined within the EU's various treaties. EU member states agree to not only cooperate with one another across some sectors, but to pool their sovereignty to the EU in others. By way of example, in all matters of trade policy the EU has exclusive competence. The EU therefore has supranational authority to negotiate on behalf of its member states in all trade negotiations. The EU is subsequently at its most state-like in international trade politics, having the competence to act and negotiate as one actor. In other fields, however, such as matters pertaining to the Common Foreign and Security Policy, member states are far more guarded about pooling their sovereignty to the EU. The EU, therefore, has only special competence in foreign and security matters, and can only act in a coordinating and facilitating role as directed by its member states.

Important also to note is that the EU's model of 'ever closer union' is somewhat unique among regional organizations, the majority of whom have followed very different paths to that of the EU. The African Union, for example, was originally designed to be deliberately weak as an intergovernmental body and purposefully avoided supranationalism. When the organization was created in 1964, many African states had only just regained their independence as former colonies, and thus sought to protect their new-found sovereign independence. The OAU Charter, therefore, explicitly states a determination to 'safeguard and consolidate the hard-won independence as well as the sovereignty and territorial integrity of our states, and to fight against neo-colonialism in all its forms'. Similarly, the 'ASEAN-way' is expressly one of regional cooperation with non-interference. In 1976,

Sovereignty pooling
The sharing or pooling of decision-making powers between states in a system of international or regional cooperation.

Integration
The process by which states progressively deepen their cooperation so that their decision-making, laws, legal and political systems are shared.

Federalism
A mixed mode of government where power is shared between a central government and regional governments. As a philosophy, Federalism advocates for the creation of federal forms of government.

Liberal intergovernmentalism
A theory of European integration which argues that states continue to play a central role in integration and that, through processes of intergovernmental bargaining, states will advance their national preferences to the European level.

Neofunctionalism
A theory of European integration which argues that integration will occur through a process of spillover. As states integrate in the economic sphere, pressure will extend to integrate in other related sectors. Over time, spillover will produce more and more sectors given over to supranational decision-making.

ASEAN member states signed the Treaty of Amity and Cooperation in Southeast Asia which outlined 'mutual respect for the independence, sovereignty, equality, territorial integrity, and national identity of all nations', 'the right of every state to lead its national existence free from external interference, subversion or coercion', and 'non-interference in the internal affairs of one another' as fundamental principles. As postcolonial scholars also stress, the emphasis for many former colonial states in their pursuit of regionalism has been far less about pooling sovereignty, as it has been about protecting and reinforcing their national sovereignty (Clark 2011: 296).

When we return to the EU, we can also identify signs of strain concerning integration and sovereignty pooling. While federalism may have been in the EU's foundations, it has not always been an obvious part of its evolution. The early demise of a European Defence Community, followed by Charles de Gaulle's staunch anti-federalist resistance to the supranational authority of the EEC in the 1960s, have continued to echo throughout the EU's evolution. The UK's resistance to 'ever closer Union' was also a hallmark of its EU membership, during which time it cited UK sovereign interests on such frequent occasions that it was branded the EU's 'awkward partner'. The UK's unprecedented withdrawal from the EU was also evidence of the limitations of federalism and sovereignty pooling; with the 'Leave' campaign exerting the need for the UK to 'reclaim' its sovereignty from Brussels (pg. 87).

LINK

Image 8.2 During the 'Gilets Jaunes' (Yellow Vests) protests in France, a protester marks his vest 'Frexit' in support of France leaving the EU. In the wake of the Brexit referendum in 2016 and formal exit in 2020, several public protests and high-profile politicians called for 'exits' in other EU member states, raising fears of possible 'Oexit' (Austria), 'Nexit' (Netherlands), and 'Polexit' (Poland), for example.

Source: Kiran Ridley/Getty Images.

Consider

There has been a growing literature on European disintegration theories, with scholars increasingly focused on possible European disintegration and the extent to which EU member states will either seek more differentiation and partial exits, or which will see the EU stagnate or mutate into a looser form of regional organization where cooperation and defence of sovereignty regains ascendancy over integration and pooling of sovereignty (Krastev 2017; Taylor 2008; Webber 2018; Wurzel and Hayward 2012; Zielonka 2006).

Explore

In 2020 the Asian Development Bank produced a report on 'Disintegration of the EU and the Implications for ASEAN'. The report stressed that 'if the EU, despite 70 years of planned integration with a significant degree of success, is not immune to disintegration, then ASEAN with its still insignificant degree of integration is surely vulnerable to such a possibility, unless it seriously initiates a process to address its root causes before it is too late.' (Asian Development Bank 2020). Find out more at www.adb.org

Connect

When countries become candidate countries for EU membership, they must not only work to align their economic, financial and political systems with those of the EU, but must commit to the principle of 'ever closer Union' as signatories of the EU's treaties. New EU member states must also commit to adopting the euro (pg. 216) as their new currency after they meet eurozone criteria. For most other regional organizations, including those in Europe such as NATO, integration and sovereignty pooling is not a criterion of membership, nor will they likely become so. Revisit the 'Debating IOs' section in Chapter Seven and the discussion about whether international organizations are actors or agents (pg. 118–22). How might you apply the principal-agent model and organizational culture approach to explain why some regional organizations integrate, while others only cooperate?

Predict

Are there limits to European integration and sovereignty pooling? How far do you think EU integration (or disintegration) might go?

Scan the QR code for access to explore weblinks and more resources.

CONCLUSION

In this chapter we have considered the concept of regionalism and the proliferation of regional organizations since World War Two. Consideration has been given to the scope of regional organizations, including in security, economics and politics, and the extent to which scope expansion has occurred over time creating intricate regional networks of alliances, agreements and unions of states working cooperatively for collective gain. In this chapter we have also shone a spotlight on the origins, historical evolution and competence of the European Union as one of the most integrated and institutionalized regional organizations in the world. Yet, as the EU example has shown, an enduring question remains for scholars of international politics in asking to what extent states should not only cooperate, but in fact integrate, within regional organizations. As this discussion has reflected, while the EU model of 'ever closer Union' presents us with an impressive example of a seemingly successful integration project, the EU must also be understood as a somewhat unique form of regionalism because of this. In the EU, along with most other regional organizations, the limits of cooperation is stark. Defence of national interest, identity and sovereignty remain core concerns for states, which can in turn limit the scope of regional cooperation and likely integration with regional organizations. Why not test your knowledge from this chapter and dig a little deeper by trying the following toolkit exercise which asks, '*Was the Battle of Marawi a turning point for the ASEAN-way?*'

TOOLKIT

Was the Battle of Marawi a turning point for the ASEAN-way?[1]

THINK

- Reflect again on the concepts of internal and external sovereignty (pg. 18). How do you understand the concept of non-interference?

OBSERVE

Image 8.3 Filipino troops capture an Islamic State flag in Marawi City, July 2017.

Source: Jes Aznar/Getty Images.

- Over the 2000s the Philippines, along with numerous other states in Southeast Asia, suffered a spate of attacks by terrorist organizations (pg. 155). In 2017, Islamic State (pg. 155) besieged the city of Marawi on the southern island of Mindanao in the Philippines, declaring its intention to carve out a Southeast Asian caliphate. The Battle of Marawi, also known as the Marawi siege or the Marawi crisis, shocked both the Philippines and the region (Al Jazeera 2017). Indonesian President Joko Widodo described the Battle of Marawi as a 'wake-up' call for Southeast Asia. Terrorism went on to become the top agenda item at ASEAN's 2017 Summit.
- ASEAN members have historically favoured national, or at most bilateral, policies to tackle terrorism, seeing it as a national rather than a regional problem. While ASEAN had made some tentative steps towards closer counter-terrorism cooperation, including the 2007 ASEAN Convention on Counter-Terrorism and the 2009 ASEAN Comprehensive Plan of Action on Counter-Terrorism, not all ASEAN members have been actively involved, and the influence of these initiatives has remained marginal due to lack of enforcement or compliance mechanisms.
- Since Marawi, ASEAN defence ministers have agreed several multilateral initiatives intended to strengthen regional counter-terrorism cooperation. One landmark agreement was the 2018 'Our Eyes' intelligence sharing platform, agreed by six of ASEAN's ten members, to enable intelligence sharing to combat future threats of terrorism, radicalism, violent extremism and other non-traditional threats in the region.

[1]With special thanks to Nate Wilson whose dissertation project helped inspire this toolkit topic.

ORGANIZE

- Realists would argue that security and defence are sovereign national interests and matters of high politics (pg. 187). While ASEAN states may look to pursue some forms of economic cooperation, along with more ad hoc measures for collective regional security, any security measures will be as loose alliances where states retain full autonomy and authority in all decisions being made (pg. 119).
- Postcolonialism explains the reticence of former colonial states to relinquish national sovereignty to regional organizations, with organizations like the African Union and ASEAN deliberately established on intergovernmental structures, where national sovereignty and non-interference are mutually respected and upheld (pg. 25).
- Liberal intergovernmentalism would suggest that ASEAN members are already seeing the significant benefits of integrating more closely in economics. Initiatives like 'Our Eyes' will be a direct result of member state bargaining, recognizing the necessity for collective action, and if closer integration follows this will be because ASEAN member states recognize the need to increase the credibility of their mutual commitments, and to ensure compliance by others.
- Reflect again on the discussion of functionalism (pg. 113) and neofunctionalism in this chapter (pg. 139). What might a neofunctionalist explanation be for ASEAN's 'Our Eyes' initiative?

LINK

- *Consider*: What lessons can be drawn from the EU example of how far states will go to pursue closer regional cooperation? How might the EU example compare to ASEAN's counter-terrorism efforts?
- *Explore*: When ASEAN enlarged in the 1990s to include Vietnam, Laos, Myanmar and Cambodia, it raised concerns over a 'two-tier ASEAN' and the development gap between ASEAN's old and newer members. In 2000 the ASEAN Heads of State agreed to adopt a special programme called the 'Initiative for ASEAN Integration'. Find out more about the initiative at https://asean.org. You can also explore the background to the Battle of Marawi, as well as ASEAN's response by looking into the media coverage at https://asiaconflictwatch.com and https://theaseanpost.com.
- *Connect*: The ASEAN-way is founded on the principle of non-interference. The Initiative for ASEAN Integration was implemented as a functional response to the economic disparities between ASEAN members after its enlargement. To what extent might initiatives like 'Our Eyes' now signal a softening of the non-interference principle to facilitate greater regional cooperation in security and defence as well?
- *Predict*: How far might ASEAN member states go in pursuit of regional security cooperation or integration to address the rising threat from Islamic State?

Scan the QR code for access to explore weblinks and more resources.

SHARE

- Answer the question '*Was the Battle of Marawi a turning point for the ASEAN-way?*'

  Have you considered writing up your response to this question as a blog post? For some helpful tips on blog writing check out *How to – write a blog* (pg. 222).

HOW TO

TAKE A POSITION

The first time your tutor asks, 'What do you think?' can be just as intimidating as it is exciting, and in international politics you may well be surrounded by others who you feel have loads of opinions! Remember though that your opinion matters. The key now is to carve your opinions into informed and justified positions that will enrich your academic research and writing. Here are a few top tips to help you start developing and taking a position in international politics.

Look at all the angles

Knowledge breeds confidence, and one of the principal keys to success in developing your position is to do your research. Whether you have an opinion already or haven't yet decided, you need to read around your topic so you can get a sense of the range of viewpoints that are out there. To be able to take a position ultimately requires you to know the different positions that you *could* take. Work through the TOOLS strategy we've used throughout this book. **T**HINK about your own feelings or assumptions and **O**BSERVE the different perspectives at play. When you read a journal article, or a newspaper, or a report, therefore, reflect on what they have said. Do you agree with the arguments that they have made and the reasons they make them? Why? Be careful also to avoid **confirmation bias**. Try to push yourself to take an opinion on the things you read and listen to in international politics and then reflect on the other angles that could be presented. That is not to say you should be overly cynical or critical of others, but rather to encourage you to develop your own independent thinking, and to hone your opinions through informed reasoning.

Get off the fence!

Having done some research and started to think about your own opinions on a subject, you then need to reason out which of the different angles presents the most compelling case. **O**RGANIZE your thinking logically. Consider the available evidence. Which perspective or argument is most clearly justified by the evidence? Which theoretical perspective has the greatest explanatory power (pg. 70) in your opinion? In international politics you will find that there are often a range of possible explanations for something but that in your research and writing you are called upon to highlight which explanation is most compelling. Aim to avoid sitting on the fence and take a side. This can take some practice, especially when it feels like all sides are making equally strong or valid arguments. But by forcing yourself to take a side you are then having to think about how you will build your case, what evidence you will use to defend it, and to justify why other arguments are perhaps weaker in their explanation (which brings in your critical analysis – see *How to – develop critical analysis skills* (pg. 163)).

Confirmation bias
Where a researcher searches for, interprets, favours or recalls information that confirms their own beliefs or values.

State your case

Now you have a position, you need to present it clearly. There's very little point having a position if you can't justify it, so reflect on how you will state your case. In essay or exam questions that deliberately call for you to take a position then you want to set it out in your introduction, that is to state, 'I will argue …' You then want to use the main body of the essay to justify why you have taken the position you have, showcasing your evidence and support, and giving justification for why you feel other approaches were deemed weaker in their explanatory power. Then reaffirm your position in the conclusion, highlighting your key points (see also *How to – approach an international politics essay* (pg. 182) which includes a section on structure).

Do also be consistent in defence of your position. It's obviously good to be able to show critical reflection of other perspectives, and to even show the potential weaknesses of your own argument, but avoid undermining yourself. Take some confidence in the stance you have taken and the research behind it. Avoid switching positions halfway through because you've talked yourself out of it or getting to the conclusion and missing that chance to say, 'This is what I think and why.'

9 Non-state actors

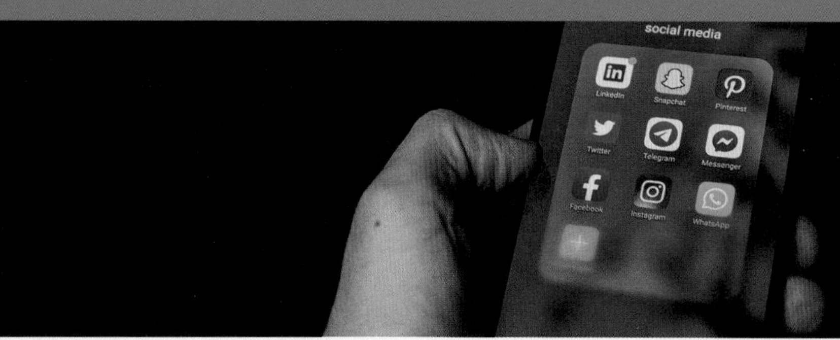

Pexels / Magnus Mueller

Abstract

In this chapter you will be introduced to the various non-state actors within today's international system. The chapter first elaborates on the concept of the non-state actor, and the evolution and spread of various types of non-state actors within international politics. From there you will address what may be considered the light and dark side of civil society, addressing the spread of international NGOs, advocacy networks and social movements, before looking at what may be defined as *uncivil* society and the various violent non-state actors that operate within our international system. The chapter then turns its focus on to multinational enterprises (MNE) and the networks of international associations representing MNE interests. The chapter concludes with a toolkit exercise asking, *'What is the power of the "Tech Titans" in international politics?'*

UNDERSTANDING NON-STATE ACTORS

In the previous few chapters of this section dedicated to actors within international politics, we have addressed the state as an actor, along with the widening architecture of international organizations (IOs) and regional organizations who can act within our international system. Already, therefore, we have seen that not only is the sovereign state a contested actor, but that actors other than states have the capacity to act in international politics. The aim of this chapter is to offer introduction to the wide network of other non-state actors at work in our international system today.

Non-state actors are organizations which are autonomous of governments and the international and regional organizations they join. According to Josselin and Wallace (2001: 3), non-state actors are those organizations 'largely or entirely autonomous from central government funding and control: emanating from civil society, or from the market economy, or from political impulses beyond state control and direction'. Non-state actors are typically transnational in their relations, often operating as networks that transcend national borders. Non-state actors also have agency – that is, they have the capacity to act within international politics (pg. 61), and therefore have the capacity to 'affect political outcomes, either within one or more states or within international organizations' (Josselin and Wallace 2001: 4).

Consider for a moment that, by 2021, Apple was one of the wealthiest companies in the world with a market capitalization – or total dollar market value – of $2 trillion: a value roughly equivalent to the gross domestic product (GDP) of Italy. Reflect further on the fact that one of the very first **non-governmental organizations** (NGOs), the International Committee of the Red Cross, established in 1863, advocated for the humanitarian treatment of wounded soldiers, and was among the first lobbyists for a League of Nations and International Labour Organization (pg. 110). Consider also, that it was an international terrorist network, Al Qaeda, that attacked the United States on 11 September 2001, causing such dramatic ripple effects in US foreign policy that we are still observing the consequences over twenty years later (pg. 155).

Non-governmental organization
Non-profit, voluntary organizations that operate largely or entirely autonomously from national governments.

In the past half-century, non-state actors have gained increasing prominence within international politics. As states began to lower their economic barriers and newly formed international economic organizations were strengthened (pg. 211–2), multinational enterprises (MNE) began to flourish. The spread of democracies, and the opening of societies after the Cold War, further enabled the growth of international NGOs and **Transnational Advocacy Networks** (TANs) to spread across borders. Increased and easier international travel further expanded non-state actor networks and facilitated the presence of growing numbers of NGOs and TANs in the various intergovernmental conferences that began to spread after the 1970s, as well as within international and regional organizations.

Transnational Advocacy Network
A network of individual NGOs, operating within and across different countries, with the purpose of advocating a common cause or issue.

As international organizations formed to address common transnational problems that individual states alone struggled to address, so too did non-governmental organizations (NGOs) who sought to influence those deliberations, rallying mass publics to ensure that citizens' voices were heard. As an example, NGO presence at the UN Framework Convention on Climate Change Conference of the Parties (COP) in Kyoto in 1997 numbered 277 NGOs. By 2021, the Glasgow UNFCCC COP included over 2,000 NGOs (UNFCCC 2022a). The communications revolution has also significantly advanced cross-border communication, information gathering and sharing, enabling non-state actors to connect more easily. Social media has particularly enhanced the ability of non-state actors to reach wider audiences. Any networked non-state actor, whatever their political purpose or ambitions, can now connect with other like-minded individuals and organizations and rally public support through Twitter/X, Facebook, WhatsApp, Telegram and other social media and instant messaging sites. The presence of non-state actors within the daily practice of international politics has therefore noticeably increased in recent decades and, with it, a growing influence and capacity to push for and even, at times, enact change within international politics.

Reflect again on Table 4.5 *Comparing theoretical approaches in international politics* (pg. 65–6). What do these different theoretical approaches tell us about the significance of state and non-state actors within international politics? What do you think?

There is a somewhat binary notion in attributing all actors other than the state into one category of 'non-state actor'. Important to highlight, however, is that the term non-state actor, in fact, captures a highly diverse grouping of different actors that we would consider autonomous from central government control. Non-state actors include not only organizations commonly associated with civil society, such as NGOs, TANs and social movements. The term is also used to describe violent non-state actors (VNSAs) associated more with *un*civil society, such as terrorist organizations, paramilitary groups, private armies and militias, or criminal gangs. Non-state actors also comprise numerous transnational economic actors as well, such as banks, MNEs and economic associations. In each variation of non-state actor, however, autonomy from the state is a common characteristic.

It would also be misleading to suggest that states and non-state actors do not frequently intersect. MNEs – such as Apple – still retain a home base for their parent company. NGOs, in addition to lobbying governments, do also often work directly with governments in providing operational services for specific programmes. MNEs also often work in public-private partnerships with governments to procure and deliver certain projects. States have also, at times, created or supported private militias or paramilitary groups as proxy forces in internal conflicts rather than using their own conventional forces (pg. 171). There can therefore be some blurring of the lines between public (governmental) and private (non-governmental) actors within both domestic and international politics. For the purposes of this chapter, though, we will focus more on distinct types of non-state actors, their main characteristics and the methods they use to exert influence within international politics.

CIVIL SOCIETY AND NON-STATE ACTORS

One of the most well-researched categories of non-state actor within international politics concerns those organizations, networks and movements commonly associated with **civil society**. Civil society is associated with the 'third sector', operating autonomously of governments and businesses, and providing a voice for the citizenry to debate and shape the future of the state and the policies enacted within it. A key function of civil society is its oversight in the management of state affairs. In fact, civil society is thought to work at its best 'in an environment of democratic governance where fundamental freedoms are guaranteed, and where open and fair participation in public affairs is the norm' (Nzau 2018: 438). Within contemporary international politics, the emergence of a *global civil society* has also played an important role in overseeing the management of international affairs.

Civil society
A society or community of citizens linked by shared interests who work collectively to pursue common actions.

The function of global civil society goes far further than oversight, however. Global civil society is also associated with forms of **direct democracy**, ensuring that the voice of the people is brought directly into international politics through debate and dialogue on issues of concern.

Direct democracy
A form of democracy in which the citizens are the ones who rule, without the need for representatives to serve as proxies.

Global civil society 'represent[s] the needs, the interests, and the immediate problems of people *over the world*' (Chandhoke 2005: 370 emphasis added). According to Germain and Kenny (2005: 1) 'the idea of "global civil society" has now become a common place term … the vision of a growing web of voluntary civic associations engaged in dialogue, debate and struggle over the unfolding direction of the economic and political organization of the world.'

Global civil society can particularly be characterized in the following ways. It is:

1. A *transnational society* of like-minded citizens, committed to working together to influence decision-makers in the furtherance of common goals.

2. A *networked society*, organized through both formal and informal organizations, networks, associations and movements.
3. A *space*, where multiple private actors operate socially to act globally, whether in cyberspace or in person at international conferences.

There are various ways that civil society organizes to bring the voice of the people into international politics. One of the most well recognized forms of civil society organization are non-governmental organizations (NGOs). As non-profit organizations, NGOs are not driven by commercial objectives – they are therefore distinctive from multinational enterprises (addressed later in this chapter) – but are created with the express purpose of advancing social, cultural, educational, environmental or other objectives. NGOs are therefore characterized as organizations who advance a particular societal cause.

NGOs can be distinguished by the scope and area of their activities. NGOs may operate at a local, regional, national or international level. The marked growth of NGOs and, more particularly, international non-government organizations (INGOs), since the 1970s and again after the Cold War, saw an increasingly transnationalized civil society spread into newly formed democracies in former communist states and the Global South. Well-known examples of INGOs include Amnesty International, Greenpeace and Oxfam. We can also distinguish NGOs by their area of activity or remit. ONGOs (operational NGOs), for example, specialize in providing specific operational functions, such as in providing humanitarian aid or development support. TANGOs are technical assistance NGOs, DONGOs are donor-organized NGOs and ENGOs are environmental NGOs, while BINGOs are business and industry NGOs, for example.

While NGOs began to flourish towards the latter quarter of the 20th century, it was not until the UN Conference on Environment and Development held in Rio de Janeiro in 1992 that they became a more established presence at international conferences. Over 2,000 NGOs participated at the Rio 'Earth Summit', now widely acknowledged as a 'breakthrough point' for NGO involvement in international politics (Kelly 2008). The Rio Earth Summit was to highlight not only the presence, but the influence of NGOs within international politics, particularly where it concerned **low politics** issues, such as in environmental and climate policy, humanitarian and development issues, and the advocation of human rights agendas (Kelly 2008: 94). Numerous studies have since focused on the authority and influence of NGOs within the UN and related international conferences. Joachim (2003), for example, argues that NGOs can influence states' interests by **framing** problems, solutions and justifications for political action. Stroup and Wong (2016) suggest that INGOs have three distinct types of authority within international politics, including *delegated* authority, *expert* authority and *principled* authority (Table 9.1) which 'allows these actors to set agendas, make, implement, and enforce rules; and then evaluate, monitor, and adjudicate outcomes' (Stroup and Wong 2016: 141).

Since 1992, NGOs have become increasingly networked, well organized and professionalized, evolving across many issue areas as Transnational Advocacy Networks (TANs). TANs are made up of multiple like-minded NGOs, operating within and across multiple different countries, working specifically towards advocacy of a common issue. In 1998, Keck and Sikkink highlighted the increasing activities of TANs as 'networks of activists, distinguishable largely by the centrality *of principled ideas or values* in motivating their formation' (Keck and Sikkink 1998: 1 emphasis added), and the various tactics TANs could use to initiate policy change. Like INGOs, TANs can also exert the same types of authority highlighted in Table 9.1.

Because of their networked nature, TANs can more strategically generate and use information in their lobbying efforts. Drawing on local testimonials, expert knowledge or

Low politics
A traditional realist framing used to describe policy fields concerned more with individual/domestic concerns such as welfare, the environment, humanitarian issues or health policy. Distinct from high politics (pg. 187) used to identify issues of concern to national security.

Framing
A persuasive tactic where information is presented in such a way as to highlight specific objectives and priorities.

Table 9.1 International NGO authority and influence within international politics

Type of INGO authority	Description
Delegated	Where an INGO is tasked by states, IOs or regional organizations to monitor implementation of a treaty or oversee the operation of a particular programme.
	Influence through oversight
Expert	Where an INGO's technical or expert knowledge places it in an authoritative position to inform international debate, shape international agendas, and influence norms and rules.
	Influence through agenda-setting
Principled	Where an INGO is perceived as legitimate in its claims, being seen as both accountable and principled in the eyes of global audiences. Also associated with moral authority.
	Influence through legitimacy

Source: Adapted from Stroup and Wong (2016).

technical expertise from among their membership, TANs can publicize and forward critical information, significantly enhancing their international advocacy efforts. TANS, which also include **epistemic communities** of experts working on common global problems, then use their expertise to inform decision-makers, making authoritative claims based on their knowledge and research. For example, it was scientific evidence provided by an epistemic community of atmospheric scientists that highlighted the necessity of banning chlorofluorocarbons (CFCs) because of the harm they caused to the ozone layer in the 1980s. The result was the Montreal Protocol – an international treaty designed to protect the ozone layer by phasing out the production of CFCs.

Epistemic community A transnational network of individuals with recognized knowledge-based expertise considered to have authority to inform decision-makers about specific problems within international politics, identify possible solutions and assess policy outcomes.

As depicted in Figure 9.1, by working collectively as networks of advocacy NGOs, TANS can also magnify civil society's contribution to international and regional organizations, not only ensuring oversight and transparency, but supplying knowledge, expertise and testimonials to inform international proceedings. More recent academic research highlights how TANs are also increasingly collaborating with other TANs across issue areas within international politics, forming 'super-networks' within civil society (Schapper and Dee *forthcoming*; Schapper 2021). These super-networks connect TANs from different policy fields, with the goal of achieving common humanitarian objectives. For example, the International Campaign to Abolish Nuclear Weapons (ICAN) includes thirty-seven TANs and 650 individual NGO members across 110 countries. Each TAN connects NGOs across multiple countries within a specific policy field, such as youth groups, faith organizations, women and gender groups, trade unions, press and media associations, health organizations, lawyers, education, science-based advocacy groups, and humanitarian and peace groups. As a super-network, ICAN brings all these TANs together under the common humanitarian umbrella of campaigning to abolish nuclear weapons. In so doing, ICAN has been able to magnify the voice of transnational civil society, pooling the respective strengths of each of

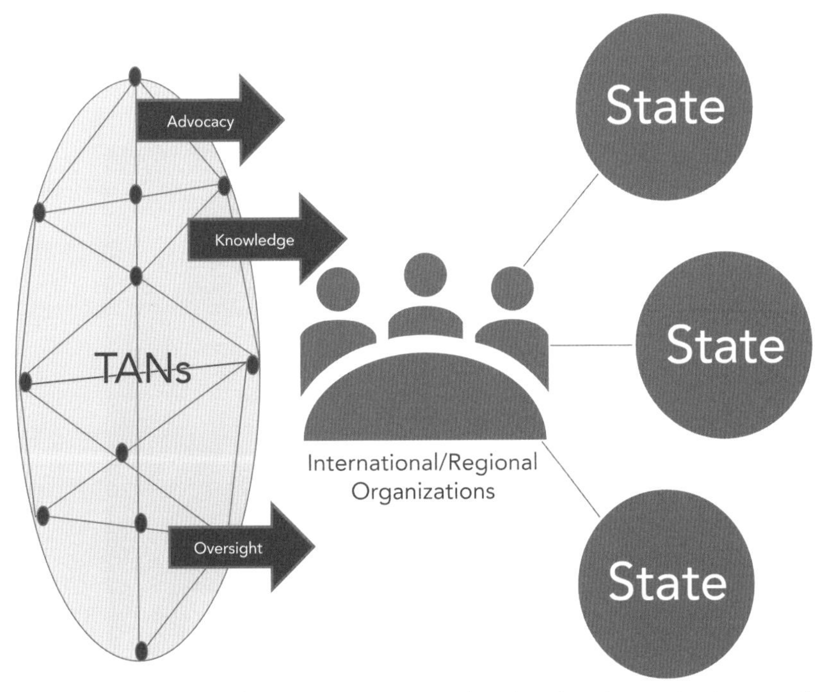

Figure 9.1 The role of TANs in international and regional organizations, and related international conferences

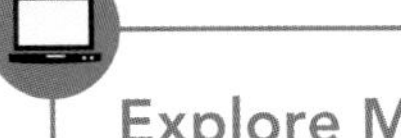

Explore More

The International Campaign to Abolish Nuclear Weapons (ICAN) is a super-network of TANs and other NGOs working together to achieve a world free of nuclear weapons. In 2019 ICAN won the Nobel Peace Prize for its campaigning role in pushing forward the Treaty on the Prohibition of Nuclear Weapons (TPNW). You can watch ICAN's Laureate speech at www.icanw.org/nobel_prize which highlights what ICAN is, how they collectively advocated for the TPNW, and now continue to lobby for its future ratification. Look also at the discussion on nuclear deterrence and disarmament, and the longer-term challenges associated with ratifying TPNW on pages x-x. You can also explore more recent developments at https://banmonitor.org/tpnw-status.

Scan the QR code for access to explore weblinks and more resources.

its TAN and NGO constituencies, enhancing their principled authority and enabling them to push for progress in global nuclear disarmament.

The networked and increasingly professionalized nature of NGOs within international politics has nevertheless also raised questions over the representativeness of a 'global civil society'. As Keane (2003: 5) identifies, for example, 'a disproportionate number (over one-third) [of INGOs] have their main offices in the European Union and Switzerland'. Other critical scholars also reflect on the 'NGOization' that has followed the professionalization of NGOs and TANs as they shift towards more hierarchical organizational structures with permanent staff, managing directors and fundraisers (Alvarez 2009) which can further reinforce power asymmetries.

OBSERVE

Image 9.1 An image depicting citizens from around the world. Do all have a voice in 'global civil society'?
Source: Parabol/Unsplash.

Critical scholars emphasize that the term 'global civil society' should be used with caution (see Keane 2003: 2), as it can be associated with Western values, Western ideals of statehood, sovereignty and the international system, and by Western-based NGOs. Neera Chandhoke, for example, highlights the exclusive and exclusionary nature of many INGOs, making global civil society 'empowering for some and disempowering for many, accessible to some and inaccessible to many' (Chandhoke 2005: 360). Cox (1999: 10–11), meanwhile, distinguishes between 'top down' and 'bottom up' conceptions of civil society. Top down conceptions are where dominant forces penetrate and co-opt popular movements, whereas bottom-up conceptions see civil society as a realm where protest and alternatives put forward by the most disadvantaged within the world economy are heard.

Social movement A loosely organized effort by a large number of people to generate societal change through collective action, typically involving protest.

Another method of organization by which civil society brings the voice of the people to bear on international politics is through the mobilization of **social movements**. A social movement is defined as 'those sequences of *contentious politics* that are based on underlying social networks and resonant collective action frames, and which develop the capacity to maintain *sustained challenges against powerful opponents*' (Tarrow 1998: 2 cited in Kelly 2008 *emphasis added*). Examples of transnational social movements include the anti-globalization movement (also referred to as the global justice movement) that protested economic globalization and the international financial organizations seen to uphold international capitalism and the corporate interest. The movement was perhaps best known for its mass protests in Seattle against the World Trade Organization (pg. 211) in 1999.

A far more recent example of a transnational social movement is Black Lives Matter (BLM) (pg. 152–3). BLM is an international social, civil and human rights movement, formed specifically to challenge the racism, discrimination and racial inequality experienced by black people around the world. The movement began in the United States following several high-profile killings of black people by police. In 2020 the movement became transnational after the death of George Floyd, who was arrested and then killed by a police officer. Using social media as a platform of influence, BLM grew both as a slogan and movement as the hashtags #BLM and #blacklivesmatter went viral around the world. According to Patrice Cullors, one of the founders of the Black Lives Matter movement, 'the role of social media democratizes voices, especially black women voices' (BBC News 2021). Social media therefore became a significant magnifier and tool for the movement, vocalizing black voices, and facilitating the coordination of mass protests. Protests using the #BLM slogan took place around the world as activists came together to protest against racism and discrimination in their own countries. Research shows that #blacklivesmatter was used roughly 3.7 million times daily between 26 May and 7 June 2020 (Pew Research 2020). The mass mobilization of support and protest resulted in many European states removing cultural symbols associated with colonialism and slavery such as statues and artworks (pg. 290). In the United States, several cities also took steps to defund the police, prioritizing health and education services.

Whether as NGOs, TANs or social movements, civil society non-state actors have exerted considerable influence within international politics. Yet they also have their limitations. Civil society has no material capability to exert force. While social movements can inspire protest, which can potentially lead to civic violence, NGOs and TANs tend not to have a coercive influence. Rather, civil society exerts influence through persuasion, and the delegated, expert and principled authority associated with their argument, advocacy, protest and the legitimacy born from representation and accountability to the citizenry they represent. Civil society's greatest attribute, therefore, is its ability to organize, network and bring international citizenry together – an attribute that has been significantly enhanced by the advent and advance of social media. As we shall see in the next section, however, those same tools have also been utilized by *un*civil society, and the rise of violent non-state actors.

*UN*CIVIL SOCIETY AND VIOLENT NON-STATE ACTORS

As Josselin and Wallace (2001: 1) reflect, 'non-state actors are heroes and villains in different narratives of international politics'. Compared to NGOs, TANs and other elements of what may be seen as the light side of civil society, we must also identify a dark side, or 'uncivil' society made up of violent non-state actors (VNSAs) within our international system. VNSAs include any private organization or armed group autonomous of government that uses violence to attain its goals. While there is some divergence within the literature about which actors constitute a VNSA, there is general agreement that they include **warlords**, **militias**, **paramilitary forces**/military companies, **insurgents**, terrorist organizations and criminal organizations/gangs (Oktav, Parlar and Kurşun 2018: 4).

VNSAs can be further divided into two categories – transcendental and transactional VNSAs. *Transcendental* VNSAs are those actors with a particular political, religious or moral cause who are willing to use violence to achieve their goals. Like NGOs, transcendental VNSAs seek to enact change. Unlike NGOs, VNSAs seek to fundamentally overhaul the system through violence, and to replace it with their own vision or philosophy (Varin and Abubakar 2017: 7). Examples of transcendental VNSAs particularly include terrorist organizations and insurgent organizations. *Transactional* VNSAs, by contrast, are those actors who are mainly concerned with economic profit maximization, and will either use violence, or trade in violence, to make that profit. Transactional VNSAs include, for example, criminal organizations or gangs who trade in people and/or black-market products and services, as well as paramilitary forces/military companies.

Warlord
A military commander who exercises control over a region, typically associated with failed or fragile states where the national government is weak and does not control the use of force within all territories.

Militia
A military force raised from a civilian population either to supplement the state's conventional armed forces in an emergency, or engaged in rebel or terrorist activities in opposition to the state's armed forces.

Paramilitary force
An unofficial military force, organized in the same way as a state's conventional military force, but separate from it. May be an irregular force like a militia, an auxiliary force like a national guard, or a private company.

Insurgency
A group of individuals fighting against a government or invading force.

The increasing number and presence of private military companies (PMC) within international politics in the last twenty years is of particular significance. Examples of PMCs include the Wagner Group, DynCorp, Sandline International and Blackwater. Each has been involved in conflicts around the world. Each is a private company providing armed combat or security services, using contract soldiers and mercenaries. As transactional VNSAs, private military companies are typically considered apolitical, offering their services to any government, international organization or sub-state actors who hires them. PMCs do, therefore, tend to blur the lines between VNSAs and multinational enterprises. PMCs are also increasingly blurring the lines over state sovereignty and the state's 'monopoly over the legitimate use of force' (pg. 93). An example of this can be seen in the activities of the Russian-based Wagner Group. The Wagner Group was reportedly deployed in Russia's annexation of Crimea in 2014, and again during the war against Ukraine in 2022 when Wagner supplemented Russia's conventional armed forces. Wagner Group soldiers have also been deployed in Syria, Central African Republic, Madagascar, Libya, Venezuela and Mozambique. In 2022 Wagner Group mercenaries were also welcomed by the Malian government to provide training, support and security to Malian service members and policy officers; replacing the French military forces that had been in place in Mali since 2013. Private military companies, therefore, represent a critical new dimension both to international conflict situations and to traditional understandings of the sovereign state.

ORGANIZE

Image 9.2 Protesters hold a banner reading 'Thank you Wagner' during a demonstration in Bamako, Mali in February 2022. The demonstration celebrated the announcement that France would be withdrawing its troops from Mali, with Wagner PMC contracted to provide military training and support to the country.

Source: FLORENT VERGNES/Getty Images.

In Chapter Two we addressed the emergence of the Westphalian state system and the concept of sovereignty. Reflect again on the principle of *internal sovereignty* as applied to the state (pg. 17), particularly as it concerns the monopoly and control over the use of force.

In Chapter Six we also considered the state as an actor in international politics (pg. 96–7) and the argument that it is a state's government that is 'the legal custodian of a state's sovereignty' (Morin and Paquin 2018). Reflect again on the notion of a failed state, and the Fragile States Index concerning state fragility (pg. 101).

In what ways do VNSAs impact state sovereignty? How might the rise of VNSAs such as the Wagner Group and other private military companies impact our understanding of a Westphalian (sovereign) state system?

Various VNSAs besides private military companies can exert influence within international politics. In contrast to civil society, who influence by persuasion, VNSAs exert influence through violence, fear, corruption and the insecurity and instability they create. Terrorist organizations have particularly dominated the international agenda in the past twenty to thirty years, as organizations that have spread to become transnational networks with multiple cells of operation.

The term *terrorism* in fact comes from the Latin word meaning 'to frighten'. A key element of any terrorist organization therefore is to enact change through fear, typically with non-combatants (civilians) as the primary targets for violence. Perhaps the most well-known example of a transnational terrorist organization is **Al Qaeda,** a militant extremist Sunni Islamic terrorist network that achieved global notoriety on 11 September 2001, when members of their organization hijacked four passenger planes flying over the eastern US and aimed them at landmark buildings in New York and Washington, including the Twin Towers of the World Trade Center in New York, and the Pentagon in Washington. After that, Al Qaeda operatives and their affiliates became the top target in the United States' War on Terror (pg. 169), and for other state-led counter-terrorist operations around the world.

Islamic State (ISIS) is another transnational terrorist organization that has links to Al Qaeda. ISIS is also unique as a terrorist organization, possessing some quasi-state-like qualities. ISIS has exerted its control over large territories in Iraq and Syria and seeks further expansion of the **caliphate** (pg. 142). Through its territorial control, ISIS has also established economic self-sufficiency, drawing on the natural resources, minerals and raw materials within its territories, as well as through criminal activities, such as extortion, kidnapping and ransom. For example, ISIS is thought to have control of around 60 per cent of Syria's oilfields and uses black-market routes and smuggling networks to trade (Oktav, Parlar and Kurşun 2018: 11). We can therefore understand ISIS as both a transcendental and transactional VNSA, being capable of profiting from its activities, while also pursuing a political and religious cause. Through its territorial expansion, ISIS has also had significant impact on regional security and international agenda through its involvement in the Syrian war (pg. 173).

In 2020 the United States' Federal Bureau of Investigation (FBI) Director, Christopher Wray, informed the US House Homeland Security Committee that 'terrorism remains the [FBI's] top priority', but highlighted how the threat to the US had now evolved to include 'lone actors inspired by foreign terrorists radicalized online and motivated to attack soft targets' (CBN News 2020). Much as civil society has used the communications revolution for networking, information sharing and awareness raising, so too has the internet and social media been used by terrorist organizations for online propaganda, radicalization and recruitment. For example, Al Qaeda launched an English language digital magazine which was thought to have inspired the Boston Marathon bombers in 2010 (Ward 2018). ISIS also has utilized social media to mobilize an estimated 40,000 foreign nationals from 110 countries to join the group (Ward 2018) and was thought to have almost 90,000 supporters on Twitter (Oktav,

Al Qaeda
A militant Islamic fundamentalist group, founded by Osama bin Laden in the late 1980s, responsible for numerous terror attacks against the United States, the deadliest of which included the 9/11 attacks that resulted in nearly 3,000 deaths.

Islamic State (ISIS)
A militant terrorist organization that developed from Al Qaeda with the goal of establishing a caliphate territory under strict sharia, Islamic rule. ISIS (also referred to as ISIL or Daesh) has established territorial control over parts of Iraq and Syria.

Caliphate
An Islamic state under the rule of a caliph or Islamic steward, considered to be a successor to the Islamic Prophet Muhammad. The last major caliphate was under the Ottoman Empire which was abolished in 1924.

Boko Haram
An extremist Islamic terrorist organization located in Nigeria. Boko Haram seeks to create an Islamic state in the country ruled by sharia law.

Al-Shabaab
A jihadist insurgent group active in Somalia and Kenya. Al-Shabaab rejects Somalia's modern borders and seeks to establish a Greater Somalia with an Islamic government that follows sharia law.

Parlar and Kurşun 2018: 13). In a report published by the UN Development Programme, the rise of communication technology in Africa was also highlighted as a 'double-edged sword' being used for social, political and economic development, but also for terrorist recruitment. The report stated that Twitter, Facebook, YouTube and other social media platforms were used by terrorist and insurgent organizations such as ISIS, **Boko Haram** and **al-Shabaab** as a 'low-cost tool to attract, train and communicate with followers and potential recruits' (UNDP 2018). We can therefore observe how *un*civil society with its various violent non-state actors has also prospered from a more networked and digitally interconnected world.

MULTINATIONAL ENTERPRISES AS NON-STATE ACTORS

Multinational enterprise
A business enterprise or organization that has its home base in one country, but has activities and assets across multiple other countries.

So far in this chapter we have considered the growth and influence of non-state actors from the light and dark side of civil society. We have observed how civil society actors, such as NGOs, TANs and social movements are non-profit organizations pursuing specific causes within international politics, exerting influence through oversight, persuasion, advocacy and protest. We have also considered how transcendental and transactional VNSAs have emerged within what we may identify as *un*civil society, capable of influencing international politics through the fear, violence, insecurity and instability that they propagate. In this section we turn now to consider another non-state actor, one that has considerable impact on our global economy, environment and development and which can also influence political outcomes within international politics, namely **multinational enterprises** (MNEs).

According to the UN Conference on Trade and Development (UNCTAD), MNEs are 'incorporated or unincorporated enterprises comprising parent enterprises and their foreign affiliates' (UNCTAD 2017: 3). MNEs are also referred to as multinational corporations (MNCs) or transnational corporations (TNCs). A key characteristic of an MNE is its 'transnationality', referring to its geographic spread across a home country and one or more host countries (UNCTAD 2007: 1). One of the earliest examples of an MNE was the Dutch East India Company (VOC) (pg. 19), founded in 1602, which advanced Dutch trading interests throughout the Indian Ocean. The VOC's home country was the Netherlands, but it had an operational headquarters in Batavia, in modern-day Jakarta, and an established network of outposts across the East Indies. The VOC was itself a multinational trading enterprise, reaping the profits of monopolies, managed by force, of trade routes and commodities around the East Indies.

Foreign direct investment
The acquisition of stakes in a foreign company or project by a business from another country.

Value chain
The progression of activities by which a business delivers a final product or service, with each part of the chain an identified step at which value is added such as sourcing, manufacturing and marketing.

MNEs oriented more towards the production of goods began to emerge and prosper during the second industrial revolution between 1870 and 1910. These MNEs drew heavily on colonial resources and bases, with the production of raw materials through mining, and commodities such as bananas, rubber and oil. Fast-forward to the 21st century and today four of the top ten MNEs, ranked by their foreign assets, are involved in mining, quarrying and petroleum, including Shell plc, TotalEnergies SE, Exxon and BP (Table 9.2). The number of MNEs has further increased since the turn of the 21st century, from around 37,000 parent companies in the early 1990s (with around 170,000 foreign affiliates), to 78,000 parent companies by 2006 (with at least 780,000 foreign affiliates) (UNCTD 2007: 12). Employment in foreign affiliates of MNEs has also subsequently increased nearly threefold since 1990 (UNCTAD 2007: xvi), with **foreign direct investment** (FDI) increasing year on year.

A massive 80 per cent of global trade is linked to MNEs and the **value chains** (pg. 213–4) they create across their transnational network of operations (UNCTAD 2013). Today, the combined total assets of the world's top ten non-financial MNEs ranked by foreign assets (Table 9.2) accounts for nearly $3.4 trillion – more than the individual GDP of France, the United Kingdom, Italy and Canada – all of whom are represented at the G7 as the world's wealthiest, most advanced developed nations. Since the Covid-19 pandemic, digital MNEs, such as Meta, Twitter/X, Uber, Amazon and Alibaba, have also grown at a remarkable speed and are having an increasing impact on international trade and investment (UNCTD 2022).

Explore More

Find out more about global trends in foreign direct investment (FDI), including the countries which receive the most FDI, the inward and outward flows between developed and developing economies, and the impacts of COVID on world FDI. The UNCTD e-Handbook of Statistics includes loads of interactive and easily accessible information that you can explore at https://hbs.unctad.org.

Scan the QR code for access to explore weblinks and more resources.

Table 9.2 The world's top ten non-financial MNEs, ranked by foreign assets, 2021

				Assets (millions of $)	
Rank	Corporation	Home economy	Industry	Foreign	Total
1	Shell plc	United Kingdom	Mining, quarrying and petroleum	367 818	404 379
2	Toyota Motor Corporation	Japan	Motor vehicles	319 475	522 471
3	TotalEnergies SE	France	Petroleum refining and related industries	298 425	332 380
4	Volkswagen Group	Germany	Motor vehicles	262 835	598 719
5	Deutsche Telekom AG	Germany	Telecommunications	259 466	318 979
6	Exxon Mobil Corporation	United States	Petroleum refining and related industries	197 420	338 923
7	Stellantis NV	Netherlands	Motor vehicles	194 548	194 548
8	BP plc	United Kingdom	Petroleum refining and related industries	191 516	287 272
9	Anheuser-Busch InBev NV	Belgium	Food and beverages	179 313	217 627
10	British American Tobacco PLC	United Kingdom	Tobacco	172 480	185 153

Source: From UNCTAD World Investment Report, ©2022. Reprinted with the permission of the United Nations.

With their remarkable presence and overall impact on the global economy, MNEs are non-state actors that also have a marked influence within international politics. First, consider that MNEs have their parent company located in a home economy. As Table 9.2 reflects, three of the top ten MNEs in 2021 were based in the UK, two in Germany, and one each in Japan, France, the United States, Netherlands and Belgium. When you cast the net wider to consider the top 100 MNEs ranked by foreign assets, you find that only 1.4 per cent of the top 100 MNEs in 2021 were located in China, Hong Kong, Taiwan, Malaysia, Singapore, Korea and Saudi Arabia. Most of the top 100 MNEs have their parent company located in Japan, Europe or North America. Consider also, that in 2021 the United States accounted for 23 per cent of the total outward stock of global FDI – more than all the developing economies combined (UNCTAD 2022: Annex 2). As we develop this in fuller detail in Chapter Twelve focused on trade and finance, we could consider the wealth and power of MNEs to merely be an extension of the wealth and power of Western governments, and the power imbalance that exists within our international system. As the example of the VOC also highlighted, there is historically more blurring of the lines between public (governmental) and private (non-governmental) realms where MNEs are concerned.

Yet, as non-state actors, MNEs are autonomous of governments. As primarily economic actors, MNEs are driven not by political motives, but by the principles of an international market economy that is both free – based on a neoliberal model that favours open borders and free trade – and restricted – in so far as states remain guardians of their own national economies (pg. 209). MNEs have both the resources and capacity to act within international politics. How they influence international politics, however, may be both *directly* – through influence exerted directly over governments, international or regional organizations – or *indirectly* through their impacts on issues of concern within international politics. Take, for example, the issue of climate change (Chapter Fourteen). Recent studies have shown that one-fifth of global CO_2 emissions come from MNE global supply chains (Zhang et al. 2020). MNEs are involved in some of the most highly polluting industrial activities i.e. petroleum production and refinery (Table 9.2). Many MNEs also have foreign affiliates in host countries that maintain the lowest environmental standards, enabling MNEs to offset their emissions to developing countries and creating 'carbon-intense' regions (Zhang et al. 2020).

MNEs therefore bear significant responsibility for the world's total carbon emissions. That corporate responsibility has seen the Organization for Economic Cooperation and Development (OECD) publish specific guidelines for MNEs to serve as 'recommendations addressed by governments to [MNEs]'. Yet those recommendations serve only to 'provide *non-binding* principles and standards for responsible business conduct in a global context' (OECD 2011 emphasis added), highlighting the autonomy of MNEs and the challenge for states in both regulating and enforcing responsible business conduct in the international economy.

MNEs are identified not only as non-state actors who have played a central role in creating transnational problems such as climate change, but as key stakeholders in solving them. For example, the Montreal Protocol banning CFC gases, while negotiated by states, was targeted at companies, who then used their technological innovation and resources to find substitutes for ozone-depleting substances (Patchell and Hayter 2013). More recently, the UN's Sustainable Development Goals programme (pg. 233–4) has also brought in both business and non-business stakeholders to develop the UN's policy responses and highlighted the 'role of the diverse private sector, ranging from micro-enterprises to cooperatives to multinationals ... in the implementation of the new Agenda' (UN 2022b).

As well as their indirect influence and more implicit political nature, MNEs have also demonstrated their capacity to influence governments through a more explicit political dimension to their activities. MNEs not only closely monitor the socio-political environment but can also seek to influence national and international politics in their public relations and lobbying. Whereas direct lobbying at the local and national political levels may be done by larger MNEs' public relations teams seeking to influence the policies of their domestic politicians and decision-makers, at the international level this is more likely achieved collectively through **international trade or economic associations** representing the common views of multiple MNEs within an industry. The Internet Association, for example, was an American lobbying association that represented companies like Facebook, eBay, Google and Amazon, and was seen as a 'powerhouse' (Politico 2021), wielding considerable influence in Washington DC.[1] Other examples of

International trade association
An international association formed by, and for, businesses operating in a specific industry across multiple countries.

international associations for MNEs include the International Association of Oil and Gas Producers, the Telecommunications Industry Association, or the International Organization of Motor Vehicle Manufacturers.

At the international level, MNEs are also particularly active within international and regional organizations. Hundreds of international trade and economic associations have their headquarters based in international hubs such as Brussels, Geneva, Paris, New York and Washington, ensuring their ease of access to the EU, UNCTAD, WTO, OECD, UN and IMF, etc. Much like TANs, these international associations use advocacy and lobbying tactics to seek to influence decision-makers. For example, international trade associations respond to government, and international and regional organizations' **consultations**, feeding in the views of their members to everything from the specifics of a bilateral trade agreement being negotiated, to the implementation of the sustainable development goals (pg. 233). The largest MNEs and international trade associations representing collective MNEs directly lobby international and regional organizations. They attend intergovernmental conferences, they host side events, and network with policymakers and other representatives of civil society to further their interests. MNEs can therefore directly contribute to debate within civil society, particularly on issues concerning development, labour and the social and environmental impacts of economic activity.

Consultations A formal process initiated by governing institutions to source the views of experts and stakeholders involved in a given issue.

Consider

How integral should MNEs and NGOs be within international and regional organizations?

Explore

Many non-profit NGOs have expressed their discontent that they do not have the same level playing field as commercial enterprises when it comes to access and recognition by actors such as the EU. The EU has sought to establish a *European Statute for Associations and NGOs* to classify and distinguish NGOs, public benefit organizations and commercial enterprises. Find out more at www.eesc.europa.eu. The European Parliament resolution on this topic can also be found at www.europarl.europa.eu or scan the barcode for the direct links. The UN Secretary-General also recommended the creation of civil society focal points in all UN entities in the *Our Common Agenda* report (pg. 117).

Connect

Reflect again on the foreign policy toolkit available in Table 6.1 and the economic instruments outlined (pg. 98). Who do you think enacts these instruments? Consider also the debate surrounding the effectiveness and legitimacy of international organizations (pg. 119–23) and connect this with the discussions within this chapter on civil society legitimacy and authority. How does civil society representation impact the effectiveness and legitimacy of international organizations?

Predict

To what extent might efforts like the *European Statute for Associations and NGOs* or civil society focal points in the UN help to address the problem of exclusion and exclusivity among INGOs (pg. 151–2)?

---

[1]The Internet Association ceased operating in December 2021.

MNEs can also use more subversive tactics to influence international and regional organizations and their state members. For example, through financing 'front' grassroot NGOs, MNEs have sought to increase their access to global conferences and international decision-makers. By way of example, in 2016 the World Health Organization (WHO) (pg. 120–1) had to revise its rules of engagement for non-state actors after several large tobacco MNEs took over the International Tobacco Growers Association – intended for small tobacco farmers in developing countries – to infiltrate the WHO and lobby against tobacco controls (Muchlinski 2021). Now the WHO distinguishes between 'private sector entities' and other NGOs and has reasserted that the 'WHO does not engage with the tobacco industry or non-state actors that work to further the interests of the tobacco industry' (WHO 2016).

CONCLUSION

In this chapter we have considered a variety of networked non-state actors within our international system. These non-state actors comprise not only the NGOs, TANs and social movements that make up a 'global' civil society, but violent non-state actors such as terrorist organizations and private military companies, as well as economic actors such as MNEs. Each of these actors can be characterized by their autonomy from the state. Each also has agency, and the capacity to affect political outcomes within international politics. In each category of non-state actor, we have considered not only their distinctive characteristics, but their respective influence, whether direct or indirect, within international politics. For civil society actors, influence is largely persuasive, founded on their delegated, expert and principled authority as representatives of national and transnational publics. For violent non-state actors, influence is coercive, founded on fear, violence and the insecurity and instability they create. For MNEs, influence comes both implicitly through their substantial impacts on the global market economy, environment and development, and explicitly in the various forms of lobbying and association used to directly influence decision-makers. As we shall see as we move on to the next section of this book, these non-state actors will continue to feature as we start to engage more deliberately with specific issues in international politics. Before that, though, take a look at the following toolkit exercise, and apply your knowledge from this chapter by asking yourself, '*What is the power of the "Tech Titans" in international politics?*'

TOOLKIT

What is the power of the 'Tech Titans' in international politics?

THINK

- Speaking to the UN Human Rights Council, Facebook's CEO, Mark Zuckerberg, stated that a free and open internet is a human right that should belong to everyone (Hempel 2015). Yet as relatively unregulated cyberspace, the internet is also a space where fake news can be spread, hate speech can be promulgated, terrorist organizations can recruit, and personal details and user data can be misused.
- For many countries around the world, the internet is freely accessible and freely used. Yet, according to Freedom House (2022), global internet freedom is progressively declining. How much control, if any, do you think governments should have over the internet? How much control do you think governments should have over how MNEs use our internet data?

OBSERVE

Image 9.3 Facebook Inc CEO Mark Zuckerberg (right) with Chinese President Xi Jinping (centre), and then Head of China's Cyberspace Administration Lu Wei (left) at a meeting of US and Chinese companies in the United States in September 2015. Zuckerberg regularly meets with world leaders, including at the United Nations and European Union. In 2021 Facebook Inc rebranded as Meta.

Source: Pool/Getty Images.

- The Tech Titans (or Tech Giants) are the biggest MNEs involved in the information technology industry. They include US-based MNEs such as Google (Alphabet), Amazon, Meta, Apple and Microsoft, as well as Asian-based Titans such as Tencent and the Alibaba Group. The Tech Titans are all dominant MNEs in their fields of information technology, i.e. e-commerce, social networking, computer and telecommunication software, etc., and each have a market capitalization ranging from $1 trillion to $3 trillion. Because they offer their services to millions of users, they also have significant influence over user behaviour and control vast quantities of user data.
- According to Freedom House (2022), China is 'the world's worst environment for internet freedom'. Under President Xi, and then Lu Wei, China's powerful Cyberspace Administration has advanced the doctrine of 'cyberspace sovereignty' where an unregulated global internet is replaced by overlapping national internets (Segal 2020). In 2022, China released draft rules for anti-trust and data protection in an effort to further regulate the biggest tech firms.
- As China's 'internet tzar', Lu Wei was once listed in *Time* magazine's 100 Most Influential People (*Time* 2015). However, in 2018 Lu was prosecuted for taking bribes and sentenced to prison for fourteen years (Xinhua Net 2018).

ORGANIZE

- In a report by the Eurasia Group in 2022, the rise of a *Technopolar World* was identified as one of the top risks now facing the world. The report stated that 'The biggest technology firms are designing, building and managing an entirely new dimension of geopolitics. In this new digital space their influence runs deep, down to the level of individual lines of code.' The report goes on to state that 'key parts of people's daily lives, and even some essential functions of the state, increasingly exist in the digital world, and the future is being shaped by tech companies'. It further argues that 'Governments can fiddle at the margins' but they will not be able to 'limit the biggest platforms' ability to invest those profits in the digital sphere where they, not governments, remain the primary architects, actors, and enforcers' (Eurasia Group 2022). How does the idea of a *Technopolar World* relate to the realist paradigm of a bipolar, multipolar or unipolar world order (pg. 77)? Should we consider MNEs as part of a global balance of power?
- Reflect again on the economic strength of MNEs and how they can exert influence through political lobbying (pg. 158). Reflect also on the role that social media has played in helping both civil and uncivil society to network and connect across borders (pgs. 152, 155–6).
- Consider the different forms of power discussed in Chapter 6 (pg. 99–100). What forms of power do you think MNEs can exercise?

LINK

- *Consider*: In 2020 the EU unveiled two new laws – the Digital Services Act and the Digital Markets Act – intended to tackle illegal and harmful content, govern how the Tech Titans use consumer data, and limit their monopoly on digital services. In 2021 US lawmakers introduced five new bills aimed at limiting the power of the Tech Titans in the US following a sixteen-month investigation into the powers of Amazon, Apple, Google and Facebook. In 2023 the UK government also announced its plans to create a new regulator to police the dominance of the largest tech platforms, including Google, Amazon and Facebook.
- *Explore*: Scan the barcode to access various news reports on these national and regional efforts to regulate the Tech Titans. You may also want to explore Freedom House's annual Freedom on the Net report, including their interactive world map that shows internet freedom scores by country. Available online: https://freedomhouse.org/explore-the-map
- *Connect*: Revisit the definition of democratic and authoritarian states in Chapter Six (pg. 79). According to Freedom House (2022), the countries ranked 'free' in internet freedom are all democratic states, while many of the countries ranked 'not free' in internet freedom are also rated as 'consolidated or semi-consolidated authoritarian regimes'.
- *Predict*: In a political contest between the EU, the US, the UK and the Tech Titans, who do you think wins?

SHARE

- Answer the question, *'What is the power of the "Tech Titans" in international politics?'*

  You may look to approach this question as a policy brief, reflecting on a 'problem' within the topic and tailoring your brief to recommending a specific course of action. For some top tips on approaching policy brief writing, check out the following *How to – prepare a policy brief* (pg. 241).

HOW TO

DEVELOP CRITICAL ANALYSIS SKILLS

Critical analysis is one of the most important qualities that universities look for in their students and which employers find especially important in graduates. To think critically in academia is to develop a set of analytical skills that enables you to reflect on, evaluate, compare and connect the information you are engaging with in your studies (see also Brick et al. 2019: 77–80). Critical analysis is an essential skill in your development as a scholar, enabling you to move beyond the description of something, to actually analysing it. In this textbook you have in fact already begun to develop your critical analysis skills through our **TOOLS**, but let's now break this down further:

THINK

In our toolkit we use **T**HINK to consider our own opinions about issues within international politics, and to reflect on what we know. For any academic topic we tend to start with questions about what happened, when, where and who was involved (Learning Development 2010). This step is an important starting point on the path to critical analysis. Be aware, however, that if you were only to describe what happened, and your opinions about it, you would not be fully engaging in critical analysis. Of course, your tutors want to know what you think, and how well you can describe something, but they also want to see that your opinions have been informed by critical analysis. That is why this is a first, but not only, step you must take.

OBSERVE

In our toolkit, **O**BSERVE is an important means of reflecting on other perspectives, and what others might know. An important next step in developing your critical analysis skills then is to **O**BSERVE what other ideas, perspectives and arguments exist around your topic. As we know, in international politics there are often different, oftentimes competing, perspectives or arguments to a given topic. Scholars working on the same topic can also come up with starkly different arguments. As you start to explore beyond asking what happened, to advancing your understanding of 'why' something happened, you are directly engaging with critical analysis. This then becomes the foundation of your scholarship, pushing you beyond phrases like 'I think this because of that', to start showing your analysis of different ideas, such as 'Scholars disagree over *x* as evidenced by *y* and *z*.'

ORGANIZE

ORGANIZE in our toolkit enables us to make more abstract connections between events, arguments and the various concepts and theories we have engaged with. This is also an essential step in developing your critical analysis skills. As we know, different theoretical traditions offer different explanations, just as different concepts will shape how and what we prioritize in our analysis. In your coursework you should therefore be aiming to demonstrate your ability to evaluate, compare and contrast those different theories and concepts and to determine which are most relevant to your topic.

LINK and SHARE

LINK and **S**HARE in our toolkit are used to bring the threads of our analysis together and to communicate an informed argument based on our findings. These same steps apply when you have conducted your critical analysis. Once you have worked through **T**HINK, **O**BSERVE and **O**RGANIZE, you then want to reflect upon what your critical analysis tells you about the topic you are researching and the implications of your analysis. Ask yourself therefore: *Why does this analysis matter to how we understand that topic? How does this analysis inform your position?* When you are sharing the findings of your critical analysis, be that in an essay, presentation or other form of coursework, you can then show your audience how the evidence from your critical analysis informs what we know, what remains uncertain, and what you, in turn, think.

Part III

Understanding the issues

10 War and peace

Pexels / Derek French

Abstract

This first issues-oriented chapter introduces you to two prominently studied issues in international politics – war and peace. Focus first is given to how we can understand war and peace as a continuum of violence and non-violence, capturing some of the key differences between conflict and cooperation within international politics. From there we will look at the different types of war within today's international system, and the theoretical explanations for the causes of war. Our focus then turns to how states move between conflict and cooperation, and the different methods that can be used to prevent, manage and resolve conflicts. We shall then consider how peace can be understood, and the extent to which world peace is feasible. The chapter concludes with a toolkit exercise for you to try your hand at explaining the cause of Russia's 2022 invasion of Ukraine.

UNDERSTANDING WAR AND PEACE

On 24 February 2022 Russia invaded Ukraine, commencing the first major war in Europe for decades. For most observers, Russia's 'special military operation' into Ukraine was altogether unprovoked and unjustified. A total of 141 states voted in a UN General Assembly resolution deploring Russia's action. Media coverage in countries around the world immediately commenced reporting on Russia's initial advances, the devastation from bomb blasts, and the plight of Ukrainian refugees which numbered in the millions. Russia's incursion into Ukraine was perceived by the West as an aggressive push to reassert Russian influence in Eastern Europe. Ukraine's pivot towards the West, including its government's calls for Ukraine to join the EU and NATO, was seen by Russia's President, Vladimir Putin, as a direct threat to Russian security. When Russia invaded, NATO and EU member states stood behind Ukraine, stopping short of entering the war directly, but providing Ukraine's military with **lethal aid**, providing emergency humanitarian assistance, and targeting Russia's economy through **sanctions**.

The war has had profound geopolitical consequences for European and global security. During the first few months of the war, Russia threatened the West with the use of nuclear weapons if NATO allies continued to provide military equipment to Ukraine. The risk of a nuclear confrontation between Russia and NATO was thus reignited in a way the world has not seen since the Cold War. In the face of Russia's resurgence and incursion into the West, Finland and Sweden both then abandoned their neutral status and applied for NATO membership. The war has further impacted global energy supplies, sparked fears of a global food crisis, and further exacerbated a cost-of-living crisis faced by millions since the Covid-19 pandemic. It is perhaps no exaggeration to state that the Russia-Ukraine war signifies a turning point; a critical juncture which will shape analysis of international politics for many years to come.

War and conflict are intrinsic parts of the history – and likely future – of our planet, and an inherent characteristic of international politics. For better or worse, wars generate change. Wars may shift the balance of power, change territorial boundaries, alter who governs, or revise the predominant economic or political order within our international system. Peace by contrast brings the chance for growth, prosperity, stability. In its broadest sense, peace can even herald in social harmony and justice. For this reason, scholars of international politics are frequently drawn to the study of war and peace. We research the causes and geopolitical implications of **conflict**, and how it may evolve into war, and we study the chances for international **cooperation**, and the likely conditions for **peace**. While war can be understood as the very antithesis of peace, and vice versa, it can be more helpful to study them less as a dichotomy and more as a continuum (see also Davenport, Erik and Regan 2018) on which exists different degrees of conflict and cooperation within and between states and other political entities.

As Figure 10.1 reflects, war can be seen as the ultimate violent expression of conflict within our international system, much as peace is the ultimate expression of cooperation and non-violence. Yet not all conflict is violent and leads to war, just as not all cooperative efforts will result in peace. To understand these issues in international politics requires consideration of the degrees of conflict and cooperation that exist along this continuum. Focus must also be paid to the methods and processes that facilitate the prevention, mediation and resolution of conflicts, and which frequently serve as a bridge between conflict and cooperation, war and peace.

To delve closer into these issues, this chapter first introduces you to conflict and different types of war within international politics. We then consider how conflicting parties use conflict prevention, management and resolution techniques to resolve conflict, before looking at the discourse around peace within international politics. Throughout these next sections we shall also address different theoretical explanations for war, conflict prevention and peace, as well as reflecting on the actors who are involved, to help you build your understanding and develop your own toolkit for further research.

Lethal aid
Aid used for the purposes of conducting warfare such as provision of weapons or military vehicles.

Sanctions
Punitive or coercive measures imposed on a state or other political entity as punishment for certain actions. Can include economic, diplomatic or military measures.

War
Organized violent armed conflict between states or other political entities.

Conflict
Serious disagreement or argument between states and/or non-state actors, potentially leading to violence, due to incompatible interests, opinions or principles.

Cooperation
The action by states and/or non-state actors to work with others to pursue common objectives and benefits.

Peace
Understood in narrow terms as the absence of war, and in broader terms as a sense of harmony, political mutuality or social justice.

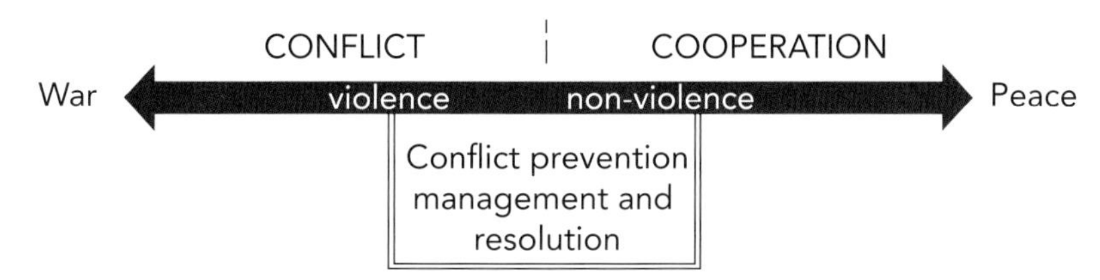

Figure 10.1 Understanding war and peace as a continuum

Are there conflicts in the world today that you care particularly about? What side of the conflict do you tend to sympathize with? Why?

Every conflict has different sides to consider. As observers, it can be easy to make judgements about a conflict based largely on reports you read or see in the news, or as an implicit bias caused by cultural or societal impressions of the conflicting parties. But be mindful of the judgements you make and why you make them. Think about the possible biases that you might have and how that shapes your perspective of the conflict you are observing.

WAR IN INTERNATIONAL POLITICS

Conflict has existed for as long as humankind has lived on this planet. As a species we are prone to disagreement and argument, and this can easily spread to conflict between groups, communities or even nations. Conflict does not always lead to violence, but when conflict becomes protracted, where national security is threatened, or where national interests are pursued through violent means, war is all too often the result. According to Carl von Clausewitz 'war is nothing but a duel on an extensive scale ... war therefore is an act of violence intended to compel our opponent to fulfil our will' (von Clausewitz et al. 2008: 12).

The first major wars were believed to have taken place more than 10,000 years ago, between prehistoric city-states in what is now modern-day Syria, Jordan and Iraq. The first historical record of war is thought to have come from Mesopotamia between Elam and Sumer around 2700 BC, with accounts of Elam's defeat being carved on stone tablets by the Sumerian victors. In 1457 BC, the first detailed history of a battle was written in hieroglyphs by the Egyptian chief military scribe Tjaneni concerning the Battle of Megiddo (located in modern-day Israel) between Kadesh and their Canaanite allies against the Egyptian Empire, led by Pharoah Thutmose III. Since then, wars have continued to be documented throughout history, being a common characteristic of the actions and interactions of city-states, dynasties, empires and the modern state itself.

As we saw in Chapter Two, the very evolution of our international system has been liberally littered and shaped by war in various forms. From the Thirty Years War that led to the Peace of Westphalia in 1648, to wars of revolution, wars of empire, world wars, the Cold War and its proxy wars, and localized civil wars. In fact, we can see that the very emergence of the sovereign state is closely interlinked to warfare. As Charles Tilly famously stated, 'war made the state and the state made war'. Consider again the concepts of internal and external sovereignty that we discussed in Chapter Two and how this related to the state as an actor in Chapter Six. The concept of internal sovereignty addresses not only a state's authority over the law and order of a clearly defined people and territory, but also the state's monopoly over the use of force by which it can uphold those laws and defend its land and people (pg. 18). External sovereignty, meanwhile, addresses a state's independence to determine its own interests and its freedom from external interference. Threats against a state's independence or any external interference in a state's internal affairs would therefore constitute a breach of state sovereignty potentially leading to war.

Image 10.1 Thutmose III smites his enemies at the Battle of Megiddo. This relief depicts what military scribe Tjaneni recorded in hieroglyphic writing on the Hall of Annals in the Temple of Amun-Re at Karnak – the first battle recorded in any such detail, including date of the battle, weapons used, force numbers and even body count.

Source: Wikimedia Commons.

As the modern state evolved, increasing reliance was placed upon its armed forces, funded by the wealth (and taxes) of its people and territories. The greater the territory, the greater the wealth, and the greater the army to defend it. The state's armed forces thus grew in both size and technological sophistication. For imperial powers, the quest for wealth was also furthered through colonization. Empires drew upon their colonies not only for material resources, but for the recruitment of soldiers, oftentimes by **conscription**.

Conscription
The compulsory enlistment of people for national service.

War on Terror
Launched by the United States government following the 11 September 2001 terrorist attacks. The War on Terror specifically targeted terrorist groups, including individual leaders and bases, located throughout the world. In 2013 US President Obama declared the War on Terror to be over, although the phrase continues to be used in US politics.

War grew noticeably more global in scope during the 20th century, particularly during World War Two where conflict waged among multiple nations and was fought out across several continents. The Cold War also – while never fought as an outright military conflict between the United States and Soviet Union – was nevertheless global in its scope of influence, shaping the international system into liberal democratic, communist and non-aligned blocs.

Since the end of the Cold War, warfare has changed somewhat, becoming more localized, often occurring within states, or between states and non-state actors. War is also more complex. Due to the globalized and interconnected nature of our international system, wars fought even in distant parts of the world with no direct bearing on our own security or interests can still have a direct impact on our lives. Consider again the Russia-Ukraine war which not only resulted in soaring gas and petroleum prices around the world (pg. 244) but sparked a global food crisis due to disruption of agricultural exports from both Russia and Ukraine that saw the global food price index increasing 58.5 per cent (Reuters 2022).

War is a global issue, regardless of where it is fought. We can also see the complexity and global impacts of war when we consider the **War on Terror** which began after the 9/11 terrorist attacks on the United States in 2001 (pg. 102). The War on Terror was an international state-led campaign against transnational networks of non-state actors made

Act of war
An act performed by one state against another with the intention of provoking war between them. Associated with the Latin phrase *casus belli* – an act or event that either provokes war or is used to justify a war.

up (primarily) of Islamic extremist sub-groups and movements. The War on Terror most notably constituted the War in Afghanistan (2001–21), the Iraq War (2003–11), as well as other high-profile military air strikes against terrorist targets in, for example, Yemen and Syria. The phrase 'War on Terror' has nevertheless been heavily criticized, and even abandoned by some governments, due to an ongoing controversy over referring to the crime of terrorism, undertaken by a non-state actor, as an **act of war**. The War on Terror does, however, highlight the nuance and complexity of war in today's globalized world.

OBSERVE

Image 10.2 Indian cavalry ride through a French village during World War One.
Source: British Library/Unsplash.

The British Empire mobilized some 1.5 million Indian soldiers during World War One (Koller 2008). Other imperial powers also recruited heavily from their colonies. French military recruitment from its colonies in West Africa, Algeria and Tunisia numbered nearly 95,000 soldiers, the vast majority by conscription (Koller 2008). In one particularly disturbing example of the racial superiority and colonial attitudes of the time, a French colonel responsible for training West Africans for the war commented in a letter to a friend that African soldiers were 'cannon fodder who should, in order to save whites' lives, be made use of much more intensively' (quoted in Koller 2008: 120).

Worth noting that in some cases, military cooperation between former colonies and empires has continued despite decolonization. For example, after India's partition and independence in 1947, four Gurkha regiments from the Indian Army were transferred to the British Army and continue to serve as the Gurkha Brigade to this day.

Types of war

When we consider war as an issue within international politics, it can be helpful to distinguish between different types of war. First, we can identify different types of war based on *who* is involved, including interstate and intrastate war. **Interstate wars** can broadly be characterized as armed conflicts between two or more sovereign states that have been formally initiated by an organized political or military act constituting an act of war. Russia's invasion of Ukraine in 2022 is one particularly high-profile example of a modern interstate war, although it is by no means commonplace. Prior to the 21st century, interstate

Interstate war
A war fought between two or more sovereign states.

wars were by far the most frequent types of warfare within our international system. Since the turn of the 21st century, however, the frequency of interstate wars has diminished, while **intrastate wars** have increased. Intrastate wars are characterized by warfare between conflicting social and political entities within a state and are largely synonymous with the more popularized term *civil war*. Examples of intrastate war include, for instance, the civil war between the Nigerian government and Boko Haram (pg. 154) over territorial controls, or the Yemeni civil war between Houthi insurgents and the Yemini government.

Intrastate war
A war fought between political entities within a state.

Another method of distinguishing between different types of war focuses more on the *scope* of wars fought. Nearly all wars are fought to change something. The *scope* of war addresses the extent of change **belligerents** ultimately strive for in war. Hegemonic war, for example, characterizes war whose outcome establishes which states will have dominance within the international system. World War Two is a prime example of a hegemonic war which saw systemic change in the defeat of Nazi Germany and the rise of a new bipolar world order dominated by the United States and the Soviet Union. World War Two is also an example of a **total war** as it was a war that saw belligerents utilize every known resource to achieve the surrender of their enemies, including the mass targeting of civilians alongside combatants.

Belligerents
Recognized in international law as those actors – typically states – engaged in a state of war and thus subject to the laws of war.

Total war
War that mobilizes every societal, economic and military resource, to the extent of prioritizing warfare over non-combatant needs, to target enemy combatants and non-combatants in order to achieve their surrender.

By contrast, **limited war** describes a war where the aim is less than the total defeat of the enemy. A limited war is closely related to the term 'proxy war' (pg. 25) developed during the Cold War, as a limited war is commonly characterized by the indirect involvement of major powers in smaller wars. As we saw in Chapter Two, during the Cold War the United States and Soviet Union regularly participated in proxy wars, not directly participating in military conflicts themselves, but indirectly supporting opposing sides in smaller wars around the world to turn the direction of the war in their favour. Limited wars are also limited in so far as major powers do not exert all their resources within the war, as we would expect to see in a total or hegemonic war. Rather, in limited war, major powers will provide military equipment or deploy limited military forces to better equip and support their favoured side in smaller conflicts.

Limited war
Small wars conducted with less than a state or other political entity's total resources to achieve goals less than an enemy's total defeat. See also **proxy wars**. (*pg. 25*)

In addition to distinguishing different types of war by *who* is fighting, and the *scope* by which wars are fought, we can also distinguish different types of warfare by focusing on *how* they are fought. **Conventional wars** are fought between the armed forces of the opposing sides. Civilians and other non-combatants are not directly targeted; therefore, destruction is limited to those national forces who are trained and authorized to attack or defend against the warring party. Conventional wars see the participants adhere to certain rules and conventions concerning the conduct of war. For example, the 1874 *Brussels Protocol* states that war should not 'inflict unnecessary suffering' upon an enemy. Between 1899 and 1907, the Hague Conferences (pg. 109) further established *The Convention on Laws and Customs of War* which set out 'to diminish the evils of war' through codes of practice for dealing with everything from treatment of belligerents, prisoners of war, the sick and wounded, to the means of injuring the enemy, to flags of truce, capitulations and armistices. Most of the interstate wars prior to World War One were conventional wars fought between professional national armies. World War One noticeably challenged the notion of conventional war, however, as it was the first time that chemical weapons were used on the battlefield, in direct contravention of Article 22–23 of the Hague Convention.[1] World War Two similarly challenged conventional warfare due to the large-scale strategic bombing used to target civilians, and with the first use of nuclear weapons deployed in war, again against non-combatants (pg. 23).

Conventional war
Wars fought using conventional military weapons and battlefield tactics that avoid targeting non-combatants.

Unconventional wars, by contrast, are wars fought using unconventional, oftentimes subversive, tactics or weaponry. Unconventional wars pay little regard to international conventions of war. They are irregular, fought instead using unconventional forces, and unconventional tactics. As former US President J. F. Kennedy neatly summarized:

Unconventional war
Wars fought using unconventional forces and tactics such as guerrilla warfare, cyber warfare or acts of terrorism.

> This is another type of warfare, new in its intensity, ancient in its origin – war by guerrillas, subversives, insurgents, assassins; war by ambush instead of by combat, by infiltration instead of aggression, seeking victory by eroding and exhausting the enemy instead of engaging him. (Kennedy 1962)

Explore More

Interested to see where in the world different types of war are taking place? There are various conflict and crisis trackers available online that you can utilize in your research. For example, the Council on Foreign Relation's Global Conflict Tracker offers an up-to-date interactive guide of the varying types of conflict currently involving or impacting the United States. Available online: www.cfr.org/global-conflict-tracker. You may also want to explore the International Crisis Group's global conflict tracker for a broader, more independent overview at www.crisisgroup.org/crisiswatch.

Scan the QR code for access to explore weblinks and more resources.

Asymmetric warfare
A type of war where the relative military capabilities of the belligerents differ significantly such that the weaker side must rely on unconventional methods to target the stronger force.

Cyberspace
A virtual environment that connects all digital and information technology.

Cyberwarfare
The offensive use of cyberattacks to target an enemy's vital computing systems.

In contrast to conventional wars which rely on professional state-led military forces to defend civilians, unconventional wars see civilians joining the fight to advance a shared goal. Guerrilla warfare is one tactic of unconventional war, which sees armed civilians work together in paramilitary units to fight a larger conventional military force using subversive tactics such as ambushes, raids or sabotage. Guerrilla 'insurgent' (pg. 153) or 'irregular' fighters use their knowledge and connections within the local area to shore up their position and legitimize their presence in the territories they hold. For example, during the Vietnam War (also referred to in Vietnam as the Resistance War or American War) (1955–75), the National Liberation Front of South Vietnam or 'Vietcong' targeted US military forces within the country using guerrilla tactics, including raids and surprise attacks. The Vietcong held support among the local population, making it difficult for American military personnel to distinguish the Vietcong from others. The Vietcong also received foreign backing from the Soviet Union and China – a characteristic of guerrilla warfare whereby guerrilla units receive military and economic aid from foreign powers who seek to advance their cause without directly entering the war.

Terrorism is also understood as a tactic of unconventional war, although acts of terrorism can be like guerrilla tactics in their method, and guerrillas can resort to acts of terrorism. A key element of any terrorist organization is that its primary targets are non-combatants. Therefore, while guerrillas look to both defend and garner the support of local citizens against combatants of a larger military force, terrorists deliberately target citizens to spread fear and notoriety around their cause. The terminology can nevertheless prove controversial and divisive. For example, the Kurdistan Workers Party (PKK) are listed as a terrorist organization by several countries including the United States and Turkey, as well as the EU, yet are also considered a guerrilla group fighting against Islamic State along Turkey's border. Where we can find similarity between guerrillas and terrorists, however, is that they both operate in domains of **asymmetric warfare**. Such asymmetry is another characteristic of unconventional war in so far as the relative military strength between the warring sides can differ significantly, such as between a state and non-state actor, as we see in the case of the War on Terror.

Since the growth of **cyberspace**, we can also include **cyberwarfare** as a method of unconventional war. Cyberwarfare has grown increasingly prominent as a domain of war with both states and non-states now using cyberattacks against enemy targets.

[1]Article 22 of the Convention Respecting the Laws and Customs of War on Land states 'the rights of belligerents to adopt means of injuring the enemy *is not unlimited*', while Article 23 expressly states 'it is especially forbidden – to employ *poison or poisoned weapons*'.

Cyberattacks may target enemy computers, computer networks, IT infrastructure and IT systems, using highly sophisticated methods ranging from malware, ransomware and phishing scams to back-door Trojans that allow an attacker to gain remote control of an IT system. In recent years, states have become increasingly oriented towards cyber defence to protect key systems as both state and non-state actors develop more sophisticated cyberattack methods. Several states are now thought to proactively utilize cyberattacks in subversive attempts to undermine and weaken the security of other states. In 2017, for example, the United States implicated Russia for cyberattacks aimed at influencing the US presidential elections. The EU, UK, US and other allies have also accused Russia of a series of cyberattacks against several targets in Ukraine following its invasion on 24 February 2022. Yet, in an interesting role reversal, Russia's governing institutions and corporations were also subject to cyberattacks from the international hacktivist collective known as *Anonymous* after its invasion of Ukraine, further highlighting how cyberspace has become a domain of unconventional war for state and non-state actors alike.

Distinguishing between different types of war can be particularly beneficial in helping identify specific characteristics of war and for comparing wars across categories, but be aware that typologies such as these do also have their limitations. For one thing, each war involves its own diverse actors, scope and tactics. Wars in the 21st century are also highly complex and can involve hybrid combinations of the different types of war outlined here. Much can therefore be missed by typecasting wars in overly simplistic dichotomies of interstate or intrastate, total or limited, conventional or unconventional war. What we can do, though, is utilize these types of war to garner a richer picture of war as the ultimate expression of conflict. Consider for a moment, *What type of war is the Syrian war (2011–)?* Pause and reflect on this question. If you are unfamiliar with the Syrian war you may want to explore the conflict trackers in the Explore More box (pg. 170) to give you some insights.

Image 10.3 In this image, smoke rises over the town of Kobani in Syria, near the Syria-Turkish border after an air strike by US Air Force fighters. At the time of writing the Syrian war remains ongoing. An estimated 400,000 Syrians have been killed in the conflict so far, with 5.7 million Syrian refugees now residing in other countries, and 6.7 million Syrians still internally displaced.

Source: Anadolu Agency/Getty Images.

Now a quick answer in response to this question would be to say that the Syrian war is an *intrastate war*. And you would – in part – be right. What began as pro-democracy protests against the incumbent Assad government in 2011 soon became a Syrian civil war between government and pro-democratic insurgents. But what began as an intrastate war soon developed an international dimension with Russia and Iran backing the Assad government, and the United States, Saudi Arabia, Turkey and others providing military support to the anti-government groups. In 2014, the conflict developed yet further complexity as the terrorist group Islamic State sought to make territorial gains in eastern and northern Syria including against the autonomous Kurdish region (Syrian/Western Kurdistan) (pg. 15). As Image 10.3 depicts, the United States and some Arab states then undertook military strikes against Islamic State. Thousands of Kurdish people were forced to abandon their homes, leading to further tensions at the Turkish border due to Turkey's concerns about YPG (Kurdish military) Units – whom Turkey links to ties with the PKK – from entering Turkish territory. This is just a snapshot of the complexity and characteristics at play in the Syrian war, but already from it we can start to see a highly nuanced picture, highlighting that the Syrian war is both a *conventional* and *unconventional* war with characteristics of guerrilla and terrorist warfare in both symmetric and asymmetric contexts. The Syrian war can also be described as a *limited war* when we consider the war from the perspective of the United States or Russia.

Theoretical perspectives on war and conflict

In addition to the types of war highlighted in the previous section, we can also draw upon different theories as tools in helping us explain the causes of war and conflict in our international system. Realism particularly highlights how war is an inevitable part of international politics. Classical realists highlight how human nature leads states to be naturally egoistic, competitive and mistrustful of others. Neorealism highlights the inevitability of war due to the anarchic structure of the international system. With no overarching authority above the sovereign state itself, states must operate within a self-help system where they can rely only on themselves to defend and advance their national interests. Offensive neorealists go further in arguing that war is inevitable due to states' inherent desire to maximize their power and reputation, including through conquest and the need for territorial gain. With their particular emphasis on the balance of power within the international system, neorealists also prioritize focus on hegemons and their economic and foreign policies. Interstate wars are thus observed through lenses of hegemonic war and the involvement of the great powers, while intrastate wars are observed through lenses of limited war and the extent to which great powers intercede in small, yet strategically significant, conflicts.

In Chapter Five we considered how the balance of power and polarity of the international system is expected to impact order and security within international politics. According to realist scholars, what form of polarity (uni-, bi- or multipolar) is most likely to create the conditions for war and conflict within the international system? Why is this?

Like realism, liberalism also focuses on states as the main units of analysis when researching war and conflict in the international system. Unlike realism, however, liberalism places its point of focus on how modernization and progress can make war avoidable through the advancement of democracy, economic interdependence between states, and the effectiveness of international organizations as forums to mitigate violence. While war may therefore be probable, due to the self-interest of states themselves, it can also be mitigated against. Liberalism pays particular attention to the characteristics of states in this regard, with democratic peace theorists arguing that democracies do not fight wars with one another – a claim grounded in empirical evidence (Doyle 1983) – and that most wars have been fought within or between non-democracies, or between democracies and non-democracies. For liberals, democracies are more likely to remain peaceful due to the voice and oversight of domestic constituencies who hold their government to account.

LINK

Consider

In Chapter Two we looked at the 1928 Kellogg-Briand Pact which sought to outlaw war (pg. 35). Many considered the Pact a failure because within a decade of its signature, every one of its signatories (with the exception of Ireland), was again at war. Yet studies have shown that the Kellogg-Briand Pact may have been effective in ending the right of conquest as a reason for countries to go to war.

Explore

'Outlawing War? It Actually Worked' was an Op-Ed by Oona Hathaway and Scott Shapiro published in the *New York Times* on 3 September 2017. You can access it online at www.nytimes.com or scan the barcode for a direct link.

Connect

According to Hathaway and Shapiro (2017), since 1928 territorial conquests rapidly declined and, in many cases, states returned territories from former conquests to pre-World War Two boundaries. With the end of the right of conquest, states no longer legally had the right to gain the spoils, territory or people from conquest. Yet, in 2014 Russia annexed Crimea, gaining control over the territory and people.

Predict

Does Russia's annexation of Crimea in 2014 and its invasion of Ukraine in 2022 symbolize a return of war for the purpose of conquest in our international system?

Constructivism places its emphasis on analysis of identities, values and beliefs in the construction of conflict and warfare. For constructivists, the anarchic condition of the international system does not constrain states to act a certain way. Conflict within our international system is rather driven by the agency of actors within the system, their identities, and the way conflict is socially constructed. During the Cold War, for example, role theory (pg. 80) first emerged as a means of identifying the different national role conceptions that states seek to perform such as 'regional leader', 'faithful ally', 'isolate', etc. (Holsti 1970). According to Holsti, such national role conceptions were socially constructed, based on differing perceptions of (internal and external) threat, the structure and power distribution of the system, as well as differing perspectives on ideology and/or nationalism. National identity is therefore considered an important driver of conflict and cooperation for social constructivists, and the likelihood that states will pursue conflictual or cooperative foreign policies with others. In contemporary international politics, we can also observe this by looking, for example, at how some states, such as Ireland or Switzerland, identify themselves as 'neutral' relative to those who pursue more overtly aggressive foreign policies, such as North Korea. Constructivism further highlights the importance of identity as a driver for conflict, not least where identities become threatened, or are left unrecognized.

Critical theories meanwhile focus their analysis and explanation on the way war has been constituted and narrated within international politics. Feminism applies a gendered perspective on war, highlighting how war is a domain of militarized masculinity where the role of women has been both subjugated and overlooked. Not only are wars predominantly fought by men, feminists argue, but notions of warfare, such as honour, nationalism, militarism, self-interest and competition are all grounded in masculinized constructs that emphasize dominion and patriarchy. Like feminism, postcolonialism also focuses on marginalized peoples in the analysis and explanation of war in international politics. For example, Khalid (2011) draws on Edward Said's *Orientalism* to show how the War on Terror is itself a replication of imperial warfare (the occident) against dissident colonies (the orient) in the way it has cast the 'East' as *Other* to the 'West'. Critical scholars do also contest what they observe as a very narrow conceptualization of violence as war within international politics. True (2000), for example, highlights that organized violence may account for the physical violence that occurs on battlefields, but it discounts the violence that happens to individuals in societies around the world, to women at risk of violence in the home, or the violence that results from displacement, or climate change, or other climate-induced disasters. These differing explanations for war, conflict and violence are further summarized in Table 10.1 towards the end of this chapter.

BETWEEN CONFLICT AND COOPERATION

While war has been a regular feature within our international system, peaceful relations between states is often a far more constant variable at work within contemporary international politics. Consider that in Western Europe there has been peace since 1945. It has been around four decades since the last interstate war in East Asia. South America has been almost war free since the end of the Cold War. As Bellamy argues, 'most people in most societies have had more experience of peacetime than wartime. Indeed, most people alive today have never experienced war and do not live in immediate fear of it' (Bellamy 2020). While conflicting interests can create the impetus for violence within our international system, they also establish the conditions for diplomacy and negotiation which can lead to cooperation and peace. War is by no means the norm for the daily interaction of states within our international system. In fact, as we saw in Chapter Six, most interstate diplomacy and foreign policy takes place through negotiation and cooperation. Negotiation then becomes the bridge between conflict and cooperation. During times of armed conflict, negotiation can often hold the key to **conflict resolution** – although it is by no means a guarantee of success. During times of peace, negotiation is also the key to navigating disputes so that violence is prevented.

Conflict resolution The process by which conflicting parties seek to resolve their differences in moving towards a lasting peace.

Conflict prevention The effort of preventing conflict through mitigation of disputes between conflicting parties, typically facilitated by a third party.

Mediation Where a, typically neutral, third party facilitates negotiations between conflicting parties in an effort to resolve their dispute.

Peacekeeping The active intervention of an international military force to stop violence between belligerent forces in order to facilitate resolution to a crisis.

There are several methods of interaction and intervention that can be used to prevent, manage and resolve conflicts. First, where conflicting parties seek to prevent the outbreak of violence, they may interact through **conflict prevention** negotiations. The UN has particularly developed this idea of conflict prevention, through the advancement of what it terms *preventive diplomacy*, referring to forms of diplomatic action taken at the earliest possible stage 'to prevent disputes from arising between parties, to prevent existing disputes from escalating into conflicts and to limit the spread of the latter when they occur' (UN 1992a). Specific methods of conflict prevention undertaken by the UN include, for example, the deployment of UN special envoys or mediation teams to help diffuse tensions and resolve local disputes, logistical support and translation services, or financial support for hosting conferences to bring disputants together.

Where conflicting parties are already engaged in violent armed conflict, interventions such as **mediation** and **peacekeeping** are also methods used for conflict management. Peacekeeping has proven a controversial topic within international politics. Since 1948 the UN has launched over seventy peacekeeping operations around the world, most of which have, since the 1980s, been in intrastate conflicts. At the time of writing, the UN has twelve peacekeeping operations (PKO) in force, from the UNTSO in the Middle East – incidentally the UN's longest standing PKO having been in operation since 1948 – to UNMOGIP in India and Pakistan, to the various operations throughout Africa including in Sudan and Central African Republic, for example. PKO are often mandated by a UN Security Council resolution, providing a certain legitimacy to the action (pg. 121). Yet the legitimacy and effectiveness of international peacekeeping operations are cause for debate.

For example, in one study of conflict and conflict termination between 1946 and 2013, Clayton and Dorussen (2022) found that mediation and peacekeeping have not only increasingly been used as the primary means of conflict management by the international community since the end of the Cold War, but that both methods have a statistically significant impact on ending conflict. Jett (2019), however, highlights the profound limitations of UN peacekeeping operations and the marginal role that peacekeepers can play. According to Jett (2019), PKO can have weak mandates often due to the more powerful interests of UN Security Council members, particularly the P5 (pg. 115). PKO may also prove unsuccessful because they may do little to address several of the key factors that underlie intrastate conflicts, such as addressing access to material and economic revenues within the state, the involvement of neighbours or other foreign powers within the conflict, and the extent to which the political leadership of the belligerent groups actually want peace (Jett 2019).

UN PKO have also been heavily criticized for their reliance on a *liberal peace* model that tends to adopt a one-size-fits-all approach to peacebuilding, which can then be blinkered to colonial legacies (Fernández Moreno, Braga and Siman Gomes 2012). Several studies have highlighted the colonial underpinnings of peacekeeping and peacebuilding efforts, highlighting how some European contributors to PKO are able to exploit interventions to foster special relations with their former colonies (see Fernández Moreno, Braga and Siman Gomes 2012; Charbonneau 2014; MacQueen 2020). For example, Portugal contributed personnel to all three UN peacekeeping missions in Timor-Leste between 1999 and 2012, with some scholars suggesting that Portugal's contribution was 'linked to an established national policy of re-engagement with the former colonies "lost" in 1974–75' (MacQueen 2020). The legitimacy of peacekeeping and peacebuilding interventions are also highly debatable due to their infringement on state sovereignty which directly encompasses the principle of non-interference – a point that many former colonies are resistant to, having regained their sovereignty after years of imperial subjugation.

Another method of moving from conflict to cooperation is conflict resolution. Conflict resolution typically occurs after various conflict management processes have achieved a cessation of armed violence and where the former belligerents seek to move forward in developing a lasting peace. Conflict resolution may take various forms, but can include *conflict transformation*, whereby former belligerents work together through numerous interactive processes to reconcile tensions, redefine interests or find common ground (Stern and Druckman 2000: 5). These processes include methods such as the Truth and Reconciliation Commission used in South Africa at the end of apartheid which served as a court-like restorative body '… to enable South Africans to come to terms with their past on a morally accepted basis and to advance the cause of reconciliation' (Truth and Reconciliation Commission 1995). Second, conflict resolution may be sought in culturally divided states through methods of *structural prevention*, such as redesigning a state's electoral system, granting certain groups or regions autonomy, providing legal guarantees of free speech and association, or ensuring civilian control over military organizations. Finally, conflict resolution can come through *normative change*. Normative change addresses the development and institutionalization of specific principles to help manage conflict and prevent violence, such as the protection of human rights, although we still arguably remain, 'a long way from a world in which what is good for humanity consistently outweighs the prerogative of states' (Stern and Druckman 2000: 7).

Explore More

Interested in how peace is agreed between conflicting parties in the international system? The PA-X Peace Agreement Database is a repository of nearly 2,000 agreements from over 140 peace processes around the world, searchable by country, entity, region, conflict type and stage of agreement. Explore More by visiting www.peaceagreements.org.

Scan the QR code for access to explore weblinks and more resources.

WHAT IS PEACE?

As we observed in the previous section, the move from conflict to cooperation is not always smooth, nor is it strictly linear. In protracted conflicts, belligerents may take decades to move beyond violence, animosity and mistrust, to achieve a conflict resolution leading to lasting peace. While the pathway to peace is not always an easy one, the destination itself is also highly ambiguous. What is peace? How do we recognize it when we see it? And is world peace possible? The very persistence of war in our world could certainly make us question whether it is possible for our planet to exist without it. But more than the deep scepticism that comes from pondering world peace as a total absence of war, let alone a world free of violence, are the many stark differences over what peace actually looks like, and how it should be conceptualized and understood.

From the realist perspective, peace is best understood in strictly narrow terms as the absence of war. To conceptualize peace as anything more than this would be unrealistic of the world in which we live, a utopian fantasy. Realism would particularly highlight that, whether due to human nature or the anarchic condition of the international system, conflict in international politics is inevitable. While realists would acknowledge that peace can be achieved, for example, in that moment when organized violence ceases because belligerents agree it is in their self-interest, or where the international system achieves a balance of power between superpowers that makes military conflict between them strategically unlikely or unwise, world peace is unfeasible. World peace can only be achieved through strong world government to oversee law and order between states. Realists would highlight, however, that the creation of a world government would never be practical or feasible while states prioritize their national over collective interests (pg. 37).

Liberal perspectives on peace are often linked with the works of Immanuel Kant who, in *Perpetual Peace*, reflected on the likelihood of eternal peace. Kant notably distinguished between truce and peace, where truce is a temporary halt to fighting, whereas peace is something lasting – a point that would seem to resonate with the UN's conceptualization of 'sustainable peace' (pg. 117). According to Kant, most peace treaties signed between nations are in effect truce treaties. For Kant, however, humankind has the capacity to bring about lasting peace among nations through federal unionism between states, and the eventual dissolution of standing armies that would make war unfeasible.

More recently, others have conceptualized 'quality peace' which can only be understood by considering two endpoints on a scale, where the negative end of the scale is political violence, and the positive end of the scale is 'political mutuality' entailing 'a quality of respect and fundamental good will between relevant actors' (Davenport, Erik and Regan 2018). Others have also argued that, more than the absence of war, peace is the ability to manage disputes peacefully through norms, institutions and practices (Bellamy 2020), thereby implying some form of 'legitimate civic order' (Bellamy 2019: 17). Only through international organizations that provide forums for negotiation and discussion, along with laws, practices and norms that establish appropriate behaviour within our international system, can cooperation be nurtured through a civic order that enables states and other non-state actors to manage disagreement and dispute without recourse to violence. The argument therefore follows that peace is itself a constitution of the orderly practice of cooperation.

Critical scholars do also favour a broader conceptualization of peace. Feminist scholars argue that if we understand peace merely as the absence of war then we must broaden our conceptual lenses to consider all forms of violence and not just organized violence (True 2020). Feminist scholarship also advocates for a more holistic understanding of peace that overcomes the social and structural injustices that can support violence both within and between societies around the world. Peace, then, can be constituted as a process of social justice that happens when the individual, the household, the community and the state become sites of non-violence, particularly for women (Cockburn 2019). These different perspectives are further summarized in Table 10.1.

Table 10.1 Theoretical perspectives on war and peace

	Realism	Liberalism	Constructivism	Critical theories
Main actors	States Hegemons	States Domestic actors	States Non-state actors	States Marginalized peoples
Causes of war	Human nature Anarchy Conquest Territorial gain	Lack of democracy, interdependence and effective IOs	Conflicting identities, values, beliefs	Militarized masculinity Imperialism
What is peace?	The absence of war	The lasting process of cooperation; political mutuality	The construction of shared norms and values constituting a common peace	Social justice and non-violence across all levels of society
Causes of peace	Self-interest of the belligerents to halt violence	Effective conflict management and resolution led by international organizations	Trust-building and reconciliation between belligerents	Addressing harmful identities, ideologies and social dynamics that support violence

CONCLUSION

In this chapter we have considered war and peace as prominent issues in international politics, that we as scholars can research through lenses of a continuum of violence and non-violence, which captures processes of conflict, conflict prevention, management and resolution, and cooperation. The aim of this chapter has not only been to inform you about war and peace within international politics, but to help you start to study and research them for yourself, considering some of the actors and theories involved. At the end of this chapter, you will find a toolkit exercise where you can apply some of your knowledge from this chapter to explore and then explain the cause of Russia's invasion of Ukraine in 2022. We will then develop further on many of these issues in the next chapter where we turn to look specifically at security in international politics.

TOOLKIT

What was the primary cause of Russia's 2022 invasion of Ukraine?

THINK

- How accurate, reliable and/or unbiased do you consider the news outlets you typically look to for your news?
- Reflect on your knowledge of the Russian invasion of Ukraine in February 2022. To what extent did media reporting leading up to and after the invasion shape your understanding of the conflict or its causes?

OBSERVE

Satellite state
A formally independent country but one whose politics, economics and military are heavily influenced or controlled by another country.

Map 10.1 A map of Ukraine.
Source: filo / Getty images

- Observe the location of Ukraine, positioned between Russia and its close ally Belarus to its north and east. To the south is the Black Sea and Crimea. To Ukraine's west are Poland, Hungary, Slovakia and Romania, all former **satellites** of the Soviet Union, and now members of the EU and NATO following the successive eastern enlargements of both organizations in 1999, 2004 and 2008 respectively (pgs. 132, 135–7).
- Crimea is formerly a sovereign territory of Ukraine but was annexed by Russia in early 2014 following the Maidan Revolution in which the Ukrainian people revolted against the pro-Russian president for refusing to sign an Association Agreement with the EU.
- In Ukraine nearly 30 per cent of the population are Russian-speaking, the majority of whom live in the east of the country. In the Donbas region in the east of Ukraine, Donetsk and Luhansk have experienced fighting between Ukrainian forces and pro-Russian separatists since 2014. After Russia's military incursion into Ukraine in February 2022 these regions announced themselves to be the *Donetsk People's Republic* and *Luhansk People's Republic*, enclaves which President Putin formally recognized as independent states, and agreed to support militarily.

ORGANIZE

- A 'levels of analysis' approach (Chapter 5) can be a useful method for explaining the different causes of war and considering their relative explanatory power (pg. 70).
- At the *individual* level of analysis, your focus may be on the decisions, identities or perceptions of individual leaders, such as President Putin or President Zelensky.
- At the *state* level of analysis, we are particularly interested in belligerent states' domestic institutions and bureaucracy, the politics of government and state economic interests, as well as the state's societal values. What then are the institutional/bureaucratic opportunities and constraints shaping both Russian and Ukrainian decision-making? What national values or ideologies are involved? What domestic interests are being protected or defended?
- At the *international* level of analysis our lens goes broader to consider the effects of the international system on the war, and vice versa. Theory can help offer explanation, such as neorealism's emphasis on the inevitability of war due to the anarchic condition of the international system, and the need to achieve security through a balance of power.

LINK

- *Consider*: Consider the types of war discussed earlier in this chapter. What type(s) of war do you think the Russo-Ukraine war is?
- *Explore*: In a radio Q&A given in April 2014, President Putin reminded listeners that the Ukrainian regions of Kharkiv, Luhansk, Donetsk, Nikolayev and Odessa were originally part of 'Novorossiya' (New Russia) having been won by Potyomkin and Catherine the Great. He stated that 'Russia lost these territories for various reasons, but the people remained'. On 24 February 2022, the day Russia invaded Ukraine, President Putin also gave a televised address concerning his reasons for the 'special military operation'. Scan the barcode to access the full transcript of both the radio and televised addresses at our companion website.
- *Connect*: In 2008, NATO leaders met for a summit in Bucharest. From that summit came the Bucharest Declaration which stated that NATO welcomed Ukraine's (and Georgia's) aspirations to one day become members of the alliance (pg. 132). In September 2014 the EU-Ukraine Association Agreement was signed and ratified. Six days after Russia's invasion of Ukraine in February 2022, Ukraine applied for EU membership. On 23 June 2022 the European Council granted candidate status to Ukraine, opening the way for its future membership.
- *Predict*: What do you think Ukraine's future is as a sovereign state?

SHARE

- Answer the question *'What was the primary cause of Russia's 2022 invasion of Ukraine?'*

  This question may strike you as reductive, but by asking you to reflect on a 'primary cause' it is deliberately pushing you to consider the relative explanatory power of the different variables shaping the conflict and to take a position. Does a particular cause stand out to you as reason for the invasion? Why? Be mindful that there is rarely a 'right' answer in international politics, but there are always good arguments, so be clear in outlining why you think a cause has more explanatory power than others. You might also want to look at *How to – take a position* (pg. 144).

HOW TO

APPROACH AN INTERNATIONAL POLITICS ESSAY

There is a high probability that during your academic studies you will need to answer an essay question as part of either a formative or summative assessment. Of course, most of you will already be familiar with how to approach essay writing but writing an international politics essay can be a little different compared to other subject areas. The following then are a few useful steps you might look to follow.

Interrogate the question

Reflect on the wording of your essay question. *Do you understand what it is asking you to do?* This may seem obvious, but it might surprise you to know that one of the most common criticisms presented by university lecturers/professors/tutors in essay feedback relates to the student *not* answering the specifics of the question. Essays that skirt around a question without fully addressing it, answer their own version of the question, or hint at an argument but never outright express an answer, are all likely to face the same negative feedback and subsequent downgrading of their mark.

When you get your essay question, therefore, first reflect on its *key words*. Key words are explicit instruction words detailed in an essay or exam question or statement that direct you in how you should answer. Regardless of how the essay question is framed, it will likely include several key words that serve as a guide to how you should go about answering. Key words may include explicit *instruction words* that provide a direct steer to how you should approach your essay. Take, for example, this question:

> *'Is Taiwan a sovereign state? Discuss with reference to current PRC-ROC relations'.*

In this example you are called upon to offer an argument/answer to the question of whether Taiwan is a sovereign state (pg. 106), but you also have the instruction word 'discuss' which directs you to offer some brief context, before discussing the different sides of the argument concerning Taiwanese statehood.

Key words also include *subject words* which direct you to address a specific subject, issue, concept or theory in your essay. In this example, a key word includes the phrase 'sovereign state' – directing you to discuss sovereignty and statehood in the body of your essay.

Key words may also serve as *limiting instructions* that guide you in how to narrow in your essay's point of focus. In this example, note that it refers to 'current PRC-ROC relations'. This again is a key word instructing you on what to focus on in your essay. As a limiting instruction you are directed to address *current PRC-ROC relations* which means you can avoid wasting word count on historical PRC-ROC relations, or ROC relations with states other than the PRC (pg. 95).

Bear in mind also that essays are intended to test your knowledge and understanding of the subject material you have been taught on your course. When interrogating your question, and reflecting on the key words included, reflect on what you have learned so far and how the essay question or statement relates to that subject material in explicit terms. This will help you tailor your answer to address the specific learning outcomes of your course assessment.

Use your TOOLS

Having interrogated the question and identified your key words, you can then start to plan for the content you want to include, and the argument you want to present. Using the **TOOLS** that we have been addressing in this book can be a helpful strategy for accomplishing this. For example:

THINK – what are *my* assumptions about this essay topic? How does this inform my argument?

OBSERVE – what *other* perspectives and arguments are out there on this topic? How do others approach this question in the existing scholarship? What alternative or critical perspectives can be found? This is an important opportunity for you to engage directly with the literature from your course reading list and in your library to show your research and wider understanding of the subject material.

ORGANIZE – what concept(s) or theories will help me frame my argument, or highlight critical reflection of counterarguments? Alternatively, how can I engage with the concept or theory detailed as a key word in my essay question to show my understanding, as well as critical reflection? You will need to be selective here. You cannot use everything so avoid overload. Part of writing a good essay is using your academic judgement in determining which concept or theory best helps support your argument and show some critical reflection.

LINK – what independent research can I do to show real-world examples and present empirical evidence to support my argument and speak to the specifics of the question?

Structure – think burger!

Having worked through your TOOLkit you should now be ready to **S**HARE your argument and begin to write up your essay. As with any academic writing, an essay calls upon you to demonstrate your effective communication skills. How you structure your essay is especially important. When structuring your essay, one top tip is to *think burger!*

Now a good international politics essay – like any good burger – includes different layers. The bun keeps your burger together, in the same way that an *introduction and conclusion* make the main points of your essay come together and act as a cohesive whole. The burger then is your *argument* (it is the best part of the burger

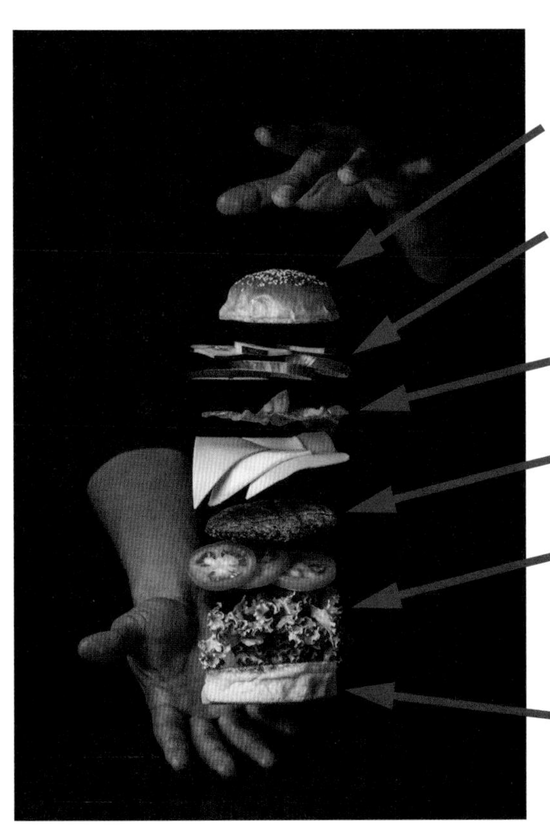

Introduction (top bun): Briefly details the essay question you will answer, introduces your argument, and outlines how you will present your case in the main body of the essay.

Section 1 (onions/pickle): Briefly sets out the context to the essay i.e. historical or political background, along with relevant scholarship that helps inform your reader and shows your knowledge of the subject material.

Section 2 (bacon): Outlines key points of any theory or concept you are utilizing. See also *How to - apply theory to your research and writing* (pg. 69).

Section 3 (cheese and burger): Showcases your empirical research, detailing clear evidence or examples that then justifies your argument.

Section 4 (salad): Offers critical reflection of your engagement with theory and empirical research, considering the limitations of your approach and alternative perspectives.

Conclusion (bottom bun): Draws main threads of your discussion together to reiterate your argument/answer to the question. Avoid just repeating yourself, but rather reflect on the implications of why your argument matters and how it relates to the wider scholarship around your topic.

Figure 10.2 Structuring your politics essay – think burger!

after all!), but the burger alone is a little unimaginative and really needs the layers to complement it and make for a richer meal. Add the onions and pickle then for some *context*, the bacon for some *theoretical or conceptual engagement*, and the cheese for some *empirical evidence* to justify your claims. The salad then comes in to offer *critical reflection*. You may then also want to think of the relish as your *citations* and overall referencing practice – showing you've done your reading, are engaging with the relevant scholarship and evidencing your claims. How you then piece it together is of course your decision as an independent scholar, but here is a very rough guide that can provide a steer:

Edit, then edit again

Once you have done the bulk of your writing, always give yourself time to edit thoroughly too. So much of good written communication comes down to editing and clarifying. Read over your essay several times before you submit the work. With each read-through aim to edit to improve the precision and clarity of your writing. This is not just about proofreading, where you look for the obvious typos, punctuation and grammatical errors. Editing means looking at every sentence and weighing up its merits as a communicative tool. Remember, you are writing to inform your reader, so look at the writing objectively, almost as if you have never read it before. When editing, you may want to follow a levels approach as follows:

Sentence-level – does each sentence make sense on its own? Could it have been written more clearly or with fewer words? Is the sentence structure easy to read?

Paragraph-level – do the sentences flow naturally one to another within each paragraph? Do your paragraph breaks make sense? Does the paragraph work as a cohesive whole?

Section-level – do the paragraphs within the main sections of your essay come together logically? Do your paragraphs connect with each other within your sections with a clear flow to your writing? Is it clear what each section of your essay is trying to do?

Essay-level – does the essay flow from introduction to conclusion following a clear and logical structure? Is your argument obvious to your reader throughout your essay? Have you answered the specifics of the question and is this obvious? Are your references accurate, with all citations listed correctly in your references list/ bibliography? (See *How to – approach referencing* pg. 126)

This can take some time but undergoing a rigorous editing process not only ensures you will submit a far tighter, more rigorous piece of academic work, but it will also pay dividends in your marking feedback and grading as well.

11 Security

Pexels / Pixabay

Abstract

This chapter introduces you to security as an issue within international politics. The chapter starts by first discussing the concept of security and the different ways it can be understood in the study of international politics, particularly considering conceptualizations of common, collective, ontological, human and national security. From there you will explore different security domains and the various new security issues that dominate security agendas today. The chapter then offers a spotlight on the proliferation and threat of the use of nuclear weapons as an international security issue which has seen considerable contestation since the Cold War, and which once again dominates international agendas. The chapter then concludes with a toolkit exercise focusing on the lessons we might draw from the Covid-19 pandemic and public health as a new security issue, addressing the question *'Should states invest in public health as a security concern after Covid-19?'*

UNDERSTANDING (IN)SECURITY IN INTERNATIONAL POLITICS

In the last chapter we observed how war and peace are long-standing issues of importance and concern for international politics scholars. Inherently interwoven with war and peace, particularly when we regard broader conceptualizations of violence, is the issue of security – and by association – insecurity – within our international system. In fact, if you were to look back at the previous chapters in this book you might notice that security has already been mentioned at numerous intervals. Flick forward to the remaining chapters and you will again find frequent references to security being made. This is because security regularly permeates discussion and analysis of international politics. As Buzan and Hansen (2009: 1) highlight, 'wherever International Relations [Politics] is taught, International Security Studies is one of its central elements'.

Security is considered important to all states, with national security often addressed as one of the highest responsibilities of government. Some scholars – particularly those who ascribe to the neorealist tradition – suggest that security is a matter of **high politics**, the epitome of a state's **national interest**, with **national security** to be strived for and rigorously prioritized due to the anarchic condition of the international system. Others, though, would suggest that states may also pursue and prioritize other values besides maximizing their security (Wolfers 1952: see also Baldwin 1997: 10–11). Writing in 1952, Arnold Wolfers argued that, like wealth or power, security is a value of great importance in international affairs. It is a value, however, 'which a nation can have more or less of and which it can aspire to have in greater or lesser measure' (Wolfers 1952: 484). As well as being a priority issue for governments, security can also be used by governments 'to justify suspending civil liberties, making war and massively reallocating resources' (Baldwin 1997: 9). Security must therefore be understood as an important political narrative and tool. When issues become **securitized** – understood as the reframing of any given issue into a security threat – they are more likely to be prioritized by governments, including in the allocation of government spending amidst various competing demands.

High politics
A traditional realist framing used to identify issues of concern to national security. Distinct from low politics (pg. 149).

National interest
Referring to the economic, military, political and societal priorities and goals of a sovereign state.

National security
Concerning the security and defence of a sovereign state from threats against its people, institutions or territory.

Securitization
The discursive process by which an issue is transformed into a security threat.

Let us again take the example of the Covid-19 pandemic. When an unknown pneumonic virus was first identified in Wuhan, China in late December 2019, most countries did not identify it as a security threat. Yet, the growing number of cases and deaths in spring 2020 and the naming of Covid-19 as a pandemic by the WHO, soon found governments around the world taking the decision to enforce localized and national lockdowns to limit the spread of the virus and protect the lives of their citizens (see BBC News 2020a for a useful overview). Citizens within these countries saw their civil liberties drastically impacted, with internal movement orders restricting when people could leave their homes, how far they could travel, and whom they could meet. Lockdowns, while suspending the civil liberties of billions of people, were justified as a necessary security measure to meet the threat that the pandemic posed to human life. During the pandemic, other national security concerns, by and large, took a back seat in government priorities. The pandemic was a singularly pressing threat, commandeering the full attention of states, large and small.

Yet, once vaccination programmes began to roll out in late 2020 and early 2021 – significantly reducing the number of deaths caused by Covid-19 – national security agendas began to gradually broaden again. Governments turned their focus to recovery, to the knock-on economic effects of national lockdowns, and to new external threats. The virus – which had so dominated headlines – became a lower-profile security issue. The virus remained, but the perception of threat had changed. Security, and securitization, therefore, must be understood as a highly fluid framing tool, prioritizing how different threats are perceived, and how governments direct and prioritize decision-making in the national interest.

DEFINING SECURITY

While recognizing the imperative of security for governments, we must also acknowledge that security is an ambiguous and, at times, heavily contested concept. What is security? Whose security are we referring to? What does international *in*security look like, and what then presents a security threat? Security is commonly understood to mean protection against threats, being then associated with defence and survival. That understanding of security has also traditionally been used within international security studies. Largely dominated by Western scholarship since its inception after 1945[1], security scholarship over much of the Cold War adopted a relatively narrow, or minimalist, conceptualization of security as that of national security, military statecraft and war (Stoett 1999; Baldwin 1997; Wolfers 1952). As Baldwin (1997: 9) reflects, 'if military force was relevant to an issue, it was considered a security issue; and if military force was not relevant, that issue was consigned to the category of low politics' (pg. 149).

During the 1970s and 1980s, a broader understanding of security – distinctive from defence or war – began to emerge. In 1982 the Independent Commission on Disarmament and Security Issues (commonly known as the Palme Commission) released its report 'Common Security: A Programme for Disarmament', which, for the first time, articulated that a state's security could not be obtained solely through its own military capabilities, but only in *common* with other states. Security, then, can be understood, not merely as a value, calculated in terms of a state's military capability relative to other states, but as a relationship of security and trust among states (McSweeney 1999: 15). In international politics, that understanding of security as a relationship may particularly be found in the make-up of various international and regional organizations that emerged in the post-World War Two era. For example, NATO (pg. 131–2) was established with the express aim of providing **collective security** for its member states, premised on a relationship of collective trust. Should one member of that alliance then be attacked, the other members would come to its aid.

Collective security
An alliance, association or other agreement between states that upholds their commitment to common action in defence of one another.

Towards the end of the Cold War, security studies saw further advancement of how security could be conceptualized, much prompted by the growth of critical security studies. For critical security scholars, security was understood not just as an action or process of national protection or defence, but as a state of 'being' – a sense of feeling secure, of being free from fear, anxiety or dread. Critical security studies advanced the concept of **ontological security** where subjects have 'the capacity to uphold a stable view of their environment and thereby "go on" with everyday life' (Delehanty and Steele 2009: 524). Ontological insecurity, by extension, signified a sense of something 'fundamentally destabilizing and challenging established world views, routines and core conceptions of selfhood' (Browning 2018: 337). In this way, ontological security approaches highlighted how even anxiety-inducing headlines concerning crime, terrorist attacks, migration crises, epidemics or threats of wars can impact our sense of security, even where we are not directly involved in those events ourselves. Security was therefore found to go beyond the state and national security, to the individual and our very sense of Self.

Ontological security
A conceptualization of security that focuses on the subject's state of being, sense of Self, and how their security is perceived and, by extension, threatened.

THINK

According to *ontological security theory*, 'being' secure is a sense of self and state of mind influenced by our environment, our day-to-day routines, our relationships of trust, and how we manage instability, anxiety and dread.

What do you think it takes for a state to feel secure? Is national security primarily a question of protection and defence, or does it concern a state's sense of self-Identity?

[1]Security was a topic of interest within the academic discourse prior to World War Two, but was characterized more as war studies, or military and grand strategy. It was only after 1945 that security became a more distinctive conceptual focal point in the literature (Buzan and Hansen 2009: 1).

Critical security scholars also challenged traditional minimalist conceptualizations that equated 'security with the sanctity of national borders' (Stoett 1999: 15). Critical scholars sought to look beyond the state as the primary object of analysis to prioritize human beings and the individual instead. Connected with this critical agenda, **human security** emerged as a new security frame in the 1990s. First developed by the UN Development Programme (UNDP) in 1994, human security was presented as a 'profound transition in thinking' away from national security and the military concerns of the state (UNDP 1994: 21). Human security placed people at the heart of the security agenda. The two major components of human security include the *freedom from want*, and the *freedom from fear* (UNDP 1994: 24). Human security then addresses security from the broad perspective of poverty, disease, hunger, unemployment, crime, political repression and environmental hazards (UNDP 1994: 23). As the report stated, 'human security is a child who did not die, a disease that did not spread, a job that was not cut, an ethnic tension that did not explode in violence, a dissident who was not silenced. *Human security is not a concern with weapons – it is a concern with human life and dignity*' (UNDP 1994: 23 *emphasis added*).

Human security
A conceptualization of security that prioritizes humankind and the survival, livelihood and dignity of the individual.

Explore More

Discover more about human security by looking at the 1994 UN Development Report that first coined and developed the concept. You can access the report at https://hdr.undp.org, paying particular attention to Chapter Two.

Scan the QR code for access to explore weblinks and more resources.

Image 11.1 During the UN General Assembly Emergency Special Session held on 2 March 2022 to debate Russia's invasion of Ukraine, several state delegations placed toys on their desks to symbolize how their vote not only concerned Ukraine's territorial sovereignty, but the wellbeing of future generations. How we understand security is often dependent upon whose security we are thinking of.

Source: TIMOTHY A. CLARY/Getty Images.

Genocide
Actions committed with the intent to destroy a national, ethnical, racial or religious group of people. A crime under international law. The term genocide comes from the Greek word '*genos*' for race/tribe and '*cide*', a Latin suffix for killing.

Ethnic cleansing
A policy designed by one ethnic or religious group to purposefully remove another ethnic or religious group from a geographic area by means of violence and terror.

Global security
A conceptualization of security that prioritizes global, transboundary and international security issues.

Humanitarianism
A philosophy, doctrine and/or policy that actively promotes the value and welfare of human life.

The human security agenda highlighted how security threats were not limited by a state's territorial boundaries. Threats to human security could come not only from beyond a state's borders, but also from and within the state itself. During the 1990s and early 2000s, horrific acts of **genocide** and **ethnic cleansing** took place in countries such as Rwanda, Somalia, Bosnia, the Congo and Sudan, drawing international attention to the security threat presented by the state to its own people (see Chapter Fifteen). In these cases, the sovereign state was not the object to be secured, but the very cause of insecurity for its citizens.

The human security agenda further highlighted how threats to humankind came from transboundary *global* issues that no one state could address alone. Issues such as economic security addressing global poverty and income inequalities, food security (pg. 191) and the threat of malnutrition and inadequate access to food, health security and the spread of infectious and parasitic diseases, and environmental security and the impacts of water scarcity, water pollution, air pollution, natural disasters and climate change therefore constituted **global security** threats.

Since the 1990s, human security has been firmly embraced by the United Nations, and adopted by several governments such as Canada, Norway and Japan. These countries coupled the human security lens with that of a humanitarian foreign policy that championed human rights, international humanitarian law and international development. Human security can therefore be associated with **humanitarianism** (Suhrke 1999) and drawn upon to prioritize any number of non-military foreign policy instruments such as in trade and development policy, or in humanitarian assistance programmes.

Yet, while national-military security frames may be criticized for being too narrow, human security has also been criticized for being overly broad in its conceptualization. As Suhrke (1999) reflects, the UNDP conceptualization of human security was almost synonymous with that of human *development* and therefore suffered from a somewhat circular illogic of where one should start and the other finish. Under that logic any issue can be considered a security issue if human life is thought vulnerable. Since the turn of the 21st century, conceptualizations of security have thus continued to develop, with growing emphasis now also being placed on specified security domains.

SECURITY DOMAINS

Despite their respective criticisms, both the minimalist-lensed conceptualization of *national security*, favoured by realists and traditional security scholars, and the maximalist-lensed conceptualization of *human security*, favoured by more critical scholars, have remained in regular use within international politics, being frequently drawn upon by policymakers and academics alike. State-centrism and the prioritization of national security has continued to play a strong role in the 21st century, as nuclear proliferation, coupled with growing concerns over international terrorism, became a focal point for new and pressing security threats against the state. Technological advancement, particularly in weapons, defensive technology and cyber warfare, has further kept the state and its respective military and intelligence capabilities to the forefront of national security deliberations. Yet, human security concerns are increasingly prioritized by international organizations, NGOs and some states, as well as by critical scholars. We can particularly see this broadening understanding of security, as both a national and human security issue, by considering the various traditional and non-traditional domains now addressed as security concerns.

A security domain is understood as any issue area and field of operation considered a security concern. Traditionally, the primary security domain of concern to states within international politics was military security, thereby aligning with the narrow conceptualization of war as organized violence (pg. 178). Interstate and conventional warfare (pg. 170–1) demanded that states maintain a strong national military capability to defend the state and fight against aggressors. Military security was concerned, therefore, with the domains of land, air and sea with an emphasis on armed forces capable of maritime, air and land defence. After World War Two, the military domain then also became concerned with the dawn of the nuclear age and the spread of **nuclear weapons**. The threat of nuclear proliferation, particularly to non-state actors, also meant that terrorism became a prominent security domain, with enhanced arms controls and counter-terrorist measures being implemented by states around the world.

Nuclear weapon
An explosive device that derives its destructive power from nuclear reaction, causing widespread injury and death both from the immediate blast and radiation. The first nuclear weapons developed used nuclear fission (atomic or A-bomb), whereas later weapons used nuclear fusion (thermonuclear, hydrogen or H-bomb).

Cyberspace (pg. 172) has also become a security domain of concern to states, with cyber security concerning the threats from state and non-state actors attacking national and international cyber systems and their associated infrastructures. In 2019, NATO also formally declared that space was now considered one of its operational domains, alongside land, air, sea and cyberspace. Space security has increasingly drawn the attention of states in recent years due to concerns of space weaponization, including developments in anti-satellite weaponry which could put any of the estimated 2,000 orbital satellites – needed for intelligence gathering, GPS navigation, communications, weather forecasting, air travel and banking – in jeopardy.

Security has also extended into other more non-traditional domains associated less with military and national security, and more with human security and threats to individual human lives. First highlighted as security domains in the 1970s, economic security and environmental security have today become pressing security concerns in international politics, and are frequently linked to other security domains such as development. For example, the World Bank's 2011 World Development Report stated that 'war is development in reverse' (World Bank 2021). The UN further advocates an integrated sustainable peace agenda (pg. 117) directly linked with the UN Sustainable Development Goals (pg. 234). In 2021 NATO too endorsed its own *Climate Change and Security Agenda*, seeking to raise awareness of the impacts of climate change on security, and setting out adaptation and mitigation measures for its members to implement in addressing climate as a security domain. The environment is also a security domain linked with food security, and the risks associated with food supplies, and addressing poverty and hunger. Energy has also increasingly been recognized as a security domain, with energy security now a key concern for governments and individuals alike (pg. 243–4).

Health security is another domain that has evolved since the 1990s, with pandemics increasingly associated with national security (Davies 2013). In 1995, for example, the World Health Organization set out to revise its International Health Regulations to take 'effective account of the threat posed by the international spread of new and re-emerging diseases' (WHO 1995). Global health security, with its emphasis on the prevention and detection of disease outbreaks, along with the definition and conceptualization of what constitutes a health emergency or threat (Harman 2021), has since become a thriving field of study within international politics. Covid-19 further shone a light on health as a security domain, highlighting how human security issues have become more salient in national security agendas – see also toolkit at the end of this chapter.

SPOTLIGHT ON NUCLEAR WEAPONS

As we have discussed so far, security can be conceptualized in multiple different ways, spanning multiple, oftentimes overlapping, traditional and non-traditional domains. In this section we turn a spotlight on to the possession, threat of use and renunciation of nuclear weapons as an issue that has not only come to dominate security agendas since 1945, but which particularly highlights the multifaceted, and at times overlapping, nature of security as a concept, domain and issue within international politics. Shining a spotlight on nuclear weapons is also helpful as nuclear weapons span a diverse range of security domains ranging from traditional military security to human security, health security, energy security and environmental security. Nuclear weapons are also a highly divisive security issue in contemporary international politics, and noticeably highlight some of the challenges that follow from competing national and human security agendas. Also, nuclear weapons are not, as some have argued, a relic of the Cold War and a '20th century weapon' (Burt 2011). Today, nuclear weapons are increasingly being highlighted in the news as well as in popular discourse, following threats of use (particularly by Russia after its invasion of Ukraine in 2022), and due to emerging technologies, both of which have significantly enhanced the ontological insecurities associated with these weapons. Nuclear-weapon states are also modernizing – and in some cases increasing – their nuclear arsenals. Nuclear security is therefore once again a point of concern for governments, and among civil society activists (pg. 150–1) around the world in a way we have not seen since the 1960s and 1970s.

Much of the insecurity associated with nuclear weapons of course relates to their status as weapons of mass destruction (WMD). A nuclear weapon is designed for indiscriminate destruction on a massive scale, with modern weapons capable of a blast damage radius of some several hundred square kilometres. Nuclear weapons are in fact thousands, and in some cases, millions of times more powerful in their explosive force relative to a conventional weapon. In addition to the damage caused by the initial shock blast, nuclear weapons generate thermal energy that causes fires and skin burns at considerable distances, and radiation that causes longer-term sickness, death and environmental degradation.

It took one B-29 heavy bomber aircraft, the *Enola Gay*, dropping one atomic bomb, named 'Little Boy', to destroy the Japanese city of Hiroshima on 6 August 1945 with an estimated 70,000 to 80,000 deaths from the immediate blast, and another 50,000 to 60,000 deaths from the radioactive fallout. It would have taken an estimated 210 B-29s carrying a bomb load of 2,100 tonnes to have produced the same destructive effect as the atomic bomb blast (US Strategic Bombing Survey 1946: 38), not then counting the longer-term radiation impacts on the people and environment. Worth noting that today's nuclear weapons are also far more powerful than the atomic bombs first developed and used in 1945.

During the Cold War the major security concerns associated with nuclear weapons related primarily to their proliferation, and possible use. Only a few years after the US deployed atomic bombs against Japan in August 1945, the Soviet Union tested its first atomic bomb (1949), followed in 1952 by the United Kingdom. France and China became nuclear-weapon states in 1961 and 1964 respectively. India then joined the nuclear club in 1971, followed by Israel in 1986 and Pakistan in 1998. At the height of the nuclear arms race in 1986, there were over 70,000 nuclear weapons in the world. Today, the global inventory of nuclear weapons stands at 12,700 warheads – now shared among nine nuclear-weapon states since North Korea tested its first nuclear weapon in 2006 (pg. 63).

National security and nuclear weapons

Developed primarily for defensive and deterrence purposes, the nuclear arms race dominated national security agendas during the Cold War. For governments developing nuclear arsenals, their national interest was the defence of their citizens and the deterrence that nuclear weapons afforded against attack. From a neorealist perspective, the development of nuclear weapons in military arsenals was in many ways an inevitable progression of the security dilemma pervading international politics (pg. 42). As Waltz argued, states would seek to maximize their security through establishing a balance of power (pg. 22). Nuclear weapons – which serve as an advanced military capability and therefore power resource – were therefore expected to spread, as other states sought to balance their power, deter attack, and achieve regional and international order and stability. Taking the example of Iran's nuclear development, and concerns over nuclear proliferation in the Middle East, Waltz in fact stated that:

> If Iran goes nuclear, Israel and Iran will deter each other, as nuclear powers always have. There has never been a full-scale war between two nuclear-armed states. Once Iran crosses the nuclear threshold, deterrence will apply, even if the Iranian arsenal is relatively small. No other country in the region will have an incentive to acquire its own nuclear capability, and the current crisis will finally dissipate, leading to a Middle East that is more stable than it is today. (Waltz 2012: 5)

Explore More

Interested in learning more about the consequences of a nuclear war in today's international system? Check out https://sgs.princeton.edu/the-lab/plan-a to see a contemporary simulation video showing a plausible escalation war between the United States and Russia that uses real nuclear force postures, targets and fatality estimates. You can also look at https://nukemap.org for an interactive map that allows you to see what impact different types and yield of nuclear weapon can have upon any location in the world. Explore https://hibakusha-worldwide.org for an interactive map of the health and environmental issues related to uranium mining and nuclear testing. Or visit www.icanw.org/storytelling for personal stories of those individuals directly impacted by nuclear testing.

Scan the QR code for access to explore weblinks and more resources.

Waltz further highlighted the example of how India and Pakistan, despite being 'historic rivals', had signed a treaty agreeing not to target each other's nuclear facilities (Waltz 2012; 5). **Mutual deterrence** had therefore ensured that they would never target each other for fear of their own destruction. Thus, 'where nuclear capabilities emerge, so too, does stability' (Waltz 2012: 5). During the Cold War, the related logic of mutually assured destruction (pg. 25) between the US and USSR also ensured that no war or conflict between the two superpowers or their respective allies escalated into a nuclear war. The very fear of nuclear weapons ever being used was therefore considered sufficient to deter conflict and thus maintain stability.

Mutual deterrence The maintenance of peaceful relations between opposing states by each having sufficient strike capability to deter the other from initiating conflict.

Over time, 'the era of nuclear crises came to be replaced by stable nuclear deterrence between the superpowers, and a more than fifty-year "tradition" of nuclear non-use emerged' (Tannenwald 2009: 6). As Cowen (2022) reflects, 'the use of nuclear weapons has now shifted into the "unthinkable" category'. A **non-proliferation** norm has also emerged within international politics (pg. 61). Much in line with the common security agenda detailed by the Palme Commission in 1982 – underwritten by the belief that 'international security must rest on a commitment to *joint survival* rather than a threat of *mutual destruction*' (Common Security 2022, emphasis added) – states have worked collectively to develop a complex network of bilateral and multilateral nuclear non-proliferation and disarmament treaties, conventions and organizations that specifically aim to control the spread of nuclear materials and weapons technology.

Non-proliferation The action or process of preventing the spread of nuclear weapons, including the commitment by non-nuclear-weapon states not to acquire nuclear weapons.

Of particular note among these treaties is the 1968 Treaty on the Non-Proliferation of Nuclear Weapons (NPT) which enshrines three pillars or commitments by its 190 States Parties:[2]

1. the commitment to pursue negotiations in good faith in pursuit of general and complete *nuclear disarmament*,
2. the commitment by all States Parties to *nuclear non-proliferation*,
3. the commitment by all States Parties to the *peaceful uses of nuclear energy*.

Explore More

You can find out about all the treaties, conventions and organizations relating to disarmament, arms control and non-proliferation of WMD, along with their key dates, signatories and objectives by visiting the Nuclear Threat Initiative at www.nti.org. You might also want to check out the UN Office of Disarmament Affairs web pages which includes a link to the disarmament treaties database, showing the status of all multilateral Arms Regulation and Disarmament agreements, including nuclear-weapon-free zones at www.un.org/disarmament.

Scan the QR code for access to explore weblinks and more resources.

The NPT has become the cornerstone of the global nuclear weapons regime, being established on a *grand bargain*: the majority of its non-nuclear-weapon states committed not to acquire nuclear weapons, along with rigorous safeguards that control the use of their nuclear materials, on the provision that the five-signatory nuclear-weapon states – the US, Russia, China, UK and France (P5) – committed to eventual nuclear disarmament. Under that bargain, states such as South Africa, Ukraine, Belarus and Kazakhstan, who had previously developed or held nuclear weapons in their territories, relinquished their weapons to join the NPT as non-nuclear-weapon states in the 1990s. Five regions around the world also committed to become nuclear-weapon-free zones, covering territories in most of the southern hemisphere and Central Asia.

When the Cold War ended, nuclear weapons remained a salient security issue. In the 1990s and early 2000s the security threat associated with nuclear weapons shifted somewhat, concerned more with the threat of **rogue states** such as North Korea, Iraq and Iran developing a nuclear weapon. After the 9/11 terrorist attacks against the United States, and the start of the War on Terror in 2001 (pg. 169), the fear further arose of terrorist groups such as Al Qaeda (pg. 155) being able to obtain the resources, technology and skill to develop a crude nuclear weapon to target the West. Whereas deterrence logics assumed that no nuclear-weapon state, acting rationally, would ever use nuclear weapons for risk of destruction, fears in the 1990s and 2000s oriented around *irrational* actors obtaining nuclear materials and developing the weapon.

Rogue state
A term originally coined by the United States to refer to those states who break international law and pose a threat to the security of others within the international system.

Other national security concerns associated with nuclear weapons have also increasingly focused on wider security domains, such as fears of cyberattacks against nuclear facilities, including nuclear energy plants designed for peaceful uses. Space also became a domain of concern, as new missile technologies developed that enabled nuclear-weapon states to mount nuclear weapons on missiles that went into space before returning to earth to meet their target. Intercontinental ballistic missiles (ICBMs) are long-range missiles that leave the earth's atmosphere before re-entry. The race for hypersonic missiles further exacerbates this fear. In October 2021, news broke that China had tested a nuclear-capable hypersonic missile. Hypersonic missiles travel at five times the speed of sound and can be used both at low altitudes and in low-orbit space before coming back to earth to meet their target. An arms race has since ensued, with Russia announcing it too had hypersonic capability in 2022.

[2]It should be noted that India, Pakistan and Israel are not members of the NPT – being unable to join except as non-nuclear-weapon states. North Korea was previously a member of the NPT but sought to withdraw from the Treaty in 2003 to pursue its nuclear weapons programme.

Human security and nuclear weapons

Nuclear weapons have a bearing on a security complex of multiple domains. Some of these domains naturally fall into traditional conceptions of national security – such as military defence, space, cyber and terrorism. Yet, as the atomic bombs in Hiroshima and Nagasaki in August 1945 both attested, the *use* of nuclear weapons creates catastrophic harm to human life, to health and to the environment. Nuclear testing throughout the Cold War had also highlighted the significant human security risks associated with nuclear weapons. The entry into force of the NPT in 1970 advanced a liberal security model grounded on multilateral efforts to prevent the proliferation of nuclear weapons, to put in place strict international controls, coordinated through a common security agreement.

By the late 2000s and early 2010s, increasing numbers of states, including from among the nuclear-armed, began to also seriously discuss the prospects for **nuclear disarmament** and of achieving 'Global Zero' – a world free of nuclear weapons (Obama 2009). Vocal advocates for nuclear disarmament among civil society also advanced this goal, supported by the *hibakusha* – or survivors of the atomic bombings in Japan – as well as individuals, many of them from indigenous populations from places such as Australia, French Polynesia, Kiribati and the Marshall Islands, who have given personal testimony to the human impacts of nuclear testing and use.

Nuclear disarmament The act of reducing or eliminating nuclear weapons from national arsenals.

Image 11.2 A photograph of ten-year-old atomic bomb survivor Yukiko Fujii is displayed at the Hiroshima Peace Memorial Museum to mark the seventy-fifth anniversary of the atomic bomb attack. Yukiko Fujii went on to have two children but died of cancer aged forty-two. She is one of thousands of people whose lives have been impacted by nuclear weapon use or testing.

Source: Carl Court/Getty Images.

Viewed through gendered lenses, the global nuclear order, with the NPT as its cornerstone, appears to 'define the bounds of acceptable nuclear possession' (Panico 2022), and only perpetuates the dominant status quo of a nuclear order and its hierarchy. Critical feminist scholars, such as Acheson (2018), particularly highlight the **patriarchy** of nuclear weapons, reflecting how representatives of nuclear-weapon states have sought to cast supporters of the prohibition treaty (TPNW) as 'delusional', and that 'caring about the humanitarian consequences of nuclear weapons is feminine, weak and not relevant to the job that "real men" have to do to "protect" their countries' (Acheson 2018: 80).

According to Carol Cohn (1987: 717), a key task for feminist scholars in fact is to 'deconstruct' the 'dominant voice of militarized masculinity and decontextualized rationality' surrounding nuclear weapons, particularly concerning the 'cold-blooded inhumanity' of nuclear planning and strategy promulgated by defence intellectuals. From the feminist perspective, therefore, rational deterrence logics and language must be explicitly countered by showcasing and telling the humanitarian impact of nuclear weapons.

Seen through lenses of human security, it is nuclear weapons that present a threat to security because of the catastrophic harm they can cause to human life. For this reason, critical perspectives highlight how nuclear weapons do not make the world safer. Instead, they perpetuate patriarchy and resist humanitarian efforts to achieve a world free of nuclear weapons.

With support for nuclear disarmament growing, in 2010 States Parties to the NPT Review Conference agreed to a Final Document that included among its key points a sentence expressing 'deep concern at *the catastrophic humanitarian consequences* of any use of nuclear weapons and [reaffirmed] the need for all States at all times to comply with applicable international law, including *international humanitarian* law' (UNODA 2010 emphasis added). The first time such a statement had been made in the context of international nuclear negotiations, from that one sentence stemmed a series of intergovernmental conferences focused expressly upon the humanitarian impacts of nuclear weapons. By 2017, following a significant snowballing of support among non-nuclear-weapon states, the Treaty on the Prohibition of Nuclear Weapons (TPNW) (pg. 151) was then approved by the UN General Assembly, essentially banning signatory States from developing or even investing in nuclear weapons or weapons technology. On 1 January 2021 the TPNW entered into force, despite deep resistance and condemnation by the nuclear-armed states and their allies. At the time of writing, none of the nuclear-weapon states or their allies have suggested they will sign the TPNW, and NATO – which upholds deterrence as a key security principle of its alliance – has stated its clear opposition to the treaty, arguing that the TPNW 'does not reflect the increasingly challenging international security environment and is at odds with the existing non-proliferation and disarmament architecture' (NATO 2020).

ORGANIZE

In Chapter Three we discussed the debate between idealists (liberals) and practical people (realists) during the interwar years. That debate heavily centred upon the merits and feasibility of military disarmament. Reflect again on the anti-pacifist cartoon (Image 3.1 pg. 36) depicting the need for an adequate US naval force as an insurance for the Kellogg-Briand Pact.

What lessons might we draw from the interwar years' debate for understanding today's debate concerning nuclear deterrence and the prospects for disarmament?

Do nuclear weapons make the world safer?

Nuclear weapons are contentious for the divisions they emphasize – not least between the nuclear 'haves' and the 'have nots'. Underlying the polarization of this debate are several competing views concerning a foundational security question – *'Do nuclear weapons make the world safer?'*

For neorealists such as Waltz (2012), even the most 'irrational' leaders would never attack a nuclear-weapon state or run the risk of war, because the threat of use of nuclear weapons deters them from provocation. Nuclear weapons thus temper the likelihood of conflict between states. While threats against the state exist – as they always will in an anarchic system – whether from superpower rivals, 'rogue' states or terrorists – a nuclear-weapon state finds its security in deterrence. As such when it comes to nuclear weapons, 'more may be better' (Waltz 2012).

From a postcolonial perspective, the global nuclear order and liberal security model enshrined by treaties such as the NPT are built on a hierarchical power structure which favours and upholds the national security of the nuclear-weapon states at the expense of Third World countries, who are placed in a position of subordination. Neatly summarized by Shampa Biswas, a postcolonial perspective of the NPT follows that 'to the extent that disarmament by existing NWS [nuclear-weapon states] remains a forever deferred goal, NNWS [non-nuclear-weapon states] always remain in the waiting room of history, never quite ready to handle the nuclear weapons that existing NWS deem necessary for their own security yet unavailable to NNWS regardless of their actual felt insecurities' (Biswas 2014: 97-8). For postcolonialists, therefore, nuclear weapons only make the world safer for nuclear-weapon states and their allies. From their position of dominance, they can defer disarmament indefinitely – perpetuating a nuclear order that is built on an entrenched cleavage between a minority of nuclear 'haves' and the majority nuclear 'have nots'.

Constructivists, while analytically neutral on the question of whether nuclear weapons make the world safer or not, do emphasize the normative tradition of non-use that has emerged among nuclear-armed states over time – developed not simply because of the logic of deterrence but by a nuclear taboo that has been constructed as a social understanding of what is deemed 'appropriate' behaviour within international politics (Tannenwald 2009). Similarly, constructivists would suggest that the norm of non-proliferation has also spread globally. That norm, moreover, deems it appropriate for states to comply with international treaties and conventions that control nuclear materials and technology, bind states to uphold nuclear safeguards, and prevent states from conducting nuclear tests. Yet, constructivists and liberals do then equally struggle to explain why states, such as North Korea, reject and withdraw from international arms control agreements, and then overtly develop and test nuclear weapons, and missile technology, in contradiction of accepted norms.

Patriarchy
A system organized along patriarchal lines, where men hold the power to the exclusion of others.

Yet, understanding security and the risk of insecurity in international politics is often a matter of perspective. When addressing the question of whether nuclear weapons make the world safer, we must therefore ask ourselves, *safer for whom*? As we saw in the last section, when we observe nuclear weapons through lenses of human security rather than as a principle of deterrence, nuclear weapons would seem to perpetuate insecurity. When used, nuclear weapons cause catastrophic harm to human life. From an ontological security perspective, the growing threat of nuclear weapons being used has also markedly increased the feeling of insecurity among individuals around the world. Nuclear weapons may then be observed as a matter of both security and insecurity in our international system.

LINK

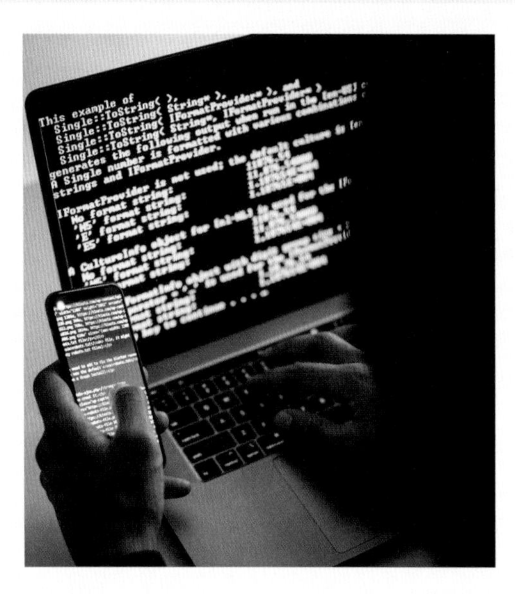

Image 11.3 Cyber connectivity is essential for sustaining our national infrastructures and key systems, including military systems, yet cyber insecurity is on the rise.
Source: Sora Shimazaki/Pexels.

Consider

Cyberspace is another issue which we may observe as a matter of both security and insecurity. According to NATO (n.d.), 'cyber threats … are complex, destructive and coercive, and becoming ever more frequent'. Consider also that ransomware attacks have increasingly targeted health services around the world, further impinging health security. By way of example, on 12 May 2017 the National Health Service (NHS) in the UK was subject to a ransomware attack known as WannaCry. The attack blocked hospital and doctors' surgeries across the country from accessing patient data, further demanding payment in bitcoin (pg. 216) to unlock the system.

Explore

The Centre for Strategic and International Studies 'Significant Cyber Incidents' timeline keeps a record of all cyber incidents dating back to 2006. Available online: www.csis.org. Also explore Joseph Nye's 2017 article entitled 'Deterrence and dissuasion in cyberspace' in *International Security* (Vol. 41. No. 3). Finally, you may also want to check out the 'NHS ransomware attack: What happened and how bad is it?' analysis by Dan Milmo in *The Guardian* newspaper from 2022. Available online: www.theguardian.com or scan the barcode for direct links.

Connect

While deterrence is traditionally connected with nuclear security, deterrence is not unique to nuclear weapons. In fact deterrence as a strategic doctrine has increasingly been connected with a growing range of non-traditional security domains, including in cyber security (Nye 2017). How states 'deter' cyberattacks is nevertheless challenging. Cyberspace is highly unregulated (pg. 216). Attributing a cyberattack to any one particular culprit is therefore notoriously difficult, thus the threat of punishment or reprisal similarly challenging to implement.

Predict

Reflect again on the toolkit exercise on the power of the 'Tech Titans' at the end of Chapter Nine, and the discussion about internet freedom and China's doctrine of 'cyberspace sovereignty' (pg. 161). To what extent do you think national security concerns justify a more heavily regulated cyberspace?

Scan the QR code for access to explore weblinks and more resources.

CONCLUSION

In this chapter we have considered security as both a traditional and critical issue within international politics, looking at security as it relates to the state, and to the individual. We have also considered the broadening security agenda and how security may be understood as an issue that spans multiple, often overlapping, security domains. As we saw when we turned a spotlight on nuclear weapons, security is a complex realm of both analysis and operation, and which can often highlight the cleavages that exist between national and human security agendas. How a state perceives threats against itself will ultimately determine how its resources are prioritized. As perceptions of *in*security widen, however, particularly across issues such as health, energy, food, cyberspace, economics and the environment, perceptions of security will also widen, placing national security agendas under a new spotlight.

As we have also seen, the traditional minimalist conceptualization of national security as a predominantly military concern is not always compatible with the maximalist conceptualization of human security as freedom from want and fear. Perceptions of threat that fall into a traditionalist national security purview, and those that come under the human security umbrella, may not always align, therefore, and can create competing priorities for governments and exacerbate cleavages within international politics. For scholars of international politics, therefore, it is important for us to consider *whose* security is of concern when addressing security threats in international politics. Common, collective, global, national, human and ontological securities give us different conceptual lenses to employ, and different priorities to emphasize. You can develop on these points and refine your understanding of security further by looking at the following toolkit exercise asking, *'Should states invest in public health as a security concern after Covid-19?'*

TOOLKIT

Should states invest in public health as a security concern after Covid-19?

THINK

- Do you think a minimalist (national) or maximalist (human) security conceptualization is best to use when thinking about public health?

OBSERVE

Image 11.4 Army personnel oversee a checkpoint in Dhaka, Bangladesh during a countrywide lockdown in July 2021. Bangladesh enacted its national lockdown after a third wave of Covid-19, rising deaths and due to fears of the spreading Delta variant which had been detected in neighbouring India. Like many countries, Bangladesh deployed its armed forces to help enforce the lockdown and oversee its citizens.

Source: SOPA Images/Getty Images.

- To date nearly 6.5 million people have died from Covid-19 according to the World Health Organization (WHO). In Bangladesh, where this image was taken, just over 2 million citizens had confirmed cases of Covid-19, with a recorded 29,314 deaths. Neighbouring India had the world's second largest number of cumulative cases of Covid-19 (behind the US) and the third highest number of Covid-19-related deaths at 527,253. In countries around the world, public health became a new national security concern as the virus spread and deaths rose.
- On 5 May 2023 the WHO announced the 'Covid global health emergency is over' (BBC News 2023). The WHO highlights, however, that the number of high-threat infectious hazards is on the rise, including epidemic-prone diseases such as yellow fever, cholera and influenza.
- In normal conditions, a state's healthcare expenditure per capita is typically far higher than its military expenditure. In 2018, the US, for example, spent approximately 14 per cent of its GDP on healthcare, compared to 3.3 per cent of its GDP on military.
- During the pandemic, governments invested heavily in vaccine development and distribution, as well as Personal Protective Equipment (PPE) and other safety measures, substantially increasing the costs of health procurement. By 2025 a further estimated $157 billion is expected to be spent by governments on Covid-19 vaccines (Reuters 2021).

ORGANIZE

- From a realist perspective, healthcare is a 'low politics' (pg. 149) issue. For a state to secure itself it must invest in its military capabilities and defence, to deter against attack from others.
- Liberalism highlights the benefits of international organizations like the WHO for addressing common health security threats. While public health remains a national government

responsibility, states can still work together to share research and develop vaccines. See also the discussion about IO effectiveness on pg. 119–20.
- Postcolonialism highlights the global inequalities in public healthcare particularly in the Third World, the lack of interest by the West when epidemics have occurred in Third World countries, and further evidenced by the slower roll-out of vaccines to the Third World during the Covid-19 pandemic.
- Reflect again on the conceptualization of human security developed by the UNDP (pg. 189–90). Do threats to our health constitute a threat to our freedom from want or fear?
- Consider again the discussion of security domains in this chapter (pg. 190–1). Which security domains do you think were most impacted during Covid-19? Does this impact how governments perceive health as a security issue?

- *Consider*: In Chapter Six we considered the various state foreign policy instruments (Table 6.1). How a state understands security can determine which of those foreign policy instruments it will best utilize and prioritize in its resource attribution and spending. A state that observes security through traditional minimalist lenses will likely prioritize its Department or Ministry of Defence, investing heavily in its defence and military-related foreign policy instruments. A state that observes security through maximalist human security lenses may be more inclined to invest in foreign policy instruments associated with aid, development or trade departments, as well as prioritizing domestic spending, such as healthcare.
- *Explore*: Explore global and national military spending relative to healthcare spending by visiting the World Bank databank at https://data.worldbank.org. Through the databank you can search for military expenditure as well as current healthcare expenditure in the search bar, showing trends over time, as well as differentiation across countries. Also explore the United States Congressional Research Service briefing entitled 'Covid-19: National Security and Defense Strategy' from 2020 which details how the United States' national security toolkit should be broadened to address the 'non-traditional' security threat presented by Covid-19. You can access this short two-page briefing at https://crsreports.congress.gov or scan the barcode to locate these links on the companion website.
- *Connect*: Securitization is the reframing of an issue into a security threat. As discussed in this chapter (pg. 187), security should be understood as a highly fluid framing tool, prioritizing how different threats are perceived and how governments in turn direct and prioritize decision-making in the national interest. If an issue can be securitized, it can also therefore be desecuritized.
- *Predict*: With an effective Covid-19 vaccine programme being rolled out around the world, to what extent do you think health will experience a process of desecuritization as a national and international security concern?

SHARE

- Answer the question – *'Should states invest in public health as a security concern after Covid-19?'*

  What theory, concepts or examples will you use to help construct your argument? What data will help you evidence your claims? You may also want to check out *How to – approach an oral presentation* (pg. 277) for some tips on approaching this sort of question as a timed oral presentation or look at *How to – prepare an academic poster* (pg. 259) for guidance on communicating your answer even more concisely using a poster.

HOW TO

APPROACH A LITERATURE REVIEW

Read any academic journal and you will likely find attention is given in the early sections to a 'literature review'. In fact, most academic research starts with a thorough analysis of what has already been written in the research field. During your studies you may also be asked to conduct your own literature review of a given topic. To help you conduct that review, included here are just a few top tips that continue to build on our **TOOLS** as a learning and research strategy.

THINK – How do you identify the relevant literature?

When you are relatively new to a field of study, it can feel overwhelming trying to familiarize yourself with all the literature that has been written about it. There are few shortcuts in academia – especially where it concerns the necessity to read and familiarize yourself with the work of scholars within your given field. But you can narrow your search using well-selected key words and other search parameters when looking to identify relevant journal articles and books in your university library or other online search engines. For example, if your literature review were about the scholarship associated with, say, global health and security, you might set your key word search as 'global health' AND 'security'. This may still return hundreds of results, but you can again narrow your search parameters using additional key words i.e. 'Covid-19', 'pandemic' or 'World Health Organization', for example.

When searching for your literature, do also pay attention to the date range of publications you are identifying using your key word search. You may find that your topic was particularly popular during a certain date range but that fewer books or articles were written on the topic after that date. Focus also on the type of publications you are identifying in your search. Are there more books or journal articles? More **grey literature** than articles? This information can also inform your literature review. Once you have identified your literature, scan the titles, abstracts and key words of each paper to filter out any papers that are less relevant to your topic. The rest you can then start to review more closely.

OBSERVE – What are the different arguments?

Start skim-reading your identified literature. With each article, or chapter, aim to catalogue what the scholar is focused on and what their main argument is. As you continue reading and cataloguing you will start to see the different perspectives being presented and – most likely (this is Politics!) – competing arguments about your given topic. This is the mainstay of any good literature review as it enables you to demonstrate the different debates within your field of research, and the competing views at play. Be aware of alternative perspectives as well. You may need to refine your key word search to identify these, perhaps looking for more critical accounts of your topic. Do also pay attention to the bibliographies of the literature you are reviewing, because these can also help you track down competing perspectives, alternative arguments or literature you may have missed in your original search. Remember, there are always other arguments and other points of view in international politics. Just because an argument is well established, or seemingly accepted in the scholarship you are reading, does not mean other views are not out there. So, take some time to reflect on alternative views, and different arguments. This is where your critical analysis also starts to come to the fore (*see also How to – develop critical analysis skills* pg. 163).

Grey literature
Literature not formally published in journals or books, such as government reports, working papers, graduate dissertations, etc.

ORGANIZE – What theories or concepts are being used or neglected?

Another important benefit of conducting a literature review is that it helps give a sense of how other scholars have used theories and concepts to analyse your topic. When reading and cataloguing your literature, therefore, take note of any theoretical framework (pg. 70) or specific concepts being used. Consider how these theories or concepts are informing the analysis and shaping the author's argument. When it comes to writing up your literature review you can then engage in discussion of the approaches used. Reflect also on any theoretical approaches that you know of, but which are perhaps less prevalent in the literature you are reviewing. Another benefit of a literature review is that they can help identify potential knowledge gaps, specifically in those areas where there is perhaps room for new research, or new approaches to be applied.

LINK and SHARE – Think forest, not trees!

By now you should have a good catalogue of different arguments and theoretical approaches being used in individual articles or books focused on your specific topic. Now you want to start to make connections between them by looking for the major themes or trends within the field as a whole. Writing a good literature review is ultimately about highlighting the major trends or themes within the field of scholarship you are reviewing. Imagine, therefore, that the field of scholarship around your topic is like a forest, with each of the individual articles and book chapters that you've read as the individual trees within it. When you communicate your literature review you want to focus on the forest itself, rather than discussing every single tree. Write your literature review focusing then on the following points:

- What are the major trends within this field of scholarship? [these may be zones within your forest that you are looking to connect with pathways]
- What are the competing perspectives/arguments? [the zones on opposite sides of your forest]
- What theories/concepts are commonly used? [these may be different types of trees that you can identify in your forest]
- What gaps may be identified? [these are the bare patches within your forest]

You may find you want to highlight books or articles that are particularly prominent in the field but avoid making your whole literature review about only very selected pieces of work. The aim here is to convey the scope and themes of the literature already written within the field of research, so go broad rather than narrow in your viewpoint.

12 Trade and finance

Pexels / Julius Silver

Abstract

Trade and finance constitute the backbone of our international economy. In this chapter you will discover more about trade and finance as essential issues of international political economy (IPE). First, we shall consider the emergence of IPE as a distinct field of academic study alongside some of the theoretical lenses that we can utilize to analyse it. From there you will be introduced to some of the international economic organizations that formed after World War Two. The chapter then turns to consider some principles of international trade and the changing politics of trade today, including the rise of global value chains, and the changing nature of international trade negotiations. The chapter then addresses several issues within international finance, looking particularly at currencies, foreign exchange, and the politics surrounding cryptocurrencies. The chapter concludes with a toolkit exercise to enable you to apply and develop some of your knowledge from this chapter, asking *'Why did the United States start the 2018 trade wars?'*

UNDERSTANDING INTERNATIONAL POLITICAL ECONOMY

Trade
The voluntary action of buying and selling goods and services between economic actors.

Where politics is associated with relationships of power (pg. 7), economics concerns relationships of wealth. If, as the adage goes, *wealth is power*, then understanding how wealth and power intersect and thus how economics and politics intertwine within our international system is of particular interest to international politics scholars. **Trade** has connected humankind for millennia. Well before the first nation-states were formed, communities were connected through markets and trade routes. The Silk Road, for example, established under the Han dynasty, spanned much of the Eurasian continent, enabling the trade of exotic goods between the 2nd century BC and the mid-15th century. As soon as money began to be used for the indirect trade of goods and services, **finance** too became a foundation on which economic relationships were built. Together, trade and finance became the bedrock on which national economies were established, and the means by which they were connected.

Today, the spread of international trade and finance have brought our world and the **international economy** closer than ever before. Since the turn of the 21st century, global **gross domestic product** (GDP) – a measurement of total economic output – increased from around $60 trillion in 2000 to just over $100 trillion in the early 2020s. In the same period, the value of world trade in goods increased from $6.45 trillion to $22.3 trillion. The total value of shares traded on stock markets around the world increased from $46.42 trillion in 2000 to $101.17 trillion in 2015. Today the top 100 largest public companies in the world account for nearly $48 trillion in revenues. As we saw in Chapter Nine, the growth and spread of multinational enterprises (MNEs) has also correlated with the growth of international trade, with 80 per cent of global trade now linked to MNEs and the value chains (pg. 156) they create.

Finance
Concerning the management, creation and study of money.

International economy
An international economic system comprising all the economic activities that take place within and between individual countries.

Gross domestic product
A measurement of the gross size of an economy that takes into account all consumer, investment and government expenditure along with net exports.

According to the Organization for Economic Cooperation and Development, multinational enterprises (MNEs) are considered 'central and dominant actors in the global economy' (Cadestin et al. 2018), accounting for roughly one third of global output and half of global exports. Important to consider, however, is that MNEs are just one type of economic actor within the international economy.

Think back to the discussion of the state (Chapter Six), international and regional organizations (Chapters Seven and Eight) and non-state actors (Chapter Nine). What other economic actors can you identify in international politics? Which actors do you think are the most 'central and dominant' in the international economy?

While the study of politics and economics can be dated back to at least the 1770s when Adam Smith first published *The Wealth of Nations*, the academic study of international political economy (IPE)[1] began to emerge as a specific sub-field within international politics in the early 1970s. The birth of IPE is often attributed to the work of Susan Strange, who in 1970 wrote of the unequal rate of change within the international political and economic systems, and argued the necessity of studying the global economy to fully understand international cooperation and organization (Strange 1970). As we also saw in Chapter Three and Four, theoretical approaches to international politics have evolved through narratives over time, often referred to as the 'great debates'. It was during the third great debate (pg. 51) that IPE developed, as scholarship began to address questions of global wealth, production, development and inequality within the international system. IPE advanced the blending of economic and international political perspectives to understand the relationship between wealth and power within our international system.

International political economy (IPE) is broadly concerned with how politics constrains and facilitates economic choices and vice versa (Walter and Sen 2009: 1). IPE views the international system as both a political and economic system, one in which 'market systems and political systems are co-constitutive' (Broome 2014: 12).

[1]Also referred to as Global Political Economy (GPE).

IPE is particularly interested in the political processes and outcomes associated with all activities in the international economy. Traditionally, though, two key areas of interest in IPE concern the political processes and outcomes associated with international trade and finance.

We need only revisit the historical evolution of the international system to see how trade and finance have moulded the world in which we live. Consider that the European Age of Discovery (pg. 16) in the 15th and 16th centuries was largely driven by incentives of wealth, with Europe's empires flourishing through the conquest and colonization of new lands in Africa, Asia and America, the creation of new trade links, and the procurement of new commodities to buy and sell. Mercantilism (pg. 19) drove much of the imperial era as European states sought to control an ever-wider network of colonies, thereby maximizing their exports, minimizing their imports, and growing rich on the gold they acquired.

OBSERVE

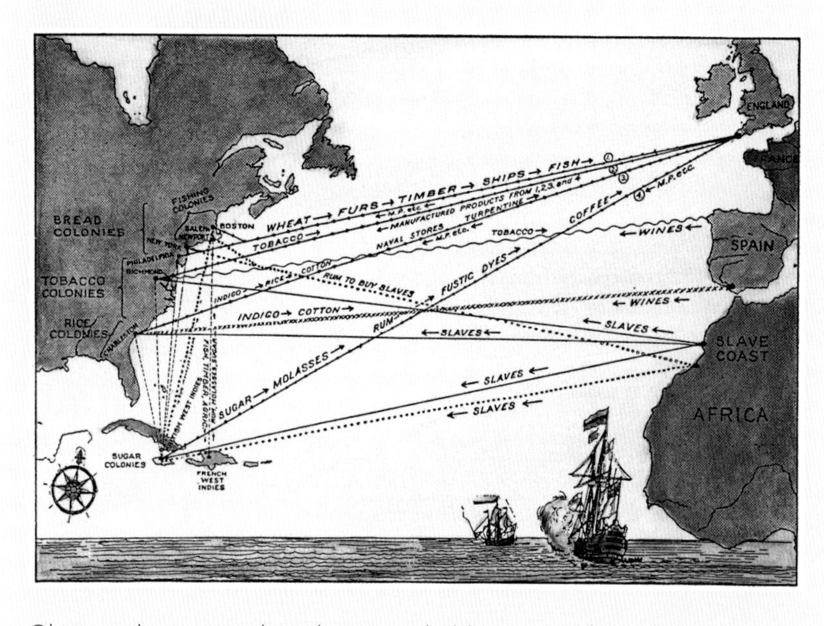

Map 12.1 A trade map from the 17th century. The map highlights the triangular trade routes between Britain, its American colonies and Africa. Slaves were transported from Africa to America who then worked to produce the rice, wheat, cotton, dyes, sugar, coffee, tobacco and timber which were transported from America back to Britain.

Source: The Granger Collection/Alamy.

Observe the commodities being traded between Africa, the British West Indies (Caribbean) and America in this map of trade routes used by the British Empire in the 17th century. Slave ships arriving in the Caribbean from Africa would unload and sell their cargo of enslaved people before reloading with sugar, rum and coffee to make the return journey to Britain.

As discussed in Chapter Two, imperialism in the 18th and 19th centuries was largely driven by mercantilism, a policy which associated the power of the state with the pursuit of wealth. Mercantilism is the economic policy associated with export maximization and import minimization. For empires – like the British Empire – this meant drawing on the resources of their own colonies, rather than importing from competitors, thereby augmenting their economic position at the expense of their rivals.

For critical scholars, the economic policies established during the age of empire remain embedded in the contemporary international system. Dependency theorists particularly emphasize how former imperial powers continue to exploit the labour and resources of their former colonies, locking them into a relationship of dependency and underdevelopment (pg. 54).

Today, the proliferation of multinational enterprise (MNEs) and the spread of foreign direct investment (pg. 156) have continued to connect governments, banks and businesses in a complex global economic network. That network operates at both the physical and digital level. In the physical, the international economy is grounded and connected in a global infrastructure of roads, railways, waterways and ports that cross and connect national economies. Consider that many of the same trade routes that connected human settlements and empires in centuries past continue to connect states today. For example, since 2013 the Chinese government has proactively pushed forward efforts to resurrect the Silk Road through its **Belt and Road Initiative** (BRI). Through the BRI, China has invested in nearly 150 countries and international organizations, enhancing infrastructure projects across land and sea in an effort to enhance connectivity and cooperation on a transcontinental scale.

Belt and Road Initiative
A transcontinental development and infrastructure strategy advanced by the Chinese government after 2013 to stimulate economic development and markets across Eurasia. The 'Belt' refers to the overland corridors that replicate and extend the old Silk Road. The 'Road' refers to the maritime road of shipping lanes connecting China to Europe.

As well as its physical infrastructure, the international economy is also built upon a global network of digital infrastructure that facilitates the movement of money around the world. Consider that in 2020 only 7 per cent of the world's money was physical money i.e. coins and banknotes. A massive 93 per cent of the world's money is non-physical, held in checking and savings accounts, funds and deposits, etc. Today we use card payments, apps and websites to move our money and pay for products, with individuals, businesses, banks and governments regularly engaging in cross-border payments through digital financial transactions.

Our international economy is heavily reliant upon a digital infrastructure of financial messaging and bank transfers facilitated by international communication technology. SWIFT, or the Society for Worldwide Interbank Financial Telecommunication, for example, was established in 1973 specifically to facilitate secure financial transactions around the world. In September 2022 alone, SWIFT recorded an average of 44.8 million financial messages *per day* (SWIFT 2022). CIPS, or the Cross-Border Interbank Payment System, is another such system, set up as a Chinese alternative to SWIFT and which processes payments in Chinese yuan. According to the Bank of England, cross-border payments have not only markedly increased in the last few decades, but the total value of global cross-border payments is also estimated to increase from almost $150 trillion in 2017 to $250 trillion by 2027 (Bank of England 2022). As international trade and **e-commerce** boom and MNEs continue to expand their assets abroad, our reliance on both the physical and digital infrastructure that facilitate international trade and finance will only deepen.

E-commerce
The buying and selling of goods and services over the internet.

Explore More

The international economy relies upon a vast network of trade routes which ensure that physical goods reach their destination. Each year the world shipping industry alone transports 11 billion tonnes of goods, including nearly 2 billion tonnes of crude oil, 1 billion tonnes of iron ore and 350 million tonnes of grain (International Chamber of Shipping 2022). You can find out more about the volume, type and reach of global cargo shipping, including key routes, using this interactive map at www.shipmap.org.

Consider also what happens when trade routes are blocked. In 2021 the Suez Canal – which sees around 12 per cent of all global trade pass through it each day – was blocked when the cargo ship *Ever Given* ran aground. Cargo ships had to either wait or divert around the Cape of Good Hope, adding approximately ten days to their journey times to Europe. The delays were estimated to have held up around $9.6 billion of trade each day that the *Ever Given* remained aground. Explore news and analysis of these events by scanning the barcode and visiting the companion website for more links.

Scan the QR code for access to explore weblinks and more resources.

THEORETICAL PERSPECTIVES

As a scholar of international politics, it is important to understand the relationships of wealth and power within our interconnected international economy, as well as how economic changes impact politics and vice versa. IPE theoretical approaches can help us to understand, explain, predict and critique the actors, events, issues and relationships within IPE. As we covered in Chapter Six, the sovereign state has become the main organizing unit of peoples and territories within the contemporary international system. Territories within defined borders are governed by national governments, who have authority to raise taxes, issue currency and oversee the welfare of their citizenry. Yet, in the study of economics, it is markets that are more often the primary focus. The reason for this point of focus is that the international economy operates on the principles of a **market economy**, 'one in which goods and services are exchanged on the basis of relative prices ... where transactions are negotiated and prices are determined' (Gilpin 1987: 18). Drawing upon the theories outlined in Chapters Three and Four, we can also observe how different theoretical perspectives similarly emphasize different actors and issues within IPE; perspectives which we can then use in our own research and analysis.

Market economy
An economic system based on market principles of freedom, competition and efficiency.

Consider that from a Marxist IPE perspective, economics is assumed to be a primary driver of politics (pg. 55). Marxism particularly emphasizes the disparity of wealth distribution in a free-market economy and highlights how capitalist processes generate class conflict between the capitalist elite (the owners and managers of wealth) and the subordinate proletariat (the workers). From a Marxist IPE perspective, therefore, a major point of analysis is less to do with markets or the state itself, and more about the social relations between owners and workers within the international economy. For example, Marxist scholarship in IPE addresses actors such as the increasing transnationalization of trade unions (Cox 1971) or issues such as the rising gap between higher productivity and stagnating wages (Karanassou and Sala 2014). Marxist and postcolonial scholarship has also emphasized the issue of class exploitation within IPE (Chibber 2013) and draws particular attention to the dependencies and inequalities embedded within the international economy.

Marxist IPE perspectives do also give account to, and critique of, the role of the state in IPE. From a historical materialist perspective (pg. 52) both the state and capitalism must be understood as a historically specific phenomena that may in time shift as capitalism changes. For some Marxist scholarship, the transnational and interconnected nature of the international economy has already seen a retreat of the state – a point mirrored by Strange (1988) who reflected upon the growing power of the global market relative to the nation-state. The state is therefore observed to have some purpose as 'transmission belts into local arenas for global capital' (Dunn 2015: 307; see also Cox 1996), but as a territorially bound actor, the state is also considered limited in the face of globalization and the mobility of global capital. Marxist scholarship also provides an important critique of the capitalist state, observing the state itself as an extension of the interests of the ruling economic elite who seek to perpetuate capitalism because they prosper the most from it. Marxist IPE approaches also reflect how interstate competition continues to characterize international political economy. Marxist IPE perspectives further showcase that the various international economic organizations established after World War Two (which we will turn to in the next section), 'continue to operate as tools of a few powerful states' (Dunn 2015: 313).

According to Griffin (2016) feminists also 'do' political economy, yet 'in distinctive, diverse and important ways'. Similar to Marxism, feminist IPE examines socioeconomic processes within the international economy. But whereas Marxist IPE tends to prioritize research of class relations, feminist IPE research focuses more explicitly on gender in economic processes, and the gendered inequalities inherent to IPE. Feminist IPE particularly exposes gendered divisions in labour, for example, the economic inequalities associated with sex and social reproduction. For example, Mezzadri, Newman and Stevano

(2022: 1783) demonstrate how the Covid-19 pandemic 'forcefully remarked the relevance of social reproduction as a key analytical lens through which we can interrogate and analyse contemporary capitalist processes, their features, outcomes and crises'. Feminist IPE also draws upon postcolonial lenses in emphasizing the 'gendered, sexualized, classed and racialized oppression and exploitation' (Nair 2018) within IPE, and thus the necessity to direct research explicitly towards the socioeconomic margins, to people themselves (Benería 2003), and to the impacts that legacies of imperialism and colonization continue to have in the international economy.

Observed from a realist IPE perspective, the state is the primary unit of analysis in IPE. Markets help facilitate the extension of state wealth and power. But how markets operate, and the rules that economic actors must follow within the international economy, are ultimately governed by states. Realist IPE perspectives highlight how state behaviour within the international economy is shaped first by rational self-interest, and second, by the distribution of material capabilities among states. As the international system is assumed to be anarchic, and the relations between states invariably competitive and mistrustful, realist IPE approaches emphasize how international economic interactions are a zero-sum game. The objective of a state's economic policy is therefore to enhance their relative power by competing with other states to maximize their gains. Great powers (pg. 22), by extension, will then go further in establishing regional or international economic systems that sustain their hegemonic position.

Realist IPE perspectives have commonly been associated with *economic nationalism*, a theory connected with the economic policies of Alexander Hamilton (1779) who championed the role of government as facilitators of economic growth, and shields to protect new or growing industries from outside competition. Mercantilist (pg. 19) and **protectionist** (pg. 29) policies are also both associated with economic nationalism. The state will implement policies to champion domestic industries, seeking their competitive advantage and relative gain within the international economy, while also seeking to protect them, using protectionism where necessary to shield domestic industries and jobs from outside competition.

Protectionism
The economic policy of restricting imports from other countries through means of tariffs, quotas or other non-tariff barriers, in order to protect national industries.

By contrast, liberal IPE perspectives emphasize the need for a diminished state role in the international economy. In contrast to realism's assumptions of an anarchic international system driven by competition, relative gains and zero-sum games, liberal IPE perspectives observe the international system as an interdependent economic space, which, while competitive and driven by self-interest, is shaped by a logic of absolute gains and non-zero-sum games. *Economic liberalism*, commonly associated with the works of the classical liberal economists Adam Smith and David Ricardo who challenged the claims of economic nationalism, assumes that protectionism impoverishes states, while free and open markets create economic growth and prosperity for all. From an economic liberal perspective, therefore, governments should adopt a laissez-faire ('allow to do') non-interventionist approach in their economic policies, enabling markets to function freely, without government restrictions such as high taxation, heavy regulation or protectionist policies that restrict competition.

In today's international economy we can see many of these liberal principles advocated within the liberal international order, not least by the various international economic organizations established after World War Two (see next section). From a liberal IPE perspective these international economic organizations are important agents for international cooperation and for solving collective action problems. As we address more fully in Chapter Thirteen, neoliberalism has also become a prominent thread woven through the economic development strategies pursued by many Western states and international organizations, particularly in the 1980s and 1990s.

These different theoretical perspectives are further summarized in Table 12.1.

Table 12.1 Comparing theoretical perspectives in IPE

	Realism	Liberalism	Constructivism	Marxism	Feminism	Postcolonialism
Main actors within IPE	The state	States and markets IOs, MNEs, individuals	The state, IOs, MNEs, NGOs	Global capitalist elites within governments and MNEs, trade unions	Individuals	The state Global North and South
Main assumptions	The international system is anarchic and competitive. States are rational actors who pursue their national interests and seek relative gains. States are concerned with the distribution of material capabilities.	The international system is interdependent. States are rational actors who pursue their national interests and seek absolute gains. International organizations facilitate international cooperation.	The international system is a social realm. IPE is a social construct made up of norms, identities and interests.	Capitalism is the main driving force of the international economy. Societal change follows changes in economic wealth and development. Capitalism induces class conflict.	The international system is gender-hierarchical. Gender is constitutive of IPE yet neglected in mainstream IPE approaches.	The international system is hierarchical. Colonial relations underpin the processes and formation of the international economy. IPE is dominated by Western centrism.
Associated concepts/ theories	Mercantilism Economic nationalism	Laissez-faire Economic liberalism	Identities Norms	Capitalism Imperialism Hegemony	Patriarchy	Race Dependency Colonialism
Common arguments	States facilitate economic growth. States will shield national industries from foreign competition where necessary.	An open market economy enhances growth, wealth and peace for all. States may referee markets but not interfere directly in them.	The social desires, preferences and identities of different actors shape the rules, norms and practices of the international economy.	Capitalism generates uneven development. The core will increase their wealth and growth at the expense of the periphery.	The international economy is premised on exploitative power relations, and the subordination of certain social groups particularly women.	The Global North dominates the global economy at the expense of the Global South.

INTERNATIONAL ECONOMIC ORGANIZATIONS

In the last section we discussed some of the different theoretical lenses that can be adopted when researching IPE, and the respective importance they place on states, markets and other socioeconomic actors. Important also to consider when researching IPE is the rise of international economic organizations after World War Two. As we identified in Chapter Seven, the post-World War Two period was hallmarked by the proliferation and emanation of international organizations, with the realm of international economy being no exception. Running in tandem to efforts to establish the United Nations (pg. 114), in 1944 delegates from forty-four states came together in Bretton Woods, New Hampshire in the US for the United Nations Monetary and Financial Conference – more commonly known as the Bretton Woods Conference. The purpose of the conference was to discuss the formation of a post-war international monetary system which sought to establish a new liberal international order (pg. 38) based on open markets, sustained economic cooperation, growth and stability.

The Final Agreement of the Bretton Woods Conference instigated three pillars that would become a foundation of the new liberal international order (Figure 12.1) and the governance of the international political economy. These pillars – each an established international organization – include the International Bank for Reconstruction and Development (IBRD), now part of the World Bank, the International Monetary Fund (IMF) and the General Agreement on Tariffs and Trade, which became the World Trade Organization (WTO).

The International Bank for Reconstruction and Development was established to provide financial assistance to war-torn and developing states after World War Two. Today, the World Bank continues to provide traditional loans, interest-free credits and grants directly to states seeking to pursue development projects. The second pillar, the International Monetary Fund (IMF), was established to oversee a new international monetary system built on a fixed exchange rate, with currencies being **pegged** to the **gold standard** and US dollar.

Pegging
When a currency is fixed to another country's currency or to a commodity currency such as gold.

Gold standard
A currency measurement system that uses gold to set the value of money. The gold standard formed the basis of the international monetary system from around the 1870s up to around World War Two.

Originally formed among forty-four founding members, the IMF today has 190 member states, who in turn finance the IMF's resources through capital subscriptions (or quotas). Each member of the IMF is assigned a quota based on their relative wealth and position in the global economy, highlighting again the link between wealth and power and the

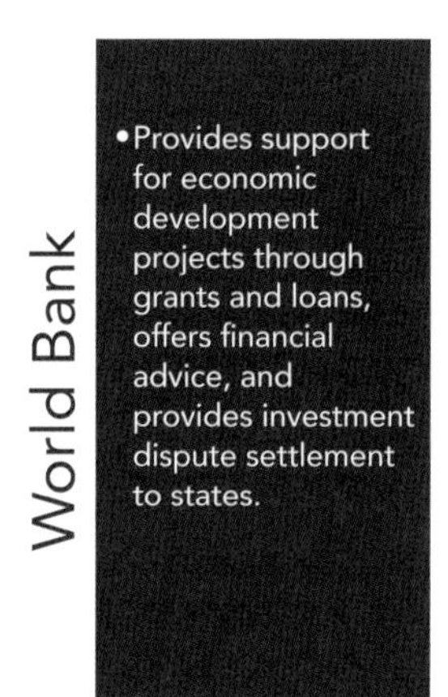

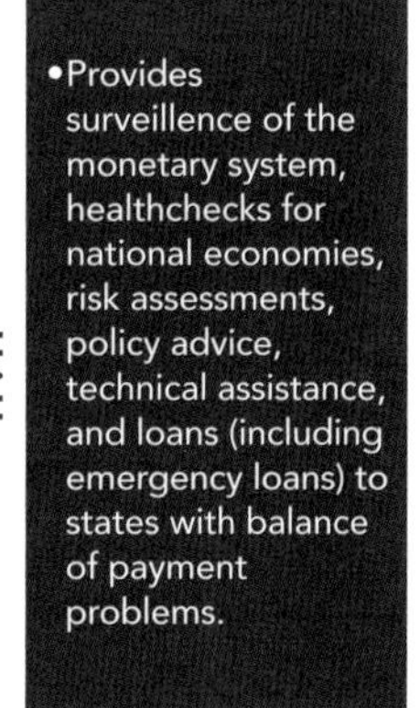

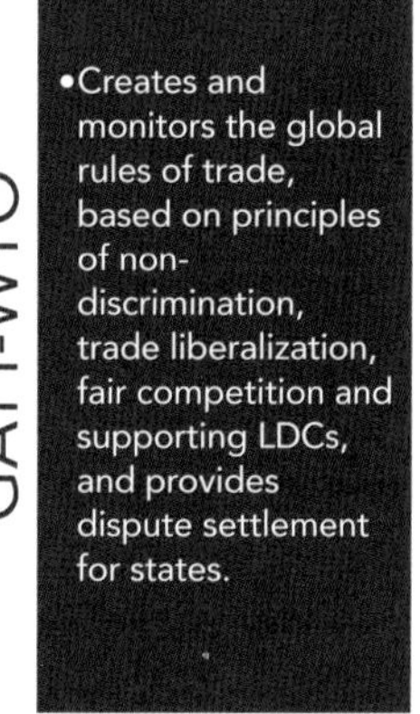

Figure 12.1 The Bretton Woods institutions

established hierarchies within the international economy. Quotas determine the maximum amount states are obliged to pay the IMF, which in turn translates into voting power within the organization, as well as the maximum amount of loans they can seek from the IMF. For example, the United States has the highest IMF quota at 17.43 per cent relative to states such as Belize, Djibouti, The Gambia, Guinea-Bissau, Lesotho, Montenegro, San Marino and Timor-Leste who have the lowest quotas at 0.01 per cent. The IMF is responsible for surveillance of the international monetary system and international economy more broadly. The IMF surveys individual national economies to check their general economic health, oversees global economic trends and assesses global capital markets and financial imbalances within the system. The IMF is also perhaps best recognized for its role in providing emergency financial support to states when impacted by financial crisis.

The third pillar of the Bretton Woods Conference was the recommendation that governments seek to reduce barriers to international trade, with the proposal to establish an International Trade Organization (ITO). While the ITO failed to come to fruition, twenty-three contracting parties agreed to establish the General Agreement on Tariffs and Trade (GATT). The GATT operated as a provisional multilateral trade agreement for nearly fifty years, overseeing multilateral **trade liberalization** on nearly 95 per cent of world visible trade (Hyett 1996: 91). In 1995 the World Trade Organization (WTO) was then created which replaced the GATT and is now responsible for monitoring the international trading system, including facilitating multilateral trade negotiations, upholding and settling disputes between members concerning the rules of international trade, and ensuring that trade flows freely and smoothly between them.

Trade liberalization The removal or reduction of tariff and non-tariff barriers to trade between states, including, for example, duties, surcharges, subsidies and quotas.

The WTO stands upon several core principles such as ensuring fair competition, but also for providing support for least developed countries (LDCs), ensuring predictability and transparency in trade, and upholding non-discrimination within the trading system. The WTO also upholds the principle that states should not discriminate between trading partners, nor should they discriminate between domestic and foreign products and services within their markets. The **most-favoured nation** principle requires that a WTO member providing preferential terms of trade access to one trading partner must extend the same terms of access to all WTO members; although it is noted that WTO members may still offer better trading terms to some countries using regional free trade agreements (FTAs). We shall continue to investigate the role of the WTO in the next section.

Most-favoured nation A WTO principle of non-discrimination whereby a WTO member providing favourable access to one trading partner must offer the same terms to all WTO members.

PRINCIPLES OF INTERNATIONAL TRADE

Trade has been an integral part of our world since humankind first started bartering. Over millennia, trade has expanded from exchanges between individuals, to local markets, to transcontinental trade routes, to being the primary driver of growth in the international economy. Since the latter half of the 20th century, international trade has connected every country of the world, facilitated the global exchange of goods and services, and significantly increased the value of the international economy. According to the UN Conference for Trade and Development (UNCTAD 2022), the value of global trade reached a record level of $28.5 trillion in 2021. Between 1970 and 2020 the sum of international exports and imports increased from 25 per cent to more than 50 per cent of total global output (World Bank 2022a). As international trade has expanded, so too has global economic growth, with global GDP increasing 100-fold in the past two centuries.

While the international economy can often seem like a borderless world, with goods and services regularly crossing borders with relative ease, we must also observe national economies as individual hubs, with each national economy shaped by the goods and services it both produces and consumes. Governments too have the authority to determine how much (or little) support they will give to their domestic industries, which industries to support, whether they will allow products and services from other countries to have free or restricted access to their economy, and which countries they may seek to pursue preferential trade relationships with. Those decisions are ultimately shaped by various principles of international trade and broader macroeconomic trends.

For example, within a market economy, businesses can trade with relative liberty, which creates an **opportunity cost**. Businesses will evaluate the trade-offs of producing more of one or other product at the expense of others. Those with the lowest opportunity costs in a specific product or service in turn develop a **comparative advantage**. Through this system, states will determine which goods and services they are best served to import or export.

Whereas imports result in an outflow of funds from the state, as products are purchased from abroad rather than domestically, exports lead to an inflow of funds as goods produced domestically are then sold abroad. A state's **balance of trade** is therefore important. Consider that in 2021, China – the world's top exporting nation – had a **trade surplus** of $103.25 billion. Compare then the United States – the world's top importing nation – who in 2021 had a **trade deficit** of $859.1 billion. Whereas China thus exported more than it imported, giving it a positive balance of trade, the United States imported more than it exported, giving it a negative balance of trade. The balance of trade does not obviously communicate the health of a state's economy or its prospects for growth (consider that the United States had a GDP of $23 trillion in 2021, despite its trade deficit, while Japan, who has a healthy trade surplus, has seen declining growth). The balance of trade is nevertheless relevant in shaping the decisions governments make in terms of their trade policy. Governments will, for example, seek to lower their trade deficit, particularly any bilateral trade deficit where the state imports more goods and services from one state than it exports to them in return.

By way of example, in 2018, the United States implemented a series of **tariffs** intended to make it harder for its largest trading partners – including China, the EU, Canada, Mexico and South Korea – to sell specific products to the US market, thereby bolstering US domestic industries and jobs. The result was one of the largest **trade wars** in decades (see also the toolkit exercise at the end of this chapter), which saw China, the EU and others retaliate against the US decision with their own tariffs being applied against imports of American products. While perhaps an extreme example, the 2018 trade wars nevertheless highlighted the importance of trade balance to governments, and how trade policies can be used for political purposes. In fact, despite often being treated in isolation, a state's trade and foreign policies are closely intertwined. Government trade departments represent an important wing of a state's external relations and statecraft, with its foreign policy often executed through economic foreign policy instruments and trade diplomacy – a trend we can also associate with the growth in international trade agreements between states and regional blocs (pg. 133).

Opportunity cost
The cost or benefit of giving up on one activity at the expense of another.

Comparative advantage
Where an economic actor can produce a good or service at a lower opportunity cost relative to others.

Balance of trade
The difference between the value of a state's exports and its imports over a defined period.

Trade surplus
When a state exports more than it imports within a fiscal year.

Trade deficit
When a state imports more than it exports within a fiscal year.

Tariffs
A tax or duty charged by governments on goods or services being imported to their country.

Trade wars
An economic conflict based on protectionist trade policies and retaliation between countries.

THE CHANGING POLITICS OF TRADE

In the past few decades, the politics of trade has also undergone substantial changes. In the space of forty years, China has jumped from thirtieth in the world to the world's leading merchandise exporter. Part of China's remarkable economic rise can be connected with its involvement in global value chains (GVCs). The World Bank defines GVCs as 'the series of stages in the production of a product or service for sale to consumers. Each stage adds value, and at least two stages are in different countries' (World Bank 2020: 17). According to the WTO, today 'more and more products are "Made in the World" rather than made in just one economy' (WTO 2023b). While the rise of global value chains (GVCs) were originally associated with outsourcing by MNEs in the Global North to affiliates located in developing countries (North-South trade) (pg. 158), between 1988 and 2013 the share of trade in parts and components between developing countries (South-South trade) increased from 6 per cent to 25 per cent and is growing (WTO 2014: 6). GVCs have further boosted the development of poorer countries, who have been able to grow their economies by joining a value chain, 'thereby eliminating the need to build whole industries from scratch' (World Bank 2020: xi).

The growing significance of GVCs in the international trading system has also added complexity to international trade negotiations. All eight of the multilateral trade negotiations conducted under the General Agreement on Tariffs and Trade between 1947 and 1994 addressed traditional 'at the border' barriers to trade by cutting tariffs, customs barriers and subsidies mainly on industrial products, textiles and agricultural products. Under the WTO, however, multilateral trade negotiations became broader and deeper. In 2001 the WTO launched the Doha Development Agenda (or Doha Round) which was intended to be the largest round of multilateral trade negotiations in history. The Round covered everything from telecommunications, rules of origin and competition policy to investment measures, services and environmental and labour standards – all issues which, unlike previous trade rounds, sought to address 'behind the border' issues (Young and Peterson 2006) and the various non-tariff barriers that governments and domestic industries are responsible for, including domestic standards and regulations.

ORGANIZE

In Chapter Nine we discussed how the value chains associated with multinational enterprises (MNEs) constitute a massive 80 per cent of global trade (pg. 156). Global value chains (GVCs) noticeably intensified over the 1990s and 2000s, particularly in regions such as East Asia, North America and Western Europe, and particularly in sectors such as machinery, electronics and transportation (World Bank 2020: 14). GVCs slowed somewhat after the global financial crisis (2007 to 2009) but continue to have a transformative effect on the international economy.

Scholars such as Barrientos, Gereffi and Pickles (2016: 1215), for example, highlight how the increase in South-South trade in intermediate goods has not only enhanced the role and power of firms in the Global South in GVCs, but has substantially bolstered the economic growth of the emerging economies in Asia, South America and Asia. Gereffi (2014: 29) goes further in suggesting that GVCs are moulding a new international economic order where an expanding number of rising powers now constitute the major centres (or poles) of economic growth.

Reflect again on the levels of analysis approach detailed in Chapter Five, particularly as it concerns the *international* level of analysis (pg. 75–9). How might the effects of GVCs inform our understanding of power and the distribution of power within the international system?

When the Doha Round struggled to find agreement – in fact being declared dead on numerous occasions (Herman and Hufbauer 2011, *Financial Times* 2015) – states began to seek the removal of tariff and non-tariff barriers through preferential free trade agreements (FTAs) with key trading partners instead. The spread of economic regional organizations and regional FTAs particularly multiplied after the mid-2000s (pg. 133). Regional trade blocs now cover vast geographic regions and account for significant shares of global GDP. Between 2018 and 2022 alone, three new regional trade blocs were launched – covering the African continent, the Trans-Pacific region and the Asia-Pacific region – adding further complexity to the already intricate cobweb of overlapping preferential FTAs now criss-crossing the globe.

The broader global picture that these changing trade dynamics point to is not only of an increasingly complex and dense international trading system, but of an international trading system in which the role of the WTO is increasingly brought into question. The WTO was created as much to facilitate multilateral trade liberalization as it was to oversee the global rules of trade and settle disputes between WTO members. By its twenty-fifth anniversary in 2020, the WTO had overseen a quadrupling in the dollar value of world trade. Through its accession process, dozens of new states joining the WTO undertook economic reforms to facilitate market opening, in turn helping to reduce average tariffs from 10.5 per cent to 6.4 per cent (Azevedo 2020). Yet multilateral trade liberalization and action to continue tackling tariff and non-tariff barriers through the WTO has required a dramatic rethink since the Doha Round's demise.

At the 2017 WTO Ministerial Conference in Buenos Aires, WTO members agreed to launch three new initiatives to advance talks on selected issues – addressing e-commerce, investment facilitation and micro, small and medium-size enterprises. What was revealing about these three initiatives was that they were proposed by smaller groups of willing WTO members rather than representing the whole WTO membership. As former WTO Director General, Roberto Azevedo (2020), stated, 'the WTO's negotiating functions are now seeing a phase of experimentation', signalling a demotion of multilateral trade liberalization efforts within the WTO, in favour of plurilateral and regional trade negotiations among smaller numbers of states – see Table 12.2.

Table 12.2 Pros and cons of multilateral, plurilateral and bilateral trade negotiations

	Multilateral trade negotiations	Plurilateral trade negotiations	Bilateral trade negotiations
Pros	Cover a large trade agenda, enabling states to offset concessions made in one area for gains in others. More likely to include development issues as part of the agenda.	Enables willing states to reach agreement on selected trade issues where common ground can be found.	Enables trading partners to negotiate preferential trade access based on their respective trading interests.
Cons	Based on a single undertaking therefore nothing is agreed until everything is agreed. Easy for some states to block progress on the whole agenda.	Can be exclusionary, favouring the advanced, developed economies. May undermine the WTO's MFN principle.	MFN principle applies, meaning preferential access needs to then be extended to all WTO members.

CURRENCIES AND FOREIGN EXCHANGE

Our international economy is not only shaped by the movement of goods and services across borders, but also by financial markets and capital flows dealing in values far beyond the output of trade in merchandise. In the early 1970s, the international monetary system shifted from one of fixed exchange rates pegged to the US dollar and gold standard to one of floating exchange rates. The foreign exchange market (also known as the forex, FX or currencies market) is the largest financial market in the world by trading volume, being valued at approximately $2.4 quadrillion, with a daily turnout of over $6.6 trillion. Forex is critical to international trade as it determines the rates at which currencies may be exchanged, while enabling currencies to be converted for payments and investments.

Forex can nevertheless be volatile. Exchange rates can change with currencies appreciating or depreciating based on the respective strength of the economies involved.

One European solution to exchange rate volatility in the 1980s and early 1990s was to establish a European Monetary System built upon a European Currency Unit (ECU) and European Exchange Rate Mechanism (ERM). While the European Monetary System created some imbalances between Europe's national economies in its initial phases, it also marked the first step in establishing a common monetary system among the EEC – and later EU – member states. In 2002 the euro was introduced as a common currency among eleven EU member states and has since replaced the national currencies of twenty EU member states (Map 8.1 pg. 138). Today, the euro is the second most traded currency in the world, behind the US dollar.

As with other national currencies, like the US dollar, Japanese yen or British pound, which are overseen by a national **central bank**, the euro is backed by the European Central Bank (ECB). The ECB is tasked with keeping prices stable within the euro area of supervising national banks, providing recommendations for risk reduction, and managing and overseeing the market infrastructure for monetary transfers within the eurozone.

Central bank
A bank with privileged authority for controlling and overseeing a state's currency and monetary policy, as well as regulating commercial banks within the country. Examples of central banks include the Bank of England, Bank of Japan or the US Federal Reserve.

The launch of the euro as a new form of supranational (pg. 134) currency was a remarkable development both for the EU and for the international monetary system. Not only did the euro signify the end of multiple national European currencies, including the powerful deutschmark, but highlighted how 'the link between state and money [could] no longer be considered to be self-evident' (Noyer 2000). Within a few short years, the link between the state and money was again brought into question with the innovation of cryptocurrency.

Cryptocurrency

On 31 October 2008 a White Paper penned by an anonymous individual or group of individuals, known only as Satoshi Nakamoto, proposed Bitcoin as a 'peer-to-peer electronic cash system' (Nakamoto 2008). Unlike state-backed currencies which require banks and other financial institutions to serve as trusted third parties to process electronic payments, Bitcoin was created to deliberately remove the third party in financial transactions, facilitating direct payment between two willing parties who would instead trust in **blockchains** of transparent digital signatures as proof of payment and receipt.

Blockchain
A distributed or linked database or ledger (blocks) that securely store time-stamped information in a digital format. Blockchains can be used for exchanging, recording or broadcasting transactions between individual users with internet access.

Bitcoin became the first cryptocurrency to operate a time-stamped ledger of user-verified transactions in monetary-like 'coin' in 2009. Since then, cryptocurrencies have diversified and spread. At the time of writing there are more than 13,000 cryptocurrencies in existence, worth just over $1 trillion in value. Cryptocurrencies – while established as an alternative to state-backed currencies which have traditionally driven the international monetary system – are now also becoming increasingly integrated into the international economy, with Bitcoin, for example, now accepted for financial transactions by a growing number of businesses.

While cryptocurrencies appear to be becoming a norm of our international economy, they are also highly volatile (IMF 2021: 41). At the time of writing, 474 cryptocurrencies had been reported 'dead' – indicating they've been reported as, or soon to be, worthless (99bitcoins 2023), while cryptocurrency exchanges have been rocked by near collapse, bankruptcy and allegations of fraud. Cryptocurrencies do also attract attention 'for their wildly fluctuating values as well as implication in international monetary laundering, Ponzi schemes and online trade in illicit goods and services across borders' (Campbell-Verduyn 2018). For this reason, cryptocurrencies, while seen to offer considerable economic opportunities, are also considered to pose considerable risks to the international economy, with the IMF (2021: 41) highlighting the 'inadequate operational and regulatory frameworks' associated with cryptocurrencies, and the urgent need for global standards and regulations over crypto assets.

LINK

Image 12.1 After Russia's invasion of Ukraine in February 2022 the Ukrainian government and NGOs advertised their bitcoin wallet addresses online, enabling them to receive millions of US dollars in financial aid through cryptocurrency.

Source: Art Rachen/Unsplash.

Consider

Cryptocurrencies are essentially borderless, established on the grounds that money could be exchanged between individuals or entities without the involvement of governments or central banks to serve as third-party intermediaries. Because of this, cryptocurrencies have often been treated as the international economy's 'Wild West' (Burcher 2018), being unregulated and open to criminality. Russia's invasion of Ukraine in 2022 has also raised questions over the neutrality of cryptocurrency, with governments and firms alike highlighting the good and bad roles that cryptocurrencies have played in the conflict (Crypto 2023).

Explore

Not only did Ukraine manage to receive millions of US dollars in bitcoin donations immediately after Russia's invasion (BBC News 2022b), but reports also circulated that pro-Russian groups solicited donations in crypto to support paramilitary operations in Ukraine (Asmakov 2022) (see also pg. 154–5). The war also raised fears that Russian officials would seek to use cryptocurrencies to evade sanctions. According to Dermarkar and Hazgui (2022), the conflict in Ukraine 'is not just a war of bombs and bullets. It is also a digital war of which cryptocurrency is just one of many components.' Find out more about the role that cryptocurrencies have played in the conflict by scanning the barcode for relevant news reports and analyses.

Connect

Revisit Chapter Eleven and our discussion about ontological security and insecurity (pg. 188). To what extent do you think cryptocurrencies generate ontological insecurity? Reflect again on the state's foreign policy instruments outlined in Table 6.1 (pg. 98). Can governments use cryptocurrencies to serve their national economic interests and security?

Predict

The IMF has warned of the need for a global response to regulate cryptocurrencies (Narain and Moretti 2022). While some states are increasingly accepting of cryptocurrencies as a form of tender, in others, such as China, cryptocurrencies are heavily regulated to prevent any threat to the yuan (Wolfe 2022). Revisit the discussion of why international organizations (IO) first formed (pg. 109–10) and the debate around IO authority to act (pg. 118–9). How likely is it that states will look to the IMF to regulate cryptocurrencies? What are the obstacles to this?

CONCLUSION

In this chapter we have considered the related issues of international trade and finance within the international economy while introducing IPE as a field of study and the different theoretical perspectives we can utilize in our research. We have addressed new developments in international trade, such as the growing significance of global value chains and in international finance with the creation of cryptocurrencies. Both developments create opportunities and risks in an increasingly globalized and interconnected economic system and bring the desire for regulation ever more to the forefront of international agendas. In the next chapter we shall continue to delve further into IPE by looking at the imbalances and inequalities within the international economy and the challenges associated with economic growth and development. Before turning to the next chapter, however, why not test and apply your knowledge from this chapter by trying the following toolkit exercise asking, *'Why did the United States start the 2018 trade wars?'*

TOOLKIT

Why did the United States start the 2018 trade wars?

THINK

- As a consumer, would you support a government policy that sought to protect domestic industries and producers by making it more expensive for you to buy foreign goods?

OBSERVE

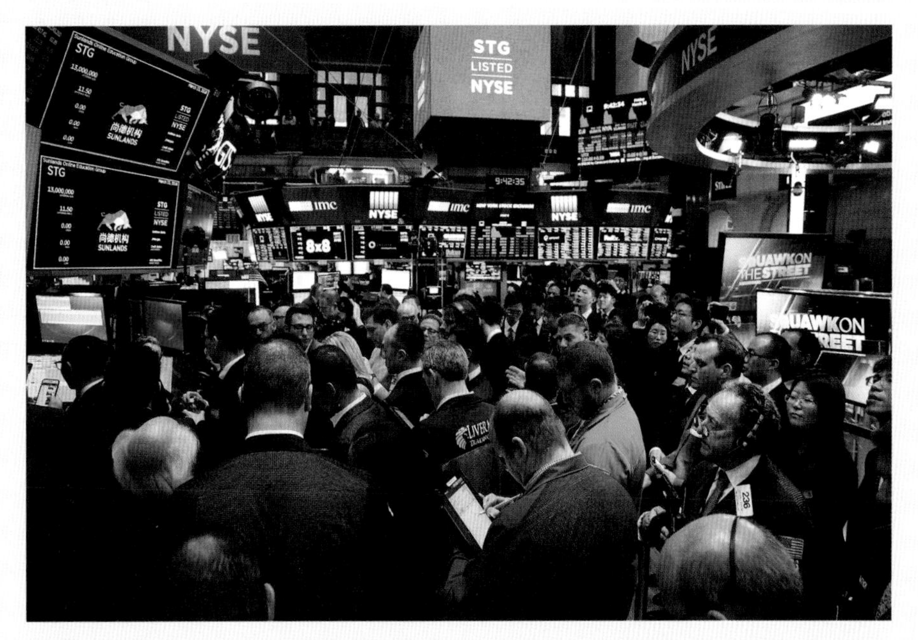

Image 12.2 Traders on the floor of the New York Stock Exchange the day after the Dow plunged in reaction to the announcement that new tariffs would be imposed, sparking fears of a trade war with China. The Dow (or Dow Jones Industrial Average) is one of the most closely observed stock indexes in the world, being considered an important indicator of the health of the US economy.

Source: Spencer Platt/Getty Images.

- When Donald Trump was elected as US president in 2016, he promised that his government would cut the trade deficit and create 25 million new jobs for the US economy. On 23 March 2018 the United States government imposed a 25 per cent steel tariff and a 10 per cent aluminium tariff on all countries exporting over $10.2 billion and $7.7 billion of products respectively.
- In April 2018 China retaliated by applying tariffs on aluminium waste and scrap, pork, fruit and nuts and other US products. By June 2018 US tariffs were applied also to the EU, Canada and Mexico, who in turn retaliated with their own tariffs. EU tariffs specifically targeted iconic US goods including bourbon whiskey, Harley Davidson motorbikes and blue jeans, for example. The 2018 trade wars applied tariffs to billions of dollars of goods.

- According to one study, sub-Saharan African countries were hurt by the trade wars despite being 'innocent bystanders' (Devermont and Chiang 2019). The study warned of a 2.5 per cent reduction in GDP for resource-intensive African countries as an impact of lowering commodity prices and the economic distress then placed on these developing countries (Devermont and Chiang 2019).
- The trade wars were eased in January 2020 when the US and China signed a Phase One trade deal. It is nevertheless worth highlighting that, at the time of writing, many of the tariffs introduced during 2018 remain in force.

ORGANIZE

- A levels of analysis approach (Chapter Five) is helpful when seeking to explain events or behaviours within international politics and to understand why something has happened. In asking why the US started the 2018 trade wars you could then apply a levels of analysis approach that draws upon IPE theoretical perspectives to help direct your research as follows:
- At the *international level of analysis*, you might consider the balance of power between the United States and China, and their respective economic strengths, particularly as it relates to the United States' own trade deficit with China and the US's balance of trade (pg. 213). Consider also how economic instruments form a crucial part of statecraft and a state's foreign policy tools (pg. 97–8) in advancing its interests and power.
- At the *state level of analysis*, you could reflect more on the role of the US government, the strengths and weaknesses of the US economy, the domestic industries that the US government was seeking to protect from foreign competitors (pg. 209), or the domestic politics that was shaping the US government's hard line towards not only the US's main trade competitors (the EU and China), but its closest neighbours (Mexico and Canada).
- At the *individual level of analysis*, you may want to direct your research to the language of President Trump himself, his background as a businessman, and his economics and attitudes towards China particularly. For example, according to President Trump, 'trade wars are good and easy to win'.

LINK

- *Consider*: Reflect again on the discussion about ontological security (pg. 188) and securitization (pg. 187). The United States tariffs on steel and aluminium were based on Section 232 of the 1962 United States' Trade Expansion Act which enabled tariffs to be imposed on goods in the interest of *national security* (pg. 187). National security-based tariffs are also exempt from WTO review. China nevertheless brought a dispute against the United States to the WTO and in 2020 they ruled that US-imposed tariffs on Chinese goods were considered 'inconsistent' with international trade rules (BBC 2020b). In response to the ruling the US Trade Representative stated that the US 'must be allowed to defend itself against unfair trade practices' (BBC 2020b).
- *Explore*: Explore more about the Trade War tariffs, effects and WTO ruling by visiting the companion website for related news and analysis. You may particularly want to look out analysis at www.piie.com and www.brookings.edu, as well as the WTO's response at www.wto.org.

- *Connect*: Trade wars are not typically won quickly, and can often outlive government Administrations. The 'banana wars', which involved a trade dispute between the EU and ten Latin American countries over the EU applying lower tariffs to bananas from African and Caribbean nations, lasted for twenty years until an agreement was finally settled in the WTO in 2012. In the case of the 2018 trade wars the tariffs applied by the Trump Administration remained in force under the Biden Administration.
- *Predict*: How likely is it that the United States will again lower its tariffs for Chinese steel and aluminium products?

Scan the QR code for access to explore weblinks and more resources.

SHARE

- Answer the question, *'Why did the United States start the 2018 trade wars?'*

  When addressing this question, give some thought to how you might utilize IPE theoretical approaches (check out *How to – apply theory to your research and writing* on pg. 69). You might also want to revisit the *How to – use the levels of analysis* approach on pg. 69 for a refresh on how to implement this approach. Consider also what position you might adopt in answering this question, ensuring that you present a clear and robust argument to the question. For more tips check out *How to – take a position* on pg. 144.

HOW TO

WRITE A BLOG

Blog writing has become an increasingly popular activity for communicating complex political issues to general audiences. Within universities, blogs have also become a popular assessment type for multitudes of different subject areas, and international politics is no exception. Blogs enable you to showcase your familiarity and understanding of an issue in international politics. Blog assignments further test your concision and precision of argument and your ability to communicate effectively and deliberately. Writing a good blog post, whether for publication or for assessment purposes, nevertheless requires you to consider a few key attributes. Below are ten top tips on writing a blog in international politics.

1. Think audience

Always write a blog post with your audience in mind. Even if you are writing your blog for an assignment, you should write as if for the kind of audience likely to read the blog were it posted online. A useful way to navigate this is to write as if for an informed audience, but one that is not necessarily expert in all things politics. Be prepared, therefore, to tailor your writing to clearly explain key terms, limit the use of technical terminology, and be concise and precise in your narrative. Never assume prior knowledge on the part of your reader. Write to inform.

2. Think purpose

Why are you writing the blog post? Consider the purpose. Are you looking to shape debate? To present opinion? To share ideas? More than this, why is what you have to say important? The purpose of a blog post should address these questions, particularly why it matters. This is also important when it comes to writing your post as the purpose impacts the way you write and communicate your key messages to your audience. Be sure to make it obvious why your post matters and why it is important to read, to engage with, and to share.

3. Keep it simple, keep it focused

Aim to keep your point of focus obvious and your writing simple. It is pretty easy to get bogged down in minutiae in politics, but this can make for pretty tedious reading for a general audience. What is your point of focus? This is your main topic, argument or organizing principle that the whole post is primarily intended for. When you communicate that purpose, you should keep your writing simple and always stay on point. Don't get pulled off on tangents.

4. Write in your voice

The tone of a blog is really important. Aim for your writing to be professional but personal, i.e. not overly formal. Write in the first person as this is your position, your voice.

5. Voice opinion: Keep it professional

Writing a blog post in politics allows you to present your own individual voice and opinions, but it is important to recognize that in politics your opinion is one of many. *Informed opinion* is the bread and butter of good politics blogging, but what makes opinion informed is not just adherence to facts and surety about your topic. Informed opinion is also about critical reflexivity of the diversity of opinions around your topic and a recognition of the 'other' when voicing the opinions you have as your 'own'. Keep your writing professional and your narrative respectful.

6. Edit, then edit again

Don't underestimate the amount of editing a blog post requires. Most blog posts will be around 500 to 1,000 words in length. This requires you to hone your skills in precision and concision of narrative. Heavy editing is required to achieve this. Be prepared to look at every sentence and question its utility. Is it needed or can it be cut? Is your message communicated simply and clearly? Look again at your grammar and syntax – is it understandable? Does the post follow a clear line of enquiry? Do sentences make sense and are paragraphs used correctly? Go through this process once, then do it again. The output will be a far more streamlined, clear and punchy blog post than you had before you started.

7. Think title

If you actually want people to read your blog then you need a title that not only informs the audience but grabs them in the process. Avoid titles that include random phrases that do not mean anything. Avoid titles that only make sense to someone who has actually read the blog post itself. Instead, you want your title to capture the very essence of your blog post so that the reader understands what they are getting into *before* they even start reading. Then play around with the title so that it is snappy and grabs the audience's attention.

8. Hyperlinks help

A good blog signposts their reader to sources of information and further reading through well-embedded hyperlinks. This relates to the point that good politics blogging is based on informed opinion. Blogs are unlikely to require the same level of referencing as an academic essay, but you still need to show your research by linking to those websites where information has been found – with an emphasis on reliable sources (see *How to – identify quality sources* pg. 106).

9. Be prepared to have your work reviewed (and critiqued)

Blogging puts your work on public display so be prepared for people reading your work, reviewing it and yes, critiquing (even criticizing) it. This is why you want to ensure you have communicated clearly, fact-checked and supported your major claims through evidence.

10. Enjoy

Goes without saying but blogging is meant to be enjoyable! This is about honing your communication skills, presenting informed opinion and engaging with others about international politics! Enjoy!

13 Equality and development

Pexels / Ahmed akacha

Abstract

This chapter advances your knowledge of international political economy (IPE) by introducing you to some of the stark inequalities within our international system, and the myriad of challenges associated with international equality and development. The chapter sets out international development as a multi-dimensional concept, highlighting the contrasts between economic and human development approaches and how they shape our understanding of equality within the international system. From there we will consider migration as a cross-cutting issue, focusing on trends within international migration, and how migration can be observed as a development, equality and security issue within international politics. The chapter then considers international efforts to achieve sustainable development, with a focus on the UN's Sustainable Development Goals, before concluding with a look at the politics of international aid. The chapter finishes with a toolkit exercise asking, '*When is a country "developed"?*'

UNDERSTANDING EQUALITY AND DEVELOPMENT

Low-income economy The World Bank's classification of economies with a Gross National Income (GNI) per capita of $1,085 or less (2021 calculation).

Today nearly half (43 per cent) of the world's total wealth is owned by 1 per cent of the world's total adult population, yet just over half (53 per cent) of the total adult population owns only 1 per cent of the world's total wealth (Figure 13.1). In 2020, 720 million people lived in extreme poverty, existing on less than $2.15 per day (World Bank 2022b). Nearly 44 per cent of the citizens of **low-income economies** lived below the poverty line at the turn of the 2020s, while in **high-income economies** that figure was just 0.6 per cent. Also consider that in 2020 Luxembourg's **GDP per capita** (by **purchasing power parity**) was $134,754. In Burundi it was $793.

Now reflect on the fact that the average life expectancy at birth for the citizens of Western Europe, Canada, Israel, Japan, South Korea, Australia, New Zealand and Chile is between eighty and eighty-four years of age, while for the Central African Republic, Somalia, Mozambique and Chad, life expectancy at birth is between fifty-three and fifty-nine years of age. Consider that only 21 per cent of citizens in South Sudan complete a primary level education, while for most Western states well over 90 per cent of their citizens complete primary and secondary level education. Finally, think about the fact that citizens of countries with very high levels of **human development** are more likely to be able to travel visa-free to around 85 per cent of all other countries worldwide, while citizens of countries with very low levels of human development meet with regular visa restrictions and must look to irregular migration pathways if they want to work in another country (IOM 2022).

When you consider these facts and figures, it is perhaps unsurprising that equality and development have become such pressing issues in international politics. While, as we saw in the last chapter, international trade and finance have done much to bolster the health and wealth of the international economy, which is now richer and more integrated than ever before, we must also recognize the stark inequalities not only still present, but in fact widening in the world around us. Development has also become a hotly debated and contested issue within international politics.

In this chapter we shall consider the related issues of equality and development and the challenges they present within international politics. We begin with an overview of the different perspectives of equality and development, resuming our discussion of the different international political economy (IPE) approaches we touched upon in Chapter Twelve. We then turn a spotlight on migration as a cross-cutting issue in equality, development and security studies. From there we shall address the sustainable development agenda and the linkages between development and the environment. The chapter then takes a look at the politics surrounding foreign aid before concluding with a toolkit exercise for you to try and expand your knowledge further, asking '*When is a country "developed"?*'

High-income economy
The World Bank classification of economies with a Gross National Income (GNI) per capita of $13,205 or more (2023 calculation).

GDP per capita
An economic measure that divides a country's gross domestic product by its total population, allowing you to compare the prosperity of countries with different population sizes.

Purchasing power parity (PPP)
An economic measure that calculates how much it would cost to purchase goods if all countries used the same currency – a useful tool for comparing living standards between countries.

Human development
An approach to development that focuses on the quality of people's lives, their education, their standard of living and the choices available to them.

According to Credit Suisse's Global Wealth Report, global wealth totalled $463.6 trillion in 2021, with the average global wealth per adult reaching $87,489 – three times what it was at the turn of the 21st century. Yet global disparities in wealth are pronounced. In Africa the average wealth per adult in 2022 was just $8,419 compared to North America where the figure stands at $560,846 (Credit Suisse 2022). What do you think explains this geographical disparity in wealth?

PERSPECTIVES FROM IPE

In the last chapter we considered how different theoretical perspectives approach international political economy (IPE) and the actors and issues they tend to prioritize. We noted how neoliberalism has particularly informed understandings of **international development** with the logic following that where market economies (pg. 208) flourish – with free trade, free markets, floating exchange rates and macroeconomic stability – **economic development** will follow. Such logics were also shaped by the history and

International development
A multidimensional concept broadly denoting the idea that countries have different levels of economic and human development.

Economic development An approach that prioritizes economic growth as a primary indicator of a country's development.

Industrialization The widescale development of industries in a country or region. Typically associated with economies shifting from an agrarian-based to an industrial-based society.

legacy of the Industrial Revolution where the economies of the UK, much of continental Europe and the United States grew rapidly during the 18th and 19th centuries due to **industrialization**. Where industry and manufacturing grew, productivity increased, wealth expanded, incomes rose and so did standards of living.

With the emergence of the liberal international order (pg. 38) after World War Two, development was similarly observed through largely economic lenses, with economic growth the core objective. All three of the Bretton Woods international organizations (pg. 211) addressed economic development in some guise. The International Bank for Reconstruction and Development (IBRD) (now part of the World Bank Group) (pg. 211) provided low-cost loans for development projects aimed, for example, at improved infrastructure, health or education services. The International Monetary Fund (IMF) supported low-income economies to develop strong, sustainable economic growth through tied loans. And the General Agreement on Tariffs and Trade (now the World Trade Organization – WTO) supported developing countries to better integrate into the international trading system. During the 1980s, development was largely pursued through a market-led strategy that championed certain prescribed economic policies to achieve economic growth – an approach which became known as the **Washington Consensus** in homage to the IMF, World Bank and US Department of the Treasury being located in Washington DC. Developing countries were encouraged to pursue these prescribed policies, such as introducing fiscal discipline, deregulation, privatization of nationalized industries, trade liberalization, and giving equal treatment to foreign and domestic businesses, for example. Development support was also linked to the Washington Consensus, with the IMF and World Bank granting low-cost loans through **structural adjustment programmes** that would see developing countries implement prescribed economic policies in exchange for financial assistance.

Washington Consensus A set of market-led economic policy recommendations for developing countries to follow to achieve economic growth.

Structural adjustment programme Conditional loans provided by the IMF and World Bank to developing countries. Low-interest loans are granted on the condition that the recipient state implement economic reforms such as privatizing government industries, deregulating the banking sector, devaluing currencies and removing barriers to free trade.

Emerging economies An economy characterized by rapid economic growth with significant industrialization, high productivity and marked increases in foreign direct investment.

As we saw in the last chapter, since the mid-20th century, the international economy has experienced remarkable economic growth. Increasing numbers of countries became integrated into the international economy, raised their standards of living, lowered barriers to trade and foreign investment, and traded competitively in global markets. Perhaps the best sung examples of countries that have experienced rapid development include the **emerging economies**. Brazil, Russia, India, China and South Africa – named the BRICS[1] by Jim O'Neill at Goldman Sachs who identified them as the emerging economies with the largest growth potential at the turn of the 21st century – have since leapfrogged their way into positions of strength within the international economy (pg. 205).

Yet, economic growth and the example set by the emerging economies tells only part of the tale of international development and, from a more critical perspective, tends also to bypass some of the common critiques of the neoliberal economic development model. A critical challenge of neoliberalism is the assumption that development follows a 'one-size-fits-all'[2] model which sees developing states implement prescribed economic policies and trusting the market to achieve economic growth. The rise of the BRICS in fact highlights this. While each of the BRICS adopted selected neoliberal economic policies, intended to open themselves up to the international economy and drive forward economic growth, they did so while also defending their own various *state-led* development policies (Bank and Blyth 2013). China's government, for example, has maintained extensive state-owned

[1]The original BRICs identified by Jim O'Neill included Brazil, Russia, India and China. South Africa was later added to the grouping, now commonly referred to as the BRICS.

[2]Scholars have also critiqued the claim that neoliberalism is a one-size-fits-all approach. Broome (2014: 22), for example, highlights that neoliberalism has essentially become 'caricatured' in IPE, and should be considered a 'broad cluster of theoretical perspectives'.

enterprises and pursues several forms of state intervention in its economy in clear contradiction to the Washington Consensus's focus on privatization. Critical perspectives further highlight that not only are many low-income economies not best suited to the sort of market-led economic growth policies pushed by the IMF and the World Bank, but that structural adjustment programmes resulted in negative effects not only on economic growth, but on human development (Vreeland 2003; Rodwan Abouharb and Cingranelli 2006; Shandra, Shandra and London 2010).

Critical scholars further highlight the entrenched historical explanations for the development challenges facing individual states and why some states achieve economic growth while others do not. Dependency theorists signpost to the systemic dependency of 'peripheral' former colonies to 'core' states within the international system, such that 'economic development and underdevelopment are the opposite faces of the same coin' (Frank 1967: 9) (pg. 54). Postcolonial scholars further emphasize the 'uneven character of global capitalism ... [as] a fundamental feature of the postcolonial world' (Kayatekin 2009: 1115). From a postcolonial perspective, the power imbalance between former colonies relative to their former colonizers is only perpetuated by mainstream neoliberal narratives associated with the very concept of *under*development itself.

Critical IPE perspectives also highlight the stark inequalities within the international economy, drawing attention to global poverty and the widening gap between the world's richest and poorest. The global wealth pyramid (Figure 13.1) highlights the marked disparity between the world's richest and poorest individuals – a disparity that has only widened over time, with the aggregate wealth of millionaires growing fivefold since 2000. By contrast, around 80 per cent of individuals counted within the lowest wealth bracket come from low-income economies where 'life membership of the base tier is often the norm' (Credit Suisse 2022: 22).

Global inequality is not only prevalent in terms of wealth disparities, but also in terms of opportunity, access to basic services, as well as ecological and gender inequality. Feminist approaches particularly highlight the correlation between gender inequality and poverty, for example. According to UN Women and the UN Development Programme, more women live in extreme poverty than men, with nearly 84 per cent of the world's

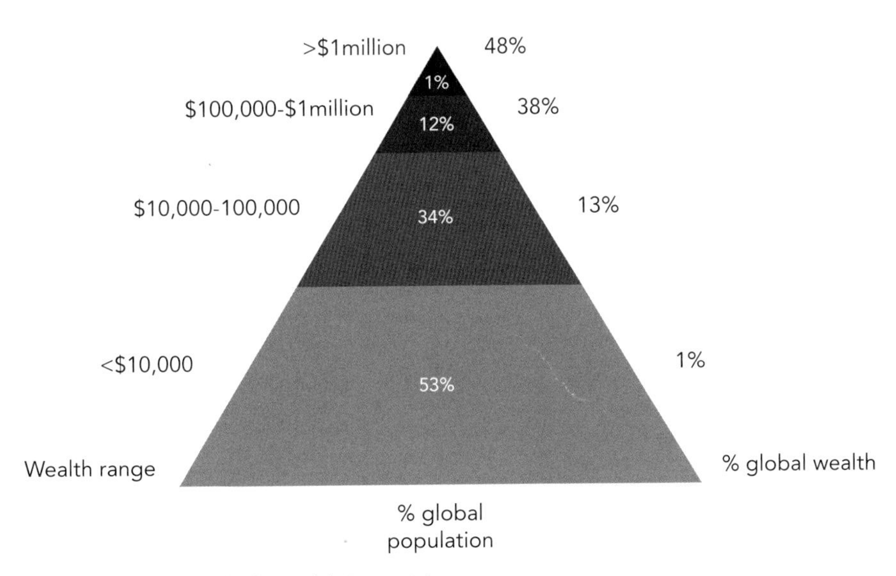

Figure 13.1 The Global Wealth Pyramid

Source: Author's compilation drawn from figures/data from the Global Wealth Databook 2022 (Credit Suisse 2022: 21).

extreme poor women and girls living in sub-Saharan Africa and Central and Southern Asia (UN Women 2022). Women in developing countries are also considered more likely to bear the burden of the 'double day' combining employment with responsibilities for housework and childcare, have fewer education opportunities, and fewer rights and protections than men (Nussbaum 2000: 1). For Feminist-IPE scholars, international development should not be oriented solely towards economic growth but towards developing human capabilities – that is 'what people are actually able to do and to be' (Nussbaum 2000). Emphasis then is placed on the need for human development to tackle social as well as economic inequalities, and to empower and engage women in that process.

OBSERVE

Image 13.1 Women cooking food in a slum area of the city of Ghaziabad in India in January 2022. Close to New Delhi, Ghaziabad is one of the fastest-growing urban centres in the world, with an annual population growth rate of just over 5 per cent.

Source: SOPA Images/Getty Images.

India is one of the fastest growing economies in the world but ranks poorly on gender equality indicators. For example, compared to men and boys, women and girls in India have a higher mortality rate, are more likely to receive lower wages, have a greater likelihood of developing anaemia, are more likely to be married before they are aged eighteen, and are less likely to own land holdings. Of the nearly 87 million people living in extreme poverty in India, 47 million are women, compared to 40 million men.

Such gender inequalities bring to the forefront the debate as to whether development should be predominantly a measurement of economic growth, or whether a society's quality of life and gender equality must also be factors.

HUMAN SECURITY AND DEVELOPMENT: A SPOTLIGHT ON MIGRATION

As we have seen, international development can be observed not only as a process of economic growth, but as a concern with individual standards of living, quality of life, education and gender equality. In 1990 the UN Development Programme (UNDP) introduced the **Human Development Index** (HDI) as a new measurement system to evaluate the level of individual human development within countries. The HDI was generated alongside the first Human Development Report in which it was stated that development 'is about more than GNP growth, more than income and wealth and more than producing commodities and accumulating capital ... Human development is a process of enlarging people's choices' (UNDP 1990). Concerned with the choices individuals have in how they live, where they work, their access to healthcare, to education, and their standard of living, human development directly sought to address inequalities within societies and advocated what the UN would a few years later conceptualize in its human security framework as the *freedom from want* (pg. 189).

Human Development Index
A worldwide ranking system that takes a summary measure of average achievement in key dimensions of human development including life expectancy at birth, years of schooling and standard of living by GNI per capita.

Human security and development agendas are now closely intertwined. In 2022 the UN Secretary-General highlighted that the world was facing a 'development paradox. Even though people are on average living longer, healthier and wealthier lives, these advances have not succeeded in increasing people's sense of security' (UNDP 2022: iii). Findings from the UN Development Programme's *Index of Perceived Insecurity* revealed that while human insecurity is high across the globe in the 2020s, it is especially high in those countries who are ranked low on the Human Development Index (HDI). For low and middle HDI countries particularly, 64 per cent of those surveyed said that they felt 'very insecure', compared to 37 per cent of respondents in very high HDI countries (UNDP 2022: 15–16).

Table 13.1 Key migration terms and definitions

Term	Definition
Internal migration	The movement of people within a state involving the establishment of a new temporary or permanent residence.
International migrant	From the perspective of the country of arrival, a person who moves into a country other than that of his or her nationality or usual residence, so that the country of destination effectively becomes his or her new country of usual residence.
Migrant worker	A person who is to be engaged, is engaged or has been engaged in a remunerated activity in a State of which he or she is not a national.
Forced migration	A person or group(s) of persons who have been forced or obliged to flee or to leave their homes, in particular as a result of or in order to avoid the effects of armed conflict, situations of generalized violence, violations of human rights or natural or human-made disasters. Also known as *forced displacement*.
Refugee	A person who, owing to a well-founded fear of persecution for reasons of race, religion, nationality, membership of a particular social group or political opinion, is outside the country of his nationality and is unable or, owing to such fear, is unwilling to avail himself of the protection of that country; or who, not having a nationality and being outside the country of his former habitual residence as a result of such events, is unable or, owing to such fear, is unwilling to return to it.

Source: Definitions drawn from UNHCR and International Organization of Migration. Available online: www.unhcr.org and www.iom.int/key-migration-terms.

Migration is one issue that especially highlights the relationship between human security and development agendas. According to the International Organization for Migration (IOM), the term migrant is something of an umbrella term, generally meaning 'a person who moves away from his or her place of usual residence, whether within a country or across an international border, temporarily or permanently, and for a variety of reasons' (IOM 2022). Migration nevertheless accounts for several different types and causes of people's movement, entailing numerous distinct terminologies ranging from immigrant to refugee.

As the key terms and definitions in Table 13.1 highlight, migration can be both a voluntary pursuit and an involuntary action due to events beyond a person's control. In recent years our newsfeeds have been dominated by crises of involuntary migration. Regions around the world, from Central America to North Africa and Europe to Southeast Asia, have all experienced **migration crises** triggered by events, be that natural disasters, war or political violence, that result in sudden peaks of migrating refugees who have been forcibly displaced from their homes. Consider that 41 per cent of migrants from Central America's Northern Triangle cited insecurity of violence as one of the main reasons for migration (IOM 2022). The war in Syria (pg. 173–4) has also resulted in 6.6 million refugees fleeing the country. Social and political instability coupled with a humanitarian crisis in Venezuela since 2014 resulted in Latin America's largest external displacement crisis, with more than 5 million refugees finding shelter in countries across Latin America and the Caribbean. Another 6 million refugees fled the war in Ukraine in 2022.

Migration crisis
An event or series of events triggering the large-scale movement of immigrants beyond normal migratory flows.

Forced migration is not only a result of conflict, but also a consequence of **food insecurity**, as well as natural and human-made disasters. For example, in 2018, 3.2 million people were at risk of food insecurity in El Salvador, while 310,000 people in Guatemala and 175,000 people in Honduras were displaced during the hurricane season in 2020 due to the impacts on agriculture and fishing in the region (IOM 2022). Across the world in 2020, 30.7 million people were internally displaced due to natural disasters, 40 per cent of whom were in East Asia and the Pacific who were impacted by typhoons, floods, earthquakes and volcanic disruptions (IOM 2022). While extreme environmental events can often be a cause of sudden population movements, there is also the increasing awareness that longer-term climate-induced environmental problems, such as droughts, regular flooding and rising sea levels, are becoming 'push-factors' for international migration (IOM 2022). As we shall see in the next section (and consider further in the following chapter), there have been increasing international efforts to address the environment in international migration and development agendas.

Food insecurity
The state of having unreliable or insufficient access to food to meet one's basic needs.

More than just an effect of human insecurity, migration is also an important dimension of the development debate. In 1970 there were around 84 million international migrants worldwide. By 2020 around one in thirty persons – that is 281 million people – were immigrants. Unlike forced migration, international migration – as a voluntary process – is particularly associated with the pursuit of economic advancement. As the International Organization for Migration (2022: 191) highlights, 'people migrate for better lives'. While countries in the Global South have broadly experienced higher levels of growth in recent decades, inequalities between low- and high-income areas continue to grow, further incentivizing international migration (Benería, Deere and Kabeer 2012: 2), with the largest **migration corridors** being from developing countries to larger developed economies.

Migration corridor
Established patterns of migratory movement, typically between countries that have developed over many years.

The relationship between migration and development is nevertheless complex. International migration is often thought to boost economic development due to migrants sending home remittances that can total more than international development assistance itself (DeWind and Ergun 2016: 5). **Remittances** are considered to increase the general prosperity of a migrant's country of origin and offer a 'lifeline' to the poorest households (IOM 2022: 247). Remittances are also thought to be a less volatile capital flow into

Remittance
Private international monetary transfers made by migrants living abroad to family or community members in their country of origin.

developing countries than foreign direct investment (FDI) or foreign aid (Vargas-Silva 2012). Yet scholars also highlight that remittances only bolster economic growth in receiving areas where there are already favourable conditions for incomes to be invested (De Haas 2005: 1274–5). Where there are already unfavourable conditions for investment in a country, recipient families will only retreat from the local economy (De Haas 2005).

It should also be noted that while the value of remittances worldwide has increased by a factor of six between 2000 and 2020, now totalling around $702 billion, inequalities between sending and recipient countries remain stark. High-income economies are almost always the main source of remittances, yet the top five remittance recipients (India, China, Mexico, the Philippines and Egypt) are **middle-income countries**. Important also to note that the cost of sending remittances to some regions around the world remains far higher than in others. Sub-Saharan Africa – which has one of the highest rates of extreme poverty in the world – is also the most expensive region in the world to send money to due to high transaction costs[3] (World Bank 2021). The economic impact of remittances for low-income economies which make up many of the poorest regions of the world thus remains questionable.

Middle-income country
A World Bank group classification that includes all lower middle-income economies (GNI per capita between $1,086 and $4,255) and upper-middle income economies (GNI between $4,256 and $13,205) *(2023 fiscal year calculation).*

Explore More

You can find out more about international migration, migration corridors, remittances and the impact of COVID on migration by looking at the International Organization for Migration's World Migration Report at https://worldmigrationreport.int. The website includes a useful interactive tool for visualizing key facts and figures.

Scan the QR code for access to explore weblinks and more resources.

ORGANIZE

Image 13.2 Migrant workers from Mexico harvest strawberries in Dover, Florida in April 2019. The United States has been the main country of destination for international migrants since 1970, with the Mexico-US migration corridor one of the largest in the world. Many high-income economies have come to rely on low-wage, unskilled and informal workers, particularly in industries like agriculture where migrant workers often make up the majority workforce.
Source: Jeff Greenberg/Getty Images

[3]In 2020 South Asia had the lowest remittance costs at 4.9 per cent. For sub-Saharan Africa, remittance costs were 8.2 per cent (World Bank 2021).

The movement of labour across borders, particularly from low-income to high-income economies, often faces obstacles. Migrant workers face considerable labour insecurities. Many migrant-receiving countries implement visa restrictions or limit the duration of contracts for low-paid occupations, which also suffer from the lowest working conditions and labour standards.

From a postcolonial perspective, international migration is thought to have its roots in colonialism and the international division of labour it created. According to Basso (2015: 86), 'immigrant workers ... have become the global prototype of the precarious, "flexible", super-exploited worker of the neoliberal era'.

Reflect again on Table 12.1 (pg. 210) and the different theoretical approaches to IPE we've discussed in Chapter Twelve and Thirteen. What do you think a liberal-IPE argument might be for explaining the rise of migrant workers, compared to say a Marxist or feminist IPE response?

Brain drain
The concern that educated and skilled individuals will migrate to other countries in pursuit of better wages and living standards thereby depriving their country of origin of their human capital.

International migration has also been raised as a potential problem for developing countries in so far as it can result in **brain drain**, and the general decline of the country's own human capital and labour force (De Haas 2005: 1273). Studies do also highlight, however, that where individuals see that there is financial reward in obtaining a full education to migrate abroad in the future, more individuals will become educated – achieving a net brain *gain* for the developing country. It is worth also considering that international migration can be a two-way process, with skilled migrants – such as doctors, nurses, engineers and scientists, for example – returning to their country of origin after some years abroad and taking their lived experience and skills with them. From a human development perspective, migration can also be found to facilitate more than just the transfer of money and skills back to countries of origin, but also the transfer of ideas, norms and values (De Haas 2005: 1272).

What is clear is that human mobility has become a central issue in both development and security agendas and remains an important dimension of the international economy. Migration is both a motivator for economic and human development, and an effect of underdevelopment and the inherent inequalities within the international economy. Migration too is an effect of increasing insecurities within the world around us and a consequence of war and violence as well as environmental degradation, food insecurity and natural disasters. As we shall see in the next section, human development and human security issues, as well as migration more specifically, continue to be emphasized as the international development agenda has evolved.

SUSTAINABLE DEVELOPMENT AND THE SDGS

So far, we have considered international development as a multidimensional concept addressing both economic and human development perspectives. Over much of the second half of the 20th century, economic development was equated with economic growth and measured through increased gross domestic product (GDP) and other economic indicators. By the early 1990s international development began to be viewed through human development lenses, with an emphasis on quality of life and available choices, largely measured using the Human Development Index (HDI). As the development discourse broadened and evolved, with human development advancing more integrated approaches, emphasis has also turned to consider the impacts of development on the environment. **Sustainable development** – defined by the UN as 'development that meets the needs of the present without compromising the ability of future generations to meet their own needs' – is now a widely utilized term in international politics and has become firmly integrated into development narratives.

Sustainable development
The pursuit of development today that does not deplete the earth's natural resources for the future.

First clarified in 1987 in a report by the World Commission on Environment and Development, entitled 'Our Common Future' (also known as the *Brundtland Report*), the concept of sustainable development treated the environment and development as one and the same issue. The report stated that 'the "environment" is where we all live; and "development" is what we all do in attempting to improve our lot within that abode. The two are inseparable' (World Commission on Environment and Development 1987). The report particularly highlighted the intrinsic concerns associated with the world's economic activity on the biosphere and the world's natural resources. Five years later, in 1992 at the Rio Earth Summit (pg. 149), 178 countries went on to adopt a comprehensive plan of action intended to build a global partnership for sustainable development aimed at improving human lives (linked to human development), and protection of the environment. In contrast to human development – which can be considered a principle of development – sustainable development was advanced as a specific plan for action in tackling development and sustainability as one and the same issue.

In 2000, UN member states adopted the Millennium Development Goals (or MDGs). The MDGs comprised eight broad-ranging goals that would serve as targets for all states and international organizations to meet by the year 2015, including:

1. eradicating extreme poverty and hunger
2. achieving universal primary education
3. promoting gender equality and women's empowerment
4. reducing child mortality
5. improving maternal health
6. combatting HIV, AIDS, malaria and other diseases
7. ensuring environmental sustainability, and
8. pursuing a global partnership for development.

According to the UN's own report card, the MDGs not only 'produced the most successful anti-poverty movement in history' but 'was largely successful across the globe' (UN 2015). In another report card, the MDGs were found to have saved at least 21 million lives, the majority of whom were in sub-Saharan Africa, due to the accelerated progress they induced (McArthur and Rasmussen 2017). Others highlighted how global child mortality rates, alongside rates in HIV and malaria, all declined during the MDG period from 2000 to 2015 (WHO 2018). Yet these reports also highlighted the uneven distribution of success rates for the MDGs, with some regions benefitting from progress while others continued to lag (UN 2015; McArthur and Rasmussen 2017; WHO 2018). The MDGs were also criticized for not being inclusive of the views from developing countries and how they did not do enough to connect international development efforts with the commercial and business world (*The Guardian* 2015).

In January 2015 work began anew to determine what a post-2015 development agenda would look like. Following in the steps of the MDGs, the UN once again pursued a goals and targets approach. In September 2015 at the UN Sustainable Development Summit, 193 States agreed the *2030 Agenda for Sustainable Development*. The new Agenda outlined seventeen Sustainable Development Goals (SDGs) – detailed in Table 13.2 – with each goal comprising between five and nineteen specific targets (totalling 169 targets overall) to be achieved by the year 2030. Both developed and developing countries were involved in the deliberations of the 2030 Agenda, and businesses are now directly linked to the process through the **UN Global Compact**.

UN Global Compact A global corporate sustainability initiative, intended to mobilize a global movement of sustainable companies and stakeholders built on ten principles of responsible business.

The SDGs bring together economic and human development approaches alongside environmental concerns. Tackling inequality is also integrated into the SDGs, with Goal 5 addressing targets to tackle *gender inequality*, while Goal 10 is explicitly focused on *reducing inequalities within and between countries*. We can also see how migration has been integrated into the SDGs. Target 8.8, for example, aims *to protect labour rights and promote safe and secure working environments for all workers, including migrant workers, in particular women migrants, and those in precarious employment*. Target 10.7, meanwhile, aims to *facilitate orderly, safe, regular and responsible migration and mobility of people*, while target 10.c aims *by 2030 to reduce to less than 3 per cent the transaction costs of migrant remittances* – in recognition of the costs of financial transfers to some of the poorest regions in the world.

Table 13.2 The Sustainable Development Goals

Goal 1	No poverty	End poverty in all its forms everywhere
Goal 2	Zero hunger	End hunger, achieve food security and improved nutrition, and promote sustainable agriculture
Goal 3	Good health and well-being	Ensure healthy lives and promote well-being for all at all ages
Goal 4	Quality education	Ensure inclusive and equitable quality education and promote lifelong learning opportunities for all
Goal 5	Gender equality	Achieve gender equality and empower all women and girls
Goal 6	Clean water and sanitation	Ensure availability and sustainable management of water and sanitation for all
Goal 7	Affordable and clean energy	Ensure access to affordable, reliable, sustainable and modern energy for all
Goal 8	Decent work and economic growth	Promote sustained, inclusive and sustainable economic growth, full and productive employment and decent work for all
Goal 9	Industry, innovation and infrastructure	Build resilient infrastructure, promote inclusive and sustainable industrialization and foster innovation
Goal 10	Reduced inequalities	Reduce inequality within and among countries
Goal 11	Sustainable cities and communities	Make cities and human settlements inclusive, safe, resilient and sustainable
Goal 12	Responsible consumption and production	Ensure sustainable consumption and production patterns
Goal 13	Climate action	Take urgent action to combat climate change and its impacts
Goal 14	Life below water	Conserve and sustainably use the oceans, seas and marine resources for sustainable development
Goal 15	Life on land	Protect, restore and promote sustainable use of terrestrial ecosystems, sustainably manage forests, combat deforestation, and halt and reverse land degradation and halt biodiversity loss
Goal 16	Peace, justice and strong institutions	Promote peaceful and inclusive societies for sustainable development, provide access to justice for all and build effective, accountable and inclusive institutions at all levels
Goal 17	Partnerships for the goals	Strengthen the means of implementation and revitalize the Global Partnership for Sustainable Development

Source: Drawn from the United Nations. Available online: https://sdgs.un.org/goals.

As this shows, the international development agenda championed by the UN and many states today is far broader than that of the neoliberal model championed in the 20th century, although economic growth remains a powerful narrative within the sustainable development discourse. Question marks nevertheless remain as to the expected effectiveness of the Sustainable Development Goals, the extent to which they can even be measured or monitored, and if they will be able to tackle global inequalities while also advancing economic growth. According to the *Economist* (2015), for example, the SDGs 'would be worse than useless', being 'so sprawling and misconceived' as to 'amount to a betrayal of the world's poorest people'. As we shall see in the next section this debate has only heightened with the effects of the Covid-19 pandemic and the effects on official development assistance – or foreign aid.

Explore More

According to the World Bank, Covid-19 dealt 'the biggest setback to global poverty in decades' (World Bank 2022b: xiii), such that it is no longer possible to meet the Sustainable Development Goals by 2030. Covid-19 resulted in a 70 million increase in the number of people living on less than $2.15 per day (at 2017 prices). Covid-19 caused a historic reversal in global income convergence, with the poorest bearing the greatest burden of the crisis due to income loss, rising prices and interruptions to health and education services. The income losses of the world's poorest nations were in fact twice as high as the world's richest, while advanced developed nations are recovering far faster from Covid-19 than low- and middle-income countries. Explore more about Covid-19's impacts on the Sustainable Development Goals at https://sdgs.un.org, and on global inequality more broadly by looking at the World Bank 2022 *Poverty and Shared Prosperity Report* Available online: www.worldbank.org.

Scan the QR code for access to explore weblinks and more resources.

THE POLITICS OF DEVELOPMENT ASSISTANCE

In May 2022 the UN Secretary-General raised alarm bells when he said there would be 'direct, negative impacts' on the world's ability to meet the Sustainable Development Goals (SDGs) if governments did not do more to provide 'predictable and additional funding' in **official development assistance** (UN 2022c). His statement came in response to several high-income donor countries cutting their overseas aid budgets during the period 2020 to 2021 and which once again brought to the foreground the various political challenges associated with international development aid.

Official development assistance Government aid aimed at promoting economic development and fighting poverty in developing countries.

Official development assistance (ODA) is the main source of financing for development aid. Most of the major donors of official development assistance are considered high-income economies, being members of the Development Assistance Committee (DAC) within the Organization for Economic Cooperation and Development (OECD). In 1969 all DAC members agreed to spend 0.7 per cent of their Gross National Product (GNP) on foreign aid as a long-term objective – a commitment that was subsequently reaffirmed by a UN General Assembly resolution in 1970. In 1993 that commitment was updated to reflect Gross National Income (GNI) as an equivalent concept. Today each DAC member's foreign aid spending is measured against the target of their spending a minimum of 0.7 per cent of their GNI. Yet only seven donor countries have ever actually met or exceeded that target.

Total official development assistance was in fact equivalent to just 0.33 per cent of the DAC's combined GNI in 2021, despite the overall volume of aid being at an all-time high.

The domestic politics associated with foreign aid in donor countries can be fraught with controversy. Governments must balance their responsibilities and commitments to provide foreign aid to other countries with their domestic economic interests, pressures and concerns. For this reason, aid budgets can often be a casualty of budget cuts when donor countries experience economic shocks, decline or recession. At the international level the politics associated with foreign aid is equally as controversial, though tends to be oriented more towards debates concerning the effectiveness of aid, and to what extent aid should be conditional. These debates are in fact interlinked as they both relate to the broader debate surrounding the Washington Consensus. As we saw earlier in this chapter, development assistance in the latter half of the 20th century was largely delivered through structural adjustment programmes that required developing countries to implement prescribed economic policies thought to facilitate economic growth. Developing countries could therefore access much needed capital but only on the condition that they pursued the same market-led economic policies championed by most of the Western high-income economies, the IMF and the World Bank.

Conditionality did not stop there, however. Development assistance was also linked to trade through tied aid, where donor governments provided bilateral loans or grants on the condition that the recipient country then bought goods and services from them or the donor's choice of countries. Many donor governments – in addition to the European Union who is a leading actor in international development and collectively provides more than half of the world's foreign aid – have also linked development assistance with the recipient countries meeting certain political conditions such as human rights, education, labour and environmental targets, ensuring the rule of law, good governance or promoting democracy. Where recipient states fail to meet those conditions, donor countries can withdraw their development assistance. For example, in 2016 the EU suspended direct financial assistance to Burundi on the grounds that they were non-compliant with essential elements of their partnership agreement regarding human rights, democratic principles and the rule of law. The suspension was repealed in 2022 following Burundi's peaceful elections in 2020 and the Burundian government's commitments to follow a road map for improvement in these areas (European Council 2022).

Arguably tied and conditional foreign aid can be a catalyst for both economic and human development. The injection of capital can help poorer countries develop their economies. Loans and grants linked to infrastructure projects – such as railways and ports – can bolster economic activity while providing the physical network for goods and services to move more freely in accessing wider markets. Aid linked to political conditions can also incentivize governments in recipient countries to uphold human rights, promote good governance and enshrine political and press freedoms, for example.

Yet as we have seen, 'one-size-fits-all' development strategies have also been roundly critiqued. By the turn of the 21st century, structural adjustment programmes were particularly being brought into question. Research highlighted that while aid flows had increased, economic growth in the poorest parts of the world remained negligible and, in some cases, had even declined. In one article published in *the Journal of Policy Reform* in 2002, William Easterly highlighted that while foreign aid to Africa had increased between 1970 and 1999, the GDP growth per capita for recipient countries had decreased – the opposite effect of what the aid had been intended for. The reason why foreign aid was so unproductive in Africa, Easterly argued, was due to the unsatisfactory performance of aid bureaucracy, the fact that programmes were designed poorly or implemented without due recognition of the economic and governmental conditions within the recipient country, or where feedback and criticism were not then acted upon. As Easterly (2002: 244) emphasized, '[p]oor nations include an incredible variety of cultures and histories ... The whole idea of summing up all this diversity into a "Third World" waiting to be "developed" by outside altruists has little connection to reality'.

Tied aid has also been criticized for forcing developing countries to pay higher prices because of lack of competition, and for the heavy administrative burden they placed on recipient countries (Carbone 2007). Critics further highlighted the aid dependence that development assistance can create for the poorest countries – a point dependency theorists would particularly support. Conditional aid can also be criticized for essentially 'conditioning' developing countries to adopt Western liberal democratic norms, representing a form of neo-imperialism (pg. 27). Such critiques not only bring to the foreground questions of sovereignty and how external interference should be understood in development discourses, but also to what extent official development assistance perpetuates Western hegemony within the international economy.

How money is distributed to those communities most in need is another point of debate surrounding aid conditionality and effectiveness. Concerns over corruption within recipient governments, coupled with the need for donor countries to demonstrate that their foreign aid budgets are well spent, have only increased the need for anti-corruption mechanisms within official development assistance (Dávid-Barrett et al. 2020) and ratcheted up the targets and conditions needed to measure aid's effectiveness. While measuring aid effectiveness is notoriously difficult, the effort alone adds further bureaucracy to foreign aid. In critiquing the bureaucratization of foreign aid, Easterly (2002: 247) suggested the need for alternative non-bureaucratic channels such as providing cash grants to the poor. While the idea of cash transfers has been slow in gaining political support, in recent years there have been increasing calls for aid budgets to be directed as cash directly given to households or individuals (Matthews 2022; Sturge 2017).

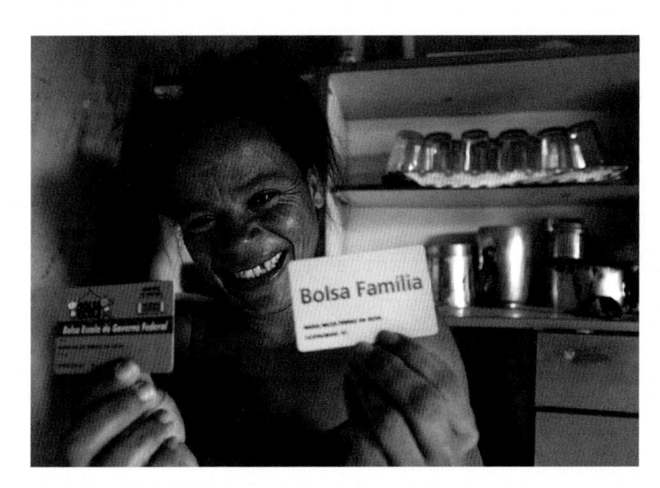

Image 13.3 In Brazil the Bolsa Família programme provided direct cash transfers to poor Brazilian families. In return, families had to ensure their children attended school and were vaccinated. The programme was implemented by the Brazilian government with financial and technical support from the World Bank. It has been widely recognized as a model for Conditional Cash Transfer (CCT) programmes.

Source: VANDERLEI ALMEIDA/Getty Images.

Consider

Most of the world's foreign aid is distributed as payments from donor organizations or governments to recipient governments. Recipient governments are then responsible for spending the aid in accordance with the conditions set out by the donors. In some countries – such as in Brazil and the Philippines – financial assistance is provided direct to the poorest individuals and households through conditional cash transfers, enabling individuals to choose how the finance should be spent or invested once they have met education and health conditions. But these programmes are rare. In 2016 the World Humanitarian Summit agreed that providing cash payments and vouchers to individuals requiring humanitarian assistance should be increased. *Do you think cash transfers paid directly to individuals or households would be a more effective model for distributing foreign aid?*

Explore

Find out more about the Bolsa Família programme at www.iadb.org. The charity ActionAid has also done research into the benefits of conditional cash transfer (CCT) programmes, particularly as it relates to improving women's agency and empowerment – see www.actionaid.org.uk. The charity GiveDirectly, meanwhile, champions the use of *un*conditional cash transfers (UCT), arguing that UCTs best enable and empower people who are most in need. Explore the evidence they draw upon at www.givedirectly.org.

Connect

Development is a multidimensional concept. Reflect again on the definitions of economic development (pg. 225), human development (pg. 225) and sustainable development (pg. 232). What conceptualization of development do you think is most useful in understanding the benefits of cash transfers?

Predict

If all donor countries met their target of providing a minimum of 0.7 per cent of their GNI in official development assistance by 2030, would it help address global poverty and inequality?

Scan the QR code for access to explore weblinks and more resources.

CONCLUSION

In this chapter we have considered the various issues, concepts and challenges associated with equality and development within international politics. As we have seen, international development is far more than just an economic issue, with development fundamentally addressing issues of equality as well as human insecurity. While economic development remains an important part of efforts to tackle global poverty and facilitate economic growth in developing countries, human development discourses have also become increasingly important in highlighting the necessity to direct development assistance towards tackling poverty and improving standards of living, education, health, ecological and general equality. A focus on equality also draws our attention to the disparities between countries within the international system, and the need for more inclusive, equitable and tailored development agendas that serve the needs of individual developing countries. In this chapter we have also seen how the UN's Sustainable Development Goals have developed to improve economic and human development, help the environment, improve conditions for migration and human mobility, and tackle inequality within and between states. Whether states will be able to achieve all 169 targets of the Sustainable Development Goals is a debate international politics scholars will continue to have, along with discussion over the effectiveness of foreign aid, what conditions should be attached, and whether new methods of distributing aid – such as the use of cash transfers – should be advanced further. These are issues and debates that will hopefully stoke your own interest in international development, equality and international political economy more broadly, and which you can continue to develop with the following toolkit exercise.

TOOLKIT

When is a country 'developed'?

THINK

- Think about this statement from the Brundtland Report: '"development" is what we all do in attempting to improve our lot' (World Commission on Environment and Development 1987). What do you think this means in understanding international development more broadly?
- Status (pg. 81) matters in international politics. Think about the status of 'developing country' and what you understand it to mean. How does this status relate and compare to other commonly used references in international politics such as 'Least Developed Country', 'emerging economy', or 'high-income economy'?

OBSERVE

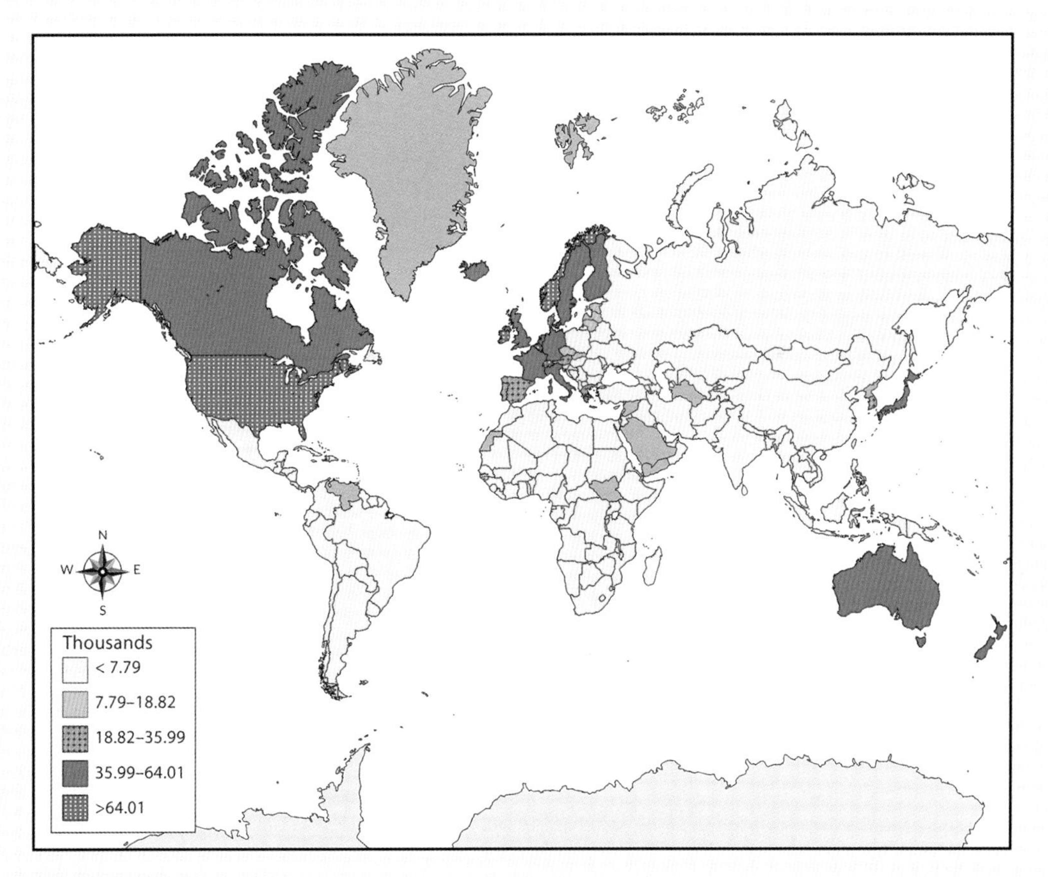

Map 13.1 A map showing country GNI per capita (Atlas method in current US$ for the year 2021).

Source: International Comparison Program, World Development Indicators database, World Bank. Eurostat-OECD PPP Programme.

- There are various categories and rankings used by states and international organizations to describe developing countries. Prior to 1989 the World Bank distinguished countries as 'developing economies' and 'industrial countries'. Since 1989, however, the World Bank distinguishes countries by income as a measure of GNI per capita. Low-income economies and middle-income economies (the palest blue countries on the map) are considered developing countries. The countries in the darkest shades of blue on this map are all classified as 'high-income economies'. The OECD also uses the World Bank's low-income and middle-income categories to determine who is included on its recipients list for Official Development Assistance.
- Another category is the Least Developed Countries (LDCs) list which include 'low-income countries confronting severe structural impediments to sustainable development' and who are considered 'highly vulnerable to economic and environmental shocks and have low levels of human assets' (UNDESA n.d.). At the time of writing there were forty-six LDCs listed by the UN. The UN's Committee for Development Policy keeps under review the list of Least Developed Countries (LDC) and determines the threshold for countries 'graduating' from LDC status. The LDC categorization is also significant as LDCs receive special international support measures such as better official development assistance, easier access to climate change finance, and reduced contributions to the UN and other international organizations' budgets, for example.

ORGANIZE

- From a neoliberal perspective, today's developing countries can be understood as those economies still undergoing the process of industrialization who will become developed as they modernize their economies and integrate into the international economy.
- Realist approaches would highlight that the post-World War Two international order and the various international organizations that formed were shaped by high-income economies to serve their economic interests and sustain their economic dominance.
- Social and critical theories would highlight how development narratives construct and reinforce meanings and identities within international politics, particularly as they concern relationships of power and dominance. Consider the meanings around 'First World' and 'Third World', for example (pg. 6). What would a postcolonial view be of the meanings associated with 'developed' and 'developing' country?

LINK

- *Consider*: In 2004 ten new Central and Eastern European (CEE) states joined the EU (pg. 134–6). Prior to their accession, the CEE states were considered developing countries in so far as their economies were just opening up after being part of the centrally planned Soviet economy. Through their candidacy and accession procedures to the EU, each state had to commit to various political conditions concerning their economic and monetary policies, rule of law, good governance and democratic practices. While these states are not yet as wealthy as the EU's older member states, since joining the EU the CEE countries have experienced significant economic growth and now rank alongside the rest of the EU as *high-income economies* as well as *very-high countries* on the Human Development Index (HDI). For example, Poland – the largest of the CEE states – increased its income per capita from £1,731 (classifying it as a low-middle income economy) in 1990 to £17,840 (classifying it as a high-income economy) in 2021.

- *Explore*: Bulgaria is another Eastern European country that joined the EU in 2007. While lauded for its impressive economic growth rate since joining, Bulgaria also has the highest poverty rate and worst income inequality in the EU. You can explore more of the data associated with Bulgaria's development at https://data.worldbank.org/country/bulgaria. For access to more research and analysis scan the barcode to visit our companion website.
- *Connect*: Does economic growth – measured by indicators and thresholds associated with a country's GDP and GNI – alone reveal if a country has 'developed'? What other measurement criteria can or should be used?
- *Predict*: North Macedonia is classified by the World Bank as a middle-income country. It is listed on the OECD Development Assistance Committee's recipients list and in 2020 2.4 per cent of its Gross National Income was derived from foreign aid. In 2020 North Macedonia joined NATO (pg. 131–2). North Macedonia is also a candidate country for joining the EU, although there is not yet a clear date for its accession. When will North Macedonia have 'developed'?

SHARE

- Answer the question '*When is a country "developed"?*'

  There are several different approaches you could take when answering this question, so take a moment to reflect on the different angles you've worked through so far and the lines of enquiry you find most compelling. You may want to make your answer more theoretical in orientation, drawing on different theories to explain and critique the concept of development itself. Or you could turn this into more of an empirical analysis with discussion of the indicators used to define and distinguish developed from developing countries, for example. Once you've decided your approach, though, make sure to think about your argument and the counterarguments that may be put across. You might also want to check out *How to – approach a literature review* (pg. 202) for some tips on identifying and consolidating your knowledge of the scholarship around your topic.

HOW TO

PREPARE A POLICY BRIEF

Policy briefs have become common means by which civil society actors share their expertise with governments and international organizations and seek to shift the political agenda. They are also increasingly used as methods of assessment in universities. The purpose of a policy brief is specifically to design and advocate a *feasible measure* for a specific *audience* (e.g. a government or international organization) confronted with a significant *problem* or issue. These also make up the three core components of a policy brief – a problem, an audience and a solution (Figure 13.2).

Imagine, for example, that you are tasked with writing a policy brief on behalf of the civil society super-network ICAN (pg. 150–1). You want more states to support and sign the Treaty on the Prohibition of Nuclear Weapons (TPNW) (pg. 195). Your problem, then, might be the fact that the world's nuclear-weapon states continue to uphold, and in some cases advance, their nuclear arsenals. Who then do you target as an audience for your brief? Narrowing in your focus to a specific audience will help you tailor your policy brief more easily. In this case, you might target the Secretary-General of NATO as your audience. NATO is a defensive alliance (pg. 131) built on a doctrine of nuclear deterrence, so it is, in many respects, part of the problem you have identified. Yet NATO is an alliance of thirty-one member states. Several NATO allies – including Norway and Germany – have also expressed interest in participating in the TPNW Meeting of the Parties as observers.

With a problem and audience now in mind, you can then start to develop your 'solution' – a practical and feasible recommendation that you believe your intended audience can implement. In our example, recommending that the NATO Secretary-General advise all NATO members to sign the TPNW – while perhaps desirable, is less practical or feasible considering NATO's formal stance on nuclear deterrence. But a more feasible solution might be to recommend that the NATO Secretary-General participate as an observer at the next TPNW Meeting of the Parties. In so doing your solution is to enhance dialogue and transparency, facilitating closer ties between TPNW signatories and NATO itself, along with civil society who actively participates in TPNW meetings. That

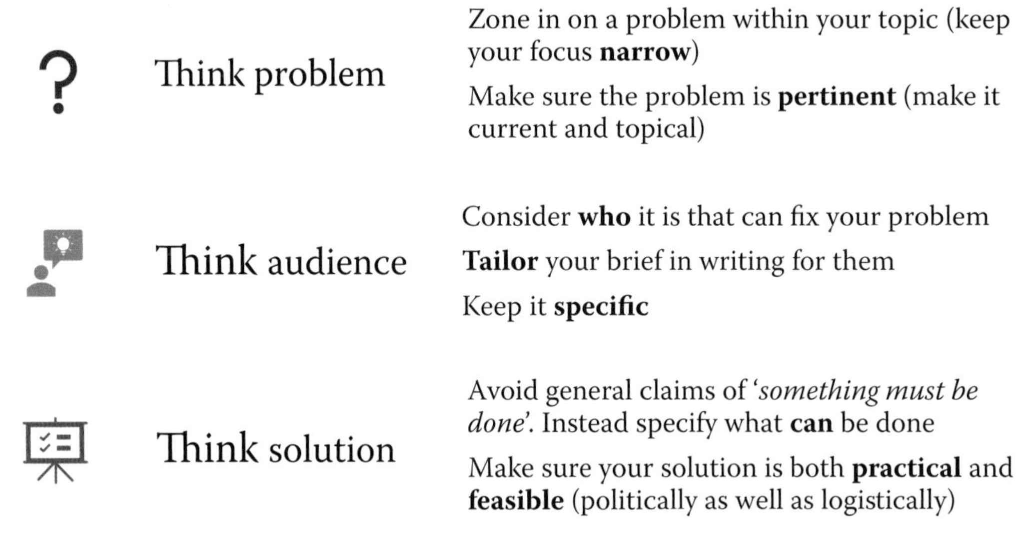

Figure 13.2 The key elements of a policy brief

Special thanks to Professor Paul Cairney for his guidance on approaching and structuring a policy brief.

is admittedly a small step, but a meaningful one. In this way your solution is targeted, and practical, and gives your audience a clear course of action.

Bear in mind that policy briefs are meant to be focused and succinct. Whoever your intended audience, they are likely to have limited time to read tomes of information but will want to glean precise information and a clear message easily and accessibly. Remember, also, that civil society (of which academia is also a key part), draws legitimacy and authority from its knowledge and expertise. Policy briefs should therefore be evidence-based, providing key facts and supporting evidence to highlight key arguments and reinforce your commentary, and with all source material clearly referenced.

Policy briefs must also be understandable and accessible, using clear language that avoids too much jargon. You can also help your audience by dividing your policy brief into clear sections, so they can easily access the information they seek. Typically, a policy brief might include the following main sections:

Executive Summary (approximately 150 words)

Like an article abstract, your executive summary should summarize the main points of your policy brief as a whole. This should include a very brief description of the problem, a statement of why something needs to change, and your recommendation. If your audience only reads this summary, they should be able to take from it the main problem and your recommended solution that is then detailed more fully in the brief.

Situation Brief (approximately 500 words)

The situation brief should provide background information explaining the significance of your problem, and the actors and interests involved. It should include key data, or diagrams that help to highlight the pressing nature of the problem you have identified.

Policy Options (approximately 500 words)

The policy options should outline and evaluate possible alternatives that your target audience might look to enact that move beyond the status quo. The policy options should be supported by evidence, with discussion of their credibility and feasibility in addressing the problem outlined in the situation brief.

Recommendation (approximately 150 words)

The recommendation is where you explain and justify your proposed solution and persuade your audience as to its validity.

Scan the QR code for access to explore weblinks and more resources.

14 Energy and the environment

Unsplash / Matthew Henry

Abstract

In 2022 the world faced a global energy crisis. Triggered by Russia's invasion of Ukraine, the global energy crisis placed energy markets and the security, reliability and sustainability of the world's energy supplies squarely onto international political agendas. In this chapter you will be introduced to energy and the environment as interlinked issues in international politics. The chapter first develops your understanding of energy and the environment as global commons, along with the associated theoretical perspectives we can utilize in explaining the prospects for collective action in protecting and sustaining the earth's climate and natural resources. The chapter then focuses on global efforts to tackle climate change, before addressing some of the more specific challenges associated with resource scarcity. The chapter concludes with a toolkit exercise for you to then apply your knowledge, focusing on the question *'What are the main obstacles to achieving global net zero by 2050?'*

International Energy Agency
An international organization established in 1974 to coordinate a collective response to major disruptions in oil supply. The IEA now facilitates energy cooperation among thirty-one member states, all of whom are also members of the OECD (pg. 235).

UNDERSTANDING ENERGY AND THE ENVIRONMENT

In 2022 the **International Energy Agency** (IEA) stated that the global energy crisis was 'a shock of unprecedented breadth and complexity' (IEA 2022). Triggered by Russia's invasion of Ukraine which began on 24 February 2022, the crisis threw global energy markets into turmoil. The crisis disrupted, and even reversed, long-standing government energy policies, and impacted billions of individuals who were faced with skyrocketing energy costs.

As the world's largest exporter of **fossil fuels,** Russia has considerable influence within global energy markets. When Russia invaded Ukraine, oil prices peaked to their highest level since 2008. Natural gas prices around the world peaked to their highest level on record. Coal prices also hit record levels. High gas and coal prices then placed upward pressure on electricity costs which also soared (IEA 2022). Global supply chains were further impacted. Sanctions, such as those introduced by the EU, banned the import of Russian oil and coal. Many European countries declared their intention to phase out reliance on Russian natural gas, pivoting instead towards the importation of **liquefied natural gas** (LNG) from the United States. Russia responded by curtailing and even turning off its gas exporting pipelines to Europe, redirecting more of its energy exports towards China and India.

Due to the integrated and interconnected nature of the international economy (pg. 205), the impact of the war on Ukraine was soon felt around the world. Fossil fuels account for around 80 per cent of the global **energy mix** (IEA 2022). Eighty per cent of the global population also lives in a country that is a net importer of fossil fuels – that's around 6 billion people who are dependent on fossil fuels produced in another country and who are therefore vulnerable to fluctuations in global energy markets (UN 2023a). Households across the world were subsequently faced not only with rising costs at the pump and in their household energy bills, but with the knock-on price hikes for food and other products impacted by rising transportation costs. While fossil fuel producers made a $2 trillion profit in 2021, some 100 million people in 2022 also found themselves unable to afford rising energy prices and were forced instead to rely on firewood for cooking (IEA 2022).

The global energy crisis sparked by the 2022 Russia-Ukraine war, while pertinent and pressing for all scholars and practitioners of contemporary international politics, is also significant in that it highlights a far deeper, historical energy and environmental crisis that the world has been on the precipice of for some decades. Ever since the Industrial Revolution (pg. 156), states have relied upon coal, gas and oil to drive their economic development (pg. 225). That reliance has, however, come at a high cost. Fossil fuels are not only **non-renewable,** with a finite supply, but, when burned, fossil fuels release high quantities of carbon dioxide (CO_2) into the atmosphere. Worldwide demand and consumption of fossil fuels has also grown dramatically over the 20th and early 21st centuries. All countries rely in some part on fossil fuels as part of their energy mix. China, for example, the world's fastest growing economy, is also the world's largest emitter of CO_2 due to its reliance on coal for industry and electricity production. Couple to this the fact that, between 1990 and 2020, the world lost a net area of 178 million hectares of forestry – that's an area the size of Libya – due to **deforestation**, further removing essential carbon stores that naturally absorb CO_2.

Climate scientists have long linked the burning of fossil fuels with global warming (IPCC 2023). Anthropogenic global **greenhouse gases** (GHG) – which include CO_2 as well as other gases that trap the sun's heat in the earth's atmosphere – have increased year on year since records first started in 1850, largely driven by industrialization and economic growth. In 2021 atmospheric CO_2 concentrations were higher than at any time in at least 2 million years, while global temperatures have increased faster since 1970 than in any other fifty-year period over at least the last 2,000 years (IPCC 2021). In fact 2016 and 2020 were tied as the hottest years on record, a trend that is only persisting as global surface temperatures continue to rise. Glaciers are retreating in the Alps, Himalayas, Andes, Rockies, Alaska and across Africa. Summer Arctic sea ice areas have also shrunk by nearly 13 per cent per decade, while sea levels are now at their highest in 3,000 years. The acidity of the oceans has also increased by 30 per cent since the Industrial Revolution. Rising global temperatures have further resulted in extremes of high and low temperatures, heavy rain, droughts and tropical cyclones (IPCC 2023).

According to the Intergovernmental Panel on Climate Change (IPCC) – an organization established by the UN in 1988 to provide scientific information to

Fossil fuels
Naturally produced organic deposits found in the earth's crust which, when extracted and combusted, provide energy, such as coal, oil and natural gas.

Liquefied natural gas
A natural gas that has been cooled to a liquid state. When liquefied, LNG is 600 times smaller than natural gas, and can be transported and stored in large containers, rather than relying on gas pipelines.

Energy mix
The combination of fossil fuels, nuclear energy and renewable energy sources required to meet energy needs.

Non-renewable
A fuel source that is single use, and once used cannot be replenished.

Deforestation
The purposeful removal of forestry in order to use the wood for fuel or manufacturing, or to convert the land to other uses, such as grazing or other agricultural uses.

Greenhouse gases
Gases that cause heat from the sun to be trapped in the earth's atmosphere. GHG emissions include water vapour (H_2O), carbon dioxide (CO_2), methane (CH_4), ozone (O_3), nitrous oxide (N_20) and chlorofluorocarbons (CFCs).

governments and international organizations for use in developing climate policies – 'it is unequivocal that human influence has warmed the atmosphere, ocean and land' (IPCC 2023: 5). The IPCC has found that the primary source of anthropogenic **climate change** is from fossil fuel combustion and industrial processes, which contributed around 78 per cent of total greenhouse gas emissions from 1970 to 2010 (IPCC 2014). Energy is also found to have significant impacts on other issues of environmental concern. For example, the world's reliance on fossil fuels has led to increased demand on extraction through mining and drilling operations, including through controversial methods such as **fracking**. These extraction methods are also found to have adverse impacts on local habitats and have led to an accelerating loss in **biodiversity** (Goklany 2021; Harfoot et al. 2018).

Climate change
A change in normal global or regional climate patterns. The term has, since the mid to late 20th century, become more commonly used to describe the effects of global warming as a result of burning fossil fuels.

Fracking
A technique whereby liquid is injected at high pressures into subterranean rock formations to open fissures for the extraction of oil or gas.

Biodiversity
Referring to the variety of plant and animal life in a particular habitat. In global contexts it refers to the variety of plants, fungi, bacteria and animals living on the earth.

The major political problems thus associated with the world's energy mix, humankind's reliance on fossil fuel, and demand for the earth's natural resources more generally, are fundamentally environmental problems. Yet, while the environment has become an increasingly prominent issue in international politics since the first Rio Earth Summit in 1992 (pg. 233), energy politics has received comparatively limited attention (Van de Graaf 2013). A result of the 2022 global energy crisis, however, is that it has placed energy markets and the security, reliability and sustainability of the world's energy supplies squarely on to international political agendas: further highlighting the inextricable link between energy and the environment.

This chapter is aimed at developing your understanding of energy and the environment as related issues of importance in international politics. In the next section we turn to address energy and the environment as global commons and some of the theoretical tensions between national interests in using the earth's resources, relative to collective international interests in protecting the environment. From there you will consider some of the politics associated with efforts to tackle climate change at the international level, before turning to look at the political tensions that exist around resource scarcity, competition and conflict. The chapter concludes with a toolkit exercise for you to apply your knowledge that asks, *'What are the main obstacles to achieving global net zero by 2050?'*

Climate change can be a polarizing political issue, being treated by many as fact, yet for others as a theory to be proven. Others still consider climate change a hoax, or misinformation.

Your perceptions and beliefs about climate change, and the extent to which global warming is a direct result of human activities, will invariably impact the importance you place on energy and environmental issues within international politics. As with any political issue, however, it is important to reflect on your own assumptions and the different perspectives that are out there. Due to the polarizing nature of climate change, misinformation has arguably coloured the debate (see Treen, Williams and O'Neill 2020). Be sure to therefore probe claims and test the quality and reliability of the sources you are using to inform your research in this area (see also *How to – identify quality sources* on pg. 106).

You may also want to take some time to look at the evidence that informs international approaches to climate politics by exploring the Intergovernmental Panel on Climate Change website at www.ipcc.ch. Take a look also at Björnberg et al. (2017), 'Climate and environmental science denial: A review of the scientific literature published in 1990–2015', *Journal of Cleaner Production*, 167: 229–241 for a useful review of the literature on climate science denial.

ENERGY AND THE ENVIRONMENT AS GLOBAL COMMONS

Our environment is essential for sustaining life on this planet. Without clean air, water and land to live off, few species would be able to survive. Without the earth's natural resources, be that fossil fuels or other **renewable energy** sources such as solar, wind, wave, geothermal or biomass power, we would not have the energy that is the lifeblood of our societies (Van de Graaf 2013: 1). Energy and the environment have particular significance in international politics, moreover, because our environment and many of the earth's natural resources are **global commons**, shared among all people, plants and animals on the planet. Global commons do not belong to any one state. The sustainability and health of the polar ice caps, oceans and the air we breathe matter for everyone's survival. The effects of pollution or the depletion of key resources does not limit itself to one state, but is a transboundary problem.

Renewable energy
Energy that comes from sources that are easily replenished i.e. solar, wind, wave/tidal power. Also known as 'clean' energies as they have zero emissions so do not add to air pollution.

Global commons
Resources that do not come under any state's national jurisdiction, but are of value and necessity to the whole planet.

While states may possess **national jurisdiction** over the natural resources within their own territories, some resources – such as the planet's woodlands and forests – are also too important to the planet's ecosystem not to be of concern to all states. The Brazilian government, for example, has faced considerable international pressure over the rate of deforestation in the Amazon rainforest, including through illegal logging activity by organized crime gangs. The Amazon, which covers over 2 million square miles, is the largest tropical rainforest in the world, absorbing more greenhouse gases than any other tropical rainforest. Deforestation of the Amazon is also a major contributor to global warming. While a natural resource of global concern, a large proportion of the Amazon falls under Brazilian national jurisdiction. The Amazon, therefore, serves as an important natural resource for Brazil to be able to utilize, yet also to manage, protect and preserve.

National jurisdiction
A nation's sovereign authority to administer justice over the territories, resources and people within its borders.

One of the greatest challenges that the earth's environment and natural resources present from an international politics perspective is how to ensure that all global commons are utilized sustainably, fairly and with the collective good in mind. Yet where there are global commons, the **tragedy of the commons** is found to follow. As articulated by Garrett Hardin in 1968, the tragedy of the commons refers to the principle that people faced with a common resource will overuse the resource to maximize their own gain. A commonly used metaphor to explain the tragedy of the commons is where there exists a piece of common land. Every farmer – being thought rational and seeking to maximize his or her own gain – will seek to utilize the resource by adding one more cow to their herd. For every cow that individual farmer adds, the more profit the farmer will receive. Those farmers who may seek to protect and preserve the common resource by limiting their herd, or by working with others to try to manage the resource sustainably, will only be faced by **free riders** who continue to use the commons for their own end. It is then in the self-interest of each farmer to add one more cow, then another, and another to best utilize the land and maximize their individual gain. The consequence is overgrazing and depletion of the resource needed to sustain them. For Hardin (1968), the tragedy is that, while the commons are a freely accessible resource, they cannot be jointly or mutually managed due to the self-interest of the individuals who would want to use if for their own gain.

Tragedy of the commons
The principle that self-interested individuals will exploit a global common at the expense of others to gain an advantage, even if that places the health and sustainability of the common at risk.

Free riding
A principle which sees some actors benefit from resources, public goods or collective agreements without having contributed to them.

By way of a contemporary example, we can observe the tragedy of the commons in fishing. Fish are a global common in so far as they are a resource of food and oils freely available in the world's oceans. While coastal states have national jurisdiction over their own territorial waters,[1] two-thirds of the world's oceans are international waters that are beyond the jurisdiction of any one state, and which are open to utilization – and exploitation – by any actor capable of open-ocean fishing. Extensive overfishing has been found to negatively

[1]Under the Law of the Sea, coastal states exercise sovereignty over the sea immediately adjacent to their shores, typically up to 12 nautical miles (22km) from their coastline. Beyond these national maritime zones are international waters that no state has national jurisdiction over.

impact the health and sustainability of both fish stocks and oceanic habitats. According to the Food and Agriculture Organization (FAO 2020), one-third of the world's fisheries have been pushed beyond their biological limit and are becoming unsustainable. Overfishing also has an impact on human populations dependent on fish for food, and on fishing for their livelihoods. Yet despite the risks associated with overfishing, fishing continues, even in depleted stock areas, due to high demand. This is the tragedy of the commons.

From a theoretical perspective, we can see how the tragedy of the commons closely relates to the classical realist tradition in international politics (pg. 35–7). From a neorealist perspective we can also observe that, while states can look to regulate the businesses and individuals who live and work in their national jurisdiction – such as the New Zealand government, for example, who sets out very clear legal requirements for commercial fishing enterprises in New Zealand's national waters – due to the anarchic condition of the international system, there is no overarching authority that can hold states accountable for upholding international regulations or to ensure they do not opt out of international agreements (pg. 18). In fact, continuing the fishing example, regional and global fisheries governance is considered notoriously weak (Schaeffer 2023), and even when states do sign agreements to address illegal fishing practices, monitoring compliance remains a pressing issue (Pew Trusts 2017).

From the realist theoretical tradition, survival and security are also paramount to an individual's – and state's – interests. A rational actor will therefore pursue those resources necessary for their survival and security. It is for this reason that energy is commonly treated more as a matter of national security (pg. 187) than of environmental concern. Energy is observed as a strategic necessity (Van de Graaf 2013); a good that is essential to the security and continued prosperity of a state and its citizens, and its continued supply a matter of keen national interest. Ensuring an accessible and reliable energy supply, particularly for the majority of states who are net importers of energy, is therefore a particular point of concern. When, in 2011, Iran threatened to block the Strait of Hormuz – a vital shipping lane linking the Gulf's oil-producing states including Bahrain, Kuwait, Qatar, Saudi Arabia and the United Arab Emirates to the Indian Ocean – analysts not only highlighted that the impact could raise the price of oil by more than $50 a barrel (*New York Times* 2012), but that it would leave stranded 17 million barrels of oil a day, sending a supply shock around the world. Energy can therefore be observed not only as an important foreign policy instrument (pg. 97–8) for energy importing states, but as a major national security concern where energy supplies are threatened or disrupted. Similarly, resource scarcity is not only a domestic concern for states but has become a potent source of international dispute – a point we shall return to later in this chapter.

Explore More

Overfishing is one of the most significant causes of oceanic decline. Overfishing is also connected with illegal, unreported and unregulated fishing which has become a pressing problem for many parts of the world. In a landmark moment, on 5 March 2023 the United Nations agreed the High Seas Treaty after twenty years of talks. The High Seas Treaty is specifically aimed at protecting the world's oceans by placing international waters into marine protected areas (MPAs). Activities within these MPAs can only occur provided it is consistent with conservation and marine biodiversity, meaning that fishing, shipping and exploration activities could be limited. Explore more news and analysis about the Treaty, along with other international efforts to overcome the tragedy of the commons, by scanning the barcode and visiting our companion website.

Scan the QR code for access to explore weblinks and more resources.

Important to also note is that the tragedy of the commons as observed through realist lenses is but one perspective of how we can understand – and manage – the global commons. Consider that in a bid to mitigate overfishing, states have also pursued and implemented national and international shipping and fishing regulations, often working through regional fisheries management organizations (RFMO) to work collectively to regulate fishing and sustain fishing stocks. We can also identify countless examples of global efforts to regulate the world's natural resources, from international biodiversity regulations to climate change mitigation, to climate finance for developing countries to facilitate more sustainable development (pg. 232–5). The liberal theoretical tradition would particularly emphasize how states are capable of cooperating through international and regional organizations to manage the global commons. Collective gain over the global commons is therefore feasible, especially where international laws and regulations are agreed and upheld by states.

Where it concerns energy, liberal IPE perspectives would also emphasize the interconnected nature of global energy markets, and how, through trade liberalization (pg. 212), energy interdependence between states has fostered conditions of international peace rather than conflict. Liberal IPE perspectives also observe how energy, like any commodity, is sold in a market economy that is subject to principles of competition and efficiency (pg. 208). As a result, energy producers must constantly strive to not only meet demand but to provide an efficient commodity in a market where 'clean', 'green', renewable energy sources are increasingly sought after. As we also saw in Chapter Nine, it was through the technological innovation of multinational enterprises in developing substitutes for the ozone-depleting chlorofluorocarbon (CFC) gases in the 1980s that CFCs were eventually banned (pg. 150). The UN Global Compact (pg. 233) is another example of the importance placed on market actors in meeting the UN's Sustainable Development Goals (SDGs). From a liberal perspective, therefore, we can see how both market and state actors can help to both sustain and regulate the global commons and facilitate a transition to greener economies.

Constructivist approaches would highlight how sustainable development has become a globally accepted norm since it was first introduced in the Brundtland Report in 1987 (pg. 233). Epistemic communities (pg. 150), such as the Intergovernmental Panel on Climate Change, have also played an important role in shaping the discourse around climate change. In so doing, discourse and knowledge have shaped a growing acceptance of the need for sustainable development and for temperance when it comes to the economic development and associated energy practices pursued by states and businesses alike. Sustainable development policies are thus observed as an appropriate form of state behaviour (pg. 62), while states who persistently opt out of international environmental pacts are seen as 'pariahs' (Gupta 2019). Over time, therefore, socially constructed norms and discourses have informed and influenced societal perceptions of the global commons, and the inappropriateness of exploiting them.

More critical perspectives further highlight how the 'tragedy' of the commons is largely hegemonic (pg. 22) in nature, being shaped by the logic that the most powerful win, and the weak lose (Gupta 2019). From a postcolonial perspective, the wealthiest states and multinational enterprises have sought to appropriate and colonize resources of a global common, using their status as 'first comer' to justify their monopoly over a resource (Gupta 2019). Large MNEs 'acting as an extended arm of their governments when interests merge' (Gupta 2019: 22) thus commandeer access to resources which should be open to all, be that fossil fuel rich lands or seabeds or fishing grounds. The result, according to Gupta (2019: 22), is that the *tragedy* of the commons is a *tragedy of inequality and injustice* in which the rich benefit and the poor suffer the consequences. Local and indigenous populations have particularly experienced the negative impacts of mining and other extractive projects by large MNEs and state enterprises, including the devastation of biodiversity and local habitats. Whereas Hardin (1974: 1246–7) argued that 'injustice is preferable to total ruin', Gupta (2019: 22) highlights that the more important question is 'total ruin and injustice for whom?'

Image 14.1 In October 2021 the indigenous people of the Waorani community in Ecuador marched on Ecuador's Constitutional Court demanding the annulment of a decree that would authorize new oil exploration projects in the Amazon. In February 2022 the Constitutional Court published a landmark ruling that recognized, for the first time, 'the right of indigenous communities to have the final decision over oil, mining and other extractive projects that affect their lands' (Amazon Frontlines 2022).

Source: Agencia Press South/Getty Images.

Fifty years after Hardin first published his 1968 article on the Tragedy of the Commons, Joyeeta Gupta set out to revisit his claims. In her analysis, Gupta highlights the neoliberal and hegemonic logics that ultimately shape the tragedy of the commons principle, as evident in the push by big businesses and powerful states to be the 'first' to capture natural resources. In critique, Gupta highlights the colonial legacies informing the tragedy of the commons logic that not only creates winners and losers, but is 'used to justify the concentration of wealth in the hands of the first comer and to push the ladder away so that no one can climb up' (Gupta 2019: 22). For Gupta, change can only happen through 'mutual agreement, mutually agreed upon' including the direct involvement of local communities and indigenous populations over the use of natural resources. Gupta further recommended reframing the principle as the 'puzzle of sustaining the global commons' (Gupta 2019) rather than highlighting its tragic end.

GLOBAL EFFORTS TO TACKLE CLIMATE CHANGE

Our climate is a global common. Climate change impacts all people, everywhere, regardless of national borders. In contemporary international politics, changes in the world's climate have become increasingly pressing, pertinent and a matter of deep concern. Actors at every level of our international system, from international and regional organizations, to governments, businesses and civil society actors, to individuals themselves, are increasingly aware of the necessity for climate action. Climate change has become an increasingly dominant issue of 'high politics' (pg. 187) on international agendas. As the effects of global warming become more pronounced – with extremes of temperatures, extreme weather patterns and rising sea levels felt around the world – climate change has become increasingly securitized (pg. 187), particularly from an ontological insecurity perspective (pg. 188). In this section we address global efforts in climate action starting in the 1990s with the 1992 Rio Earth Summit.

The 1992 Rio Earth Summit, or the United Nations Conference on Environment and Development, was a major breakthrough international conference for several reasons. As we saw in Chapter Nine and Chapter Thirteen, Rio not only provided the 'breakthrough moment' for civil society to access international conferences (pg. 149), but the conference also brought the concept of sustainable development squarely into the international spotlight (pg. 232–3). At the Summit, delegates agreed that balancing economic, social and environmental interests was vital for sustaining human life on the planet. Sustainable development was considered an attainable goal for all people in the world, spanning local, national, regional and international levels (UN 1992b). Since the Rio Earth Summit, sustainable development has become widely mainstreamed on local, national, regional and international agendas spanning issues as broad as trade, finance, energy, development and security. The UN Sustainable Development Goals (pg. 233–4) have also been widely integrated and enacted around the world.

The Rio Earth Summit was also significant for launching three closely connected Conventions addressing international environmental protections: the Convention on Biological Diversity, aimed at conserving and sustaining biological diversity, the UN Convention to Combat Desertification, aimed at protecting and restoring land for sustainable future use, and the UN Framework Convention on Climate Change (UNFCCC), intended to 'stabilize greenhouse gas concentrations in the atmosphere at a level that would prevent dangerous anthropogenic interference with the climate system' (UN 1994). At the international level, the UNFCCC, which formally launched in 1994 and now has 198 Parties, serves as the foremost multilateral decision-making body for global climate action with states and observers meeting annually at a Conference of the Parties (COP) to negotiate multilateral responses to climate change.

According to the original Convention text, Parties to the UNFCCC recognized 'that human activities have been substantially increasing the atmospheric concentrations of greenhouse gases, that these increases enhance the natural greenhouse effect, and this will result on average in an additional warming of the earth's surface and atmosphere and may adversely affect natural ecosystems and humankind' (UN 1994). The Convention acknowledges that states have a 'sovereign right to exploit their own resources pursuant to their environmental and development policies', but that they also have 'responsibility to ensure that activities within their jurisdiction or control do not cause damage to the environment of other States or of areas beyond the limits of national jurisdiction' (UN 1994). As part of their national responsibilities, the UNFCCC requires all Parties to develop, update and publish national inventories of the sources and removals of greenhouse gases within their territories, while obligating them to also formulate, implement, publish and regularly update national and regional measures intended to **mitigate** climate change (UN 1994). Parties to the Convention are, moreover, expected to cooperate in preparing for **climate adaptation**, including by supporting areas most affected by drought, desertification and floods (UN 1994).

Climate mitigation Referring to efforts to tackle the causes of climate change by reducing the sources of greenhouse gas emissions and/or increasing the supply of carbon sinks (also known as stores) that absorb greenhouse gases.

Climate adaptation Referring to efforts to respond to the existing effects of climate change, particularly as it relates to rising sea levels and extremes of weather and temperatures.

Another important element of the UNFCCC is that it explicitly highlights the 'common and differentiated responsibilities' (UN 1994) of Parties to the Convention. Developed country Parties to the Convention are not only expected to 'take the lead in combatting climate change and the adverse effects thereof' but are expected to 'bear a disproportionate or abnormal burden under the Convention' based on 'equity and respective capabilities'; recognizing also that developing countries are more vulnerable to the effects of climate change (UN 1994). Parties to the UNFCCC are subsequently categorized by their economic development status (see also pg. 239). *Annex I* countries include the advanced industrialized countries, while *Non-Annex I* countries include all developing countries. This categorization has been significant in shaping international climate agreements since the first UNFCCC Conference of the Parties (COP) in the late 1990s.

ORGANIZE

According to the UN Conference on Environment and Development (UN 1992b), the involvement of local, national, regional and international levels was considered necessary in tackling climate change and achieving sustainable development if we are to sustain life on our planet.

Reflect again on the levels of analysis approach in Chapter Five. What actors are necessary to enact change in addressing climate change at the *individual*, *state* and *international* levels?

From Kyoto to Paris

The first major international climate agreement to be negotiated under the UNFCCC was the *Kyoto Protocol*, agreed at the UNFCCC COP in Kyoto, Japan in 1997. Under the Kyoto Protocol, all *Annex I* countries were required to make 'meaningful' reductions of CO_2 emissions, using a target baseline of 1990, by no later than 2012. The Kyoto Protocol was significant as the first international agreement to ever commit industrialized countries to meet binding targets of around an average 5 per cent reduction in greenhouse gas emissions. Individual countries were nevertheless able to agree individual limits, to adopt climate mitigation policies, and to report regularly on their national implementation. The Kyoto Protocol was limited in its effectiveness, however. Not only was the reduction rate of greenhouse gas emissions low, being the most that all UNFCCC Parties could agree to, but not all UNFCCC Parties then signed or ratified the agreement.

Due to various challenges in its ratification, the Kyoto Protocol did not enter into force until 2005. Crucially, the United States, one of the world's largest emitters of greenhouse gases, did not ratify the agreement and was therefore not bound to limit its emissions in line with the other *Annex I* countries. *Non-Annex I* countries – which also includes large emerging economies such as India and China who make a significant contribution to global greenhouse gases – were also not obliged to make emissions reductions in the Kyoto Protocol. More than this, even though legally bound to limit their greenhouse gas emissions by the targets agreed, very few *Annex I* countries in fact met their national targets by 2012. The result was that the Kyoto Protocol had no obvious impact on rising CO_2 emissions (*The Guardian* 2012).

Over the course of the 2000s and early 2010s, parties to the UNFCCC re-energized efforts to negotiate a successor agreement to the Kyoto Protocol. In 2015 the UNFCCC Conference of the Parties met in Paris where the *Paris Agreement* was negotiated and agreed. In contrast to the Kyoto Protocol which required that only the developed countries reduce emissions, the Paris Agreement highlights that all Parties to the Agreement must seek to reduce their emissions. Specifically, the Paris Agreement requires that all Parties to the Agreement submit an updated national climate action plan – known as Nationally Determined Contributions or NDCs – every five years. Paris also committed *Annex I* states to provide developing countries **climate finance** to adapt to climate change and enhance their capability to adapt to climate impacts.

Climate finance
Finance that supports climate mitigation and adaptation policies and measures.

A core objective of the Paris Agreement was that states would each work towards set national targets with the goal of keeping global temperatures 'well below' 2°C (3.6°F) above pre-industrial times and to 'endeavour to limit' them even more, to 1.5°C. Paris further set out to commit countries to reach a peak in greenhouse emissions 'as soon as possible', and to strike a balance between output of man-made greenhouse gases and absorption – by forests or the oceans – 'by the second half of this century' (UNFCCC 2015).

Explore More

According to the Intergovernmental Panel on Climate Change, human activities are estimated to have caused 1°C of global warming above pre-industrial times and will likely reach 1.5°C between 2030 and 2052 if temperatures continue to rise at their present rate. Find out more about the importance of limiting global temperature rises by looking at the IPCC's latest Assessment Report. Available online: www.ipcc.ch. You may also be interested in checking out the *Climate Clock*, available online at https://climateclock.world. Like the Doomsday Clock, the Climate Clock highlights the urgency for global climate action if humankind is to prevent the worst effects of climate change from becoming irreversible.

Scan the QR code for access to explore weblinks and more resources.

Limits to global climate action

While the Paris Agreement went much further than the Kyoto Protocol in setting out a clear, and increasingly ambitious, plan for global climate action, it too has its limitations. According to the UN Environment Programme (UNEP 2022), there remains a stark gap between the emissions reductions promised by Parties to the Paris Agreement, and the reductions actually needed to limit global warming to 2°C, let alone 1.5°C. This **emissions gap** means that, if no additional action is taken, the result will be global warming of 2.8°C over the 21st century (UNEP 2022). As the UNEP (2022: xvi) states, 'incremental change is no longer an option: broad-based economy-wide transformations are required to avoid closing the window of opportunity to limit global warming to well below 2°C, preferably 1.5°C'. The UNEP goes further in highlighting that, in order to meet the goal of limiting global warming to 2°C, countries would need to *triple* the level of their commitments made under the Paris Agreement and *quintuple* their commitments to limit global warming to 1.5°C (UNEP 2018).

Emissions gap
Defined by the UN Environment Programme as the difference between the estimated total global greenhouse gas emissions resulting from the implementation of Nationally Determined Contributions, and the total global greenhouse gas emissions that limit global warming.

Net zero
The goal of fully negating the amount of greenhouse gas emissions produced by human activity through reduction targets, energy efficiency measures and the creation of carbon sinks.

There therefore remains a clear gulf between what states have pledged to do, and what scientists believe needs to be done to tackle rising global temperatures and the impacts of climate change. While many states have now committed to adopt **net zero** pledges, translating pledges into real action is challenging. Even though 'only a fraction of proven fossil fuel reserves can be burned if we are to keep [the] temperature rise to 1.5°C' (UN 2023b), fossil fuels remain the cheapest option for many consumers, fossil fuels remain in high demand by states around the world, and fossil fuel emissions continue to soar. The Paris Agreement markedly offered no direct mention to the use of fossil fuels. Civil society activists further highlight the prominent presence of the fossil fuel industry both at climate negotiations and through direct lobbying of government ministers (*The Guardian* 2021a; 2017, see also pg. 158).

In seeking to further advance global climate action, however, at the UNFCCC COP26 in Glasgow in 2021, Parties to the Convention agreed to the *Glasgow Climate Pact*. The Glasgow Climate Pact is the first international agreement that explicitly targeted fossil fuels as a key driver of global warming. Specifically, the Pact:

> *Calls upon* Parties to accelerate the development, deployment and dissemination of technologies, and the adoption of policies, to transition towards low-emission energy systems, including by rapidly scaling up the deployment of clean power generation and energy efficiency measures, including accelerating efforts towards the phasedown of unabated coal power and phase-out of inefficient fossil fuel subsidies, while providing targeted support to the poorest and most vulnerable in line with national circumstances and recognizing the need for support towards a just transition. (UNFCCC 2021: pt.36)

While the Glasgow Climate Pact was significant in providing a broad mandate for states to start to cut the use of coal power, it was also significant for the political tensions that ensued over the language used. Note the mention to 'the *phasedown* of unabated coal power'. This framing was in fact a watered-down version of earlier draft language which had stipulated the '*phaseout* of unabated coal production'. The change in language followed a last-minute intervention by India and China who objected to there being explicit mention to a 'phaseout' of coal. According to India's environment and climate minister, the revision reflected the 'national circumstances of emerging economies' (*The Guardian* 2021b) and their national interests to continue to utilize coal power in their energy mix for development purposes. Glasgow thus noticeably highlighted the ongoing tensions in climate politics between states' 'sovereign right to exploit their own resources pursuant to their environmental and development policies' and their 'responsibility to ensure that activities within their jurisdiction or control do not cause damage to the environment of other States or of areas beyond the limits of national jurisdiction' (UN 1994) – a point we shall return to in the toolkit exercise at the end of this chapter.

UNDERSTANDING RESOURCE SCARCITY

Resource scarcity
Where, whether due to geological availability, range of reserves or price, the supply of natural resources is unable to meet demand.

When industrialization first began, the earth's natural resources were thought to be in infinite supply. Today, just as we have become keenly aware of climate change, so too are we keenly aware that the earth's natural resources are finite. Another pressing political challenge associated with energy and environmental politics in contemporary international politics therefore concerns **resource scarcity.** According to the WTO (2011: 46), natural resources are 'stocks of materials that exist in the natural environment that are both scarce and economically useful in production or consumption' and include both renewable and non-renewable sources. Resource *scarcity* is distinct from resource *rarity.* While some natural resources are rare, natural resources are considered *scarce* principally where demand for the resource outweighs supply.

As we have already seen, states have national jurisdiction over the natural resources in their territories. Important to reflect upon, however, is that the earth's natural resources are not evenly distributed, nor do states have equal access to resources. The United Arab Emirates (UAE), for example, is estimated to hold the seventh largest proven oil and gas reserves globally, yet has little to no coal, lead, zinc, gold, limestone, salt, arable land, etc. With most of the UAE's oil and gas companies state-owned, 30 per cent of the country's GDP (pg. 205) is directly based on its oil and gas output. The UAE subsequently had a GDP of just over $358 billion in 2020.

By way of comparison, the Democratic Republic of Congo (DRC) has far more natural resources than the UAE, including cobalt, copper, niobium, tantalum, oil, diamonds, gold, silver, zinc, manganese, tin, uranium, coal, hydropower and timber resources. Yet, much of the DRC's gold, cobalt and copper reserves remain untapped due to a lack of infrastructure. More than this, while the DRC was the largest producer of cobalt in 2020, many of the mining enterprises in the DRC are foreign-owned (pg. 54). In 2020 the DRC's GDP was just over $48 billion.

The inequality of distribution and access to natural resources is further challenged by the fact that many of the world's most sought-after primary commodities are also found in states that are more likely to be politically fragile (UNEP 2009: 11), undemocratic (Ross 2001) or 'failed' (Chauvet and Collier 2008). Such states are believed to suffer from what Auty (1993) described as the 'resource curse' where resource-rich countries were found to have less economic growth and responded poorly to economic development efforts compared to states who had fewer resources. Critical perspectives have challenged these claims, however, highlighting the considerable variation among resource-rich states (Porter and Watts 2017) that makes the resource curse thesis ungeneralizable. Others have challenged the very concept of the resource curse, especially as it is believed to relate to 'undemocratic' and 'failing' states (Schwarz and de Corral 2013, pg. 100–2). Marxist theoretical perspectives further highlight the imbalances and inequalities associated with natural resources as commodities. From a Marxist perspective the international economy is stratified into dependencies where countries that are resource-rich – many of which were former colonies for the very reason of their resources – remain locked into the role of resource supplier and exploited for the advancement of capitalist states today (Van de Graaf 2013: 15). Postcolonial perspectives emphasize less the resource curse and more the systemic failures of neoliberal economic development policies, particularly through structural adjustment programmes (pg. 226), to reform resource-rich countries (Porter and Watts 2017).

Where it concerns conflict specifically, natural resources are found to prolong civil unrest, generate revenue for violent non-state actors (pg. 153–5) and generally undermine peacekeeping efforts (pg. 176–7) (UNEP 2009). According to the UN Environment Programme Expert Advisory Group on Environment, Conflict and Peacebuilding, 'as the global population continues to rise, and the demand for resources continues to grow, there is significant potential for conflicts over natural resources to intensify in the coming decades' (UNEP 2009). Conflict is not only to be expected over resources such as minerals or oil, but over clean water and water systems. According to the Pacific Institute's Water Conflict Chronology, between the years 2000 and 2009 a total of eighty local conflict situations occurred around the world where dispute over the control of water or water systems was a trigger or root cause of the conflict. Between 2010 and 2019 that figure had increased to 294. Between 2020 and 2022 the figure was already at 140 conflict situations triggered by disputes over access to water resources (Pacific Institute 2022).

Water conflict has also generated significant focus on international agendas. One example of this is the Grand Ethiopian Renaissance Dam project which began construction in 2011 and started generating electricity in 2022. According to Ethiopian Prime Minister Abiy Ahmed, the mega-dam serves 'Ethiopia's main interest ... to bring light to 60 per cent of the population who is suffering in darkness, to save the labour of our mothers who are carrying wood on their backs in order to get energy' (Al Jazeera 2022a). But the dam project has caused dispute between Ethiopia and its neighbours Sudan and Egypt who fear they will suffer from severe water shortages. Egypt especially is dependent on the Nile for irrigation and drinking water. Despite efforts by the African Union (pg. 133) to mediate the dispute since 2011, with emphasis on finding agreement for how Ethiopia will fill and operate the dam, at the time of writing no agreement has been reached. The mega-dam thus serves to highlight the marked competition and potential for conflict over natural resources, especially where national energy interests are at stake.

CONCLUSION

The earth's natural resources are a lifeblood for our societies, yet their protection, management and sustainability represent critical and challenging issues in international politics. Our climate serves to sustain life on this planet, yet global warming and climate change has become an increasingly pressing issue on international agendas and a cause of deep concern for people everywhere. For scholars of international politics, one of the major tensions we must, in turn, identify when researching energy and the environment concerns is the capacity for global actors to work together to manage and sustain the global commons. While the collective global interest is to preserve and protect the earth's resources for the benefit of all, individual, business and national interests will seek to utilize those resources for their own economic gain. As this chapter has further highlighted,

Greenwashing
The process of using misleading information or disinformation to convey and market a false public image of being environmentally friendly and responsible.

competition and the potential for conflict are expected where resources are scarce and demand outstrips supply. Energy is especially found to present a keen national interest and security concern for states, a driver for potential international conflict, and a blocking issue where it concerns ambitious and effective global climate action. You can explore these elements of international politics further in the following toolkit exercise, which asks *'What are the main obstacles to achieving global net zero by 2050?'*

LINK

Image 14.2 The Grand Ethiopian Renaissance Dam is Africa's largest hydropower dam. Built by the Ethiopian government, the mega-dam project has been the source of more than a decade-long dispute between Ethiopia, Egypt and Sudan.
Source: Anadolu Agency/Getty Images.

Consider

Hydropower is a green energy source that uses the flow of water to produce electricity. Ethiopia is the second most populated country in Africa, yet at the turn of the 2020s two-thirds of its people were not connected to the electricity grid. Hydroelectricity therefore provides an important means by which Ethiopia can develop and become a green economy.

Explore

Find out more about the background and politics of the mega-dam project by scanning the barcode for links to relevant news and analysis.

Connect

In the dam dispute, Ethiopia accused Egypt of trying 'to maintain a colonial-era grip over the Nile's waters by imposing rules over the dam's filling and operation' (Al Jazeera 2022b). This is in reference to the 'Scramble for Africa' (pg. 20) when the British Empire sought to control the source of the Nile. In 1902 the British Empire and Ethiopia agreed a Treaty in which Ethiopia agreed not to block the flow of the Nile. In 1929 the British Empire and Egypt also agreed a Treaty which prevented Britain's East African colonies (including Sudan) from using the Nile's waters without Egypt's consent (Tekuya 2020).

Predict

What are the prospects of achieving an international agreement over the Nile's waters now that the Grand Ethiopian Renaissance Dam is operational?

TOOLKIT

What are the main obstacles to achieving global net zero by 2050?

THINK

- To keep global warming to no more than 1.5°C the Paris Agreement called for greenhouse gas emissions to be reduced by 45 per cent by 2030 and to reach net zero (pg. 253) by 2050. Net zero means cutting greenhouse gas emissions to as close to zero as possible, with remaining emissions then absorbed by the oceans and forestry. Global net zero will require all, but especially the largest emitters, to make drastic cuts in their emissions and soon. How likely do you think it is that states and businesses will act to achieve this target? What obstacles can you envisage that might prevent or delay action?

OBSERVE

Image 14.3 China is the world's largest contributor of carbon emissions, consuming more than half of the world's coal. The Chinese government has pledged to peak its CO_2 emissions by 2030 before reaching carbon neutrality by 2060. As part of these efforts, in 2021 the Junliangcheng power plant in Tianjin (pictured) was converted from a traditional coal power station to a natural gas-fired plant with the goal of helping 'push the country toward zero carbon' (GE Gas Power n.d.).

Source: Wikimedia Commons.

- At the 2021 Glasgow Climate Summit, tensions were high over the language concerning the 'phasedown' of coal power in the Glasgow Climate Pact (pg. 253).
- Over 70 countries have pledged to reach net zero by 2050 covering around 76 per cent of global greenhouse gas emissions. China has pledged to reach carbon neutrality by 2060, and India by 2070. Yet despite the Glasgow Climate Summit calling on all countries to revisit and strengthen their 2030 commitments by the end of 2022, only twenty-four countries responded with new or updated plans. Projections suggest that there will be an *increase* in greenhouse gas emissions by 2030 (UN 2023c).
- According to the 2022 Net Zero Global Stocktake Report, there was a surge in national net zero targets being set in domestic legislation, increasing from 10 per cent of total GHG coverage at the end of 2020, to 65 per cent in June 2022. More than one-third of the world's largest publicly traded companies now also have net zero targets. However, the report highlights that one-fifth of net zero targets set by national and sub-national governments, and 65 per cent of targets set by companies, do not yet meet minimum procedural standards of robustness. As the report reflects, 'while the rapid uptake of net zero targets is encouraging, we need much more clarity from actors on how they plan to get there' (Oxford Net Zero 2022).

ORGANIZE

- Reflect again on the tragedy of the commons and Gupta's critique of the tragedy of the commons, particularly as it relates to colonial and postcolonial legacies and to inequalities within the international economy (pg. 247–50).
- Realist theoretical approaches emphasize that any international agreement on climate action can only succeed if states believe they themselves will benefit from it. For net zero to be reached, the most powerful states particularly must see that their national interests are met by it. This was arguably evidenced by the United States when it withdrew from the Kyoto Protocol in the early 2000s, and again from the Paris Agreement in 2016 (pg. 252). Is it in China's interests to phase out coal and push for an earlier net zero target? What interests matter most from a realist perspective?
- Reflect again on the discussion of Marxist approaches in IPE (pg. 208). From one Marxist perspective, while the goal of achieving net zero 'reflects a consensus held by the majority of the world's business and political elite', the problem is their 'inability to actually act on the consensus' (Sweeney 2016). Net zero targets are increasingly being implemented both by governments and companies, but are targets enough? According to Oxford Net Zero (2022), 'failure to improve commitment to targets with better governance and transparency might leave companies and governments open to **greenwashing** allegations'.
- Liberal theoretical approaches would highlight that international climate agreements can deliver collective action where states see there are absolute gains to be achieved. International organizations, not least the UN and the UNFCCC, are then 'essential agents of international cooperation that provide an important check on the unilateral exercise of power by one state over another, as well as helping both public and private actors to solve collective action problems' (Broome 2014: 23).

LINK

- *Consider*: India and China may constitute the world's first and third largest emitters of CO_2 in the 2020s, but under the terms of the UNFCCC and its principle of 'common but differentiated responsibility', both China and India are categorized as *non-Annex I* countries (pg. 251).
- *Explore*: The Net Zero Tracker at https://zerotracker.net. You can also access more news and analysis of international efforts to move towards net zero, along with data on the annual CO_2 emissions produced per country by year by scanning the barcode for more links and resources.
- *Connect*: Reflect on the relationship between economic development (pg. 225), industrialization (pg. 226) and greenhouse gas emissions. The world's top seven emitters – China, the US, India, the EU, Indonesia, Russia and Brazil – accounted for about half of global greenhouse gas emissions in 2020. The G20 (pg. 78) are responsible for about 75 per cent of global emissions (UNEP 2022).
- *Predict*: What would need to happen for governments and companies to not only adopt, but implement, net zero targets by 2050?

SHARE

- Answer the question, *'What are the main obstacles to achieving global net zero by 2050?'*

  When addressing this question, think about the *problem-audience-solution* approach used when crafting a policy brief – see *How to – prepare a policy brief* (pg. 242). If you were writing this up as a policy brief, what is the primary problem you would seek to identify to your reader? What solution might you then recommend?

HOW TO

PREPARE AN ACADEMIC POSTER

Academic posters are a great way to share your research. In sharp contrast to an essay where you must present several pages worth of detailed text and analysis, an academic poster is just one page of information designed to capture the attention of passers-by, while communicating a clear message, quickly and accessibly. Not dissimilar to an abstract for an article or chapter, an academic poster requires you to determine the key takeaways from the materials you have researched and the information you have gleaned. Key takeaways may include, for example, your main argument or point, specific controversies or competing perspectives, data or other evidence, as well as points for future research.

A further benefit of academic posters is that they follow no fixed structure but enable you to inject your own creativity into the process. Posters should, above all, be visually appealing. When designing your academic poster, you should therefore aim to use a mixture of graphics and text, combining charts, figures, graphs, infographics or photos with short bursts of text that will help guide and inform your viewer of your key takeaways. Be sure that your text is easily readable, in an accessible font and size. You may have a word count to follow or not, but as a rule err towards brevity with your texts. Imagine you are crafting the executive summary with the key highlights from your policy brief (pg. 242). Then weave your choice phrases or short sentences into an illustrated summary. The rest of the poster's design will be easier if you build around your text as well. You may want to use different font sizes to highlight levels of importance for the information being presented. Headers in larger font size should direct to the key information that your audience can take away even if they don't read smaller text included on the poster.

Be mindful also of your colour scheme. Simple can often be best, combining a couple of complementary colours or sticking to one colour and using different shades. You should avoid making the poster too 'busy' with colours that shout at rather than complement each other. When you come to select images, or other graphics, be mindful also that images are subject to copyright laws, so you need to be careful of how you use and cite materials. It is recommended that you use images that have a Creative Commons licence which grants copyright with various conditions. You can access Creative Commons image banks at websites such as https://pixabay.com, https://unsplash.com, or www.pexels.com for example.

15 Rights and responsibility

Unsplash / Pyae Sone Htun

Abstract

This chapter introduces you to rights and responsibility as two distinct, yet intertwined, issues within contemporary international politics. The chapter engages first with the distinctions between collective and individual rights. Focus is then paid to the emergence of an international human rights framework within international politics, how human rights became codified in international law and upheld by international organizations and courts, and addressing some of the contentions that have surrounded the perceived universality of human rights within international politics. Our discussion then turns to consider the debate around human rights norms and the inviolability of state sovereignty, focusing on the concept of humanitarian intervention and the 'Responsibility to Protect'. The chapter concludes with a toolkit exercise asking, '*Why was there no humanitarian intervention during the 2017 Rohingya crisis?*'

UNDERSTANDING RIGHTS AND RESPONSIBILITIES IN INTERNATIONAL POLITICS

As we touched upon in the last chapter, responsibility is a pervasive theme in global climate politics. Responsibility has been discussed as a *historic* responsibility, referencing the legacy of industrialization among the developed countries as largely bearing the responsibility (that is, culpability) for climate change today (pg. 251), as an *environmental* responsibility referencing the perceived imperative for all states to address climate change to save future generations, as a *corporate* and *individual* responsibility referencing the specific obligations of businesses, enterprises and individuals themselves towards climate action, and as a *moral* responsibility, referencing the necessity to do the right thing for the good of life on this planet. As we also observed, the UN Framework Convention on Climate Change (UNFCCC) enshrines the principle of 'common and differentiated responsibilities' (UNFCCC 1994). For example, at the 2022 UNFCCC Conference of the Parties, China submitted a paper in which it stated that, 'the developed countries failed to fulfil their promised responsibilities and obligations' (UNFCCC 2022b). As this quote highlights, *differential* responsibility is a pervasive theme in climate politics, associated with developed, or *Annex I*, countries taking the lead, acting first and providing greater resources in the form of finance or aid (Bernstein 2020: 12), while developing countries hold them accountable.

Responsibility is not unique to climate politics, however. In fact, responsibility has become 'a central part' (Hoover 2012: 235) of international politics, with 'the shift to hold individuals and regimes accountable to universal obligations' signifying 'a remarkable change' (Hoover 2012: 233) in our contemporary international system. According to Clark and Reus-Smit (2013: 241) responsibility 'necessarily involves accountability: that is, the right of others to call us to task for performance or non-performance'. Responsibility draws our focus to the conduct of actors within international politics, the appropriateness, or the standards by which they act (pg. 62), as well as assigning duty, and blame, for actions taken or not taken.

As we saw in Chapter Five, responsibility in international politics is often observed as the purview of the great powers (pg. 76). According to Bull (1980: 437 *emphasis added*), a great power is not only 'a member of the club of powers that are in the front rank in terms of military strength, but also that it regards itself, and is regarded by other members of the society of states, as having *special rights and duties*'. Neorealist and neoliberal perspectives emphasize that it is rational self-interest and power that shape the responsibility that great powers are themselves willing to take on and which they subsequently exercise over others. Great powers take on responsibility for international order and security because it consolidates, legitimizes or sustains their hegemonic position within the international system. As great powers they in turn exercise control over that system. Yet the scholarship addressing the special responsibilities of great powers within international politics also frequently emphasizes great power *ir*responsibility and the shirking of great power obligations (Bernstein 2020; Bull 1980).

Typically absent from these more system-level (pg. 75–7), positivist (pg. 38–41), theoretical perspectives, is reference to responsibility as 'being answerable for a particular act or outcome in accordance with what are understood to be *moral imperatives*' (Erskine 2008: 700 *emphasis added*). It took the emergence of social and critical theoretical perspectives in international politics to really shift this point of focus, and today there is a burgeoning scholarship surrounding morality, ethics and the social construction of responsibility within international politics, not least as it concerns **rights**.

Rights
A moral or legal entitlement that someone or something can claim to have or do.

Rights are moral, social, ethical or legal principles that an actor is entitled to, and which can be claimed and exercised when threatened. The active promotion of rights as a matter of international concern has grown exponentially since the end of World War Two. Respect for human rights has itself become a 'universal obligation' and 'moral imperative' within contemporary international politics. Upholding and protecting human rights has become an integral part of the practice of international politics, with human rights now increasingly part of the discourse of non-state actors, states and international and regional organizations. Yet as we shall see in the following sections, human rights can also court controversy as well as contestation within international politics, not least where it concerns the question of who bears responsibility for upholding them.

In the following sections, focus then is given to rights and responsibility as distinct yet interrelated issues within international politics. First, we distinguish individual and collective rights within international politics as they relate to the right – and duty-bearer. From there attention is given to the emergence of human rights as a matter of international politics and law, and the international organizations established to monitor them. Focus is then given to some of the critical theoretical perspectives that have shaped discussion over the universality of human rights. Finally, the chapter turns to the intersection between responsibility and rights, shining a spotlight on the specific issue of humanitarian intervention and the 'Responsibility to Protect', a principle which has brought traditional conceptions of sovereignty and the right to non-interference directly into question. The chapter concludes with a toolkit exercise asking, *'Why was there no humanitarian intervention during the 2017 Rohingya crisis?'*

DISTINGUISHING RIGHTS AND DUTY

When approaching the related issues of rights and responsibilities in international politics it is first helpful to distinguish between different types of rights, as well as between those who possess rights (right-bearer), relative to those who have a duty to uphold rights (duty-bearer).

Collective rights are those rights held by a group, such as the state, nation, tribe or ethnic group. When we consider collective rights in international politics, we may particularly consider the equal rights attributed to independent sovereign states. As we saw in Chapter Two, *internal sovereignty* assumes that a state has authority over the law and order of a clearly defined people and territory (pg. 18). *External sovereignty* meanwhile assumes that all states are independent, free from the interference of other authorities or powers (pg. 18). Over time these sovereign principles have become established in international norms, conventions and laws. For example, all independent sovereign states possess certain diplomatic rights as enshrined by the 1961 **Vienna Convention on Diplomatic Relations**.

Vienna Convention on Diplomatic Relations An international treaty that codifies the practices and principles of diplomatic relations between states. The Convention, which was signed in 1961 and formally entered into force in 1964, today has 193 States Parties, which include the majority of UN member states (with the exception of South Sudan and Palau) and with the addition of the State of Palestine and Holy See.

The UN Charter (1945) also stipulates the principles of 'equal rights and self-determination of peoples'. In 1952 the UN General Assembly further enshrined 'the right of self-determination of all peoples and nations' (UNGA 1952). As we shall see later in this chapter, the state's right to non-interference is also widely discussed within international political discourses.

Individual rights, by contrast, are rights possessed by an individual regardless of their citizenry. Since the late 20th century, international politics has been transformed by the rise of human rights as an issue, discourse and political-legal practice. Human rights are those rights that every human being possesses courtesy of the fact that they are human. Human rights empower individuals because they are an entitlement that every person has, and which every individual can therefore claim when that right is threatened (Donnelly 2013: 9).

When we consider rights, we must also recognize that there is a distinction between a right-bearer and duty-bearer (Donnelly 2013: 8). You are a right-bearer. You possess basic human rights because of the simple fact that you are human. Rights such as the right to life, security and freedom are therefore your rights regardless of your citizenship. As a citizen of a country, you also possess certain collective rights, as well as protections for rights that your national government will have signed and ratified. For example, if you are a woman living in any one of the 189 states that have signed and ratified the Convention on the Elimination of Discrimination against Women (see next section), then your right to vote, your right to non-discrimination in education and employment, your right to shared responsibility for child-rearing by both sexes, to name but a few rights you are afforded, are enshrined in international law.

Recognizing, respecting and protecting those rights is then the duty of a diverse array of actors at the local, national, regional and international levels within our international system. For example, your education provider or employer bears the duty of responsibility to respect and uphold your rights. Your national government is also a primary duty-bearer, bearing ultimate responsibility to protect your rights. As we shall see in the next sections, however, much of the debate surrounding rights and responsibilities in international politics have developed from contestation in the construction and interpretation of individual and collective rights, as well as what then happens when states, as duty-bearers, fail to protect the human rights of their people.

HUMAN RIGHTS IN INTERNATIONAL POLITICS

It has become a pervasive Western narrative that **human rights** stemmed from the American and French revolutions of the 1780s (pg. 20). The argument follows that the French and American revolutions led to a political-legal construct that guaranteed individual rights both in principle and in law, which rulers were compelled to respect. National courts, independent of government and political parties, further upheld the personal rights of the individual. The very emergence of the democratic state was formed on these principles, where personal rights matter and public authorities respect the personal autonomy and preferences of the individual (Forsythe 2018). These same principles are considered to have shaped the post-war liberal international order (pg. 38) including the formation of the United Nations (pg. 114–8).

Human rights
Fundamental rights inherent to every human being regardless of their nationality, age, sex, religion or other beliefs.

In fact, human rights narratives can be traced across a vast array of religions, cultures and territories dating back centuries (Mende 2021). Consider, for example, that the Haitian revolution in 1792 signified one of the first major pushes for political participation for persons of colour, and for the abolition of slavery. We can also identify the importance of fundamental values of freedom, liberty and tolerance in Buddhism, Confucianism, Mandarin and Braham traditions, for example (Mende 2021).

The internationalization of human rights, however, can broadly be attributed to the emergence of international organizations and the push towards collective international action in the post-World War Two era. Notably, in the preamble to the UN Charter, all members of the UN determined 'to reaffirm faith in fundamental human rights, in the dignity and worth of the human person, in the equal rights of men and women and of nations large and small' (UN 1945). At the first UN General Assembly Session in 1946, UN members further agreed to complement the UN Charter with a document intended to guarantee human rights for all peoples. On 10 December 1948, the Universal Declaration of Human Rights was approved.

International Covenant on Civil and Political Rights
An international treaty enshrining the universal civil and political rights of individuals everywhere, such as equality before the law, the right to a fair trial, freedom of thought, etc. The Covenant also includes two optional protocols adopted in 1976 and 1989.

International human rights law

The Universal Declaration of Human Rights (UDHR) became the foundation for what is now a rich body of international human rights law laying out the obligations of governments to act in certain ways or to refrain from certain acts, in order to promote and protect human rights and fundamental freedoms of individuals or groups. In 1966 the UDHR was reinforced by the adoption of the **International Covenant on Civil and Political Rights** and the **International Covenant on Economic, Social and Cultural Rights** (Table 15.1) The International Covenants advanced many of the rights already enshrined in the UDHR but made them binding on the states that ratified them. The Covenants identify the responsibilities placed on states to respect, protect and fulfil those rights. Together with the UDHR, these International Covenants and their optional protocols, make up what is commonly referred to as the *International Bill of Human Rights.*

International Covenant on Economic, Social and Cultural Rights
An international treaty which ensures the enjoyment of economic, social and cultural rights, including the rights to education, fair and just conditions of work, an adequate standard of living, the highest attainable standard of health, and social security.

Table 15.1 Rights enshrined by the International Covenants

International Covenant on Civil and Political Rights	International Covenant on Economic, Social and Cultural Rights
• Freedom from discrimination • Right to equality between men and women • Right to life • Freedom from torture • Freedom from slavery • Right to liberty and security of person • Right to be treated with humanity in detention • Freedom of movement • Freedom of non-citizens from arbitrary expulsion • Right to fair trial • Right to recognition before the law • Right to privacy • Freedom of religion and belief • Freedom of expression • Right of peaceful assembly • Freedom of association • Right to marry and found a family • Right of children to birth registration and a nationality • Right to participate in public affairs • Right to equality before the law • Minority rights	• Freedom from discrimination • Right to equality between men and women • Right to work • Freedom to choose and accept work • Right to just and favourable conditions at work • Right to form trade unions • Right to strike • Right to social security • Right of mothers to special protection before and after birth • Freedom of children from social and economic exploitation • Right to an adequate standard of living • Freedom from hunger • Right to health • Right to education • Freedom of parents to choose schooling for their children • Right to take part in cultural life • Right to enjoy benefits of science • Right of authors to moral and material interests from works • Freedom to undertake scientific research and creative activity

Source: UN Office of the Human Rights Commissioner. Available online: www.ohchr.org/en/what-are-human-rights/international-bill-human-rights.

Explore More

The Universal Declaration of Human Rights set out for the first time the fundamental human rights to be universally protected, including the right to life, liberty and security of person. Take some time to explore the UDHR, reflecting upon the human rights it enshrines, at www.un.org. You can also explore the status of ratification for eighteen of the core international human rights treaties deposited with the UN, including those states that have ratified, signed but not ratified, or taken no action at https://indicators.ohchr.org.

Scan the QR code for access to explore weblinks and more resources.

The International Bill of Human Rights has been further supplemented over time by numerous international laws oriented towards specific human rights protections. These include, for example, the International Convention on the Elimination of All Forms of Racial Discrimination (1969), the Convention on the Elimination of Discrimination against Women (1979), the Convention against Torture and Other Cruel, Inhuman or Degrading Treatment (1987), the Convention on the Rights of the Child (2002), the Convention on the Protection of the Rights of All Migrant Workers and Members of Their Families (2003), the International Convention on the Rights of Persons with Disabilities (2008), and the International Convention for the Protection of Persons from Enforced Disappearance (2010).

In conjunction, the end of World War Two also saw important advances in the codification of international humanitarian law through the 1949 **Geneva Conventions** which updated the rules and personal protections afforded to all persons, including non-combatants, during conflicts. Following the 1949 Convention, **war crimes** also became identified in international law as acts that are in 'grave breach' of the Geneva Convention including, for example, wilful killing, torture, taking hostages, or unlawful deportation or unlawful confinement (UN 1998). The late 1940s also saw codification of the 1948 Convention on the Prevention and Punishment of the Crime of Genocide (the *Genocide Convention*) recognizing genocide (pg. 190) as a crime – a direct response to the Holocaust and the systematic murder of Jews during World War Two (pg. 23).

Geneva Conventions
A series of international treaties that built upon the 1864, 1906 and 1929 Geneva Conventions, along with the 1907 Hague Convention (pg. 109) but which went further in affording protection to civilians, including in occupied territories.

War crimes
Violations of the laws of war, as set out in the 1949 Geneva Conventions, which constitute a criminal act.

Responsibility for monitoring the various conventions that make up the corpus of international human rights and humanitarian laws are various international and regional organizations and courts, operating at different levels and with distinct purviews. For example, the Council of Europe (pg. 134) has its own European Convention on Human Rights overseen by the **European Court of Human Rights** which rules on both individual and state applications concerning allegations of violations of civil and political rights. At the international level the UN family comprises various bodies in overseeing international human rights and humanitarian law. The UN High Commissioner for Human Rights holds primary responsibility for all UN human rights activities and is mandated to respond to serious human rights violations. The High Commissioner is further supported by the Office of the High Commissioner for Human Rights (OHCHR) who also acts as Secretariat to the UN Human Rights Council. The UN Human Rights Council, established in 2006, is an intergovernmental body, comprising forty-seven state representatives who are tasked with strengthening and promoting human rights worldwide, and for making recommendations where human rights violations occur. The UN is also served by a Human Rights Committee and the Committee on Economic, Social and Cultural Rights who have responsibility for monitoring the International Covenants.

European Court of Human Rights
A court established in Strasbourg by the Council of Europe (pg. 134) in 1959 charged with supervising the enforcement of the European Convention on Human Rights.

The International Court of Justice (ICJ) (pg. 114–5) is the principal judicial organ of the UN and also has purview over any human rights issues brought to its attention by UN member states as it concerns international law. For example, in November 2019 the Republic of The Gambia filed an ICJ Application against Myanmar, concerning violations of the Genocide Convention by Myanmar's security forces perpetrated against the Rohingya Muslim population (see also toolkit exercise pg. 275). Myanmar's government challenged the allegations, raising several formal objections to the case brought by The Gambia. In July 2022, however, the ICJ ruled that the Application was admissible, enabling the case to move forward as legal proceedings before the Court (ICJ 2022).

The International Criminal Court (ICC) is another important actor in upholding international human rights law. In contrast to the International Court of Justice, which decides disputes between countries, the ICC is a criminal court that prosecutes individuals. Established by the **Rome Statute** in 1998, the ICC is considered the court of last resort for the prosecution of serious international crimes, including genocide and war crimes. According to Article 1 of the Rome Statute, the ICC has 'the power to exercise its jurisdiction over persons for the most serious crimes of international concern'. As the Court states, its

Rome Statute
The international treaty, adopted on 1 July 1998 in Rome, that serves as the foundation and governing document of the International Criminal Court.

aim is 'to hold those *responsible accountable* for their crimes and to help prevent these crimes happening again' (ICC n.d. emphasis added).

Since it began operation in 2002, the ICC has tried thirty-one cases and issued ten convictions and four acquittals. The ICC's cases are all brought against individuals – including some national leaders, including former and sitting presidents – accused of gross human rights violations against people in, for example, the Democratic Republic of Congo, the Central African Republic, Uganda, Sudan, Kenya, Libya and Côte d'Ivoire. In 2019 the ICC also instigated an investigation following accusations of genocide against the Rohingya population. In March 2023 the ICC also issued an arrest warrant for Russia's President Putin over war crime allegations regarding claims that Russian forces unlawfully deported children from Ukraine to Russia in 2022.

THINK

Image 15.1 ICC judges preside over the hearing of Thomas Lubanga for war crimes for enlisting and conscripting child soldiers during a conflict in the Democratic Republic of Congo from 2002 to 2003. In July 2012 Lubanga was tried and convicted.

Source: ED OUDENAARDEN/Getty Images.

The Rome Statute and the ICC enshrines a system of individual criminal responsibility, the significance being that individual persons are tried and punished for international crimes of concern rather than any collective authority i.e. governments or violent non-state actors. The International Court of Justice by contrast rules on legal disputes between states. States may therefore apply to the ICJ for ruling against another state, as observed in the case of The Gambia vs Myanmar.

Reflect again on the distinction between individual and collective rights, and the respective jurisdiction of the ICC and ICJ. What do you think are the merits of punishing international human rights crimes of concern by targeting individual perpetrators? What do you think the challenges might be of trying to punish human rights violations perpetrated by states themselves?

While the ICC is oriented towards the prosecution of individual persons for 'serious crimes of international concern', it is important to highlight that it too remains 'complementary to national criminal jurisdictions' (ICC 2011: Art 1). The ICC can only exercise its jurisdiction over individuals where they are a national of, or committed the crime in the national territory of, a state that has signed and ratified the Rome Statute (ICC 2011: Art 12). At the time of writing there were 123 States Parties to the Rome Statute. Worth highlighting in the case of human rights abuses against the Muslim Rohingya population, is that Myanmar is not a party to the Rome Statute and is not therefore subject to ICC jurisdiction. The ICC's own investigation of criminal acts against the Rohingya is therefore being conducted in relation to crimes committed against the Rohingya population with reference to the territory of neighbouring Bangladesh where most Rohingya fled to, and who has been party to the Rome Statute since 2010. Russia is also not a signatory of the Rome Statute, noticeably diminishing the chances that President Putin will be brought to trial by the ICC.

The ICC is also reliant upon states for enforcement. For example, when the ICC issues an arrest warrant, it is dependent upon the cooperation of national governments and law enforcement that individuals are then arrested and detained. The ICC cannot try an individual that is not present in court, nor do they imprison criminals once convicted. For example, the Congolese militia leader, Thomas Lubanga, the first man to be convicted of war crimes by the ICC, was surrendered by the Congolese authorities in March 2006. In July 2012 he was sentenced by the ICC to fourteen years' imprisonment and transferred back to a prison in the DRC to serve out the remainder of his sentence.

Are human rights universal?

Already we can observe that monitoring and enforcing international human rights law involves a careful balancing act between national and international responsibilities, particularly as it concerns the state as duty-bearer and international organizations and courts tasked with their oversight. Another challenge we can also observe when researching human rights in international politics concerns how such rights are themselves constructed and subsequently interpreted. From a constructivist perspective, we can see that 'rights still have to be identified – that is constructed – by human beings and codified in the legal system' (Forsythe 2018). Because rights are constructed and then codified, they are also subject to interpretation. Consider that while all member states of the UN recognize 'the equal and inalienable rights of all members of the human family' (UN 1948), this near-universal recognition 'neither confirms that such rights exist nor guarantees their effectiveness' (Reidy 2005: 8). The very universality enshrined by the Universal Declaration of Human Rights (UDHR) and the wider body of international human rights laws is particularly open to critique, as well as being an ongoing debate within international politics scholarship.

One particular point of contention concerning the universality of human rights is that the institutionalization of human rights in the post-war era is considered broadly cognizant with a narrow Western construction and interpretation of individual rights (Forsythe 2018; Bagchi and Das 2012). A dominant view is that Western liberal states created the UDHR and that newly decolonized states supported it largely to emphasize their own sovereignty (Mende 2021). An argument follows, however, that the universal human rights enshrined by the UDHR and broadly accepted in Western cultures are in contrast with the prioritization of collective rights favoured in many non-Western cultures (Bagchi and Das 2012: 8). Countries in the Global South particularly are argued to prioritize the wellbeing of the society as a whole rather than that of the individual (Bagchi and Das 2012: 8) and that prioritizing individual over collective rights, 'would lead to breakdown of social order and family structure and an erosion of traditional values in that society' (Bagchi and Das 2012: 8). Such arguments are further grounded in the importance of **cultural relativism** and the necessity of observing cultural difference and diversity in setting standards of obligation and moral imperative.

Cultural relativism
The claim that historical, cultural, religious or ethical practices differ among cultures. Claims of what constitutes right or wrong practices are therefore relative.

Others go further in arguing that the West's framing of universal human rights ignores cultural diversity and 'seeks to supplant all other traditions while rejecting them' (Mutua 2002; xi). Human rights are then observed as a 'Eurocentric construct for the reconstitution of non-Western societies and peoples' (Mutua 2002: 6). Some postcolonial scholars further highlight how the universality of human rights ignores the legacy of colonialism. Frick (2012), for example, argues that 'the claim whereupon the classical human rights values and norms are universal or even constitute a consensus of mankind, dashes against postcolonial realities that reject the West's hegemony in moral and political terms'. For others, the process of decolonization itself shifted the focus of debate away from violation of rights by colonizers, and on to a liberal vision of human rights (Bagchi and Das 2012).

Some critical scholars further signpost to human rights discourses such as the African (Banjul) Charter on Human and People's Rights (1981), the Cairo Declaration on Human Rights in Islam (1990), and the Bangkok Declaration prepared by a regional meeting of Asian states approaching the UN World Conference on Human Rights in 1993, to showcase distinctions between Western and Global South human rights perspectives. In the Bangkok Declaration, for example, Asian states recognized the 'principles of respect for national sovereignty, territorial integrity, and non-interference in the internal affairs of states' – highlighting the imperative of collective rights – while stressing 'that the promotion of human rights should be encouraged by cooperation and consensus and not through confrontation and the imposition of incompatible values' (UN 1993). The Bangkok Declaration also stated that 'while human rights are universal in nature, they must be considered in the context of a dynamic and evolving process of international norm-setting, *bearing in mind the significance of national and regional particularities and various historical, cultural and religious backgrounds*' (UN 1993 emphasis added) – highlighting the importance of cultural relativity.

On the other side of the debate, however, countries in the Global South have been highlighted for their commitment to human rights, their multilateral efforts in driving forward political and legal change, and for providing key voices in shaping the UN's global human rights framework, even before the Universal Declaration of Human Rights was agreed (Mende 2021). While in some narratives Western powers are broadly credited for driving forward the international human rights agenda, other accounts emphasize how nations from the Global South played a pivotal role. Egypt, for example, introduced a resolution to the UN in 1947 against racial and religious persecution, supported by South American, Asian and African states. Cuba, India and Panama, moreover, highlighted the issue of genocide (Mende 2021). Countries such as Jamaica, Liberia, Ghana, the Philippines and Costa Rica have also been identified for being proactive in shaping the UN's human rights frameworks, engaging NGOs and brokering human rights conventions, such as the International Convention on Elimination of all Forms of Racial Discrimination (Jensen 2016). These states maintained a strong level of commitment to universal human rights, even in the face of opposition from the West and the Soviet Union who were at that time invoking principles of non-intervention and state sovereignty (Mende 2021). As Jensen argues, 'the real story of the UN human rights system, seen from a 1960s and a Global South perspective, is one where progress was driven by developing countries and, in essence, that progress was then "left on the doorstep" of the 1970s to be taken up by the West'.

The construction, interpretation and enforcement of international human rights law has since become a pervasive – if oftentimes disputed – force in international politics. Since the end of the Cold War, human rights have become firmly integrated in nearly all intergovernmental issues within international politics. Consider, for example, that human rights principles are now integral to the UN Sustainable Development Goals (pg. 234). The UNFCCC also now includes human rights principles in its Paris Agreement (pg. 252). The conceptualization of human security in the 1990s (pg. 189) also showcased the importance of human rights and dignity in international security agendas, as well as the responsibility of states themselves to protect and defend human life.

OBSERVE

Image 15.2 Leaders at the Bandung Conference in 1955. The Conference is broadly accredited as a milestone in decolonization, being the first time the leaders of twenty-seven newly independent former colonial states from across Asia and Africa met, and the foundation of the Non-Aligned Movement (pg. 27) Among the principles agreed at the Bandung Conference was a declaration on the promotion of world peace and cooperation, including respect for fundamental human rights.

Source: Wikimedia Commons.

The debate over universal human rights and the Global South is also relevant when we consider the 1955 Bandung Conference (pg. 25). According to one historian, Bandung's 'anti-Western "mood"' meant that the 1948 Universal Declaration of Human Rights was characterized as 'an instrument of neocolonialism and in attacks on its universality in the name of cultural integrity, self-determination of peoples, or national sovereignty' (Glendon 2001: 215). Bandung has therefore been observed as signalling the start of a steady decline in support and respect for the human rights embodied in the UDHR (Glendon 2001: 216).

Others, however, challenge this perspective, arguing that Bandung constituted a 'highpoint' in Third World enthusiasm for human rights (Burke 2006: 962). Two of the architects behind the UDHR, Carlos Romulo of the Philippines and Charles Malik of Lebanon, were both delegates at the Bandung Conference. Human rights were an important part of the political dialogue at Bandung, especially concerning discussion on colonialism and freedom (Burke 2006: 950). Speaking after the conference, Malik is reported to have stated that 'to some of us ... freedom was much larger and much deeper than mere liberation from foreign rule. To us freedom meant freedom of mind, freedom of thought, freedom of press, freedom to criticize, to judge for yourself – freedom, in short, to be the full human being' (Malik 1955, cited in Burke 2006: 959).

HUMANITARIAN INTERVENTION

Human rights have not only been prevalent in international discourses but in practice. The end of the Cold War was thought to have heightened expectations of multilateral diplomacy and collective action in addressing international challenges, including collective action in the defence of common humanity (ICISS 2001: 1). Over the course of the 1990s, as the world observed what seemed like a rising tide of human rights atrocities around the world, coalitions of states, working multilaterally through the UN or NATO, undertook military interventions with the stated aims of preventing human rights violations in other states.

ORGANIZE

Different theoretical approaches in international politics offer competing explanations and critiques of why states undertake humanitarian interventions. Cheikh (2013), for example, draws upon Marxist approaches to neocolonialism to argue that humanitarian intervention is connected to 'new forms of colonialism' and that intervention is encouraged by 'realist interests'. According to Cheikh (2013: 154) the controversy surrounding humanitarian intervention 'is not alleged to stem from the imperative "to intervene or not to intervene", but rather from the question "what interests were intervening states possibly pursuing"?' Forsythe (2018) reinforces this argument suggesting that 'the international law of human rights is based on liberalism, but the practice of human rights all too often reflects a realist world'. Constructivist scholarship by contrast stresses the evolution of norms surrounding interventionism and the increasingly global acceptance of intervention on humanitarian grounds (Bellamy 2011; Vaughn and Dunne 2015).

Feminist and postcolonial scholarship, however, observe humanitarian intervention more as an act of colonial violence directing research and analysis to 'how the production of gendered, racialized, and sexualized identities have facilitated colonial violence' (Vernon 2022: 2). For postcolonial scholars particularly, Western interventions in non-Western societies are justified by a 'pathology of the savior mentality' (Mutua 2002: 6). Feminist scholars further critique how interventions are legitimized on the justification that they will protect 'women and children'. Enloe, for example, argues that in the minds of those intervening states, 'women are family members rather than independent actors, presumed to be almost childlike in their innocence about international *realpolitik*' (Enloe 1993: 166 see also Kolmasova and Krulisova 2018).

Reflect on the case of *Operation Restore Hope*. Do you think this was an example of US self-interest or moral imperative? Whom did the intervention protect? What and whose interests were advanced?

Image 15.3 A US Marine CH-53 Sea Stallion delivers food to the village of Maleel in Somalia. The US was the main pillar of the international peacekeeping effort, codenamed *Operation Restore Hope*.

Source: Wikimedia Commons.

Humanitarian intervention is defined as 'coercive – and particularly military – action against another state for the purpose of protecting people at risk in that one state' (ICISS 2001). Humanitarian intervention involves breaching a state's sovereign right to non-interference from foreign powers, on the grounds of protecting human life within that state. In the case of Somalia in late 1992, for example, nearly half a million Somalians had died because of famine, regional conflict and civil war. Hundreds of thousands more were at risk of starvation due to breaks in supply lines or humanitarian supplies being seized by local warlords. In response to the crisis, the international community intervened. *Operation Restore Hope* was a multinational operation led by the United States with support by the UN. The operation saw the US send upwards of 30,000 military personnel to Somalia, alongside 10,000 personnel from another twenty-four UN member states to secure supply lines. *Operation Restore Hope* commenced on 9 December 1992, just six days after the UN Security Council passed Resolution 794 (1992) authorizing the intervention in Somalia 'in order to establish a secure environment for humanitarian relief operations'. Military intervention was further justified by the US and UN by the magnitude of human tragedy in Somalia, along with reports of widespread violations of international humanitarian law (UNSC 1992).

Humanitarian intervention
The use or threat of armed force by a state, group of states or international organization to prevent gross violations of human rights among nationals of a target state without that state's consent.

'No more Rwandas'

Shortly after *Operation Restore Hope* in Somalia, events were soon to unfold which brought humanitarian intervention into an even sharper focus. In 1993, 2,500 UN peacekeepers had been sent into Rwanda to oversee a ceasefire between the Hutu government and the Tutsi liberal movement, the Rwandan Patriotic Front. The UN's peacekeeping mandate was limited, being intended to oversee the ceasefire but not to directly intervene. On 6 April 1994 the Rwandan president was killed. Within hours, several thousand Tutsis and members of the political opposition were killed by a Hutu paramilitary organization known as the *Interahamwe*. When ten Belgian peacekeepers who were part of the UN peacekeeping mission were also killed, nations involved in the UN peacekeeping force began to evacuate their nationals from Rwanda. Over 100 days, almost 1 million Tutsis, along with moderate Hutus, were slaughtered in one of the worst, most rapid genocides in modern history.

The genocide in Rwanda is now widely acknowledged as a failure of humanitarian intervention and of collective *in*action. It is also seen as one of the darkest chapters in the UN's history (pg. 122). A report of the genocide being perpetrated against the Tutsis was not relayed by the UN Secretariat to the UN Security Council (UNSC). Even when the massacres were known, the UNSC failed to acknowledge the genocide, or to act, despite still having UN peacekeepers on the ground who could have mitigated the slaughter that followed. In short, Rwanda 'laid bare the full horror of inaction' (ICISS 2001: 1) by the international community and has been recognized as 'a failure of international will – of civic courage – at the highest level' (ICISS 2001: 1).

The events in Rwanda marked a turning point in international politics. After the genocide the UN, along with numerous states, made the commitment that there should be 'no more Rwandas'. Large-scale human rights violations in Haiti, Kosovo, East Timor and Sierra Leone were all responded to by direct military interventions intended to protect civilians and preserve life.

The humanitarian intervention into Kosovo in 1999 was, however, to signify another 'watershed event' (Doyle 2016: 17) that brought the controversy surrounding humanitarian intervention within international politics to a head (ICISS 2001: vii). In 1989, Serbia – then a part of Yugoslavia – imposed direct rule over Kosovo, which included a predominantly ethnic Albanian population. The move sparked increasing tensions and eventual violence between the Kosovo Liberation Army and Serb and Yugoslav forces. By February 1999 reports were circulating of war crimes being committed against ethnic Albanians in

Kosovo. When diplomatic efforts failed, and with fears of ethnic cleansing (pg. 190), NATO launched air strikes against Serbian military targets in March 1999.

While in both Somalia in 1992 and Haiti in 1994, humanitarian interventions had been authorized by the UN Security Council, in the 1999 Kosovo intervention, this did not happen. Intervention into Kosovo was instead led by NATO, without a UNSC resolution. As the UN Secretary-General, Kofi Annan, later stated, '[t]he genocide in Rwanda showed us how terrible the consequences of inaction can be in the face of mass murder. But ... Kosovo raised equally important questions about the consequences of action without international consensus and clear legal authority' (UN Secretary-General 1999).

LINK

Consider

The NATO-led intervention in Kosovo, named Operation Allied Force, involved a seventy-eight-day period of air strikes against Serbian forces with the intent of halting ethnic cleansing against Kosovar Albanians. The air strikes proved controversial. Yugoslav forces responded to NATO air strikes by displacing hundreds of thousands of Albanians from Kosovo who fled into neighbouring Macedonia. By June 1999 a peace accord was agreed between NATO and Yugoslavia that included Serbia's troop withdrawal and the return of Kosovo's ethnic Albanians. In 2001 an *Independent International Commission on Kosovo* was tasked with reporting on the intervention by NATO. It famously concluded that the intervention was 'illegal but legitimate'.

Explore

Explore the commission's report, available online at https://reliefweb.int. Reflect on the report's claim of illegality in the case of NATO's intervention (p. 2) as well as the threshold principles it outlines for legitimate humanitarian intervention (p. 4).

Connect

A major concern associated with the legitimacy of humanitarian intervention after Kosovo was that powerful states could take unilateral action to intervene in other states' affairs even if the UNSC could not or would not act. Kosovo was therefore seen, particularly by states in the Global South, as setting a dangerous precedent for future interventions. For some states, Kosovo sparked fears that humanitarian intervention might be used 'as a pretext for imperial intervention' (Doyle 2016: 16–17). See also pages 100–02 where we discussed critical views on the labelling of failed and fragile states to justify interference.

Predict

Reflect again on the challenges associated with UNSC decision-making (pg. 112). The UNSC can legitimately authorize a humanitarian intervention, but what is to happen when the UNSC can't or won't decide?

Scan the QR code for access to explore weblinks and more resources.

The Responsibility to Protect

The events of the 1990s raised fundamental questions not only about why states had been willing to protect lives and intervene in some internal conflicts, but not others, but over the legitimacy of intervening in another state's internal affairs at all. In September 2000 the Canadian government sought to respond to some of these challenges by establishing an *International Commission on Intervention and State Sovereignty.* The Commission was tasked with trying to forge a new consensus on the competing principles of human rights and state sovereignty. The Report outlined two basic principles upon which understandings of humanitarian intervention should be hinged. First, that the primary responsibility for the protection of a state's people lies with the state itself (ICISS 2001: xi). And second, that where a population is suffering from serious harm, and where the state in question is unwilling or unable to halt or avert it, 'the principle of non-intervention yields to the international *responsibility to protect*' (ICISS 2001: xi emphasis added).

The **Responsibility to Protect** (or R2P) has since become an established – if still heavily contested – norm in contemporary international politics. R2P is distinctive for several reasons.

Responsibility to Protect
A guiding principle within international politics, that places the responsibility to protect citizens first with the state, but then with the international community where the state fails in its duty.

First, R2P constituted a radical shift in understanding sovereignty. Rather than sovereignty being addressed merely as control or authority over a people and territory, sovereignty became conditional upon a state's responsibility to protect its people.

Second, R2P stipulated that it is the responsibility of the international community to assist states in fulfilling their responsibility to protect. Emphasis is therefore placed on multilateral efforts to use appropriate diplomatic, humanitarian and other peaceful means to help states protect their populations from gross violations of human rights.

Third, R2P clarified that where a state fails in its responsibility to protect, the responsibility then falls to the international community. The ICISS report particularly stipulated that military intervention for human protection purposes should be 'exceptional and extraordinary measures', warranted only where there was 'serious and irreparable harm occurring to human beings, or imminently likely to occur' (ICISS 2001: xii) including large-scale loss of life or large-scale ethnic cleansing (ICISS 2001: xii).

In 2005 the UN World Summit further consolidated the R2P principle when world leaders made a unanimous historic commitment to protect populations from genocide, war crimes, ethnic cleansing and **crimes against humanity**. In 2009 the UN adopted a three-pillar R2P implementation strategy that further clarified: 1. the protection responsibilities of the state, 2. the concomitant responsibility of the international community to provide assistance and capacity-building to support the efforts of states to meet their R2P responsibilities, and 3. an international commitment to a timely and decisive response to protect populations from atrocity crimes.

Crimes against humanity
First used with reference to the slave trade but now codified under the 1998 Rome Statute with reference to crimes including murder, extermination, enslavement, deportation or forcible transfer of population, imprisonment or other severe deprivation of physical liberty, torture, various forms of sexual violence, persecution against any identifiable group, enforced disappearance of persons, apartheid and other inhuman acts intentionally causing great suffering.

For some scholars the success of the Responsibility to Protect ultimately rests in its legitimization of armed intervention, its defining of the scope of forcible, multilateral protections that the international community provides, and of how it allows for the care of both vulnerable populations and national sovereignty (Doyle 2016: 15). Between 2006 and spring 2023, the UN Security Council had referenced R2P in ninety resolutions and presidential statements, most serving to remind states of their responsibility to protect their civilians when human rights concerns arise (GCR2P 2023). R2P has also been invoked to justify international actions such as the enforcement of a no-fly zone in Libya in 2011, and an arms embargo against the Central African Republic in 2018.

For others, however, while R2P remains a 'normative innovation' in international politics, the actual practice of R2P has proven rather more restricted (Bellamy and Luck 2018). Despite atrocity crimes still taking place within our international system, the international community's willingness, and capacity to offer a timely and decisive response, has been limited. The Responsibility to Protect thus remains a contentious issue. Despite the efforts to conceptualize R2P and to legitimize humanitarian interventions where atrocity crimes have been committed, humanitarian interventions over the 2010s and 2020s have been few – a point we shall return to in the toolkit exercise at the end of this chapter.

Explore More

Find out more about the Responsibility to Protect, including some of its key documents and strategies, by visiting www.un.org/en/genocideprevention. You may also be interested in the work of the Global Centre for the Responsibility to Protect (GCR2P), an advocacy group formed of governments, foundations and individuals campaigning for the implementation, strengthening and institutionalization of R2P to prevent atrocities and protect human rights. You can explore more about the Centre's analysis of populations currently at risk from human rights abuses using this interactive map at www.globalr2p.org/populations-at-risk.

Scan the QR code for access to explore weblinks and more resources.

CONCLUSION

In this chapter we have considered rights and responsibilities within international politics. We have addressed collective and individual rights and the emergence of an international human rights framework. We have also looked at how human rights were embedded in the foundations of the UN, codified in international law, and are today monitored and overseen by various international and regional organizations and courts. And we have seen how human rights have established a universal obligation and moral imperative on states as duty-bearers to protect their people and uphold their human rights.

Much as rights have become integral to international politics, so too has responsibility become a pervasive theme. Yet as we have also seen in this chapter, the intersection of rights and responsibility sparks notable contentions. Contestation between human rights norms and the inviolability of the sovereign state, along with the legitimacy and willingness of the international community to intervene where there are gross violations of human rights, have been especially marked in the debate surrounding humanitarian intervention and the Responsibility to Protect. R2P has not only constituted a fundamental reframing of how we understand sovereignty itself; establishing sovereignty's conditionality on the state's responsibility to protect its own people. R2P has also legitimized international intervention into a state's internal affairs where atrocity crimes against its people are being committed. Determining the extent to which the norms enshrined by R2P are then exercised by the international community nevertheless remains a matter of continued debate for us as scholars of international politics, particularly around why, despite having legitimate grounds to act, the international community does not intervene to prevent atrocity crimes more often. You can continue to engage with these issues by trying the following toolkit exercise, asking '*Why was there no humanitarian intervention during the 2017 Rohingya crisis?*'

TOOLKIT

Why was there no humanitarian intervention during the 2017 Rohingya crisis?

THINK

- Whose responsibility do you think it is to protect and uphold individual human rights?

OBSERVE

Image 15.4 Cox's Bazar in Bangladesh – today the world's largest refugee camp and home to 950,000 Rohingya.

Source: Allison Joyce/Getty Images.

- Rohingya Muslims have faced discrimination and targeted violence in Rakhine State, Myanmar for some decades, forcing many to flee into neighbouring countries. In August 2017, however, Rohingya Arsa militants launched attacks against police stations across Rakhine. Myanmar's security forces responded with a systematic attack against the Rohingya, burning their villages and attacking and killing civilians. By 2022, an estimated 1 million Rohingyas continued to reside in refugee camps in neighbouring Bangladesh, many at Cox's Bazar, here pictured.
- NGOs reporting from Myanmar and Bangladesh during the crisis suggested that nearly 7,000 Rohingya were killed between August and September 2017. The government of Myanmar put that figure at 400, claiming that its 'clearance operations' targeted militants and not civilians (BBC News 2020c).
- The UN Security Council passed no resolution, nor authorized any intervention. The UNSC's formal response was a presidential statement given on 6 November 2017 condemning attacks against the Myanmar security forces by the Arakan Rohingya Salvation Army, and expressing grave concerns over reports of human rights violations and abuses, including by the Myanmar security forces, against the Rohingya population. The Statement went on to stress the Council's 'strong commitment to the sovereignty, political independence, territorial integrity and unity of Myanmar' while highlighting 'the primary responsibility of the Government of Myanmar to protect its population' (UNSC 2017).

ORGANIZE

- A 2019 report to the UN's Human Rights Council found that the events that transpired in Rakhine State indicated 'genocidal intent' by Myanmar against the Rohingya (UNGA 2019). In 2022 the US government also acknowledged that the Rohingya had been subject to genocide and crimes against humanity. Reflect again on the four atrocity crimes (pgs. 190, 265, 273) and the principles established by the Responsibility to Protect (pg. 272–3). What conditions must be met for the international community to legitimately intervene in another state's internal affairs?
- The realist theoretical tradition highlights that states act out of self-interest and are therefore unlikely to intervene to 'save strangers' unless it serves their national interest. Sovereignty and a state's security are also considered paramount. Reflect again on the politics of decision-making in the UN Security Council (pg. 112). How might realist logics have impacted the UN Security Council's willingness to authorize an intervention in this case? Which UNSC members might have resisted efforts to intervene in Myanmar?
- Reflect again on the critical theoretical perspectives of humanitarian intervention (pg. 270). How might non-intervention be justified from these perspectives?

LINK

- *Consider*: Humanitarian intervention can come in different forms. While most humanitarian interventions in the 1990s involved direct military interventions coordinated by the UN or NATO – such as in Somalia or Kosovo – since the turn of the 21st century interventions have tended to involve arms embargoes, other targeted sanctions or enforcing no-fly zones, in order to protect civilians. States also try to hold governments and individuals to account for their actions, such as The Gambia's application concerning Myanmar to the International Court of Justice (pg. 265). Consider also that an international response can also come in the form of providing humanitarian aid for refugees.
- *Explore*: Explore more about Myanmar (including more recent developments within the country) at www.globalr2p.org. Scan the barcode also for more news and analysis, and to access the UN Security Council's statement on the 2017 Rohingya crisis.
- *Connect*: According to a UN Special Rapporteur, 'it has been cultivated for decades in the minds of the Myanmar people that the Rohingya are not indigenous to the country and therefore have no rights whatsoever to claim' (UN Human Rights Office of the High Commissioner 2017). Because the Rohingya have been denied citizenship by the Myanmar government they do not benefit from the same collective rights (pg. 262) attributed to other nationals. Worth highlighting that the 1954 UN Convention on Statelessness, which sets out minimum standards for the treatment of stateless persons with regards their basic rights such as a right to education, housing and employment, defines a 'stateless person' as someone 'not recognized as a national by any state under the operation of its law'. Neither Myanmar nor Bangladesh are parties to the UN Convention on Statelessness.
- *Predict*: Whose responsibility is it to protect the Rohingyas' basic human rights?

SHARE

- Answer the question '*Why was there no humanitarian intervention in the 2017 Rohingya crisis?*'

  Critical analysis is an important part of your skills development as a scholar, but also in shaping your argument to questions such as these. Check out *How to – develop critical analysis skills* (pg. 163) for some helpful tips in using critical analysis to address this question.

HOW TO

APPROACH AN ORAL PRESENTATION

In your studies you may be called upon to present your work to others as an oral presentation, whether as a formative or summative assessment, or a regular practice you are asked to do during seminars. When approaching an oral presentation, however, a few top tips are worth keeping in mind.

Prepare for the presentation as you would an essay

An oral presentation is much like any piece of written work you prepare at university, the only difference being that the emphasis is placed on your oral rather than written communication skills. If you have been given an oral presentation on a set topic or question, you should still prepare for it as you would any piece of written work, like an essay (see also *How to* – approach *an international politics essay* pg. 182). Pay particular attention therefore to what your argument is, what evidence you will use, what theory or concepts you will draw upon to frame your discussion. Think also about how you would then structure your presentation if it was written out as an essay. Like any essay, an oral presentation still requires an introduction, some background and context, details concerning a particular case or example, and a summative conclusion. Start to pull this out into a list of things you want to highlight in your presentation and in what order. Having a clear plan will help ensure you address all the key points you wish to get across to your audience, while preventing you from going off on tangents (which can happen far more easily when talking than when writing!)

Use slides to complement your presentation

Consider using PowerPoint slides as a complementary tool to capture your audience's interest, and signpost them to the key messages you want them to understand from your presentation. Try to avoid having multitudes of slides with nothing but text on them as this can result in your audience just reading your slides rather than listening to you. Try also to avoid just reading straight off your slides as this can become rather tedious for your audience. Instead think about the structure of your presentation and key messages you want your audience to take away from each section. For each section and key message prepare one slide. For that one slide think carefully about what would complement your key message best. Rather than including lots of text, consider using a descriptive image or data easily presented in a simple table or diagram, for example. Make your headers simple and clear. The slide needs to reinforce your key message so that your audience can easily follow your line of enquiry. Do also pay attention to things like font size and colour contrast. Aim for your slides to be accessible and easy to view by anyone. PowerPoint has its own accessibility checker which can help you tailor your design so that those with low vision can still see the content.

Speak clearly

Give time to practise your presentation, thinking about how you are communicating as you practise. Our natural talking speed can often be a little too fast for a presentation – and we often speak more quickly when we get nervous – so think about slowing your pace down a little. Reflect on your articulation, and how clearly you are pronouncing words and phrases. If you are speaking to an international audience, think about how you could present your work so that everyone can understand you. Remember also to look at your audience. Make eye contact with them. This is especially helpful for those who may be hearing impaired.

Watch your time

It is very easy to go under or over time in an oral presentation. Two issues you particularly want to avoid are *1.* going off on tangents, by giving unprompted examples, or reflecting on issues that are less relevant to your presentation, and *2.* reading directly off a script you've prepared in advance. Going off on tangents can result in you losing valuable minutes and risks pulling you off topic. But reading off a script – while safer in terms of ensuring you've included everything you wanted to say – risks losing your audience. Try listening to someone reading an essay to you. It can be monotonous because our reading voice is not our natural speaking voice. You can avoid both problems by preparing talking points on cue cards in advance. Talking points can just be a few bullet points for each of your PowerPoint slides and serve as short cues to remind you of the issues you wished to highlight for each slide. For each card, bear your time in mind. Stay on point so you won't deviate and waste precious seconds.

16 Race, religion and identity

Unsplash / Haley Rivera

Abstract

In this concluding chapter, we address how race, religion and identity have been addressed in the study of international politics. Attention is paid first to how identity has been addressed by the different theoretical approaches within international politics. From there we consider race and racism as issues that have been largely neglected in the study of international politics, but which now are increasingly a point of focus, both in scholarship and practice. The chapter then addresses religion and its resurgence as an issue in the study of international politics since the Cold War, paying particular attention to religion as a cause for both international conflict and cooperation. The chapter then brings us back full circle to how this book began by refocusing on you, and your research, and how what you Think, Observe, Organize, Link and Share can continue to shape international politics as a discipline in the future.

UNDERSTANDING RACE, RELIGION AND IDENTITY

In this book we have touched upon several topics that address race, religion and identity in international politics. For example, race has been discussed in terms of colonialism (pg. 18), decolonization (pg. 6) and postcolonialism (pgs. 27, 55–8). Identity has been highlighted as it relates to social constructivism (pg. 61–3), or the individual level of analysis (pg. 82–6). Religion has also been touched upon in discussions of terrorism (pg. 155) or civil wars (pg. 171). What may also strike you when reading the preceding chapters, however, is the extent to which race, religion and identity have *not* featured. Indeed, race and religion have not always been obvious characteristics in the study of international politics, with scholarship concentrated on matters of anarchy, sovereignty, national interests, the rise of international organizations, the international economy, or with interdependence, power, security, and conflict and cooperation. These issues in many respects form the bedrock of our discipline, and yet, as critical scholars emphasize, have been noticeably absent in engaging with issues of race (Vitalis 2015; Chowdhry and Nair 2002) and are markedly **secular** in their approach (Shah and Philpott 2011). In fact, race and religion have been largely downplayed in conventional international politics discourses, particularly during the Cold War when the major point of scholarly interest was less on cultural issues, and more on power (Moaz and Henderson 2021: 9–10).

Secularism
Being unconnected with religious or spiritual matters.

The apparent marginalization of race and religion within international politics scholarship only really started to change after the Cold War, when cultural and religious issues began to be addressed in the study of international conflict and cooperation, along with the internal politics and conflict within 'failing states' (pg. 100–1). Al Qaeda's attack on the United States, in the events of 9/11 (pg. 102), further ignited interest – even concern – over religion's role in international politics, with a growing emphasis on religious fundamentalism and its link to violent non-state actors.

Race and racism have also become pressing issues in international politics, and increasingly so. The 2010s and early 2020s saw numerous migration crises (pg. 230), alongside rising concerns over immigration that have placed race and racism front and centre on national and international political debates (Dumbrava 2022; Fox News 2019). Consider that at the end of the Cold War there were roughly a dozen border walls and fortifications erected worldwide. By 2022 that number had sextupled to seventy-four, with fifteen more in the planning stages. Each wall has been erected by states at their territorial borders to prevent illegal migration, smuggling and to combat terrorism (Vallet 2022), but which are also observed as racially charged, being erected to keep 'others' out (García 2019). In the 2010s and early 2020s, Black Lives Matter also fought against domestic racism and police brutality, becoming a transnational social movement and sparking protests around the world (pg. 152–3). Across university campuses, race and racism have also become a central point of debate among staff and students alike, with increasing calls to remove former colonial symbols and legacies within universities, and to decolonize the curriculum (Bhambra, Gebrial and Nişancıoğlu 2018).

In 1900 the activist and historian W. E. B. Du Bois claimed that the problem of the 20th century would be the problem of the **colour line**. Over a century later and concerns of a hardening global colour line have been reignited (Carrozza, Danewid and Pauls 2017). Academic focus is increasingly turning to race, and racial realities in a discipline that has studiously ignored racism (Carrozza, Danewid and Pauls 2017). The rise of critical theories, and of postcolonialism, however, has done much to shine light on the importance of race and racism in understanding international politics. For example, race and racism are seen to shape the construction of discourses around Global North and South, of the West and Third World. Race and racism are also considered intrinsic of national identities and are found to shape the politics of immigration and security. The construction of race can therefore also be identified as one of the 'pivotal features of the contemporary economic, political and cultural dominance by the West of the Third World' (Chowdhry and Nair 2002: 18).

Colour line
Referring to the social, economic and political barriers that exist between different races.

The aim of this final chapter then is to offer a timely refocus on the importance that race, religion and identity play in international politics. Attention in the following sections is paid first to identity, revisiting some of the theoretical approaches we have been discussing so far to consider the extent to which identity matters in international politics. From there we will consider race, racism and international politics, looking particularly at some of the discussion points concerning efforts to decolonize international politics as a discipline. The chapter then considers religion in international politics, addressing some of the controversies over religion as a cause of conflict, relative to its influence in shaping cooperation and peace. Finally, as we started this book with the axiom that 'all politics starts with you', so too do we conclude, turning to you and how your identities and beliefs will continue to shape not only your own world view, but your research as you continue to advance in your study of international politics. We conclude with a toolkit exercise that offers you an opportunity for self-reflection over the issues addressed in this book, asking '*What does decolonization mean to me?*'

William Edward Burghardt Du Bois, born 1863, was a black American sociologist, historian and Pan-Africanist civil rights activist. In his essay 'The Present Outlook for the Dark Races of Mankind' he stated:

'It is but natural for us to consider that our race question is a purely national and local affair, confined to 9 million Americans and settled when their rights and opportunities are assured, and yet a glance over the world at the dawn of the new century will convince us that this is but the beginning of the problem – that the color line belts the world and that the social problem of the twentieth century is to be the relation of the civilized world to the dark races of mankind' (Du Bois 2015: 112).

To what extent do you think this statement, made well over a century ago, relates to race relations in the 21st century?

THE IMPORTANCE OF IDENTITY IN INTERNATIONAL POLITICS

Does identity really matter in international politics? For the realist theoretical tradition, identity has not been an issue of significant concern. Any scholar adopting a realist theoretical approach to their research is primarily concerned with national interest, security and the behaviour of the state as a primary actor within an anarchic international system. For the neorealist particularly, identity is not a salient feature when determining states' interests. Neorealism, like other positivist theoretical approaches (pg. 38), would also challenge the extent to which identity can be measured as a discernible and verifiable variable when researching international politics (pg. 38). Yet despite realism's seeming disinterest in identity as a point of explanation in international politics, an implicit assumption follows that identity is itself a characteristic, even by-product, of the state. From the realist tradition we can therefore observe that, where identity does matter, it is inherently state-oriented, linked to national citizenship, and is therefore intrinsically connected to sovereignty and a state's territorial borders. Our citizenship establishes our common national identity with all other citizens of our country, while delineating 'us' from 'them'. Emphasis, therefore, is placed upon the sanctity of state borders to protect the national identity and interests – a logic that has also been used to justify anti-immigration stances, and the erection of border walls (Trump 2019; Rigby and Crisp – see also pg. 56).

Liberal theoretical approaches have also tended to downplay the importance of identity within international politics. The liberal tradition observes identity as a predominantly individual concern. Our identities are personal to us as individuals because we are each unique. While liberalism tends not to focus on the specifics of those identities, how they are formed, or their influence upon the world in which we live, liberalism does assume that all individuals share the same universal identity as members of the human race – an

OBSERVE

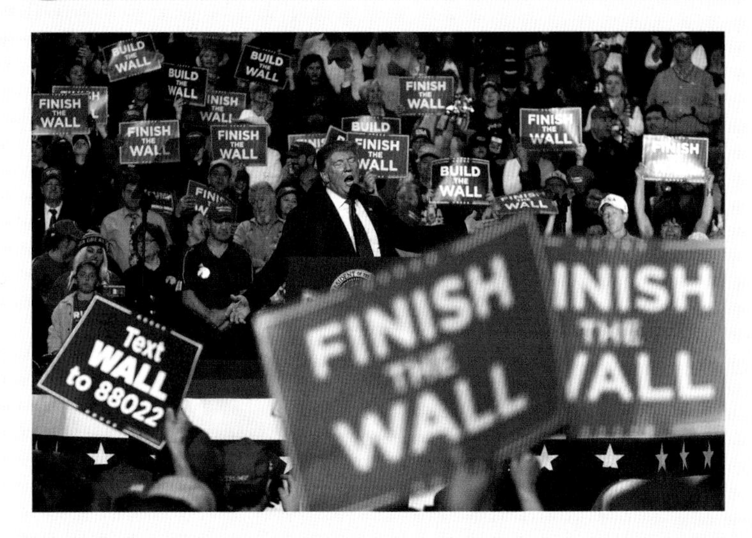

Image 16.1 In 2019, then US President Donald Trump speaks at a Make America Great Again rally in El Paso, Texas where he pressed forward his campaign to erect a border wall between Texas and Mexico.

Source: Joe Raedle/Getty Images.

The border between the United States and Mexico is over 3,000 kilometres, and is considered to be one of the most frequently crossed borders in the world (pg. 230). The United States Border Patrol began constructing barriers along its southwest border in the early 1990s. In 2006 the US Senate voted to pass the Secure Fence Act which authorized the construction of physical infrastructure to secure the border. In 2017, under the Trump Administration, the border wall system was revamped, and the border wall refunded and extended. According to a press release from the US Department of Homeland Security in October 2020, 'The Border Wall System is Deployed, Effective, and Disrupting Criminals and Smugglers' (US Department of Homeland Security 2020).

In this image President Trump speaks to a rally of people carrying banners in support of the wall being built in El Paso, Texas. At the same time as the Make America Great Again rally was taking place, a 'March for Truth' protest was also being held outside the conference centre. Protesters in the march involved various community partners and NGOs, including Border Network for Human Rights. Speaking at the March for Truth, Democratic Congressman Beto O'Rourke stated to the crowd that 'We know that walls do not save lives. Walls end lives … There is no bargain in which we can sacrifice some of our humanity to gain a little more security' (Cequea 2019).

important driver for the universalism of human rights (pg. 267–9). Thus, our identities are at once individual, but also universal. The liberal focus therefore tends to negate the significance of other forms of collective identity, such as class, gender, race, ethnicity or religion.

Social and critical theories, by contrast, place special emphasis on the importance of identity in the study of international politics. Social constructivism stresses the relevance of identity in shaping interests in international politics – with socially constructed national identities particularly imperative to how a state's national interests are subsequently forged and shaped (pg. 61–3). A state's role or its status within international politics are also connected with conceptions of its national identity (pg. 80). Identities can, moreover, be shaped and changed through social interaction with others.

Marxism, meanwhile, would emphasize the significance of class identity, arguing that people identify themselves first and foremost by their economic class. Marxism further assumes that the major fault lines within the international system are between the working class (the proletariat), and the capitalist elite (the bourgeoisie), and that a classless society will only be feasible when international capitalism has been abolished (pg. 55). Gramscian-inspired approaches would also emphasize how the collective identity of capitalist societies are subtly being controlled by the capitalist elite through popular culture. Emphasis then is placed on dissidents and resistance movements who then challenge such cultural hegemony (pg. 53) (Balci 2017; Dodds 2005: 175).

Feminist scholarship, by contrast, emphasizes the importance of gender and identity, adopting gendered lenses to understand what, why and how we study international politics. Along with other critical theories, feminism is particularly concerned with offering alternative conceptualizations of power and relationships within international politics, and highlighting unequal power relationships, particularly where it concerns social injustice for those whose gender, but also ethnic, tribal, religious or sexual identities have left them under-represented or subordinated (pg. 60–1).

Postcolonial scholarship has also played a significant role in highlighting the importance of race, class, indigenous and gender identities within international politics. Postcolonialism especially emphasizes the dominance of the Western story in international politics, as well as the effect of 'othering' or 'worlding' of the Third World which remains prominent in international narratives today (pg. 57–8). Debate surrounding national identity, and the *threat* of migration, are thus observed from a postcolonial perspective as a discursive act of othering that places the role of the migrant in the role of 'them' to a national construction of 'us'. As we can observe in the case of the US-Mexico border wall, but also in other examples such as Brexit in the UK (pg. 87), immigration has often been framed using negative connotations that associates migrants with 'smugglers', 'criminals' or 'terrorists'. Postcolonialism calls out that framing and has become an important lens by which to understand identity politics, particularly where it concerns racial identity, oppression and racism.

RACE, RACISM AND INTERNATIONAL POLITICS

In the last section it was asked, *Does identity really matter in international politics?* As we have seen, different theories place different levels of salience on the issue of identity in the study of international politics. While social and critical theories have embraced the study of identity and stress its importance in shaping international politics, more traditional theoretical lenses, including realism and liberalism, tend to downplay identity, emphasizing instead the importance of the individual, the nation-state or the universalism of the human race.

Racism
The belief, practice and policy of prejudice and domination against an individual or group based on their race.

When we turn to consider race and **racism**, however, we can observe widening fissures between these different theoretical camps, as well as some of the blind spots in our discipline's evolution and its more established concepts, theories and approaches. As discussed in Chapter Three, our discipline has evolved out of multiple narratives and spaces (pg. 34), of which race relations has been a foundational – yet at times, all too implicit – component. Consider that one of the foremost journals of the discipline, the *Journal of International Relations* (now *Foreign Affairs*), was originally the *Journal of Race Development* (Vitalis 2015: ix). Yet the popularized story of our discipline highlights its foundations in the birth of a university department, and the subsequent evolution of theoretical great debates where the state, power, conflict and cooperation were of foremost concern. Within that discourse, race and racial relations have been largely absent. Imperialism was also seemingly ignored, or at the very least downplayed. As Doyle (1986: 11) stated in *Empires*, '[i]nternational relations scholars, for their part, tend to place imperialism in a minor position, as one of many possible policies that a powerful state can employ'. Imperialism, when addressed, has conventionally been seen as a strategy of power, an extension of the state, with the racial realities of imperialism and colonialism, grounded as they have been in racist assumptions of white supremacism – then neglected or silenced (Persaud and Walker 2001: 374).

Yet as postcolonialism stresses, there is no one world, and no single story, but rather multiple and overlapping worlds and narratives that shape what is known, and what is accepted. For critical scholars, race and racism have been seminal to the development of our discipline (Henderson 2013: 76), yet the dominant (Eurocentric and Anglo-American) story of our discipline has been one of 'race-blindness' (Nişancıoğlu 2020: 40). Consider that Philip Kerr – quoted in Chapter Three with reference to his comment about realists being 'practical people' (pg. 35–6) – had just over a decade previously published a chapter in one of the first *Introduction to the Study of International Relations* textbooks. His chapter was titled 'Political Relations Between Advanced and Backward Peoples'. Its opening line stated that, '[t]he problem of the relations which should exist between advanced and backward peoples has always been one of the gravest that has presented itself to mankind' (Kerr 1916: 141). The chapter went on to state in its first section on the 'Necessity of Empire' that:

> There are peoples who by reason of their character, their truthfulness and integrity, their political institutions, their sense of public responsibility, their resourcefulness and capacity progressively to improve the conditions under which they live, regard themselves as the leaders of mankind. These are, broadly speaking, the peoples of European origin. There are others who, because of their idolatry of wood or stone, the weakness of their sense of responsibility, their treatment of women, their apathy and their fatalist acquiescence in things as they are, are regarded by the civilised peoples as backward. These are, broadly speaking, the peoples of non-European origin (Kerr 1916: 141-2).

We can therefore see that Du Bois' problem of the colour line going into the 20th century was already firmly embedded in some of the earliest texts of international politics/relations over a century ago.

When we look to the history of international politics, we can clearly observe race and racism's significant real-world impacts – from colonialism and slavery (pg. 19) to **segregation** to genocide (pg. 189) to **apartheid**. Yet issues of race and racial equality have also been moderated in the formation of what we now study as the liberal international order (pg. 38) (Acharya 2022). Consider that Woodrow Wilson (pg. 34) – a liberal internationalist widely accredited with shaping the early foundations of our discipline and for championing the League of Nations (Acharya 2022: 24) – also oversaw segregation in the United States, reportedly stating that 'we cannot make a homogenous population out of people who do not blend with the Caucasian race' (Vought 1999: 29 cited in Shilliam 2021: 69). Wilson is also accredited with preventing a Japanese racial equality clause from being implemented into the League of Nations principles (Acharya 2022: 34). The Japanese proposal sought to introduce language on the equality of nations – 'making no distinction, either in law or in fact, on account of their race or nationality' (Axelrod 2019). Yet, as Chair of the League of Nations Committee, Wilson imposed a unanimity ruling that resulted in the proposal's demise even though a majority of members supported it (Axelrod 2019).

Segregation
Actions within a state that separate with a means of isolating a race, class or ethnic group.

Apartheid
Meaning 'apartness' in Afrikaans. A system or policy of institutionalized racism or discrimination on racial grounds.

The lack of references to race or colonialism in the Charter of the League's successor, the United Nations, has also been noted by critical scholars who highlight how 'anti-racism and decolonization were secondary concerns at the founding of the UN' (Acharya 2022: 37) – a point others have challenged when looking at the human rights provisions of the UN Charter (Persaud and Walker 2001: 374, also pg. 262). Racial subordination nevertheless continued to feature in the makings of the liberal international order, first in the League's mandate system, and in its continuation under the UN's Trusteeship Council.

ORGANIZE

Image 16.2 A group of delegates from the Universal Negro Improvement Association (UNIA) visit the League of Nations in Geneva in 1922 to demand independence for the former German colonies in South West Africa. The former colonies were being administered by the League of Nations' mandate system.
FPG/Getty Images

Reflect again on Image 7.1 (pg. 110) and observe the details concerning the League of Nations and its mandate system. The former German colonies in South West Africa were being administered by the League's mandate system. In image 16.2 below, representatives of the Universal Negro Improvement Association (from left to right, Jean Adam (Haiti), James O'Meally (Jamaica), George O'Marke (Sierra Leone) and William L. Sherrill (US)) attend the League of Nations to demand the independence of mandated territories with a view to founding a new republic for Africans around the world. The UNIA was founded by Jamaican political activist Marcus Garvey who advocated black pride, and black nationalism, championing a return of black peoples to Africa.

Now revisit Table 7.2 (pg. 115) addressing the functions and operation of the UN's principal organs, particularly as it relates to the Trusteeship Council. According to Acharya (2022) when the Trusteeship system was being discussed during the San Francisco Conference that launched the UN, colonialism was barely mentioned. Eleven of the twelve territories overseen by the UN Trusteeship Council were governed under mandates from the League of Nations.

Despite racism's obvious impacts in international politics, the academic telling of race and racism in international politics has been criticized for receiving the 'epistemological status of silence' (Persaud and Walker 2001). Critical scholars observe how white supremacism was not only salient in the discipline's earliest foundations but continues in the study of international politics, 'hidden in plain sight' in the theories we use, and in many of the foundational concepts that we draw upon (Henderson 2013, Nişancıoğlu 2020). Henderson, for example, argues that liberalism and realism – two major paradigms in the discipline – are 'oriented by racist – primarily white supremacist – precepts'. For Henderson, anarchy is a 'racially infused construct' used by realism to justify a hierarchical racial order that justifies imperialism and colonialism, and by liberalism to justify the primacy of individual rights, democracy, free trade and 'the imposition of a white racist order on indigenous peoples' (Henderson 2013: 85). Henderson (2013: 89) goes further in stating that the popular narrative of how our discipline evolved 'hovers outside of its own history', ensuring the '"norm against noticing" the centrality of white racism in world politics'.

As scholars of international politics, we can therefore start to address the 'epistemology of silence' and 'norm against noticing' race and racism in international politics by proactively reflecting upon and recognizing its impacts. According to Persaud and Walker (2001), the politics of race and the practices of racism within international politics can particularly be recognized in four ways.

First, in racial discourses which divide the world into binaries i.e. civilized/uncivilized, modern/backward, developed/undeveloped. *Second*, we can see race and racism's impacts on the world's demography and territories. Conquest, the carving up of territories, the displacement of indigenous populations and the supplanting of indigenous populations by white settlers have altered identities and senses of belonging. *Third*, we can observe race and racism's impact on the international economy, particularly looking at racialized labour supply and practices of labour recruitment (pg. 231–2). This not only includes the stark impacts of historic and modern slavery, but the importing of Third World domestic labour, the trafficking of sex workers, and the impacts on both legal and illegal economic migration (pg. 229–32). And *fourth*, Persaud and Walker (2011), highlight the impacts of 'othering' and the construction of racial identities that frame and reproduce difference which are prevalent both in internal conflicts, and within international interactions.

As scholars, we are therefore encouraged to reflect on the 'problem of difference' (Blaney and Tickner 2017: 267) which marks both the study and practice of international politics, and to actively acknowledge the impacts that race has had, and continues to have, upon the subject we are studying.

Explore More

Zombie narratives have become an increasingly popular way of teaching and interpreting international politics. Drezner's *Theories of International Politics and Zombies*, for example, offers a creative introduction to the different theories in international politics and how they might explain international behaviours when faced with a zombie outbreak. The 2022 'Apocalypse edition' also includes a chapter on 'Postcolonial Approaches to the Posthuman World'. Blanton (2013) has written about how to 'bring the undead' into international politics classrooms. Fishel and Wilcox (2017) have also addressed the zombie in international politics, viewed specifically through lenses of racialization and fear of the Other. Find out more about these different approaches by exploring these works yourself:

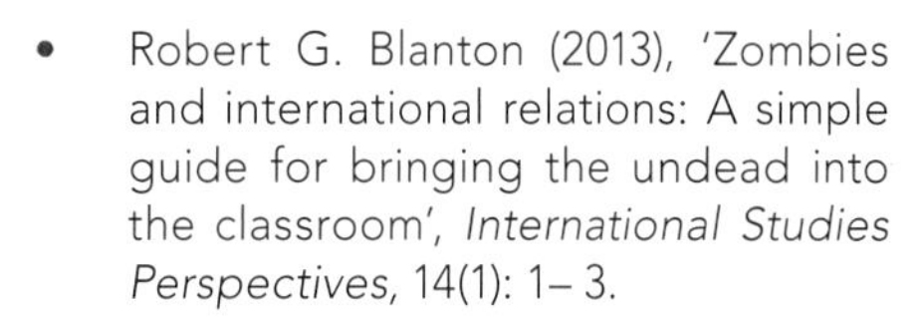

- Robert G. Blanton (2013), 'Zombies and international relations: A simple guide for bringing the undead into the classroom', *International Studies Perspectives*, 14(1): 1– 3.
- Daniel Drezner (2022), *Theories of International Politics and Zombies*, Apocalypse edition, Princeton: Princeton University Press.
- Stephanie Fishel and Lauren Wilcox (2017), 'Politics of the living dead: Race and exceptionalism in the apocalypse', *Millennium*, 45(3): 335–355.

Scan the QR code for access to explore weblinks and more resources.

RELIGION AND INTERNATIONAL POLITICS

As we saw in the last section, race has been a neglected issue within the study of international politics until recently. Religion similarly was considered something of a marginalized issue within dominant international politics discourses throughout much of the 20th century. With the end of the Cold War, however, scholarship focused on religion and international politics substantially increased, offering a new lens for observing the world in which we live (Moaz and Henderson 2020: 10–11). Religion has been observed by many as a resurgent issue within international politics, yet one that then clashes with a growing secularism in modern societies. Scholars have suggested that the world is witnessing a rising tide of secularism with religion 'waxed in its political influence over the past generation in every region of the globe' (Philpott 2007: 505). 'Giving Up on God: The Global Decline of Religion' was the title of an article in *Foreign Affairs* published in 2020 which outlined that the 'overwhelming majority' of countries studied had become less religious (Inglehart 2020). Religion, in turn, is subsequently addressed as something traditionalist – as separate from modern cultures as it is separate from governing institutions.

Others, however, have highlighted the continued salience of religion as a force in international politics: 'Religion has come to exert its influence in parliaments, presidential palaces, lobbyist offices, campaigns, militant training camps, negotiation rooms, protest rallies, city squares, and dissident jail cells' (Shah and Philpott 2011: 3). Consider that, at the turn of the 2020s, population statistics suggest that 85 per cent of the global population has a religious affiliation (CIA n.d.). Christians are the largest religious group, making up nearly one-third of the earth's population (31 per cent), while Muslims – the second largest religious group – represent nearly 25 per cent of the global population. Around 15 per cent of the global population is Hindu, just under 7 per cent is Buddhist, while 0.2 per cent is Jewish. Just under 6 per cent of the global population are also affiliated with **folk religions**, such as Chinese folk religions, traditional African religions, Aboriginal Australian beliefs and Native American beliefs. Consider also that roughly 40 per cent of countries and territories (79 out of 198 studied worldwide) have **blasphemy** laws, while 11 per cent (22 countries) have laws against **apostasy** (Villa 2022). We can therefore observe that religion is of fundamental importance not only to billions of individuals, but to large numbers of states as well.

Folk religions
Faiths associated with a particular group of people, ethnicity or tribe.

Blasphemy
Speaking or acting in a way that shows contempt, disrespect or insult against God or of people and objects deemed sacred.

Apostasy
The abandonment or renunciation of one's religious beliefs.

To what extent, then, should religion matter to scholars of international politics? According to Moaz and Henderson (2020: 2), while religion is an individual belief, personal to each one of us, 'what makes religion so relevant to social life and to international relations is that most religions – certainly the more popular ones – form and sustain communal institutions. They contain tangible elements that bind people together in profound ways.' By way of example, at the time of writing, there are roughly 1.34 billion people of Catholic faith in the world. Each of those 1.34 billion people is an individual with a personal belief in God and the Roman Catholic Church. Were we then to adopt an individual level of analysis (pg. 82–6), we might note the importance of the individual's religious beliefs in shaping their identity, or their world view, or the extent to which their beliefs impact their decisions. At an international level of analysis (pg. 75–9), however, we can observe that the Roman Catholic Church is the common institution of 1.34 billion individuals. The Head of the Catholic Church, the Pope, oversees a hierarchical transnational network of cardinals, archbishops, bishops, priests and deacons, each overseeing churches in countries around the world. The Catholic Church supports thousands of Catholic schools and colleges. More than this, the Pope, as Bishop of Rome, has jurisdiction over the Vatican and Holy See. Religion then is not a private affair, but also communal (Moaz and Henderson 2020: 2). Where religions are organized, they have a capacity to act within international politics, much like other international civil society organizations; although the Holy See is also unique among religious organizations in having sovereign jurisdiction in international law permitting it the right to enter into diplomatic relations, and to sign treaties.

And yet it has not been the capacity of religious organizations to act in international politics that has drawn the most controversy in academic and policy-making circles, but the extent to which religion is itself an issue of concern within international politics. Religion – and religious difference – speaks to the same 'problem of difference' discussed in the previous section. The history of religion, how religions formed and how they have grown, are charged by a politics of difference both within and between religions. Consider that the Abrahamic faiths – Judaism, Christianity and Islam – while sharing many of the same foundations, are divided into three distinct **world faiths**. Religions have also divided, and split within themselves, evolving over time and shaping the religious affiliations and identities of many. For example, Islam has split into several religious groups, including Sunnis, Shi'ites, Alawites and Ahmadis, for example, which have then been associated with contention and conflict. Eastern Orthodoxy and Protestantism split from the Roman Catholic Church. Buddhism was divided into Mahayana and Theravada; each split forming a new community, and a new communal religious identity.

World faiths
Faiths that are shared by people around the world and not limited to a specific territory or people.

Religions, therefore, matter not only for the common institutions they create, but the identities they construct. When those identities or institutions have been threatened, religion has then been identified as a major factor – and explanatory variable – for conflict in the international system. A common argument follows that religions have been the major cause of violence and war throughout history, from the Crusades to the Thirty Years War (pg. 16), to the conflict between Israel and Palestine, to the Troubles in Northern Ireland, to the human rights abuses against the Rohingya Muslim populations in Myanmar (pg. 275–6). Religion is considered a trigger for political instability, a fuel for **sectarian** violence, and a cause of war. Since the events of 9/11 when Al Qaeda – a **fundamentalist** Islamic terrorist organization – attacked the United States, religion has also been closely linked to the rise of terrorism, and the War on Terror (pg. 169).

Sectarianism
Associated with prejudice, discrimination and/or violence between groups, and typically linked to religious affiliation.

Fundamentalism
A conservative interpretation of religion that adheres strictly to sacred texts, dogmas or ideologies, in direct challenge to modern or more progressive interpretations of the faith.

Civilization
A human society with its own social organization and culture.

One now popularized discourse within international politics associates conflict with cultural and religious differences within the international system. In 1993 Samuel Huntington wrote the 'Clash of Civilizations?' published by *Foreign Affairs*, in which he argued that the future of world order would not be driven by clashes between First, Second or Third Worlds as during the Cold War, but between **civilizations** – 'the highest cultural grouping of people and the broadest level of cultural identity people have short of that which distinguishes humans from other species' (Huntington 1993). In his 1996 book *The Clash of Civilizations and the Remaking of World Order*, Huntington developed upon this theme highlighting that the major civilizations of the contemporary international system included the Sinic, Japanese, Indian, Islamic, Western, Orthodox, Latin American and 'possibly' African civilizations (Huntington 1996: 44–45). For each of these civilizations Huntington argued that 'religion is a central defining characteristic' (1996: 47). Civilizational differences then were considered basic, based on different views on 'the relations between God and man, the individual and the group, the citizen and the state, parents and children, husband and wife, as well as differing views on the relative importance of rights and responsibilities' (Huntington 1993). Consequently 'differences among civilizations have generated the most prolonged and the most violent conflicts' (Huntington 1993) and would constitute the major fault lines as the 'flash points for crisis and bloodshed' (Huntington 1993). Huntington went on to argue that one of the major fault lines in contemporary international politics would be between the West and Islam.

While Huntington's thesis made an impact within academia during the 1990s, the events of 9/11 noticeably amplified its argument and key message within the policy community as well – that religion would be a major cause of conflict for the West in the 21st century. After 9/11, Islamic fundamentalist terrorist organizations became the major cause of concern for the US government, and a major driver for the subsequent War on Terror (pg. 169). The Clash of Civilizations continued to be taught in universities and became embedded in political discourses, with politicians and those in high public office using the Clash of Civilizations to describe everything from terrorist violence and the War on Terror to tensions in US-China or India-Pakistan relations, to the US withdrawal from Afghanistan (pg. 102), and even more recently with reference to Russia and the conflict with Ukraine (Douthat 2022; Smith 2020).

The controversy surrounding Huntington's Clash of Civilizations soon generated studies to test his claims of whether religion is a primary trigger for war within the international system. In one study by Chiozza (2002), for example, empirical analysis highlighted that state interactions across civilizational divides were not more conflict-prone, nor were differences between civilizations associated with any greater risk of conflict. In 2014, the Institute for Economics and Peace also published the findings of empirical research into religion's impacts on conflict and peace. They found that while religion had been one of the causes of conflicts throughout history, it was not the only reason for conflict, nor was it the main cause of conflict today (Institute for Economics and Peace 2014: 2).

Consider

The Clash of Civilizations thesis has continued to resonate in political discourses far beyond the United States where it was first popularized at the turn of the 21st century. The Clash of Civilizations has become a popular framing for security dialogues, in political analysis and in government policies.

Explore

Scan the barcode to find links to Samuel Huntington's original article on the Clash of Civilizations, along with commentaries by other scholars twenty years after its publication. Huntington's thesis has also been roundly critiqued since its publication. Criticism is particularly levelled at Huntington's attempts to classify civilizations (or not, as is seen in the case of the African civilization), as well as in the lack of empirical evidence to support his argument (Chiozza 2002).

Connect

The Clash of Civilizations has particularly been criticized by postcolonial scholars for its 'othering' of races and religions, particularly of Islam by the West. For example, Edward Said remarked that the Clash of Civilizations was a 'gimmick' that dealt in such 'vast abstractions that may give momentary satisfaction but little self-knowledge or informed analysis' (Said 2001). More recently, scholars have stressed the Clash of Civilizations' racist undertones, which continues to appeal 'because of its emotive tribal appeal, setting up an us-versus-them scenario that's helped create anti-Muslim westerners and anti-westerner Muslims' (Bullock 2022).

Predict

What impact does the Clash of Civilizations have on the 'problem of difference' (pg. 285) in contemporary international politics?

Studies have further highlighted the positive effects of religion on peace (Institute for Economics and Peace 2014), peacebuilding (Coward and Smith 2004), and international cooperation (Moaz and Henderson 2020). Moaz and Henderson (2020: 269–70), for example, find that while religious similarity between states has limited bearing on economic cooperation, it can have a strong effect on security cooperation, establishing greater cohesion in organizations such as the Organization of American States, or NATO (both largely Christian states), as well as the Arab League (largely Sunni Muslim states). Others reflect on the important role that religious leaders and organizations have played in peacebuilding (Coward and Smith 2004: 3). **Religious peacebuilding** (Coward and Smith 2004: 5) has since received growing academic attention, with studies focusing on the opportunities and limits of religious peacebuilding efforts (Steen-Johnsen 2017; Wang 2014). Others highlight how religion serves to provide an important moral and symbolic voice within international politics. Chu (2012), for example, emphasizes how the Catholic Church challenged the US invasion of Iraq in 2003, classifying the action 'morally unjustifiable'.

Religious peacebuilding
The activities performed by religious actors or organizations with the purpose of resolving or transforming conflict situations.

World faiths have also played an important role in advocating world peace, including in nuclear disarmament, peacekeeping, poverty relief and tackling climate change. For example, the World Council of Religious Leaders was formed in 2002 with the goal of creating a community of world religions to assist the UN, its agencies and individual states in preventing conflict, and addressing social and environmental problems. Specifically, the World Council seeks to promote peace by 'promoting the practice of the spiritual values shared by all religious traditions' (World Council of Religious Leaders n.d.). Religion then must be observed as more than conventional binaries and presumed logics associating religion, and the religious, with conflict, while neglecting religious efforts to establish cooperation, peacebuilding and peace itself. Religion, then, much like race and identity, is complex and multifaceted. Researching these issues challenges us to therefore question our mental maps and test epistemological claims, to delve deeper and explore further. To echo Robbie Shilliam (2021: 151): *'I hope you might understand now, at the end of our journey, how important it is for us to challenge these conventional binaries – not just for morality's sake, but for the sake of better analysis too.'*

Explore More

The Institute for Economics and Peace 2014 report *Five Key Questions Answered on the Link Between Peace and Religion* offers a global statistical analysis on the empirical link between peace and religion. It addresses a number of key questions, including whether religion is a main cause of conflict today, whether countries with firmer religious or atheist beliefs determines their peacefulness, and the extent to which religion can play a positive role in peacebuilding. Explore further by reading the report. Available online: www.economicsandpeace.org

Scan the QR code for access to explore weblinks and more resources.

YOU AND YOUR RESEARCH

It has been the aim of this book not only to introduce you to the study of international politics. Its goal has been to encourage you to start to make the first active steps towards becoming a researcher of international politics. Much as we started this book with the axiom that all politics starts with YOU, so too then do we conclude. What key lessons might you as a researcher take from this book as you continue to advance in your scholarship? Well, the key lessons of this book reside in your toolkit. These **TOOLS** – **T**hink, **O**bserve, **O**rganize, **L**ink and **S**hare – will serve you not only as a learning strategy but as a researcher as you continue to advance in your study. So be prepared to...

Think

Think about your identity, your assumptions, your mental maps (pg. 3). What you think will shape your decisions as a researcher. It will shape the theories or concepts you favour, the topics you prioritize and the issues you neglect.

Observe

Your opinion, your arguments, your mental maps, are unique to you. But how do others see the topic you are researching? What contribution do others make to the scholarship? What are the dominant arguments in the field? And, crucially, what views have been marginalized or even silenced?

Organize

Throughout this book you have started to develop and hone your own analytical and theoretical toolkit for approaching the study of international politics. As you approach your research, therefore, organize what you know of the different theoretical perspectives we have covered in this book, their ontologies, methodologies and epistemologies. The theories, analytical tools and concepts introduced in this book serve as lenses by which you can start to explore, explain, predict and critique the world in which we live. Use them, test them and your research and analysis will be the richer for it.

Link

Be an active researcher. Actively look at the world in which we live. *Consider* what you know but also be prepared to *explore* further. Engage in your own independent empirical research, proactively search and enquire, test the validity of the claims you are reading. Make *connections* between what you think, what others believe, and what the existing scholarship can tell us. And be ready to *predict* what comes next. Academia is not just about learning, but about investigation and the contribution of new knowledge.

Share

As this chapter has highlighted, international politics is a discipline that has, at times, studiously neglected certain topics, while prioritizing others. Yet paradoxically, international politics is also a discipline that thrives on debate, on discourse, and on competing perspectives. As a scholar of international politics your ability to communicate, to write, discuss and inform is now imperative. Remember, as was highlighted in Chapter One, it is debate that moulds every discipline.

This is now your discipline. So shape it...

TOOLKIT

What does 'decolonization' mean to me?

THINK

- Decolonization is a term frequently used today, not only within the praxis of international politics, but in its study. Since 2015 there have been growing movements challenging colonial legacies, including those in universities and the taught curricula. Yet decolonization can involve 'a multitude of definitions, interpretations, aims and strategies' (Bhambra, Gebrial and Nişancıoğlu 2018: 2). Reflect again on the discussion about decolonization in the first chapter of this book (pg. 6–7). What wider meanings do you think should be attributed to the concept of decolonization?

OBSERVE

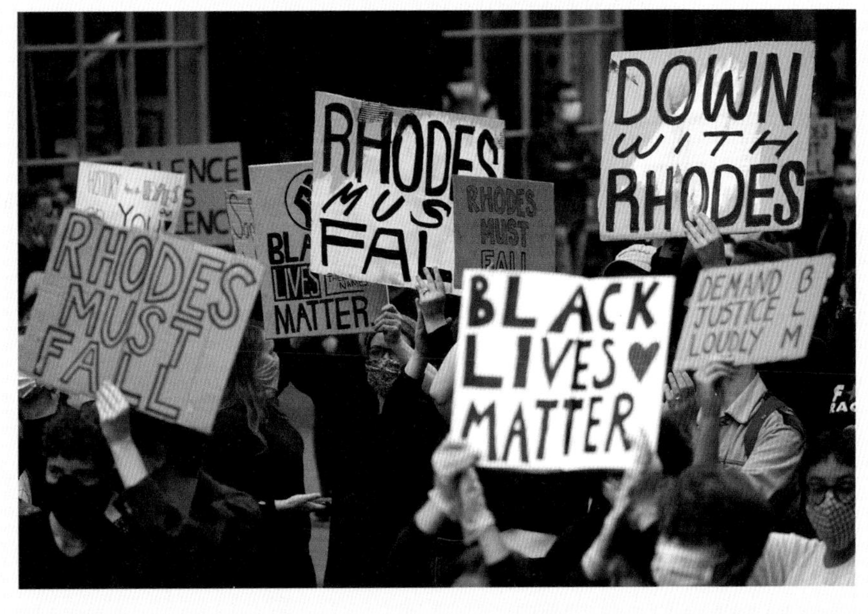

Image 16.3 Students protest at Oxford University, UK, June 2020.

Christopher Furlong / Getty Images

- In 2015 students at the University of Cape Town, South Africa, demanded the removal of a statue of Cecil Rhodes from their campus – a move that sparked an international campaign against institutional racism and with an ambition to decolonize education, known simply as #RhodesMustFall.
- Cecil Rhodes was a British businessman and politician who served as prime minister of Cape Colony from 1890 to 1896 and who made his fortune in diamond mining. As prime minister he used his power to take land away from black Africans and limited their ability to participate in elections. His legacy has been associated with the early foundations of apartheid in the country.
- In 2020 supporters of #RhodesMustFall protested at Oxford University calling for the removal of a statue of Cecil Rhodes from one of the college buildings. As this image highlights, the protest was further energized by the social movement Black Lives Matter (pg. 152).

ORGANIZE

- According to Bhambra, Gebrial and Nişancıoğlu (2018: 2) 'decolonizing' is a way of thinking about the world which takes colonialism, empire and racism as its empirical and discursive object, and which offers alternative ways of thinking about how politics is practised. Decolonization can be a contested term, however, meaning different things to different people.
- What reflections have you drawn from this chapter that shape your understanding of decolonization? Reflect also on how decolonization has been addressed in other sections of this book. Consider, for example, the history of decolonization in Chapter Two (pg. 25–7). Reflect on the importance of epistemology and what we 'know' in shaping critical theoretical approaches in international politics (pg. 33), particularly as it concerns postcolonialism (pg. 56–7). You may also want to revisit some of the 'Observe' tools from earlier chapters to consider how postcolonial and critical perspectives are used to critique and challenge colonial legacies and structural imbalances of power within international politics.

LINK

- *Consider*: Renowned Nigerian author Chimamanda Ngozi Adichie refers to 'the danger of the single story'. She states that 'stories matter, many stories matter. Stories have been used to dispossess and malign. But stories can also be used to empower and to humanize. Stories can break the dignity of a people, but stories can also repair that broken dignity' (Adichie 2009). As indigenous rights campaigner and educator Nikki Sanchez also highlights, the history of decolonization 'is not your fault, but it is absolutely your responsibility' (Sanchez 2019).
- *Explore*: Scan the barcode to access relevant resources including Adichie and Sanchez's TED talks. You can also explore more about the different meanings of decolonization, as well as how the UN addresses decolonization and indigenous peoples.
- *Connect*: Since 1945 more than eighty former colonies, comprising around 750 million people, have gained independence in the international system. Some seventeen Non-Self-Governing Territories still remain such as French Polynesia, American Samoa, Guam, Gibraltar or the Falkland Islands. Some 476 million indigenous people also live in ninety countries across the world. As Sanchez (2019) argues, many indigenous people live in what are 'occupied territories'.
- *Predict*: If decolonization is a process, when does it end? What do you think needs to occur before colonialism is a thing of the past?

SHARE

- Answer the question, *'What does "decolonization" mean to me?'*

  This toolkit offers a useful exercise in reflective thinking and writing. Reflect on your work through the different stages of this toolkit. What have you learned? What lessons can you extract that will inform your research and analysis in the future? You can also check out *How to – approach reflective writing* (pg. 293) for some tips on this.

HOW TO

APPROACH REFLECTIVE WRITING

Reflective writing is increasingly used in universities to encourage you as a scholar to actively reflect on your learning, and what you think, feel and understand from different activities. Reflective writing may be something you undertake informally in preparation for seminars, or as a formal assessment. The following are just a few tips for approaching reflective writing in your own studies.

THINK – Be reflective

Reflective writing is expressly aimed at the active reflection of an activity you have already performed, be that a presentation, review, debate, simulation or project, for example. Reflection provides opportunity for you to think back about what happened, how you engaged with certain materials, or understood the activity itself.

OBSERVE – Be evaluative

Reflective writing is importantly also evaluative. The goal in reflective writing is not simply to regurgitate facts of what you did and when, but to evaluate the learning you took from the exercise you are reflecting on. You should particularly look to evaluate the connections you have made (or not made) between what you knew, what you now know, and what lessons you extracted that you will seek to apply in the future. As yourself, therefore, what did you learn, how has this shaped your subject knowledge, and what would you do differently next time?

ORGANIZE – Structure and framing

As with any academic writing, you need to be clear in how you communicate your reflections to your audience. Try to avoid treating reflective writing like a brain dump where you just stream all your thoughts on to the paper. Work through your reflection and evaluation steps first, taking notes as you go. Then start to organize your reflections. Reflective writing is a naturally more subjective form of writing compared to your international politics essay (pg. 182) or policy brief (pg. 242) which tend to be more objective. Your structure will also likely be less rigid, but you should still think about the structure you want to present. Your structure may, for example, follow a timeline, with paragraphs organized around reflections and evaluations of different stages of your learning. You may alternatively prefer a structure where you first present reflections as a description of what happened, before then offering your evaluation and lessons for the future.

Because reflective writing is subjective, you can also use more personal framing in your choice of language. For example, reflective accounts are almost ways written in the first person because *you* are the subject of its reflection and evaluation. You are writing for an academic audience so your tone should still be relatively formal, but you are also writing as yourself so don't be shy about saying 'I think', 'I believe', 'I felt' or 'I understood'.

References

99Bitcoins (2023), Bitcoin Obituaries. Available online: https://99bitcoins.com/bitcoin-obituaries/ (accessed 11 May 2023).

Aberystwyth University (2023), 'Timeline of Events'. Available online: https://www.aber.ac.uk/en/interpol/about/centenary/interpollegacy/timelineofevents/ (accessed 21 March 2023).

Acharya, A. (2021), 'Global International Relations', in T. Dunne, M. Kurki and S. Smith (eds), *International Relations Theories: Discipline and Diversity*, 5th edn, 304–21, Oxford: Oxford University Press.

Acharya, A. (2022), 'Race and racism in the founding of the modern world order', *International Affairs*, 98(1): 23–43.

Acheson, R. (2019), 'The nuclear ban and the patriarchy: A feminist analysis of opposition to prohibiting nuclear weapons', *Critical Studies on Security*, 7(1): 78–82.

Adichie, C. N. (2009), 'The Danger of a Single Story', TED Talks. YouTube. Available online: https://www.youtube.com/watch?v=WHm7aBWoheY (accessed 14 May 2023).

Aggestam, K. and A. Towns, eds (2018), *Gendering Diplomacy and International Negotiation*, Basingstoke: Palgrave Macmillan.

Aggestam, K., A. Bergman Rosamond and A. Kronsell (2019), 'Theorising feminist foreign policy', *International Relations*, 33(1): 23–39.

Al Jazeera (2017), 'Gaining ground: The battle for Marawi', 30 October. Available online: https://www.aljazeera.com/gallery/2017/10/30/gaining-ground-the-battle-for-marawi/ (accessed 28 April 2023).

Al Jazeera (2022a), 'Ethiopia starts electricity production at Blue Nile mega-dam', 20 February. Available online: https://www.aljazeera.com/news/2022/2/20/ethiopia-electricity-production-gerd-blue-nile-mega-dam (accessed 20 December 2022).

Al Jazeera (2022b), 'Ethiopia's Blue Nile mega-dam explained', 21 February. Available online: https://www.aljazeera.com/news/2021/7/8/explainer-ethiopias-massive-nile-dam (accessed 20 December 2022).

Al Jazeera (2022c), 'Putin warns of hitting "new targets" if Kyiv gets new missiles', 5 June. Available online: https://www.aljazeera.com/news/2022/6/5/russia-to-strike-new-targets-if-kyiv-sent-long-range-rockets (accessed 25 January 2023).

Alvarez, S. (2009), 'Beyond NGO-ization? Reflections from Latin America', *Development*, 52: 175–84.

Amazon Frontlines (2022), 'Ecuador's Supreme Court Makes Historic Ruling Recognizing Indigenous Right to Consent Over Oil and Mining Projects'. Available online: https://amazonfrontlines.org/chronicles/ecuador-supreme-court-recognizes-indigenous-right-to-consent-over-oil-and-mining/ (accessed 13 December 2022).

Anderson, B. (1991), *Imagined Communities: Reflections on the Origin and Spread of Nationalism*, London: Verso.

Anievas, A. (2010), *Marxism and World Politics*, London: Routledge.

Annan, K. (2005), '"In Larger Freedom": Decision Time at the UN'. Available online: https://www.un.org/sg/en/content/sg/articles/2005-04-25/larger-freedom-decision-time-un (accessed 27 April 2023).

Asmakov, A. (2022), 'Pro-Russian Paramilitary Groups Raised $400,000 in Bitcoin, Crypto to Avoid Sanctions', Decrypt, 3 October. Available online: https://decrypt.co/111080/pro-russian-groups-raising-sanctions-evading-funds-crypto (accessed 12 May 2023).

Assassi, L. (2009), *The Gendering of Global Finance*, Basingstoke: Palgrave Macmillan.

Atkins, J. and J. Gaffney (2020), 'Narrative, persona and performance: The case of Theresa May 2016–2017', *The British Journal of Politics and International Relations*, 22(2): 145–366.

Auty, R. M. (1993), *Sustaining Development in Mineral Economies: The Resource Curse Thesis*, London: Routledge.

Axelrod, J. (2019), 'A Century Later: The Treaty of Versailles and Its Rejection of Racial Equality', *NPR*. Available online: https://www.npr.org/sections/codeswitch/2019/08/11/742293305/a-century-later-the-treaty-of-versailles-and-its-rejection-of-racial-equality (accessed 10 February 2023).

Azevedo, R. (2020), 'The WTO's 25 years of achievement and challenges'. Available online: https://www.wto.org/english/news_e/news20_e/dgra_01jan20_e.htm (accessed 8 November 2022).

Azizah, N., A. Maksum and M. A. Hidayahtulloh (2020), 'Enhancing women contribution in peace, conflict resolution and security agenda: Indonesian female peacekeepers in the United Nations peacekeeping operations', *Revista UNISCI*, 18(53): 111–29.

Bagchi, S. S. and A. Das (2012), 'Introduction: Human Rights and the Third World: Issues and Discourses', in S. S. Bagchi and A. Das (eds), *Human Rights and the Third World: Issues and Discourses*, 7–20, Lanham, MD: Lexington Books.

Balci, A. (2017), 'Writing the world into counter-hegemony: Identity, power, and "foreign policy" in ethnic movements', *International Relations*, 31(4): 466–83.

Baldwin, D. A. (1997), 'The concept of security', *Review of International Studies*, 23(1): 5–26.

Bank, C. and M. Blyth (2013), 'The BRICS and the Washington Consensus: An introduction', *Review of International Political Economy*, 20(2): 241–55.

Bank of England (2022), 'Cross-border payments'. Available online: https://www.bankofengland.co.uk/payment-and-settlement/cross-border-payments (accessed 2 November 2022).

Barkawi, T. (2016), 'Decolonising war', *European Journal of International Security*, 1(2): 199–214.

Barnett, M. N. and M. Finnemore (1999), 'The politics, power, and pathologies of international organizations', *International Organization*, 53(4), 699–732.

Barrientos, S., G. Gereffi and J. Pickles (2016), 'New dynamics of upgrading in global value chains: Sifting terrain for suppliers and workers in the global south', *Environment and Planning A*, 48(7): 1214–19.

Basso, P. (2015), 'Neoliberalism, Crisis and International Migration', in L. Pradella and T. Marois (eds), *Polarizing Development: Alternatives to Neoliberalism and the Crisis*, 86–97, London: Pluto Press.

Bates, R. H. (2008), 'The logic of state failure: Learning from late-century Africa', *Conflict Management and Peace Science*, 25(4): 297–314.

BBC News (2020a), 'Coronavirus: The world in lockdown in maps and charts'. Available online: https://www.bbc.co.uk/news/world-52103747 (accessed 24 August 2022).

BBC News (2020b), 'US China tariffs "inconsistent" with trade rules says WTO', 15 September. Available online: https://www.bbc.co.uk/news/business-54168419 (accessed 12 May 2023).

BBC News (2020c), 'Myanmar Rohingya: What you need to know about the crisis', 23 January. Available online: https://www.bbc.co.uk/news/world-asia-41566561 (accessed 20 January 2023).

BBC News (2021), 'What is Black Lives Matter and what are the aims?', 13 June. Available online: https://www.bbc.co.uk/news/explainers-53337780 (accessed 29 September 2022).

BBC News (2022), 'Millions in Bitcoin pouring into Ukraine from donors', 26 February. Available online: https://www.bbc.co.uk/news/technology-60541942 (accessed 12 May 2023).

BBC News (2023), 'Covid global health emergency is over, declares WHO', 5 May. Available online: https://www.bbc.co.uk/news/health-65499929 (accessed 28 May 2023).

Beasley, R., J. Kaarbo and K. Oppermann (2021), 'Role theory, foreign policy, and the social construction of sovereignty: Brexit stage right', *Global Studies Quarterly*, doi: 10.1093/isagsq/ksab001.

Bell, D. and S. Vucetic (2019), 'Brexit, CANZUK, and the legacy of empire', *The British Journal of Politics and International Relations*, 21(2): 367–82.

Bellamy, A. (2011), 'Libya and the responsibility to protect: The exception and the norm', *Ethics & International Affairs*, 25(3): 263–9.

Bellamy, A. (2020), 'Thinking about world peace', *Ethics & International Affairs*, 34(1): 47–56.

Bellamy, A. and E. Luck (2018), *The Responsibility to Protect: From Promise to Practice*, Cambridge: Polity Press.

Benería, L. (2003), *Gender, Development and Globalization: Economics as if All People Mattered*, London: Routledge.

Benería, L., C. D. Deere and N. Kabeer (2012), 'Gender and international migration: Globalization, development, and governance', *Feminist Economics*, 18(2): 1–33.

Bernstein, S. (2020), 'The absence of great power responsibility in global environmental politics', *European Journal of International Relations*, 26(1): 8–32.

Bhambra, G. K., D. Gebrial and K. Nişancıoğlu (2018), *Decolonising the University*, London: Pluto Press.

Bieler, A. and A. Morton (2018), *Global Capitalism, Global War, Global Crisis*, Cambridge: Cambridge University Press.

Biswas, S. (2014), *Nuclear Desire: Power and the Postcolonial Nuclear Order*, Minneapolis, MN: Minnesota University Press.

Björkdahl, A. (2002), 'Norms in international relations: Some conceptual and methodological reflections', *Cambridge Review of International Affairs*, 15(1): 9–23.

Björnberg, K. E., M. Karlsson, M. Gilek and S. O. Hansson (2017), 'Climate and environmental science denial: A review of the scientific literature published in 1990–2015', *Journal of Cleaner Production*, 167: 229–41.

Blagden, D. (2019), 'Two visions of greatness: Roleplay and realpolitik in UK strategic posture', *Foreign Policy Analysis*, 15(4): 471–2.

Blaney, D. L. and A. B. Tickner (2017), 'Worlding, ontological politics and the possibility of a decolonial IR', *Millennium*, 45(3): 267–510.

Blanton, R. G. (2013), 'Zombies and international relations: A simple guide for bringing the undead into the classroom', *International Studies Perspectives*, 14(1): 1–13.

Bøås, M. and K. Jennings (2007), '"Failed states" and "State failure": Threats or opportunities?' *Globalizations*, 4(4): 475–85.

Bremmer, I. (2018), 'The "Strongman Era" Is Here. Here's What It Means for You', *Time Magazine*, 3 May. Available online: https://time.com/5264170/the-strongmen-era-is-here-heres-what-it-means-for-you/ (accessed 18 May 2023).

Brewer, A. (1990), *Marxist Theories of Imperialism: A Critical Survey*, 2nd edn, London: Routledge.

Brick, J., N. Wilson, D. Wong and M. Herke (2019), *Academic Success: A Student's Guide to Studying at University*, London: Red Globe Press.

Broome, A. (2014), *Issues and Actors in the Global Political Economy*, London: Palgrave Macmillan.

Browning, C. (2018), 'Brexit, existential anxiety and ontological (in)security', *European Security*, 27(3): 336–55.

Budabin, A. C. and L. A. Richey (2021), *Batman Saves the Congo: How Celebrities Disrupt the Politics of Development*, Minneapolis, MN: Minnesota University Press.

Bull, H. (1980), 'The great irresponsibles? The United States, the Soviet Union, and world order', *International Journal*, 35(3): 437–47.

Bullock, K. (2022), 'Ukraine war shows it's time to do away with the racist "Clash of Civilizations" theory', *The Conversation*, 21 March. Available online: https://theconversation.com/ukraine-war-shows-its-time-to-do-away-with-the-racist-clash-of-civilizations-theory-178297 (accessed 11 February 2023).

Burcher, C. U. (2018), 'What cryptocurrencies will do to the integrity of politics', *World Economic Forum*, 16 April. Available online: https://www.weforum.org/agenda/2018/04/what-cryptocurrencies-will-do-to-the-integrity-of-politics (accessed 12 May 2023).

Burke, R. (2006), '"The compelling dialogue of freedom": Human rights at the Bandung Conference', *Human Rights Quarterly*, 28(4): 947–65.

Burt, R. (2011), 'The new geopolitics: Why nuclear weapons no longer serve US interests', *Cornell International Affairs Review*, 4(1): 19–25.

Buzan, B. and L. Hansen (2009), *The Evolution of International Security Studies*, Cambridge: Cambridge University Press.

Buzan, B. and R. Little (2000), *International Systems in World History: Remaking the Study of International Relations*, Oxford: Oxford University Press.

Cadestin, C., K. De Backer, I. Desnoyers-James, S. Miroudot, M. Ye and D. Rigo (2018), 'Multinational enterprises and global value chains: New insights on the trade-investment nexus', OECD Science, Technology and Industry Working Papers 2018/05. Available online: https://www.oecd-ilibrary.org/industry-and-services/multinational-enterprises-and-global-value-chains_194ddb63-en (accessed 10 November 2022).

Campbell-Verduyn, M. ed. (2018), *Bitcoin and Beyond: Cryptocurrencies, Blockchains, and Global Governance*, Abingdon: Routledge.

Carbone, M. (2007), *The European Union and International Development: The Politics of Foreign Aid*, London: Routledge.

Carl, N., J. Dennison and G. Evans (2018), 'European but not European enough: An explanation for Brexit', *European Union Politics*, 20(2): 282–304.

Carr, E. H. (2021), *Nationalism and After*, London: Springer Nature Limited.

Carrozza, I., I. Danewid and E. Pauls (2017), 'Racialized Realities in World Politics', *Millennium*, 45(3): 267–8.

CBN News (2020), 'FBI Director tells lawmakers terrorism is still number 1 national security threat', 17 September. Available online: https://www1.cbn.com/cbnnews/national-security/2020/september/fbi-director-tells-lawmakers-terrorism-is-still-number-1-national-security-threat (accessed 27 September 2022).

CBS News (2022), 'Russia fumes as Finland and Sweden push for NATO membership', 13 May. Available online: https://www.cbsnews.com/news/finland-nato-russia-sweden-ukraine-united-states-vladimir-putin/ (accessed 18 May 2023).

Cequea, A. (2019), 'El Pasoans march for truth during Trump visit', *Act.tv*, 10 April. Available online: https://www.act.tv/latest-news1/trump-in-el-paso (accessed 14 February 2023).

Central Intelligence Agency [CIA] (n.d.), *Field Listing – Religions*, The World Factbook. Available online: https://www.cia.gov/the-world-factbook/field/religions/ (accessed 8 February 2023).

Central Intelligence Agency [CIA] (1985), 'The Cuban presence in Angola', Interagency Intelligence Assessment, 15 November. Available online: https://www.cia.gov/readingroom/docs/CIA-RDP88T00565R000600890002-7.pdf (accessed 6 June 2023).

Chandhoke, N. (2005), 'How global is global civil society?' *Journal of World-Systems Research* 11(2): 355–71.

Charbonneau, B. (2014), 'The imperial legacy of international peacebuilding: The case of Francophone Africa', *Review of International Studies*, 40(3): 607–30.

Chauvet, L. and P. Collier (2008), 'What are the preconditions for turnarounds in failing states?', *Conflict Management and Peace Science*, 25(4): 332–48.

Cheikh, N. (2013), 'Stories behind the western-led humanitarian intervention in Libya: A critical analysis', *African Journal of Political Science and International Relations*, 7(3): 154–63.

Chibber, V. (2013), *Postcolonial Theory and the Specter of Capital*, London: Verso.

Chiozza, G. (2002), 'Is there a clash of civilizations? Evidence from patterns of international conflict, 1946–97', *Journal of Peace Research*, 39(6): 711–34.

Chowdhry, G. and S. Nair, eds (2002), *Power, Postcolonialism and International Relations: Reading Race, Gender and Class*, New York: Routledge.

Chu, L. T. (2012), 'God is not dead or violent: The Catholic Church, just war, and the "resurgence" of religion', *Politics and Religion*, 5(2): 419–40.

Churchill, W. (1946), '"Iron Curtain" Speech, "Sinews of Peace",' 5 March 1946, History and Public Policy. Available online: http://digitalarchive.wilsoncenter.org/document/116180 (accessed 20 April 2022).

Clark, M. (2011), 'Indonesia's postcolonial regional imaginary: From a "neutralist" to an "all-directions" foreign policy', *Japanese Journal of Political Science*, 12(2): 287–304.

Clarke, H., M. Goodwin and P. Whiteley (2017), 'Why Britain voted for Brexit: An individual-level analysis of the 2016 referendum vote', *Parliamentary Affairs*, 70: 439–64.

Clayton, G. and H. Dorussen (2022), 'The effectiveness of mediation and peacekeeping for ending conflict', *Journal of Peace Research* 59(2): 150–65.

Cockburn, C. (2019), 'The Continuum of Violence: A Gender Perspective on War and Peace', in C. Cockburn, G. Wenona and J. Hyndman (eds), *Sites of Violence: Gender and Conflict Zones*, 24–44, Berkeley, CA: University of California Press.

Cohn, C. (1987), 'Sex and death in the rational world of defense intellectuals', *Signs*, 12(4): 687–718.

Cohn, N. (2016), 'Why the Surprise over "Brexit"? Don't Blame the Polls', *New York Times*, 24 June. Available online: https://www.nytimes.com/2016/06/25/upshot/why-the-surprise-over-brexit-dont-blame-the-polls.html (accessed 31 January 2023).

Cole, T. (2012), 'The White-Savior Industrial Complex', *The Atlantic*, 21 March. Available online: https://www.theatlantic.com/international/archive/2012/03/the-white-savior-industrial-complex/254843/ (accessed 29 January 2023).

Common Security (2022), 'Common Security 2022: For our shared future'. Available online: https://commonsecurity.org/about-common-security-2022/ (accessed 23 September 2022).

Council of Europe (2022), 'Exclusion of the Russian Federation from the Council of Europe and suspension of all relations with Belarus'. Available online: https://www.coe.int/en/web/cdcj/-/russian-federation-excluded-from-the-council-of-europe (accessed 28 April 2023).

Coward, H. and G. S. Smith (2004), *Religion and Peacebuilding*, New York: State University of New York Press.

Cowen, T. (2022), 'Putin's Nuclear Threat Makes Armageddon Thinkable', *Washington Post*, 21 April. Available online: https://www.washingtonpost.com/business/energy/putins-nuclear-threat-makes-armageddon-thinkable/2022/04/20/d40b8fe2-c0cc-11ec-b5df-1fba61a66c75_story.html (accessed 22 September 2022).

Cox, R. (1971), 'Labor and transnational relations', *International Organization*, 25(3): 554–84.

Cox, R. (1981), 'Social forces, states and world orders: Beyond international relations theory', *Millennium*, 10(2): 126–55.

Cox, R. (1996), *Approaches to World Order*, Cambridge: Cambridge University Press.

Cox, R. (1999), 'Civil society at the turn of the millennium: Prospects for an alternative world order', *Review of International Studies*, 25(1): 3–28.

Cox, R. and T. Sinclair (1996), *Approaches to World Order*, Cambridge: Cambridge University Press.

Credit Suisse (2022), 'Global Wealth Report 2022'. Available online: https://www.credit-suisse.com/about-us/en/reports-research/global-wealth-report.html (accessed 10 November 2022).

Cross, M. (2017), *The Politics of Crisis in Europe*, Cambridge: Cambridge University Press.

Crypto (2023), 'IRS Trains Ukraine Law Enforcement to Track and Trace Russia's Cryptocurrency Moves', *Crypto Breaking News*, 11 May. Available online: https://www.cryptobreaking.com/irs-trains-ukraine-law-enforcement-to-track-and-trace-russias-cryptocurrency-moves/ (accessed 12 May 2023).

Da Vinha, L. (2019), 'Maps of War and Peace: Rethinking Geography in International Affairs', *Brown Journal of World Affairs*, 25(2): 73–92.

Daddow, O. (2019), 'Global Britain™: The discursive construction of Britain's post-Brexit world role', *Global Affairs*, 5(1): 5–22.

Das, U. (2019), 'What is the Indo-Pacific?', *The Diplomat*, 13 July. Available online: https://thediplomat.com/2019/07/what-is-the-indo-pacific/ (accessed 28 April 2023).

Davenport, C., M. Erik and P. M. Regan (2018), *The Peace Continuum: What It Is and How to Study It*, New York: Oxford University Press.

Dávid-Barrett, E., M. Fazekas, O. Hellmann, L. Márk and C. McCorley (2020), 'Controlling corruption in development aid: New evidence from contract-level data', *Studies in Comparative International Development*, 55: 481–515.

Davies, S. E. (2013), 'National Security and Pandemics', *UN Chronicle*, No. 2, Vol. L, Security. Available online: https://www.un.org/en/chronicle/article/national-security-and-pandemics (accessed 4 May 2023).

De Haas, H. (2005), 'International migration, remittances and development: Myths and facts', *Third World Quarterly*, 26(8): 1269–84.

Delehanty, W. and B. Steele (2009), 'Engaging the narrative in ontological (in)security theory: Insights from feminist IR', *Cambridge Review of International Affairs*, 22(3): 523–40.

Dermarkar, S. and M. Hazgui (2022), 'How the Russia-Ukraine conflict has put cryptocurrency in the spotlight', *The Conversation*, 6 April. Available online: https://theconversation.com/how-the-russia-ukraine-conflict-has-put-cryptocurrencies-in-the-spotlight-180527 (accessed 12 May 2023).

Devermont, J. and C. Chiang (2019), 'Innocent Bystanders: Why the U.S.-China Trade War Hurts African Economies', Center for Strategic and International Studies, 9 April. Available online: https://www.csis.org/analysis/innocent-bystanders-why-us-china-trade-war-hurts-african-economies (accessed 12 May 2023).

DeWind, J. and D. Ergun (2013), 'Development and Migration: Historical Trends and Future Research', in J. Cortina and E. Ochoa-Reza (eds), *New Perspectives on International Migration and Development*, 5–42, Columbia, NY: Columbia University Press.

Dietz, T., K. Havenevik, M. Kaag and T. Oestigaard, eds (2011), *African Engagements: Africa Negotiating an Emerging Multipolar World*, London: Brill.

Dodds, K. J. (2005), *Global Geopolitics: A Critical Introduction*, Abingdon: Routledge.

Donnelly, J. (2013), *Universal Human Rights in Theory and Practice*, 3rd edn, Ithaca, NY: Cornell University Press.

Douthat, R. (2022), 'Vladimir Putin's Clash of Civilizations', *New York Times*, 26 February. Available online: https://www.nytimes.com/2022/02/26/opinion/vladimir-putin-clash-of-civilizations.html (accessed 11 February 2023).

Downer, A. (2023), 'Morrison's legacy will turn Australia into a significant power', *Australian Financial Review*, 12 May. Available online: https://www.afr.com/policy/foreign-affairs/morrison-s-aukus-legacy-elevates-australia-above-also-ran-middle-power-20230309-p5cqmn (accessed 18 May 2023).

Doyle, M. (1986), *Empires*, Ithaca, NY: Cornell University Press.

Doyle, M. (2016), 'The politics of global humanitarianism: The responsibility to protect before and after Libya', *International Politics*, 53(1): 14–31.

Drezner, D. (2022), *Theories of International Politics and Zombies*, Apocalypse edition. Princeton, NJ: Princeton University Press.

Du Bois, W. E. B. (2015), *The Problem of the Color Line at the Turn of the Twentieth Century: The Essential Early Essays*, edited by N. D. Chandler, New York: Fordham University Press.

Dumbrava, C. (2022), 'Walls and fences at EU borders', *European Parliament Research Service*, Briefing, PE 733.692. Available online: https://www.europarl.europa.eu/RegData/etudes/BRIE/2022/733692/EPRS_BRI(2022)733692_EN.pdf (accessed 11 February 2023).

Dunn, B. (2008), *Global Political Economy: A Marxist Critique*, London: Pluto Press.

Easterly, W. (2002), 'The cartel of good intentions: The problem of bureaucracy in foreign aid', *The Journal of Policy Reform*, 5(4): 223–50.

Enloe, C. H. (1993), *The Morning After: Sexual Politics at the End of the Cold War*, Berkeley, CA: University of California Press.

Enloe, C. H. (2014), *Bananas, Beaches and Bases: Making Feminist Sense of International Politics*, 2nd edn, Berkeley, CA: University of California Press.

Erskine, T. (2008), 'Locating Responsibility: The Problem of Moral Agency in International Relations', in C. Reus-Smit and D. Snidal (eds), 699–707, *The Oxford Handbook of International Relations*, Oxford: Oxford University Press.

Eurasia Group (2022), *Top Risks 2022*. Available online: https://www.eurasiagroup.net/files/upload/EurasiaGroup_TopRisks2022.pdf (accessed 29 September 2022).

European Council (2022), 'Burundi: EU lifts existing restrictions under Article 96 of the ACP-EU Partnership Agreement', Press release, 8 February. Available online: https://www.consilium.europa.eu/en/press/press-releases/2022/02/08/burundi-eu-lifts-existing-restrictions-under-article-96-of-the-acp-eu-partnership-agreement/ (accessed 22 November 2022).

Fernández Moreno, M., C. Braga and M. Siman Gomes (2012), 'Trapped between many worlds: A post-colonial perspective on the UN mission in Haiti (MINUSTAH)', *International Peacekeeping*, 19(3): 377–92.

Fierke, K. M. and K. E. Jørgensen (2001), *Constructing International Relations: The Next Generation*, Armonk, NY: M. E. Sharpe.

Financial Times (2015), 'The Doha round finally dies a merciful death', 21 December. Available online: https://www.ft.com/content/9cb1ab9e-a7e2-11e5-955c-1e1d6de94879 (accessed 12 May 2023).

Finnemore, M. (1996), *National Interests and International Society*, Ithaca, NY: Cornell University Press.

Finnemore, M. and K. Sikkink (1998), 'International norm dynamics and political change', *International Organization*, 52(4): 887–917.

Fishel, S. and L. Wilcox (2017), 'Politics of the living dead: Race and exceptionalism in the apocalypse', *Millennium*, 45(3): 335 –55.

Florea, A. (2014), 'De facto states in international politics (1945–2011): A new data set', *International Interactions*, 40: 788–811.

Food and Agriculture Organization of the United Nations [FAO] (2020), *Global Forest Resources Assessment 2020*, Main Report. Available online: https://www.fao.org/3/ca9825en/ca9825en.pdf (accessed 12 December 2022).

Forsythe, D. (2018), *Human Rights in International Relations*, 4th edn, Cambridge: Cambridge University Press.

Fox News (2019), 'Democrats call border wall racist and immoral, deny immigration crisis', 8 January. Available online: https://www.foxnews.com/transcript/democrats-call-border-wall-racist-and-immoral-deny-immigration-crisis (accessed 10 February 2023).

Fragile States Index (2018), 'What Does State Fragility Mean?' Available online: https://fragilestatesindex.org/frequently-asked-questions/what-does-state-fragility-mean/ (accessed 24 June 2022).

Frank, A. G. (1967), *Capitalism and Underdevelopment in Latin America*, New York: Monthly Review Press.

Frederking, B. and C. Patane (2017), 'Legitimacy and the UN Security Council', *PS: Political Science & Politics*, 50(2): 347–53.

Freedom House (2022), 'Countering an Authoritarian Overhaul of the Internet: Freedom on the Net 2022 Report'. Available online: https://freedomhouse.org/report/freedom-net/2022/countering-authoritarian-overhaul-internet (accessed 30 April 2023).

Freeman, C. W. Jr. (1997), *Arts of Power: Statecraft and Diplomacy*, Washington, DC: United States Institute of Peace Press.

Frick, M. (2012), 'Universal Claim and Postcolonial Realities: The Deep Unease over Western-Centred Human Rights Standards in the Global South', in S. S. Bagchi and A. Das (eds), *Human Rights and the Third World: Issues and Discourses*, 21–33, Lanham, MD: Lexington Books.

Gallagher, P. R. (2017), 'The Holy See Perspective on Contemporary International Issues', His Excellency Paul Richard Gallagher, Secretary of Relations with States of the Holy See, Speech to Fordham University, 25 September. Available online: https://holyseemission.org/contents//statements/59ca7e772e36c.php#:~:text (accessed 11 February 2023).

Gallarotti, G. M. (2015), 'Smart power: Definitions, importance, and effectiveness', *Journal of Strategic Studies*, 3: 245–81.

Gandhi, L. (1998), *Postcolonial Theory: A Critical Introduction*, Crows Nest, New South Wales: Allen & Unwin.

García, M. (2019), 'The border wall isn't just a dividing line – it's a monument against racial progress', *The Guardian*, 25 April. Available online: https://www.theguardian.com/commentisfree/2019/apr/25/border-wall-south-texas-national-identity-exclusion (accessed 10 February 2023).

GE Gas Power (n.d.), 'Coal to gas transition: Junliangcheng Power Plant in China'. Available online: https://www.ge.com/gas-power/resources/case-studies/junliangcheng-plant-coal-to-gas-conversion (accessed 6 June 2023).

Gereffi, G. (2014), 'Global value chains in a post-Washington Consensus', *Review of International Political Economy*, 21(1): 9–37.

Germain, R. and M. Kenny, eds (2004), *The Idea of Global Civil Society*, London: Routledge.

Gilpin, R. (1987), *The Political Economy of International Relations*, Princeton, NJ: Princeton University Press.

Glendon, M. A. (2001), *A World Made New: Eleanor Roosevelt and the Universal Declaration of Human Rights*, New York: Random House.

Global Centre for the Responsibility to Protect [GCR2P] (2023), 'UN Security Council Resolutions and Presidential Statements Referencing R2P', 15 March. Available online: https://www.globalr2p.org/resources/un-security-council-resolutions-and-presidential-statements-referencing-r2p/ (accessed 14 May 2023).

Godfrey, J. (2018), *How to Use Your Reading in Your Essays*, 3rd edn, London: Palgrave Macmillan.

Goklany, I. (2021), 'Reduction in global habitat loss from fossil-fuel-dependent increases in cropland productivity', *Conservation Practice and Policy*, 35(3): 766–74.

Goldstone, J. A. (2008), 'Pathways to state failure', *Conflict Management and Peace*, 25(4): 285–96.

Granton, M. (2021), 'View from The Hill: For Morrison AUKUS is all about the deal, never mind the niceties', *The Conversation*, 19 September. Available online: https://theconversation.com/view-from-the-hill-for-morrison-aukus-is-all-about-the-deal-never-mind-the-niceties-168248 (accessed 18 May 2023).

Griffin, P. (2016), 'Feminist Political Economy', in J. Steans and D. Tepe-Belfrage (eds), *Handbook on Gender in World Politics*, 345–53, Cheltenham: Edward Elgar Publishing.

Groch, S. (2023), 'What is AUKUS and what are we getting in Australia's biggest ever defence spend?', *The Sydney Morning Herald*. Available online: https://www.smh.com.au/politics/federal/what-is-aukus-and-what-are-we-getting-in-australia-s-biggest-ever-defence-spend-20230310-p5cr2j.html (accessed 18 May 2023).

Gupta, J. (2019), 'The puzzle of the global commons or the tragedy of inequality: Revisiting Hardin', *Environment: Science and Policy for Sustainable Development*, 61(1): 16–25.

Hardin, G. (1968), 'The tragedy of the commons', *Science*, 162: 1243–8.

Hardin, G. (1974), 'Commentary: Living on a life boat', *Science*, 24(10): 561–8.

Harfoot, M., D. P. Tittensor, S. Knight, A. P. Arnell, S. Blyth, S. Brooks, S. H. M. Butchart, J. Hutton, M. I. Jones, V. Kapos, J. P. W. Scharlemann and N. D. Burgess (2018), 'Present and future biodiversity risks from fossil fuel exploitation', *Conservation Letters*, 11:e12448. DOI: 10.1111/conl.12448.

Harman, S. (2021), 'Threat not solution: Gender, global health security and COVID-19', *International Affairs*, 97(3): 601–23.

Hathaway, O. and S. Shapiro (2017), 'Outlawing War? It Actually Worked', *New York Times*. Available online: https://www.nytimes.com/2017/09/02/opinion/sunday/outlawing-war-kellogg-briand.html (accessed 31 May 2022).

Hay, C. and M. Lister (2006), 'Introduction: Theories of the State', in C. Hay, M. Lister and D. Marsh (eds), *The State: Theories and Issues*, Basingstoke: Palgrave Macmillan.

Hempel, J. (2015), 'Zuckerberg to the UN: The Internet Belongs to Everyone', *Wired*, 28 September. Available online: https://www.wired.com/2015/09/zuckerberg-to-un-internet-belongs-to-everyone/ (accessed 30 April 2023).

Henderson, E. (2013), 'Hidden in plain sight: Racism in international relations theory', *Cambridge Review of International Affairs*, 26(1): 71–92.

Herman, L. and G. C. Hufauer (2011), 'Doha is Dead', *Foreign Policy*, 26 September. Available online: https://foreignpolicy.com/2011/09/26/doha-is-dead/ (accessed 12 May 2023).

Hill, C. (2003), *The Changing Politics of Foreign Policy*, London: Palgrave Macmillan.

Hill, C. (2023), 'Debating Britain's role in the world: From decolonization to Brexit', *International Politics*. Available online: https://doi.org/10.1057/s41311-023-00454-8. (accessed 27 August 2023).

Hinsley, F. H. (1967), 'The concept of sovereignty and the relations between states', *Journal of International Affairs*, 21(2): 242–52.

HM Government (2021), *Global Britain in a Competitive Age: The Integrated Review of Security, Defence, Development and Foreign Policy*, Command Paper 403, March.

Hollis, M. and S. Smith (1990), *Explaining and Understanding International Relations*, Oxford: Clarendon Press.

Holsti, K. J. (1970), 'National role conceptions in the study of foreign policy', *International Studies Quarterly*, 14(3): 233–309.

Holsti, K. J. (1991), *Peace and War: Armed Conflicts and International Order 1648–1989*, Cambridge: Cambridge University Press.

Holsti, K. J. (1995), *International Politics: A Framework for Analysis*, 7th edn, Englewood Cliffs, NJ: Prentice Hall.

Hoover, J. (2012), 'Reconstructing responsibility and moral agency in world politics', *International Theory*, 4(2): 233–68.

Hoyoon, J. (2019), 'The Evolution of Social Constructivism in Political Science: Past to Present', Sage Open. Available online: https://journals.sagepub.com/doi/full/10.1177/2158244019832703 (accessed 21 March 2023).

Huntington, S. (1993), 'Clash of civilizations?' *Foreign Affairs*, 72(3): 22–49.

Huntington, S. (1996), *The Clash of Civilizations and the Remaking of World Order*, London: Simon & Schuster.

Hyett, S. (1996), 'The Uruguay Round of the GATT: The United Kingdom Standpoint', in N. Emiliou and D. O'Keefe (eds), *The European Union and World Trade Law: After the GATT Uruguay Round*, 91–102, Chichester: Wiley.

Ikenberry, G. J. (2017), 'The rise, character, and evolution of international orders', in O. Fioretos (ed.), *International Politics and Institutions in Time*, 59–76, Oxford: Oxford University Press.

Inglehart, R. F. (2020), 'Giving up on God: The global decline of religion', *Foreign Affairs*, 99(5): 110.

Institute for Economics and Peace (2014), 'Five Questions Answered on the Link Between Peace & Religion'. Available online: https://www.economicsandpeace.org/wp-content/uploads/2015/06/Peace-and-Religion-Report.pdf (accessed 12 February 2023).

Intergovernmental Panel on Climate Change (2014), *Climate Change 2014: Synthesis Report*, Contribution of Working Groups I, II and III to the Fifth Assessment Report of the Intergovernmental Panel on Climate Change, Geneva: IPCC.

Intergovernmental Panel on Climate Change (2021), *Climate Change 2021: The Physical Science Basis. Summary for Policymakers*. Available online: https://www.ipcc.ch/report/ar6/wg1/downloads/report/IPCC_AR6_WGI_SPM.pdf (accessed 8 December 2022).

Intergovernmental Panel on Climate Change (2023), *Synthesis Report of the IPCC Sixth Assessment Period (AR6)*. Available online: https://www.ipcc.ch/report/ar6/syr/downloads/report/IPCC_AR6_SYR_SPM.pdf (accessed 13 May 2023).

International Chamber of Shipping (2022), 'Shipping and world trade: driving prosperity'. Available online: https://www.ics-shipping.org/shipping-fact/shipping-and-world-trade-driving-prosperity/ (accessed 4 November 2022).

International Commission on Intervention and State Sovereignty [ICISS] (2001), *The Responsibility to Protect*, Ottawa: International Development Research Centre. Available online: https://www.idrc.ca/en/book/responsibility-protect-report-international-commission-intervention-and-state-sovereignty (accessed 14 May 2023).

International Court of Justice [ICJ] (2022), 'Application of the Convention on the Prevention and Punishment of the Crime of Genocide (The Gambia v. Myanmar)'. Available online: https://www.icj-cij.org/en/case/178 (accessed 15 January 2023).

International Criminal Court [ICC] (n.d.), 'About the Court'. Available online: https://www.icc-cpi.int/about/the-court (accessed 11 January 2023).

International Criminal Court [ICC] (2011), 'Rome Statute'. Available online: https://www.icc-cpi.int/sites/default/files/RS-Eng.pdf (accessed 14 May 2023).

International Energy Agency [IEA] (2022), 'World Energy Outlook 2022: Executive Summary'. Available online: https://www.iea.org/reports/world-energy-outlook-2022/executive-summary (accessed 8 December 2022).

International Labour Organization [ILO] (2021), *ILO Global Estimates on International Migrant Workers: Results and Methodology*, 3rd edn, Geneva: ILO.

International Monetary Fund [IMF] (2021), *Global Financial Stability Report. COVID-19, Crypto, and Climate: Navigating Challenging Transitions*, 21 October, Washington: IMF.

International Organization for Migration [IOM] (2022), *World Migration Report 2022*. Available online: https://worldmigrationreport.iom.int/wmr-2022-interactive/ (accessed 16 November 2022).

Iqbal, Z. and H. Starr (2015), *State Failure in the Modern World*, Stanford CA: Stanford University Press.

Jensen, S. (2016), 'How the Global South shaped the international human rights system'. Available online: https://www.universal-rights.org/blog/how-the-global-south-shaped-the-international-human-rights-system/ (accessed 16 January 2023).

Jett, D. (2019), *Why Peacekeeping Fails*, London: Palgrave Macmillan.

Joachim, J. (2003), 'Framing issues and seizing opportunities: The UN, NGOs, and women's rights', *International Studies Quarterly*, 47(2): 247–274.

Josselin, D. and W. Wallace (2001), *Non-State Actors in World Politics*, London: Palgrave Macmillan.

Kapoor, I. (2002), 'Capitalism, culture, agency: Dependency versus postcolonial theory', *Third World Quarterly*, 23(4): 647–64.

Kapoor, I. (2013), *Celebrity Humanitarianism: The Ideology of Global Charity*, Abingdon: Routledge.

Karanassou, M. and H. Sala (2014), 'The role of the wage-productivity gap in economic activity', *International Review of Applied Economics*, 28(4): 436–59.

Kayatekin, S. A. (2009), 'Between political economy and postcolonial theory: First encounters', *Cambridge Journal of Economics*, 33: 1113–18.

Keane, J. (2003), *Global Civil Society?* Cambridge: Cambridge University Press.

Keck, M. and K. Sikkink (1998), *Activists beyond Borders*, Ithaca, NY: Cornell University Press.

Keenan, G. (1946), 'Long telegram', History and Public Policy Program Digital Archive, *National Archives and Records Administration*, Department of State Records (Record Group 59), 22 February 1946. Available online: https://digitalarchive.wilsoncenter.org/document/116178 (accessed 21 April 2022).

Kelly, R. (2008), 'From international relations to global governance theory: Conceptualizing NGOs after the Rio breakthrough of 1992', *Journal of Civil Society*, 3(1): 81–99.

Kennedy, J. F. (1962), 'United States Military Academy Commencement Address', delivered 6 June, West Point, New York. Available online: https://www.americanrhetoric.com/speeches/jfkwestpointcommencementspeech.htm (accessed 8 June 2022).

Keohane, R. (1984), *After Hegemony: Cooperation and Discord in the World Political Economy*, Princeton, NJ: Princeton University Press.

Kerr, P. H. (1916), 'Political Relations between Advanced and Backward Peoples', in A. J. Grant, F. F. Urquhart, A. Greenwood, J. D. I. Hughes and P. H. Kerr (eds), *An Introduction to the Study of International Relations*, London: Macmillan and Co. Available online: https://archive.org/details/cu31924007464161/page/n11/mode/2up (accessed 10 February 2023).

Kerr, P. (1928), 'The outlawry of war', *Journal of the Royal Institute of International Affairs*, 7(6): 361–88.

Khalid, M. (2011), 'Gender, orientalism and representations of the "other" in the war on terror', *Global Change, Peace & Security*, 23(1): 15–29.

Khanna, P. (2018), 'Cartographic Conceptions for the Twenty-First Century', *Brown Journal of World Affairs*, 25(2): 25–36.

Klotz, A. (2018), *Norms in International Relations: The Struggle against Apartheid*, Ithaca, NY: Cornell University Press.

Kolb, D. (1984), *Experiential learning: experience as the source of learning and development*, Englewood Cliffs, N. JL Prentice-Hall.

Koller, C. (2008), 'The Recruitment of colonial troops in Africa and Asia and their deployment in Europe during the First World War', *Immigrants & Minorities*, 26(1/2): 111–33.

Kolmasova, S. and K. Krulisova (2018), 'Legitimizing military action through "Rape-as-a-weapon" discourse in Libya: Critical feminist analysis', *Politics & Gender*, 15: 130–50.

Krastev, I. (2017), *After Europe*, Philadelphia PA: University of Philadelphia.

Krauthammer, C. (1990/91), 'The unipolar moment', *Foreign Affairs*, 70(1): 23–33.

Krishna, S. (2009), *Globalization and Postcolonialism: Hegemony and Resistance in the Twenty-First Century*, Plymouth: Rowman & Littlefield.

Krook, M. L. and J. True (2012), 'Rethinking the life cycles of international norms: The United Nations and the global promotion of gender equality', *European Journal of International Relations*, 18(1): 103–27.

Lamont, C. (2022), *Research Methods in International Relations*, 2nd edn, London: Sage Publications.

Lamy, P. (2004), *Trade Policy in the Prodi Commission, 1999–2004: An Assessment*, Brussels: European Commission.

Learning Development (2010), 'Model to develop critical thinking', Flyer, Plymouth University. Available online: https://www.plymouth.ac.uk/uploads/production/document/path/1/1710/Critical_Thinking.pdf (accessed 20 January 2023).

Lebow, R. N. (2003), *The Tragic Vision of Politics: Ethics, Interests and Orders*, Cambridge: Cambridge University Press.

Lowy Institute (2022a), 'Security and Defence', Lowy Institute Poll 2022. Available online: https://poll.lowyinstitute.org/themes/security-and-defence/ (accessed 18 May 2023).

Lowy Institute (2022b), 'AUKUS' Lowy Institute Poll 22. Available online: https://poll.lowyinstitute.org/charts/aukus/ (accessed 18 May 2023).

MacQueen, N. (2020), 'The peacekeeping legacy in Timor-Leste: Imperial re-encounters?', *International Peacekeeping*, 27(1): 29–34.

March, J. G. and J. P. Olsen (1998), 'The institutional dynamics of international political orders', *International Organization*, 4: 943–69.

Matthews, D. (2022), 'The rise and rise of GiveDirectly', *Vox*, 31 August. Available online: https://www.vox.com/future-perfect/2022/8/31/23329242/givedirectly-cash-transfers-rory-stewart (accessed 21 November 2022).

McArthur, J. W. and K. Rasmussen (2017), 'How successful were the Millennium Development Goals?' *Brookings*, 11 January. Available online: https://www.brookings.edu/blog/future-development/2017/01/11/how-successful-were-the-millennium-development-goals/ (accessed 13 May 2023).

McSweeney, B. (1999), *Security, Identity and Interests: A Sociology of International Relations*, Cambridge: Cambridge University Press.

Mearsheimer, J. (2001), *The Tragedy of Great Power Politics*, New York: W. W. Norton.

Mende, J. (2021), 'Are human rights western – And why does it matter? A perspective from international political theory', *Journal of International Political Theory*, 17(1): 38–57.

Mezzadri, A., S. Newman and S. Stevano (2022), 'Feminist global political economies of work and social reproduction', *Review of International Political Economy*, 29(6): 1783–1803.

Mildner, S. A., S. Richter and G. Lauster (2011), *Resource Scarcity – A Global Security Threat?*, Stiftung Wissenschaft und Politik (SWP) Research Paper, Berlin. Available online: https://www.swp-berlin.org/publications/products/research_papers/2011_RP02_lag_mdn_rsv_ks.pdf (accessed 19 December 2022).

Milner, H. and A. Moravcsik, eds (2009), *Power, Interests and Nonstate Actors in World Politics*, Princeton, NJ: Princeton University Press.

Moaz, Z. and E. A. Henderson (2020), *Scriptures, Shrines, Scapegoats, and World Politics: Religious Sources of Conflict and Cooperation in the Modern Era*, Michigan: University of Michigan Press.

Morgenthau, H. J. ([1948] 1985), *Politics among Nations: The Struggle for Power and Peace*, 6th edn, revised and edited by K. W. Thompson, New York: McGraw Hill.

Morin, J. F. and J. Paquin (2018), *Foreign Policy Analysis: A Toolbox*, London: Palgrave Macmillan.

Morris, J. and N. Wheeler (2007), 'The Security Council's crisis of legitimacy and the use of force', *International Politics*, 44: 214–31.

Muchlinski, P. (2021), 'The changing nature of corporate influence in the making of international economic law: Towards "multistakeholderism"', *European Yearbook of International Economic Law*, 11: 3–20.

Mutua, M. (2002), *Human Rights: A Political and Cultural Critique*, Philadelphia, PA: Pennsylvania Press.

Nair, S. (2017), 'Introducing postcolonialism in international relations theory', *E-International Relations*, 8 December. Available online: https://www.e-ir.info/2017/12/08/postcolonialism-in-international-relations-theory/ (accessed 25 August 2022).

Nair, S. (2018), 'Postcolonial Feminism', in J. Elias and A. Roberts (eds), *Handbook on the International Political Economy of Gender*, 50–60, Cheltenham: Edward Elgar.

Nakamoto, S. (2008), *Bitcoin: A Peer-to-Peer Electronic Cash System*, White Paper. Available online: https://www.bitcoin.com/bitcoin.pdf (accessed 8 November 2022).

Narain, A. and M. Moretti (2022), 'Regulating Crypto: The right rules could provide a safe space for innovation', International Monetary Fund. Available online: https://www.imf.org/en/Publications/fandd/issues/2022/09/Regulating-crypto-Narain-Moretti (accessed 12 May 2023).

Nay, O. (2013), 'Fragile and failed states: Critical perspectives on conceptual hybrids', *International Political Science Review*, 34(3): 326–41.

New York Times (2012), 'Oil Price Would Skyrocket if Iran Closed the Strait of Hormuz', 4 January. Available online: https://www.nytimes.com/2012/01/05/business/oil-price-would-skyrocket-if-iran-closed-the-strait.html (accessed 13 May 2023).

Nişancıoğlu, K. (2020), 'Racial sovereignty', *European Journal of International Relations*, 26(S1): 39–63.

North Atlantic Treaty Organization (n.d.), Cyber defence. Available online: https://www.nato.int/cps/en/natohq/topics_78170.htm (accessed 4 May 2023).

North Atlantic Treaty Organization (2020), 'North Atlantic Council Statement as the Treaty on the Prohibition of Nuclear Weapons Enters into Force', 15 December. Available online: https://www.nato.int/cps/en/natohq/news_180087.htm (accessed 5 May 2023).

Nussbaum, M. (2000), *Women and Human Development: The Capabilities Approach*, Cambridge: Cambridge University Press.

Nye, J. (1990), 'The changing nature of world power', *Political Science Quarterly*, 105(2): 177–92.

Nye, J. (2008), *The Powers to Lead*, Oxford: Oxford University Press.

Nye, J. (2017), 'Deterrence and dissuasion in cyberspace', *International Security*, 41(3): 44–71.

Nzau, M. (2018), 'Uncivil Society and Ethnic Militia in African Politics', in S. O. Oloruntoba and T. Falola (eds), *The Palgrave Handbook of African Politics, Governance and Development*, 437–450, New York: Palgrave Macmillan.

Obama, B. (2009), 'Remarks by President Barack Obama in Prague as delivered'. Available online: https://obamawhitehouse.archives.gov/the-press-office/remarks-president-barack-obama-prague-delivered (accessed 22 September 2022).

Oktav, Ö. Z., D. E. Parlar and A. M. Kurşun, eds (2018), *Violent Non-state Actors and the Syrian Civil War: The ISIS and YPG Cases*, Cham: Springer.

Onuf, N. (1989), *World of Our Making: Rules and Rule in Social Theory and International Relations*, Columbia, SC: University of South Carolina Press.

Oppermann, K., R. Beasley and J. Kaarbo (2020), 'British foreign policy after Brexit: Losing Europe and finding a role', *International Relations*, 34(2): 133–56.

Organization for Economic Cooperation and Development (2011), *OECD Guidelines for Multinational Enterprises*, 2011 edn. Available online: https://www.oecd.org/daf/inv/mne/48004323.pdf (accessed 30 April 2023).

Osiander, A. (2001), 'Sovereignty, international relations, and the Westphalian myth', *International Organization*, 55(2): 251–87.

Oxford Net Zero (2022), 'Tracking Net Zero Progress: How Aligned Are We on the Global Path to Net Zero?' Net Zero Global Stocktake Report. Available online: https://netzeroclimate.org/innovation-for-net-zero/progress-tracking/ (accessed 14 May 2023).

Oye, K., ed (1986), *Cooperation under Anarchy*, Princeton, NJ: Princeton University Press.

Pacific Institute (2022), 'Water Conflict Chronology', Pacific Institute, Oakland, CA. Available online: https://www.worldwater.org/water-conflict/ (accessed 19 December 2022).

Panico, C. (2022), 'Making nuclear possession possible: The NPT disarmament principle and the production of less violent and more responsible nuclear states', *Contemporary Security Policy*, DOI: 10.1080/13523260.2022.2092679.

Parker, G., S. Payne, A. Klan, K. Manson, A. Gross and V. Mallet (2021), 'Aukus: How transatlantic allies turned on each other over China's Indo-Pacific threat', *Financial Times*, 24 September. Available online: https://www.ft.com/content/06f95e54-732e-4508-bc92-c3752904ba67 (accessed 17 May 2023).

Patchell, J. and R. Hayter (2013), 'How big business can save the climate: Multinational corporations can succeed where governments have failed', *Foreign Affairs*, 92: 17–23.

Persaud, R. and R. B. J. Walker (2001), 'Apertura: Race in international relations', *Alternatives*, 26(4): 373–6.

Peterson, J. and E. Bomberg (1999), *Decision-Making in the European Union*. Basingstoke: Palgrave Macmillan.

Peterson, V. S. and A. Runyan (2013), *Global Gender Issues in the New Millennium*, 4th edn, Boulder, CO: Westview.

Pew Research (2020), '#BlackLivesMatter surges on Twitter after George Floyd's death', 10 June. Available online: https://www.pewresearch.org/fact-tank/2020/06/10/blacklivesmatter-surges-on-twitter-after-george-floyds-death/ (accessed 30 April 2023).

Pew Trusts (2017), 'How to End Illegal Fishing', Issue Brief, 12 December. Available online: https://www.pewtrusts.org/en/research-and-analysis/issue-briefs/2017/12/how-to-end-illegal-fishing (accessed 13 May 2023).

Phạm, Q. N. and R. Shilliam (2016), *Meanings of Bandung: Postcolonial Orders and Decolonial Visions*, London: Rowman & Littlefield International.

Philpott, D. (2007), 'Explaining the political ambivalence of religion', *American Political Science Review*, 101(3): 505–25.

Piazza, J. A. (2008), 'Incubators of terror: Do failed and failing states promote transnational terrorism?' *International Studies Quarterly*, 52(3): 469–88.

Politico (2021), 'The end of the Internet Association', 15 December. Available online: https://www.politico.com/newsletters/politico-influence/2021/12/15/the-end-of-the-internet-association-799494 (accessed 29 September 2022).

Ponsonby, A. (1928), 'Disarmament by example', *Journal of the Royal Institute of International Affairs*, 7(4): 225–40.

Porter, D. and M. Watts (2017), 'Righting the resource curse: Institutional politics and state capabilities in Edo State, Nigeria', *The Journal of Development Studies*, 53(2): 249–63.

Putnam, R. D. (1988), 'Diplomacy and domestic politics: The logic of two-level games', *International Organization*, 42(3): 427–60.

Rachman, G. (2016), 'Trump, Putin, Xi and the cult of the strongman leader', *Financial Times*, 31 October. Available online: https://www.ft.com/content/39da343a-9f4b-11e6-891e-abe238dee8e2 (accessed 28 January 2023).

Reidy, D., ed (2005), *Universal Human Rights: Moral Order in a Divided World*, Lanham, MD: Rowman & Littlefield.

Reinharz, S. (1992), *Feminist Methods in Social Research*, Oxford: Oxford University Press.

Reuters (2022), 'The war in Ukraine is fuelling a global food crisis'. Available online: https://graphics.reuters.com/UKRAINE-CRISIS/FOOD/zjvqkgomjvx/ (accessed 8 June 2022).

Reuters (2023), 'Kremlin says U.S.-supplied tanks will "burn" in Ukraine'. Available online: https://www.reuters.com/world/europe/kremlin-says-us-supplied-tanks-will-burn-ukraine-2023-01-25/ (accessed 25 January 2023).

Richards, D., P. Diamond and A. Wager (2019), 'Westminster's Brexit paradox: The contingency of the "old" versus the "new" politics', *The British Journal of Politics and International Relations*, 21(2): 330–48.

Rigby, J. and J. Crisp (2023), 'Fortress Europe', *The Telegraph*, 11 February. Available online: https://www.telegraph.co.uk/global-health/fortress-europe-borders-wall-fence-controls-eu-countries-migrants-crisis/ (accessed 14 February 2023).

Robinson, F. (2019), 'Feminist foreign policy as ethical foreign policy? A care ethics perspective', *Journal of International Theory*, 17(1): 20–37.

Rodwan Abouharb, M. and D. L. Cingranelli (2006), 'The human rights effects of World Bank structural adjustment, 1981–2000', *International Studies Quarterly*, 50: 233–62.

Ross, M. L. (2001), 'Does oil hinder democracy?', *World Politics*, 53(3): 325–61.

Rousseau, D. (2005), *Democracy and War: Institutions, Norms, and the Evolution of International Conflict*, Stanford, CA: Stanford University Press.

Rublee, M. R. (2009), *Nonproliferation Norms: Why States Choose Nuclear Restraint*, Athens: University of Georgia Press.

Russett, B. and J. Oneal (2003), *Triangulating Peace: Democracy, Interdependence, and International Organizations*, New York: Norton.

Said, E. (1995), *Orientalism*, London: Penguin.

Said, E. (2001), 'The Clash of Ignorance', *The Nation*. Available online: https://www.thenation.com/article/archive/clash-ignorance/ (accessed 11 February 2023).

Sajed, A. (2013), *Postcolonial Encounters in International Relations: The Politics of Transgression in the Maghreb*, Abingdon: Routledge.

Sanchez, N. (2019), 'Decolonization Is for Everyone', TEDx Talks. YouTube. Available online: https://www.youtube.com/watch?v=QP9x1NnCWNY (accessed 14 May 2023).

Schapper, A. (2021), 'The "Super-Network": Fostering interaction between human rights and climate change institutions', *Complexity, Governance and Networks*, 6(1): 32–45.

Schapper, A. and M. Dee (forthcoming), 'Super-Networks shaping international agreements: Comparing the climate change and nuclear weapons arenas', *International Studies Quarterly*. Accepted for publication 5 June 2023.

Scheuermann, M. and A. Zürn, eds (2020), *Gender Roles in Peace and Security: Prevent, Protect, Participate*, Cham: Springer.

Schramm, M. and A. Stark (2020), 'Peacemakers or iron ladies? A cross-national study of gender and international conflict', *Security Studies*, 29(3): 515–48.

Schuman, M. (2021), 'What the China-Australia Spat Means for America', *The Atlantic*, 28 July. Available online: https://www.theatlantic.com/international/archive/2021/07/china-australia-america/619544/ (accessed 18 May 2023).

Schwarz, R. and M. de Carral (2013), 'Not a curse at all: Why Middle Eastern oil states fail and how it can be prevented', *Journal of Intervention and Statebuilding*, 7(3): 402–22.

Segal, A. (2020), 'China's Vision for Cyber Sovereignty and the Global Governance of Cyberspace', NBR Special Report No. 87, *The National Bureau of Asian Research*. Available online: https://www.nbr.org/publication/chinas-vision-for-cyber-sovereignty-and-the-global-governance-of-cyberspace/ (accessed 30 April 2023).

Shah, T. and D. Philpott (2011), 'The Fall and Rise of Religion in International Relations: Theory and History', in J. Snyder (ed.), *Religion and International Relations Theory*, 24–59, Columbia, NY: Columbia University Press.

Shandra, J. M., C. L. Shandra and B. London (2010), 'Debt, structural adjustment, and non-governmental organizations: A cross-national analysis of maternal mortality', *Journal of World-Systems Research*, 16(2): 217–45.

Shilliam, R. (2021), *Decolonizing Politics: An Introduction*, Cambridge: Polity Press.

Singer, J. D. (1960), 'International conflict: Three levels of analysis', Review of *Man, the State, and War: A Theoretical Analysis*, *World Politics*, 12(3): 453–61.

Sjoberg, L. (2013), *Gendering Global Conflict: Towards a Feminist Theory of War*, Columbia, NY: Columbia University Press.

Sjoberg, L. and J. A. Tickner (2013), 'Feminist Perspective on International Relations', in W. Carlsnaes, T. Risse and A. B. A. Simmons (eds), *Handbook of International Relations*, 2nd edn, 170–94, London: Sage Publications.

Smith, K. E. (2014), *European Union Foreign Policy in a Changing World*, 3rd edn, Cambridge, London.

Smith, W. S. (2020), 'Ukraine and the Clash of Civilizations', *National Interest*, 12 May. Available online: https://nationalinterest.org/feature/ukraine-and-clash-civilizations-153636 (accessed 11 February 2023).

Spivak, G. C. (1985), 'The Rani of Sirmur: An essay in the reading of archives', *History and Theory*, 24(3): 247–72.

Steen-Johnsen, T. (2016), *Religious Peacebuilding and State Context*, London: Palgrave Macmillan.

Stern, P. C. and D. Druckman (2000), *International Conflict Resolution after the Cold War*, Washington, DC: National Academy Press.

Stoett, P. (1999), *Human and Global Security: An Exploration of Terms*, Toronto: University of Toronto.

Strange, S. (1970), 'International economics and international relations: A case of mutual neglect', *International Affairs*, 46(2): 304–15.

Strange, S. (1988), *States and Markets*, London: Pinter Publishers.

Stroup, S. S. and W. H. Wong (2016), 'The agency and authority of international NGOs', *Perspectives on Politics*, 14(1): 138–44.

Sturge, G. (2017), 'Five myths about cash transfers', *The New Humanitarian*, 6 January. Available online: https://www.thenewhumanitarian.org/opinion/2017/01/06/five-myths-about-cash-transfers (accessed 21 November 2022).

Suhrke, A. (1999), 'Human security and the interests of the state', *Security Dialogue*, 30(3): 265–76.

Sweeney, S. (2016), 'Corporations call for "net zero" emissions: Do they know how to get there?', *New Labor Forum*, 25(3): 101–6.

SWIFT (2022), 'SWIFT FIN Traffic & Figures'. Available online: https://www.swift.com/about-us/discover-swift/fin-traffic-figures (accessed 2 November 2022).

Tallberg, J. and M. Zürn (2019), 'The legitimacy and legitimation of international organizations: Introduction and framework', *The Review of International Organizations*, 14: 581–606.

Tang, S. (2013), *The Social Evolution of International Politics*, Oxford: Oxford University Press.

Tannenwald, N. (2009), *The Nuclear Taboo: The United States and the Non-Use of Nuclear Weapons since 1945*, Cambridge: Cambridge University Press.

Taylor, P. (2008), *The End of European Integration: Anti-Europeanization Examined*, London: Routledge.

Tekuya, M. (2020), 'The Grand Renaissance Dam: What's at stake and what could break the deadlock', *The Conversation*, 22 July. Available online: https://theconversation.com/the-grand-renaissance-dam-whats-at-stake-and-what-could-break-the-deadlock-143018 (accessed 20 December 2022).

The Economist (2015), 'The 169 commandments', 26 March. Available online: https://www.economist.com/leaders/2015/03/26/the-169-commandments (accessed 21 February 2023).

The Guardian (2012), 'Has the Kyoto protocol made any difference to carbon emissions?', 26 November. Available online: https://www.theguardian.com/environment/blog/2012/nov/26/kyoto-protocol-carbon-emissions (accessed 18 December 2022).

The Guardian (2015), '7 Reasons the SDGs will be better than the MDGs', 26 September. Available online: https://www.theguardian.com/global-development-professionals-network/2015/sep/26/7-reasons-sdgs-will-be-better-than-the-mdgs (accessed 18 November 2022).

The Guardian (2017), 'Fossil fuel companies undermining Paris agreement negotiations – report', 1 November. Available online: https://www.theguardian.com/environment/2017/nov/01/fossil-fuel-companies-undermining-paris-agreement-negotiations-report (accessed 18 December 2022).

The Guardian (2018), 'Jacinda Ardern makes history with baby Neve at UN general assembly', 24 September. Available online: https://www.theguardian.com/world/2018/sep/25/jacinda-ardern-makes-history-with-baby-neve-at-un-general-assembly (accessed 24 January 2023).

The Guardian (2019), 'The Greta Thunberg effect: at last, MPs focus on climate change'. Available online: https://www.theguardian.com/environment/2019/apr/23/greta-thunberg (accessed 18 May 2023).

The Guardian (2021a), 'UK ministers "met fossil fuel firms nine times as often as clean energy ones"', 10 September. Available online: https://www.theguardian.com/environment/2021/sep/10/uk-ministers-met-fossil-fuel-firms-nine-times-more-often-than-clean-energy-companies (accessed 18 December 2022).

The Guardian (2021b), 'COP26 ends in climate agreement despite India watering down coal resolution', 13 November. Available online: https://www.theguardian.com/environment/2021/nov/13/cop26-countries-agree-to-accept-imperfect-climate-agreement (accessed 13 May 2023).

Tickner, J. A. (1990), *Gendering World Politics*, Columbia, NY: Columbia University Press.

Tickner, J. A. (2002), 'Feminist perspectives on 9/11', *International Studies Perspectives*, 3: 333–50.

Time (2015), 'Lu Wei', The 100 Most Influential People. Available online: https://time.com/collection-post/3823285/lu-wei-2015-time-100/ (accessed 30 April 2023).

Toft, M. D., D. Philpott and T. S. Shah (2011), *God's Century: Resurgent Religion and Global Politics*, New York: W. W. Norton.

Towns, A. (2011), *Women and States: Norms and Hierarchies in International Society*, Cambridge: Cambridge University Press.

Treen, K., H. T. P. Williams and S. J. O'Neill (2020), 'Online misinformation about climate change', *WIREs Climate Change*, 11: e665.

True, J. (2003), *Gender, Globalization, and Post-Socialism: The Czech Republic after Communism*, Columbia, NY: Columbia University Press.

True, J. (2020), 'Continuums of violence and peace: A feminist perspective', *Ethics & International Affairs*, 34(1): 85–95.

True, J. (2022), 'Feminism(s)', in R. Devetak and J. True (eds), *Theories of International Relations*, 6th edn, 142–63, London: Bloomsbury.

Truman Doctrine. (1947), 'Recommendations for Assistance to Greece and Turkey', History and Public Policy Program Digital Archive, Truman Library, 12 March 1947. Available online: https://digitalarchive.wilsoncenter.org/document/116182 (accessed 20 April 2022).

Trump, D. (2019), 'We're building the wall anyway', YouTube. Available online: https://youtu.be/5nwfL-PPD40 (accessed 14 February 2023).

Truth and Reconciliation Commission (2022), Official Truth and Reconciliation Commission Website. Available online: https://www.justice.gov.za/trc/ (accessed 31 May 2022).

United Kingdom Department of International Development [UK DfID] (2009), 'Fragile States', CRISE Working Paper No. 51. Available online: https://assets.publishing.service.gov.uk/media/57a08b62e5274a27b2000af7/wp51.pdf (accessed 24 June 2022).

United Kingdom National Archives (2022), 'Slavery and the British transatlantic slave trade'. Available online: https://www.nationalarchives.gov.uk/help-with-your-research/research-guides/british-transatlantic-slave-trade-records/?msclkid=9f804e9bc14d11eca6ca6c2a9f3c29db (accessed 21 April 2022).

United Nations [UN] (1945), 'United Nations Charter'. Available online: https://www.un.org/en/about-us/un-charter (accessed 26 April 2023).

United Nations [UN] (1948), 'Universal Declaration of Human Rights'. Available online: https://www.un.org/en/about-us/universal-declaration-of-human-rights (accessed 14 May 2023).

United Nations [UN] (1992a), 'An Agenda for Peace: Preventive diplomacy, peacemaking and peace-keeping (A/47/277 - S/24111)', 17 June.

United Nations [UN] (1992b), 'United Nations Conference on Environment and Development'. Available online: https://www.un.org/en/conferences/environment/rio1992 (accessed 15 December 2022).

United Nations [UN] (1993), 'Report of the Regional Meeting for Asia of the World Conference on Human Rights', Bangkok, 7 April. A/CONF.157/ASRM/8. Available online: https://digitallibrary.un.org/record/167021 (accessed 15 January 2023).

United Nations [UN] (1994), 'United Nations Framework Convention on Climate Change.' Available online: https://unfccc.int/files/essential_background/background_publications_htmlpdf/application/pdf/conveng.pdf (accessed 18 December 2022).

United Nations [UN] (2015), 'The Millennium Development Goals Report 2015', New York. Available online: https://www.un.org/millenniumgoals/2015_MDG_Report/pdf/MDG%202015%20rev%20(July%201).pdf (accessed 22 November 2022).

United Nations [UN] (2017a), 'System-Wide Strategy on Gender Parity Report', 6 October. Available online: https://www.un.org/gender/sites/www.un.org.gender/files/gender_parity_strategy_october_2017.pdf (accessed 27 April 2023).

United Nations [UN] (2017b), 'What does "Sustaining Peace" mean?' Available online: https://www.un.org/peacebuilding/sites/www.un.org.peacebuilding/files/documents/guidance-on-sustaining-peace.170117.final_.pdf (accessed 27 April 2023).

United Nations [UN] (2021a), 'Afghanistan on "countdown to catastrophe" without urgent humanitarian relief', *UN News*, 25 October. Available online: https://news.un.org/en/story/2021/10/1103932 (accessed 24 June 2022).

United Nations [UN] (2021b), 'Our Common Agenda – Report of the Secretary-General', New York, United Nations Publications. Available online: https://www.un.org/en/content/common-agenda-report/assets/pdf/Common_Agenda_Report_English.pdf (accessed 27 April 2023).

United Nations [UN] (2022a), 'Concluding Debate on Security Council Reform, 77th Meeting, 38th Session, GA/12473', 18 November. Available online: https://press.un.org/en/2022/ga12473.doc.htm (accessed 27 April 2023).

United Nations [UN] (2022b), 'Transforming our world: The 2030 Agenda for Sustainable Development'. Available online: https://sdgs.un.org/2030agenda (accessed 29 September 2022).

United Nations [UN] (2022c), 'Statement by the Secretary-General following the Spring session of the UN's Chief Executives Board meeting'. Available online: https://www.un.org/sg/en/content/sg/statement/2022-05-13/statement-the-secretary-general-following-the-spring-session-of-the-uns-chief-executives-board-meetings (accessed 21 November 2022).

United Nations [UN] (2023a), 'Renewable energy – powering a safer future'. Available online: https://www.un.org/en/climatechange/raising-ambition/renewable-energy (accessed 12 December 2022).

United Nations [UN] (2023b), 'Financing Climate Action'. Available online: https://www.un.org/en/climatechange/raising-ambition/climate-finance (accessed 18 December 2022).

United Nations [UN] (2023c), 'For a livable climate: Net-zero commitments must be backed by credible action'. Available online: https://www.un.org/en/climatechange/net-zero-coalition (accessed 20 December 2022).

United Nations Conference for Trade and Development [UNCTAD] (2004), 'Transnational corporations and foreign affiliates'. Available online: https://unctad.org/system/files/official-document/gdscsir20041c3_en.pdf (accessed 29 September 2022).

United Nations Conference for Trade and Development [UNCTAD] (2007), 'World Investment Report: Transnational Corporations, Extractive Industries and Development'. Available online: https://unctad.org/system/files/official-document/wir2007_en.pdf (accessed 28 September 2022).

United Nations Conference for Trade and Development [UNCTAD] (2013), '80% of trade takes place in "value chains" linked to transnational corporations, UNCTAD report says'. Available online: https://unctad.org/press-material/80-trade-takes-place-value-chains-linked-transnational-corporations-unctad-report (accessed 28 September 2022).

United Nations Conference for Trade and Development [UNCTAD] (2021), 'The Effects of the COVID-19 Pandemic on International Trade, Key Statistics and Trends in International Trade 2021 Report'. Available online: https://unctad.org/system/files/official-document/ditctab2022d3_en.pdf (accessed 15 November 2022).

United Nations Conference for Trade and Development [UNCTAD] (2022), *Global Investment Trends Monitor*, Issue No. 41, 27 April.

United Nations Department of Economic and Social Affairs [UNDESA] (n.d.), 'Least Developed Countries (LDCs)'. Available online: https://www.un.org/development/desa/dpad/least-developed-country-category.html (accessed 27 August 2023).

United Nations Development Programme [UNDP] (1994), 'UN Development Report'. Available online: https://hdr.undp.org/content/human-development-report-1994 (accessed 5 May 2023).

United Nations Development Programme [UNDP] (2018), 'Social Media in Africa'. Available online: https://www.undp.org/africa/publications/social-media-africa (accessed 27 September 2022).

United Nations Development Programme [UNDP] (2022), 'New threats to human security in the Anthropocene: Demanding greater solidarity'. Available online: https://hs.hdr.undp.org/pdf/srhs2022.pdf (accessed 17 November 2022).

United Nations Environment Programme [UNEP] (2009), *From Conflict to Peacebuilding: The Role of Natural Resources and the Environment*, Nairobi: UNEP.

United Nations Environment Programme [UNEP] (2018), 'Emissions Gap Report 2018'. Available online: https://www.unep.org/resources/emissions-gap-report-2018 (accessed 18 December 2022).

United Nations Environment Programme [UNEP] (2022), 'Emissions Gap Report 2022'. Available online: https://www.unep.org/resources/emissions-gap-report-2022 (accessed 18 December 2022).

United Nations Framework Convention on Climate Change [UNFCCC] (2015), 'Paris Climate Agreement'. Available online: https://unfccc.int/sites/default/files/english_paris_agreement.pdf (accessed 21 February 2023).

United Nations Framework Convention on Climate Change [UNFCCC] (2021), 'Glasgow Climate Pact'. Available online: https://unfccc.int/sites/default/files/resource/cma2021_10_add1_adv.pdf (accessed 18 December 2022).

United Nations Framework Convention on Climate Change [UNFCCC] (2022a), 'Statistics'. Available online: https://unfccc.int/process-and-meetings/parties-non-party-stakeholders/non-party-stakeholders/statistics (accessed 22 September 2023).

United Nations Framework Convention on Climate Change [UNFCCC] (2022b), 'China's submission to the global stocktake', 5 November. Available online: https://unfccc.int/documents/624549 (accessed 10 January 2023).

United Nations General Assembly [UNGA] (1952), 'The right of peoples and nations to self-determination', A/RES/637. Available online: https://www.refworld.org/docid/3b00f0791c.html (accessed 16 January 2023).

United Nations General Assembly [UNGA] (2019), 'Report of the independent international fact-finding mission on Myanmar', A/HRC/42/50. Available online: https://documents-dds-ny.un.org/doc/UNDOC/GEN/G19/236/74/PDF/G1923674.pdf?OpenElement (accessed 20 January 2023).

United Nations Human Rights Office of the High Commissioner [OHCHR] (2017), 'Myanmar: UN Security Council must act on Rohingya crisis – UN expert'. Available online: https://www.ohchr.org/en/press-releases/2017/10/myanmar-un-security-council-must-act-rohingya-crisis-un-expert (accessed 20 January 2023).

United Nations Office of Disarmament Affairs [UNODA] (2010), Final Document, NPT/CONF.2010/50, Vol. I. Available online: https://www.un.org/en/conf/npt/2010/ (accessed 4 May 2023).

United Nations Secretary-General [UNSG] (1999), 'Two concepts of sovereignty', Statement by Kofi Annan, 18 September. Available online: https://www.un.org/sg/en/content/sg/articles/1999-09-18/two-concepts-sovereignty (accessed 17 January 2023).

United Nations Security Council [UNSC] (1992), 'Resolution 794 (1992), Adopted 3 December 1992'. Available online: http://unscr.com/en/resolutions/doc/794 (accessed 14 May 2023).

United Nations Security Council [UNSC] (2017), 'Security Council Presidential Statement Calls on Myanmar to End Excessive Military Force, Intercommunal Violence in Rakhine State', SC/13055, 6 November. Available online: https://press.un.org/en/2017/sc13055.doc.htm (accessed 14 May 2023).

United Nations Women (2022), 'Poverty deepens for women and girls, according to latest projections', 1 February. Available online: https://data.unwomen.org/features/poverty-deepens-women-and-girls-according-latest-projections (accessed 16 November 2022).

United States Department of Homeland Security (2020), 'The Border Wall System is Deployed, Effective, and Disrupting Criminals and Smugglers', News Archive, 29 October. Available online: https://www.dhs.gov/news/2020/10/29/border-wall-system-deployed-effective-and-disrupting-criminals-and-smugglers (accessed 14 February 2023).

United States Department of State (2011), 'Signing of the US-Kosovo Agreement on the Protection and Preservation of Certain Cultural Properties, Remarks by Hillary Rodham Clinton', 14 December. Available online: https://2009-2017.state.gov/secretary/20092013clinton/rm/2011/12/178863.htm (accessed 23 June 2022).

United States Strategic Bombing Survey (1946), 'Chair's Report, 19 June'. Available online: https://info.publicintelligence.net/USSBS-NagasakiHiroshima.pdf (accessed 29 August 2022).

Vallet, E. (2022), 'The World is Witnessing a Rapid Proliferation of Border Walls', *Migration Policy Institute*, 2 March. Available online: https://www.migrationpolicy.org/article/rapid-proliferation-number-border-walls (accessed 13 February 2023).

Van de Graaf, T. (2013), *The Politics and Institutions of Global Energy Governance*, Basingstoke: Palgrave Macmillan.

van Leeuwen, H. (2021), 'Just another day in the ScoMo-BoJo bromance', *Australian Financial Review*, 16 September. Available online: https://www.afr.com/world/europe/just-another-day-in-the-scomo-bojo-bromance-20210916-p58s3q (accessed 18 May 2023).

Vargas-Silva, C. (2012), 'Migration and Development', The Migration Observatory at the University of Oxford, 16 March. Available online: https://migrationobservatory.ox.ac.uk/resources/primers/migration-and-development/ (accessed 18 November 2022).

Varin, C. and D. Abubakar (2017), *Violent Non-State Actors in Africa: Terrorists, Rebels and Warlords*, Cham: Palgrave Macmillan.

Vaughn, J. and T. Dunne (2015), 'Leading from the front: America, Libya and the localization of R2P', *Cooperation and Conflict*, 50(1): 29–49.

Vernon, P. (2022), 'Sexuality, gender and the colonial violence of humanitarian intervention', *International Studies Review*, 24(3): 1–22.

Villa, V. (2022), 'Four in ten countries and territories worldwide had blasphemy laws in 2019', *Pew Research Center*, 25 January. Available online: https://www.pewresearch.org/fact-tank/2022/01/25/four-in-ten-countries-and-territories-worldwide-had-blasphemy-laws-in-2019-2/ (accessed 13 February 2023).

Vinas, S. (2014), 'Latin women take the helm', *World Policy Journal*, 31(1): 39–47.

Vitalis, R. (2015), *White World Order, Black Power Politics: The Birth of American International Relations*, Ithaca, NY: Cornell University Press.

Vollaard, H. (2014), 'Explaining European disintegration', *Journal of Common Market Studies*, 52(5): 1142–59.

Von Clausewitz, C., M. Howard and P. Paret (2008), *On War*, Princeton, NJ: Princeton University Press.

Vought, H. (1994), 'Division and reunion: Woodrow Wilson, immigration, and the myth of American unity', *Journal of American Ethnic History*, 13(3): 24–50.

Vreeland, J. R. (2003), *The IMF and Economic Development*, Cambridge: Cambridge University Press.

Walt, S. M. (1999), *The Origins of Alliances*, Ithaca, NY: Cornell University Press.
Walter, A. and G. Sen (2009), *Analyzing the Global Political Economy*, Princeton, NJ: Princeton University Press.
Waltz, K. (1959), *Man, the State and War: A Theoretical Analysis*, Columbia, NY: Columbia University Press.
Waltz, K. (1979), *Theory of International Relations*, Reading, MA: Addison-Wesley.
Waltz, K. (1990), 'Realist thought and neo-realist theory', *Journal of International Affairs*, 44(1): 21–37.
Waltz, K. (2012), 'Why Iran should get the bomb: Nuclear balancing would mean stability', *Foreign Affairs*, 91(4): 2–5.
Wang, Y. M. (2014), 'Strategic engagement and religious peace-building: A case study of religious peace work in Jerusalem', *Approaching Religion*, 4(2): 71–82.
Ward, A. (2018), 'ISIS's Use of Social Media Still Poses a Threat to Stability in the Middle East and Africa', *The RAND Blog*, 11 December. Available online: https://www.rand.org/blog/2018/12/isiss-use-of-social-media-still-poses-a-threat-to-stability.html (access 20 April 2023).
Washington Post (2019), 'Trump shrugs as UN warns it's about to run out of money', 9 October. Available online: https://www.washingtonpost.com/national-security/trump-shrugs-as-un-warns-its-about-to-run-out-of-money/2019/10/09/568f8756-eac5-11e9-85c0-85a098e47b37_story.html (accessed 27 April 2023).
Weber, M. (1925/1978), *Economy and Society: An Outline of Interpretative Sociology*, Berkeley, CA: University of California Press.
Wendt, A. (1987), 'The agent-structure problem in international relations theory', *International Organization*, 41 (3): 335–70.
Wendt, A. (1992), 'Anarchy is what states make of it: The social construction of power politics', *International Organization*, 46(2): 391–425.
Wendt, A. (1999), *Social Theory of International Politics*, Cambridge: Cambridge University Press.
Wight, C. (2006), *Agents, Structures and International Relations: Politics as Ontology*, Cambridge: Cambridge University Press.
Wilson, W. (1919), 'Statement to the Preliminary Peace Conference 14 February 1919'. Available online: https://history.state.gov/historicaldocuments/frus1919Parisv03/d5 (accessed 27 April 2023).
Wohlforth, W. (1999), 'The stability of a unipolar world order', *International Security*, 24(1): 5–41.
Wolfe, L. (2022), 'China's War on Crypto', *Reason*, January. Available online: https://reason.com/2021/12/01/chinas-war-on-crypto/ (accessed 12 May 2023).
Wolfers, A. (1952), '"National security" as an ambiguous symbol', *Political Science Quarterly*, 67: 481–502.
Wood, E. M. (2003), *Empire of Capital*, London: Verso.
World Bank (2011), 'World Development Report 2011: Conflict, Security, and Development'. Available online: https://openknowledge.worldbank.org/entities/publication/25f2300c-f9d4-54de-8a56-30566e72003a (accessed 5 May 2023).
World Bank (2020), 'Trading for Development in the Age of Global Value Chains', World Development Report, Washington: International Bank for Reconstruction and Development/The World Bank.
World Bank (2021), 'Defying Predictions, Remittance Flows Remain Strong during COVID-19 Crisis', Press Release, 12 May. Available online: https://www.worldbank.org/en/news/press-release/2021/05/12/defying-predictions-remittance-flows-remain-strong-during-Covid-19-crisis (accessed 17 November 2022).
World Bank (2022a), 'Trade (% of GDP)'. Available online: https://data.worldbank.org/indicator/NE.TRD.GNFS.ZS (accessed 4 November 2022).
World Bank (2022b), 'Correcting Course', Overview of the Poverty and Shared Prosperity Report. Available online: https://openknowledge.worldbank.org/bitstream/handle/10986/37739/9781464818936ov.pdf (accessed 14 November 2022).
World Commission on Environment and Development (1987), 'Our Common Future'. Available online: https://sustainabledevelopment.un.org/content/documents/5987our-common-future.pdf (accessed 18 November 2022).
World Council of Religious Leaders (n.d.), 'Building An Integrated Framework for Peace'. Available online: https://www.wcorl.org/ (accessed 12 February 2023).
World Health Organization [WHO] (1995), 'Revision and Updating of the International Health Regulations, WHA48.7', 48th World Health Assembly.
World Health Organization [WHO] (2016), 'Framework of engagement with non-state actors, 69th World Health Assembly, WHA69.10, 28 May'. Available online: https://apps.who.int/gb/ebwha/pdf_files/wha69/a69_r10-en.pdf (accessed 29 September 2022).

World Health Organization [WHO] (2018), 'Millennium Development Goals (MDGs)', Fact Sheet, 19 February. Available online: https://www.who.int/news-room/fact-sheets/detail/millennium-development-goals-(mdgs) (accessed 18 November 2022).

World Health Organization [WHO] (2020), 'WHO Director General's opening remarks at the media briefing on COVID-19', 11 March. Available online: https://www.who.int/director-general/speeches/detail/who-director-general-s-opening-remarks-at-the-media-briefing-on-Covid-19—11-march-2020 (accessed 4 April 2023).

World Trade Organization [WTO] (2011), 'World Trade Report 2010: Trade in Natural Resources', Geneva: WTO.

World Trade Organization [WTO] (2014), 'World Trade Report, Trade and development: recent trends and the role of the WTO'. Available online: https://www.wto.org/english/res_e/booksp_e/world_trade_report14_e.pdf (accessed 7 November 2022).

World Trade Organization [WTO] (2023a), 'Regional Trade Agreements Database'. Available online: https://rtais.wto.org/ (accessed 28 April 2023).

World Trade Organization [WTO] (2023b), 'Global Value Chains'. Available online: https://www.wto.org/english/res_e/statis_e/miwi_e/miwi_e.htm (accessed 11 May 2023).

Wurzel, R. and J. Hayward (2012), *European Disunion: Between Solidarity and Sovereignty*, Basingstoke: Palgrave Macmillan.

Xinhua Net (2018), 'Former senior officials prosecuted for taking bribes', 30 July. Available online: http://www.xinhuanet.com/english/2018-07/30/c_137357372.htm (accessed 30 April 2023).

Yalta Conference Agreement (1945), 'Declaration of a Liberated Europe', History and Public Policy Program Digital Archive, *National Archives*, 11 February. Available online: http://digitalarchive.wilsoncenter.org/document/116176 (accessed 21 April 2022).

Yoder, J. (2010), 'An intersectional approach to Angela Merkel's foreign policy', *German Politics*, 20(3): 360–75.

Young, A. and J. Peterson (2006), 'The EU and the new trade politics', *Journal of European Public Policy*, 13(6): 795–814.

Zhang, Z., D. Guan, R. Wang, J. Meng, H. Zheng, K. Zhu and J. Du (2020), 'Embodied carbon emissions in the supply chains of multinational enterprises', *Natural Climate Change*, 10: 1096 –1101.

Zielonka, J. (2006), *Europe as Empire: The Nature of the Enlarged Union*, Oxford: Oxford University Press.

Index